PEACE MAKER
ピースメーカー

**Volume 3
by Nanae Chrono**

HAMBURG // LONDON // LOS ANGELES // TOKYO

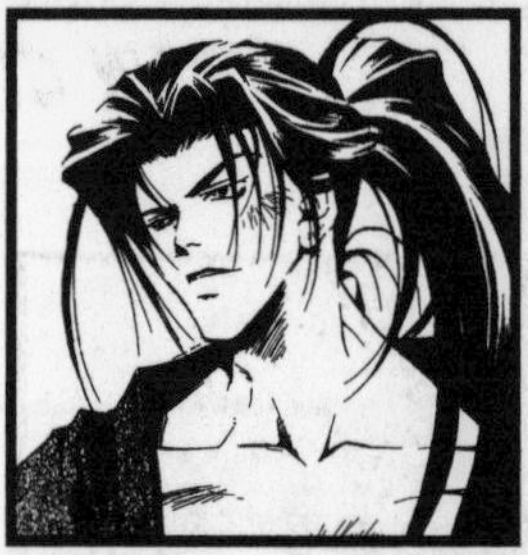

HIJIKATA TOSHIZOU

VICE COMMANDER

BECAUSE OF HIS COLD DEMEANOR AND BRUTALITY, HE IS KNOWN AS THE "DEMON VICE COMMANDER."

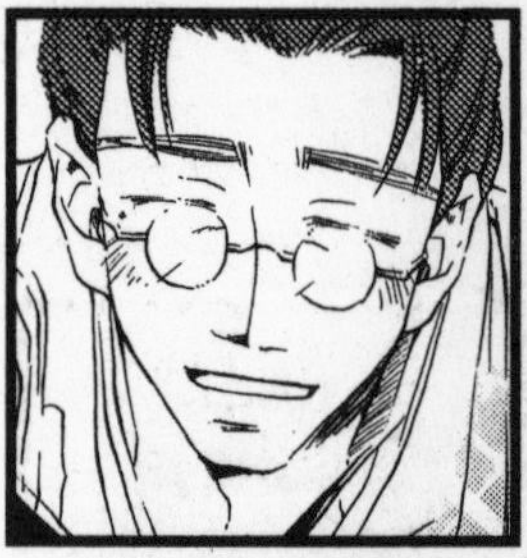

YAMANAMI KEISUKE

VICE COMMANDER

THIS BUDDHA-LIKE VICE COMMANDER COULDN'T BE LESS LIKE HIJIKATA. HE'S OFTEN SEEN CARRYING HIS ABACUS.

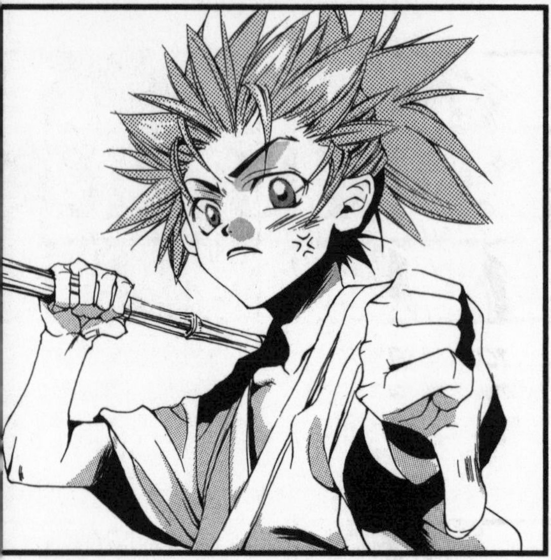

ICHIMURA TETSUNOSUKE

HIJIKATA'S PAGE

BRASH TETSU HAS JOINED THE SHINSENGUMI TO LEARN TO BECOME STRONG. HE WANTS TO GET REVENGE ON HIS PARENTS' MURDERERS, CHOUSHUU REBELS. ALTHOUGH HE JOINED THE SHINSENGUMI WITH ASPIRATIONS OF BECOMING A SWORDSMAN, HE'S BEEN ASSIGNED THE THANKLESS DUTY OF HIJIKATA'S PAGE.

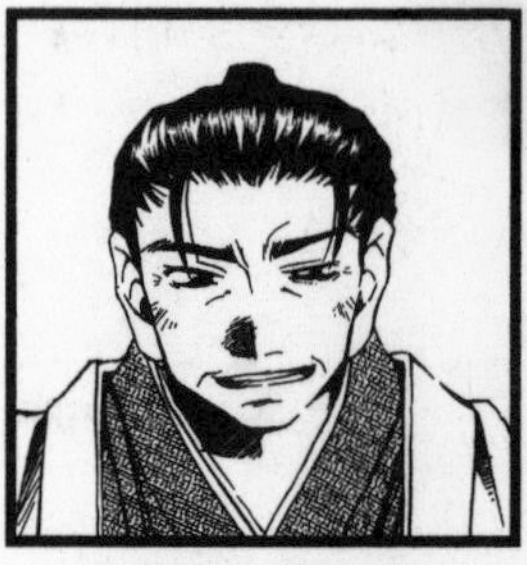

KONDOU ISAMI

DIRECTOR

A FOUNDING MEMBER OF THE SHINSENGUMI AND ALSO A MASTER AT THE SHIEIKAN DOJO IN EDO, THE MAIN DOJO OF THE TENNEN RISHIN STYLE.

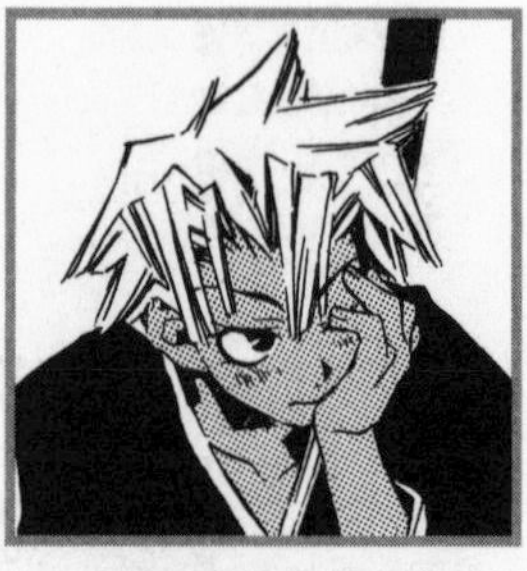

KITAMURA SUZU

A BOY WITH SILVER HAIR. HE HAS NO FAMILY AND LIVES WITH HIS MASTER, YOSHIDA TOSHIMARO. HE AND HIS MASTER OPPOSE THE SHINSENGUMI.

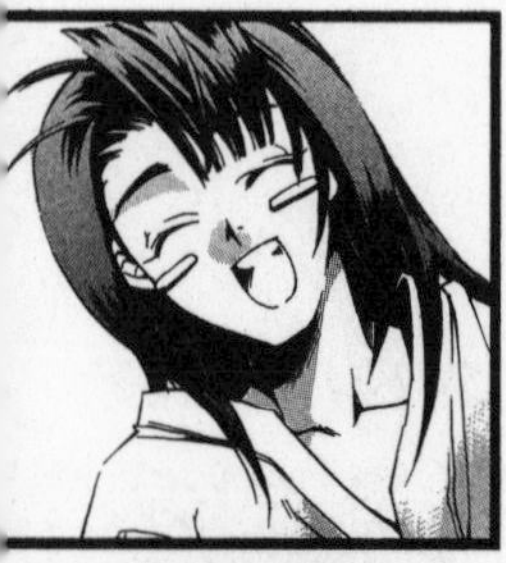

OKITA SOUJI

CAPTAIN OF THE FIRST SQUAD

THE BEST SWORDSMAN IN THE SHINSENGUMI. HE'S GENERALLY CALM AND FRIENDLY, BUT WIELDING A BLADE CAN TRANSFORM HIM INTO A HEARTLESS KILLER.

MAIN CHARACTERS

NAGAKURA SHINPACHI

CAPTAIN OF THE SECOND SQUAD

SMALL BUT STRONG. A SWORDSMAN LIKE OKITA. HE FIGHTS IN THE SHINTO-MUNEN SCHOOL STYLE.

TOUDOU HEISUKE

CAPTAIN OF THE EIGHTH SQUAD

ONE OF THE THREE STOOGES OF THE SHINSENGUMI. HE LIKES CUTE THINGS, INCLUDING TETSU.

HARADA SANOSUKE

CAPTAIN OF THE TENTH SQUAD

A GIANT AMONG MEN, HE'S A MASTER OF THE SPEAR IN THE HOZOIN SCHOOL STYLE. HE'S GOOD FRIENDS WITH SHINPACHI.

ICHIMURA TATSUNOSUKE

TETSU'S OLDER BOTHER AND GUARDIAN. HE'S ALWAYS WORRYING ABOUT TETSU. TATSU WANTS NOTHING TO DO WITH SWORDFIGHTING, AND IS A BOOKKEEPER FOR THE SHINSENGUMI.

YAMAZAKI SUSUMU

SHINSENGUMI NINJA

A SPY FOR THE SHINSENGUMI, HE REPORTS TO HIJIKATA. TACITURN AND COLD, HE HOLDS MANY SECRETS.

SAYA

TETSU SAVED HER FROM SOME RUFFIANS, AND NOW THE TWO ARE FRIENDS. SAYA CANNOT SPEAK, BUT COMMUNICATES THROUGH HAND GESTURES AND WRITING.

☐ SHINSENGUMI MEMBERS

☐ PERSONS OUTSIDE THE SHINSENGUMI

THE STORY OF PEACE MAKER

IN THE FIRST YEAR OF GENJI, 1864, JAPAN WAS IN GREAT TURMOIL. MILITANT AND XENOPHOBIC FORCES, WHICH HAD LONG OPPOSED THE TOKUGAWA SHOGUNATE, ADVOCATED EXPELLING WESTERN INFLUENCE AND RESTORING THE EMPEROR IN KYOTO TO POWER. TO PROTECT THE SHOGUNATE'S INTEREST IN KYOTO, A LEGENDARY PEACEKEEPING FORCE WAS FORMED FROM TWO HUNDRED-SOME RONIN. THEY WERE THE SHINSENGUMI. THIS IS THE STORY OF ICHIMURA TETSUNOSUKE, WHO SOUGHT TO JOIN THEM.

CONTENTS

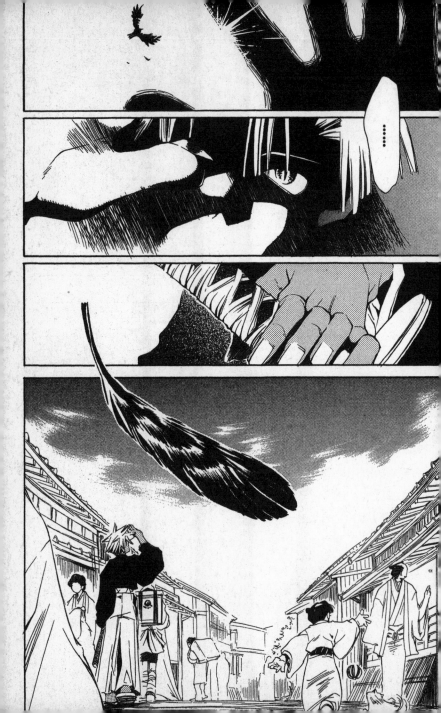

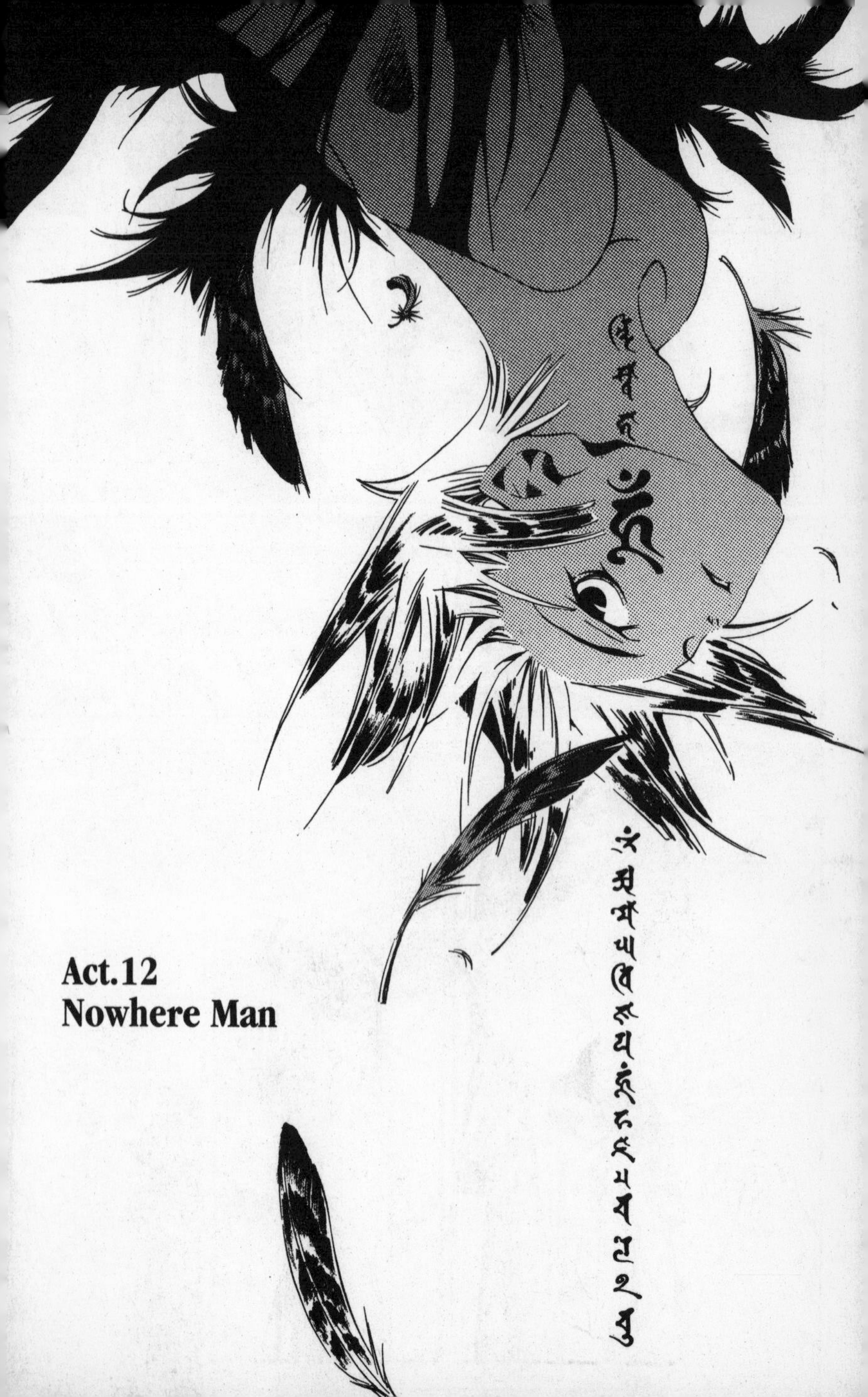

Act.12
Nowhere Man

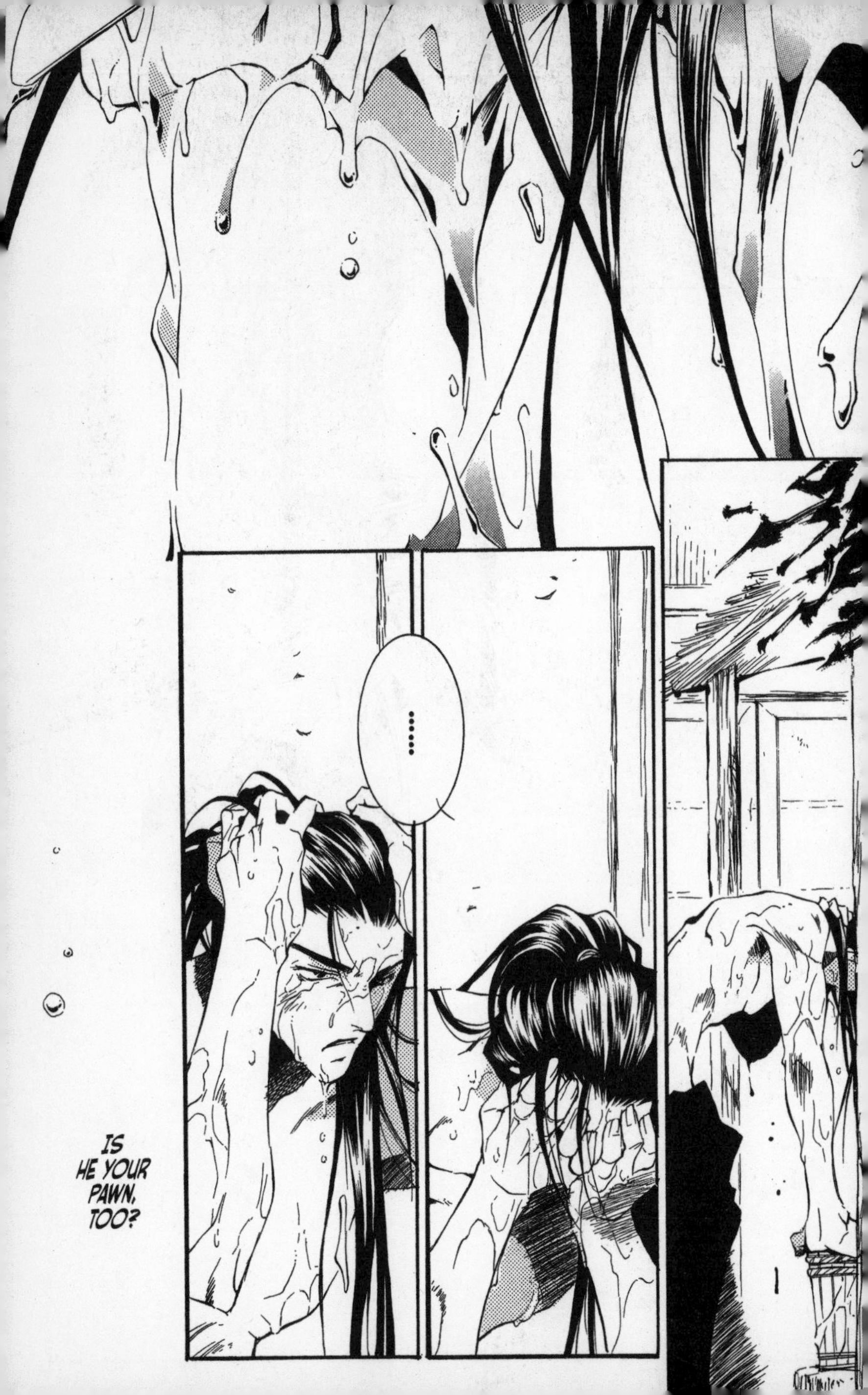
......
IS HE YOUR PAWN, TOO?

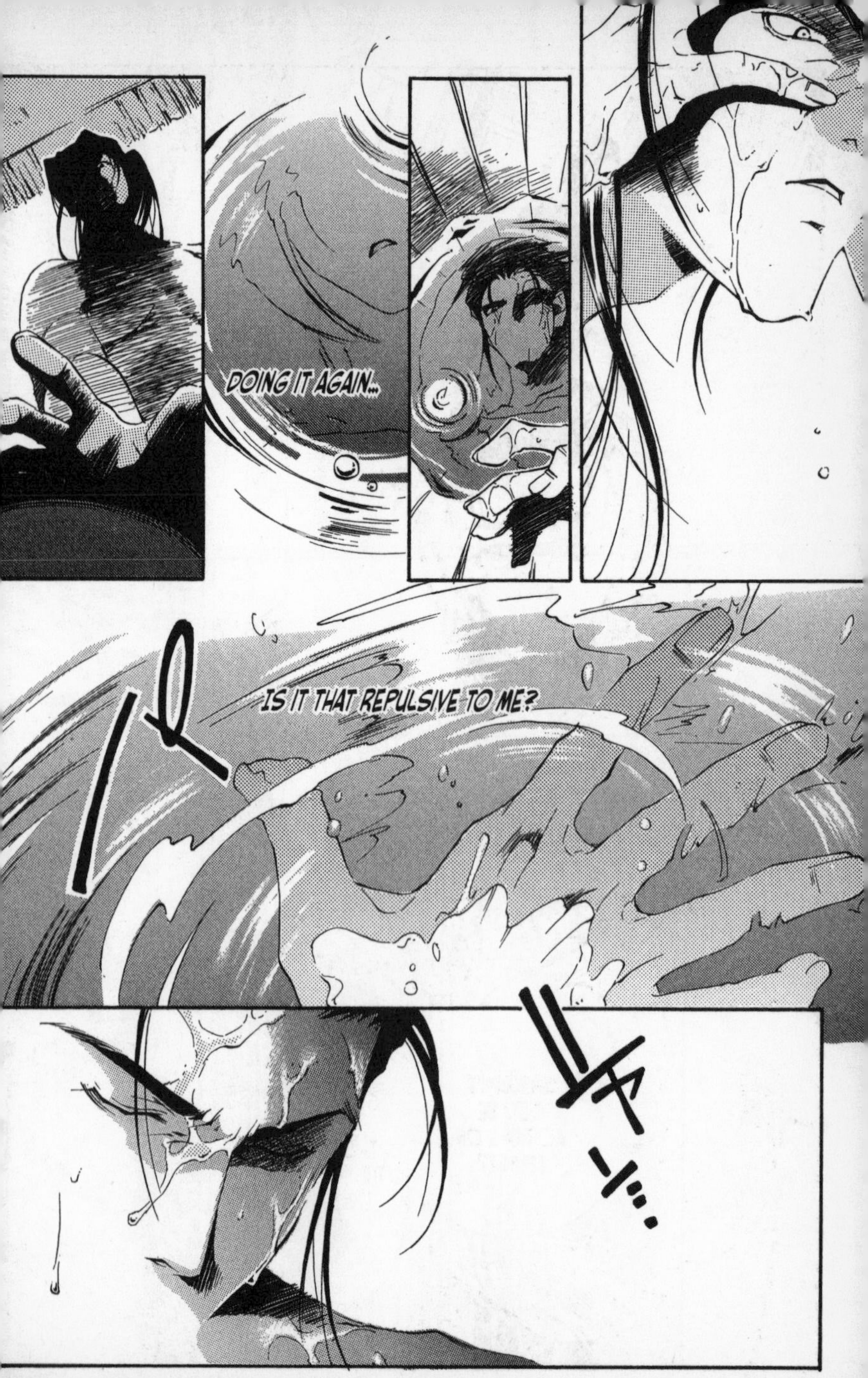
DOING IT AGAIN...
IS IT THAT REPULSIVE TO ME?

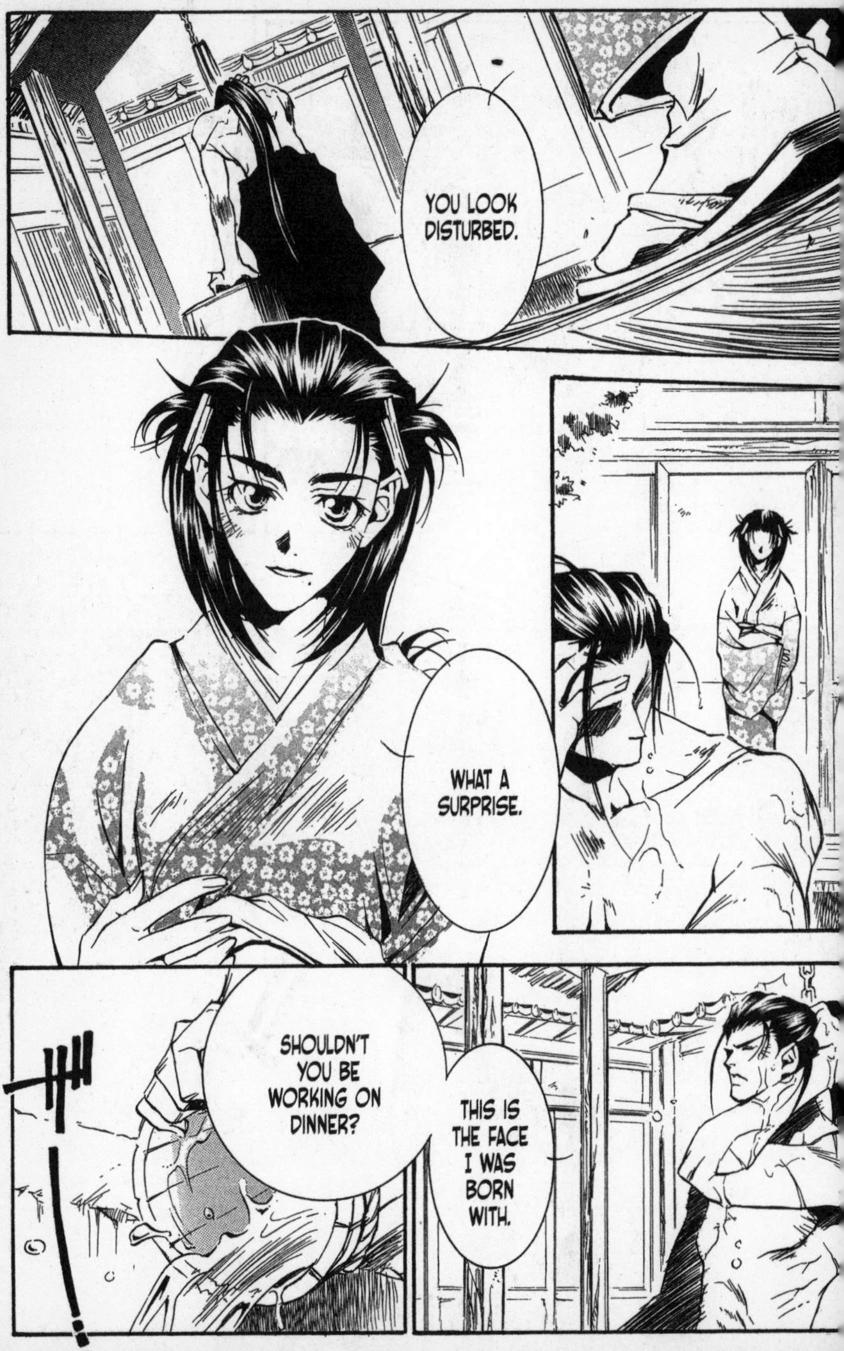
YOU LOOK DISTURBED.
WHAT A SURPRISE.
THIS IS THE FACE I WAS BORN WITH.
SHOULDN'T YOU BE WORKING ON DINNER?

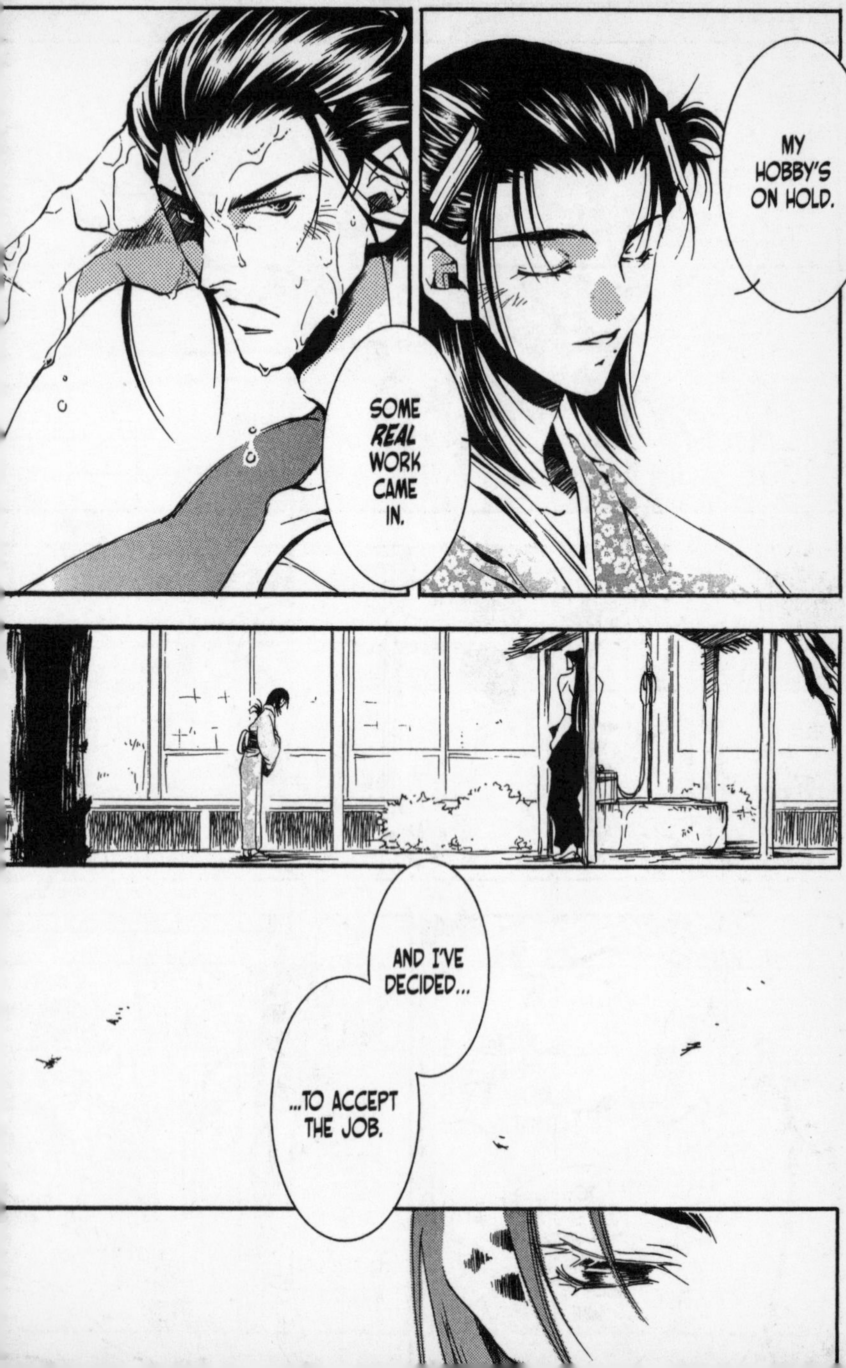
MY HOBBY'S ON HOLD.
SOME *REAL* WORK CAME IN.
AND I'VE DECIDED...
...TO ACCEPT THE JOB.

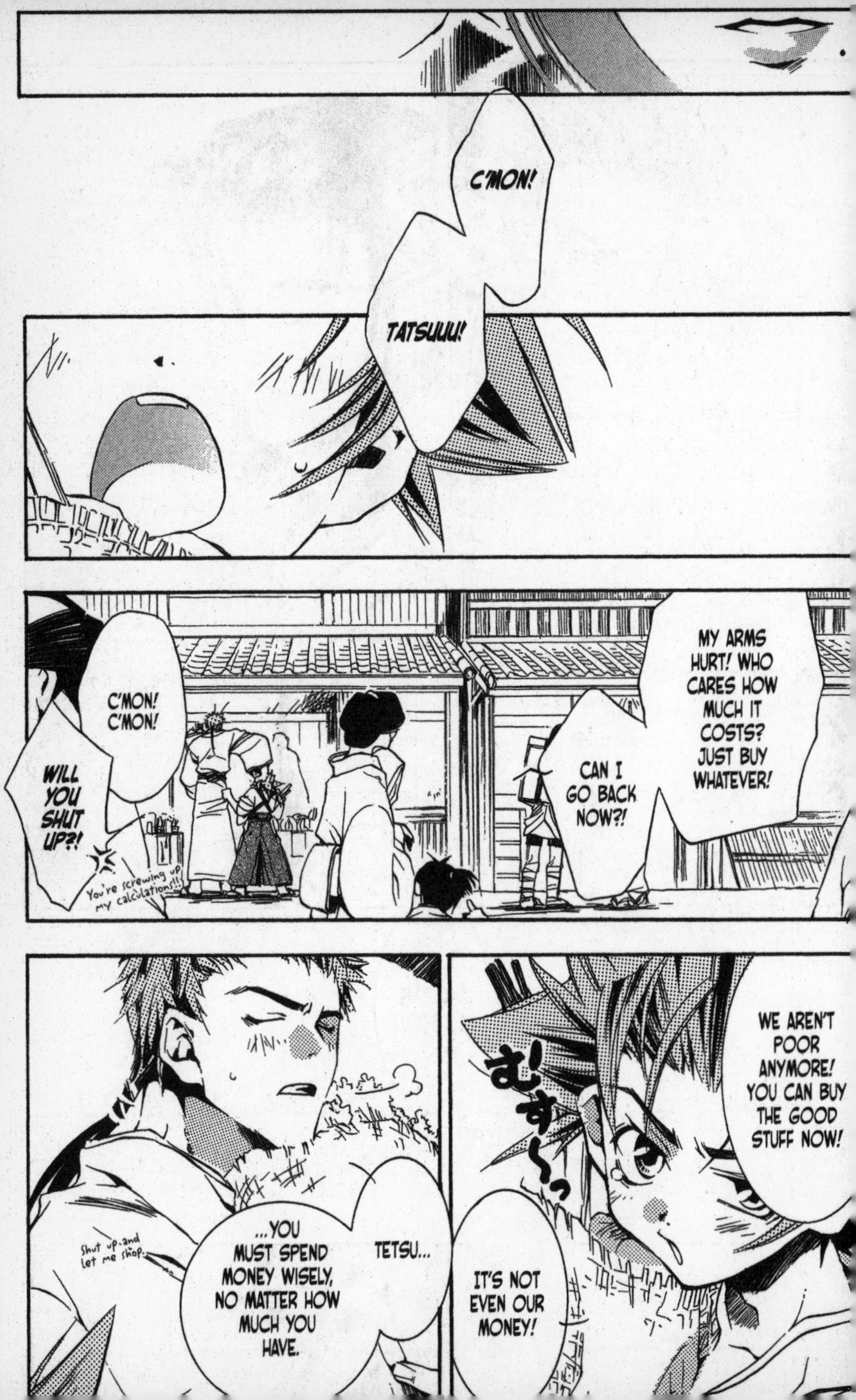
C'MON!
TATSUUU!
MY ARMS HURT! WHO CARES HOW MUCH IT COSTS? JUST BUY WHATEVER!
CAN I GO BACK NOW?!
C'MON! C'MON!
WILL YOU SHUT UP?!
You're screwing up my calculations!!
WE AREN'T POOR ANYMORE! YOU CAN BUY THE GOOD STUFF NOW!
IT'S NOT EVEN OUR MONEY!
TETSU...
...YOU MUST SPEND MONEY WISELY, NO MATTER HOW MUCH YOU HAVE.
Shut up and let me shop.

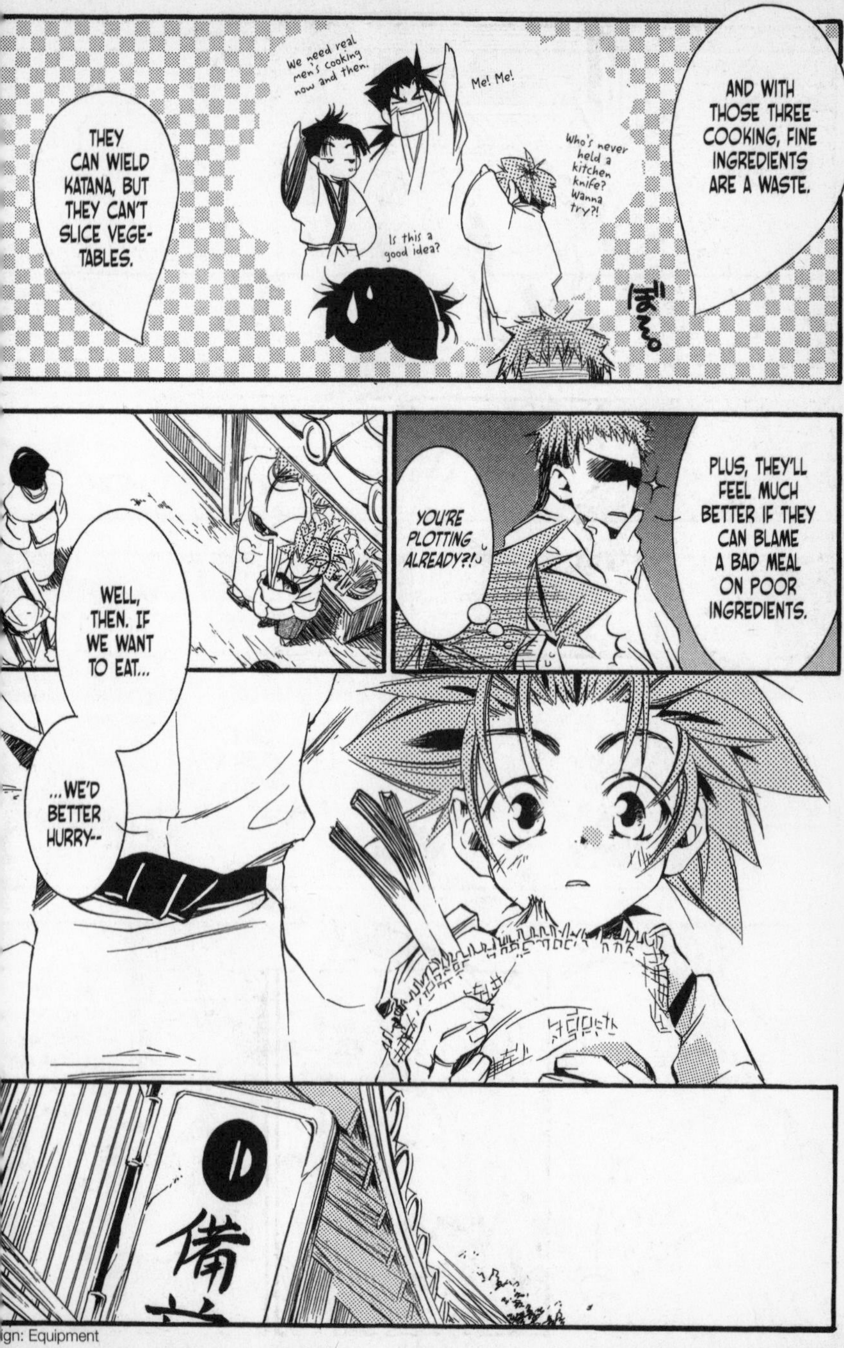
AND WITH THOSE THREE COOKING, FINE INGREDIENTS ARE A WASTE.
Who's never held a kitchen knife? Wanna try?!
Me! Me!
We need real men's cooking now and then.
Is this a good idea?
THEY CAN WIELD KATANA, BUT THEY CAN'T SLICE VEGE-TABLES.
PLUS, THEY'LL FEEL MUCH BETTER IF THEY CAN BLAME A BAD MEAL ON POOR INGREDIENTS.
YOU'RE PLOTTING ALREADY?!
WELL, THEN. IF WE WANT TO EAT...
...WE'D BETTER HURRY--
備

ign: Equipment

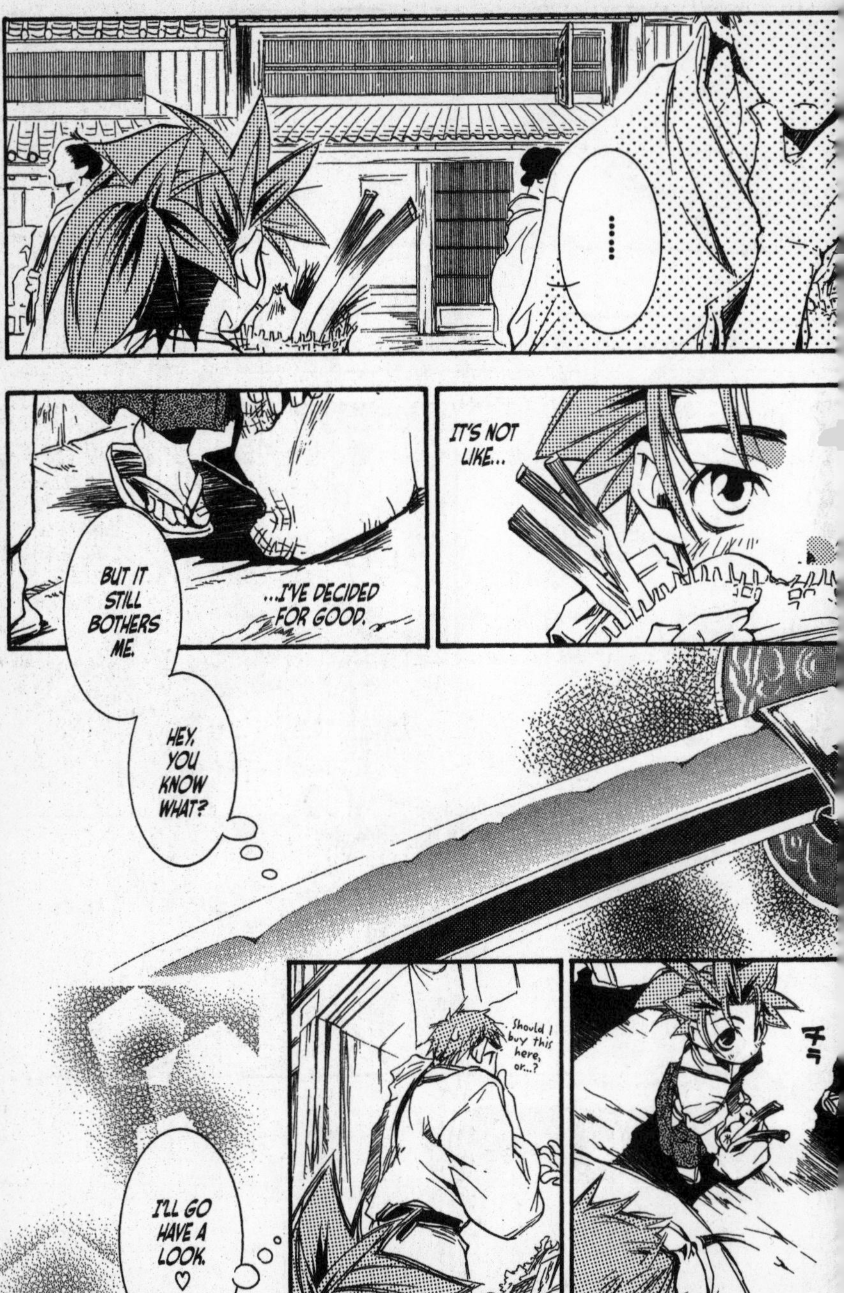
……
IT'S NOT LIKE...
...I'VE DECIDED FOR GOOD.
BUT IT STILL BOTHERS ME.
HEY, YOU KNOW WHAT?
チラ
Should I buy this here, or...?
I'LL GO HAVE A LOOK. ♡

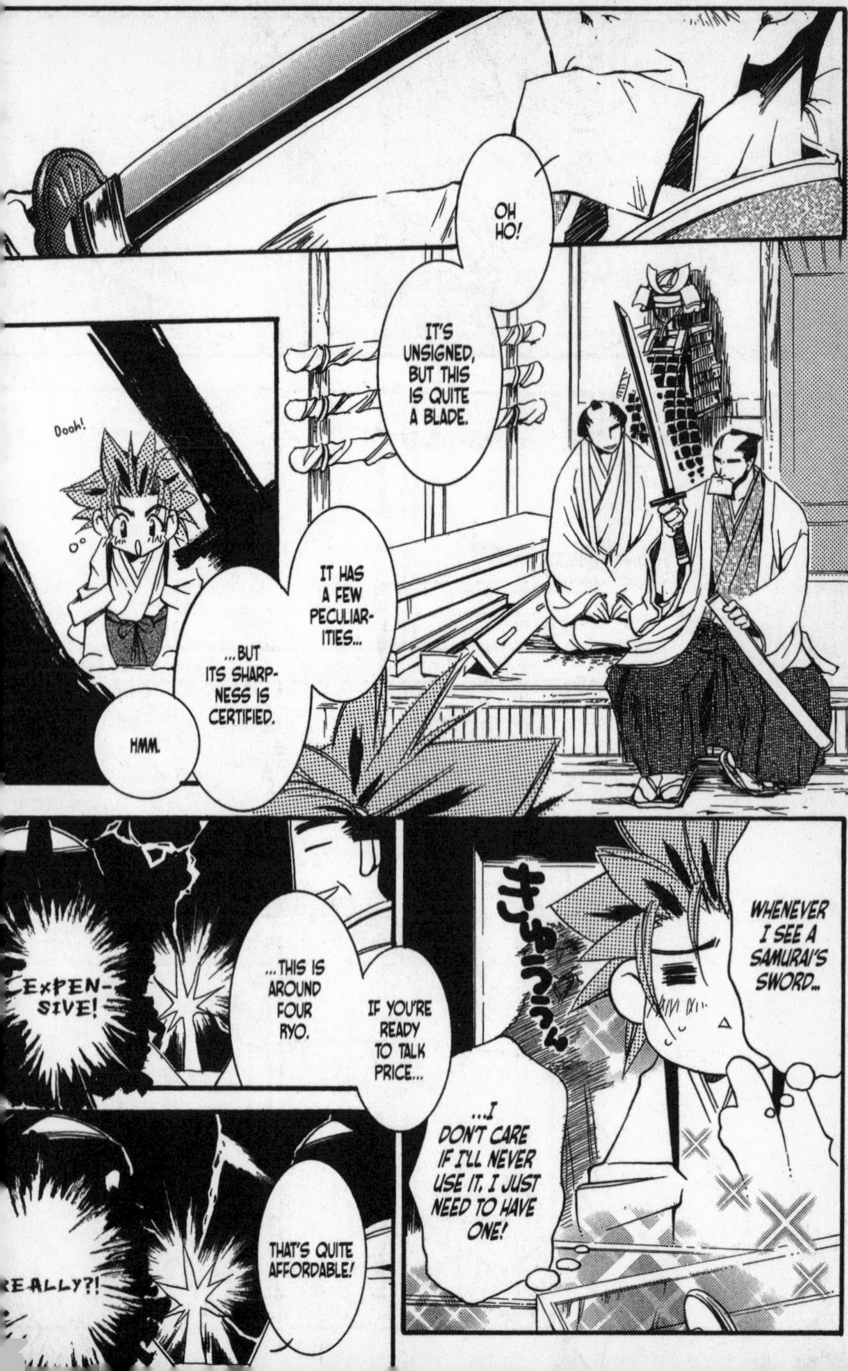
OH HO!
IT'S UNSIGNED, BUT THIS IS QUITE A BLADE.
IT HAS A FEW PECULIAR-ITIES...
...BUT ITS SHARP-NESS IS CERTIFIED.
Oooh!
HMM.
WHENEVER I SEE A SAMURAI'S SWORD...
...I DON'T CARE IF I'LL NEVER USE IT. I JUST NEED TO HAVE ONE!
IF YOU'RE READY TO TALK PRICE...
...THIS IS AROUND FOUR RYO.
EXPEN-SIVE!
THAT'S QUITE AFFORDABLE!
REALLY?!

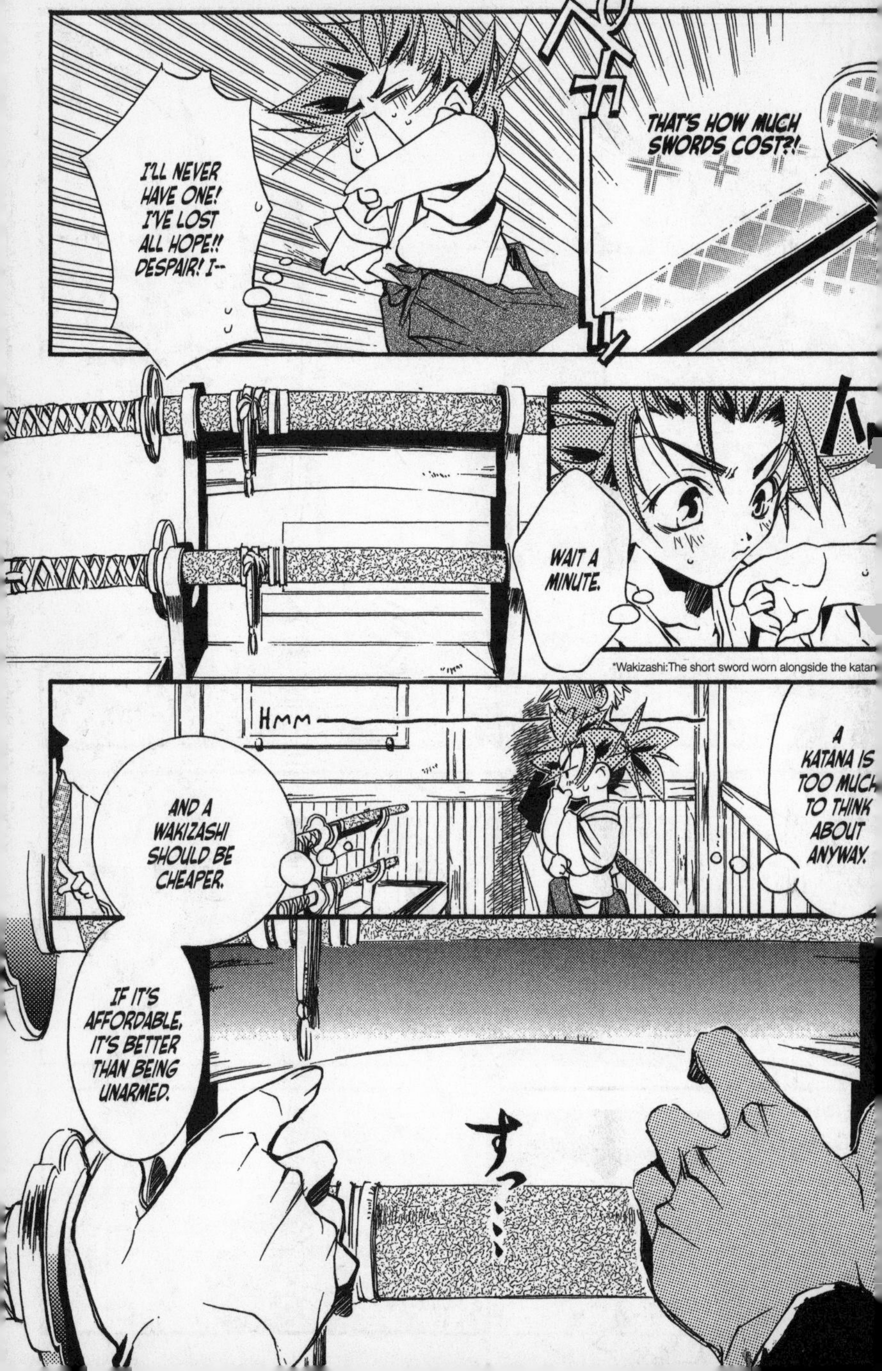
THAT'S HOW MUCH SWORDS COST?!
I'LL NEVER HAVE ONE! I'VE LOST ALL HOPE!! DESPAIR! I--
WAIT A MINUTE.
A KATANA IS TOO MUCH TO THINK ABOUT ANYWAY.
HMM—
AND A WAKIZASHI SHOULD BE CHEAPER.
IF IT'S AFFORDABLE, IT'S BETTER THAN BEING UNARMED.
すっ

*Wakizashi: The short sword worn alongside the katan

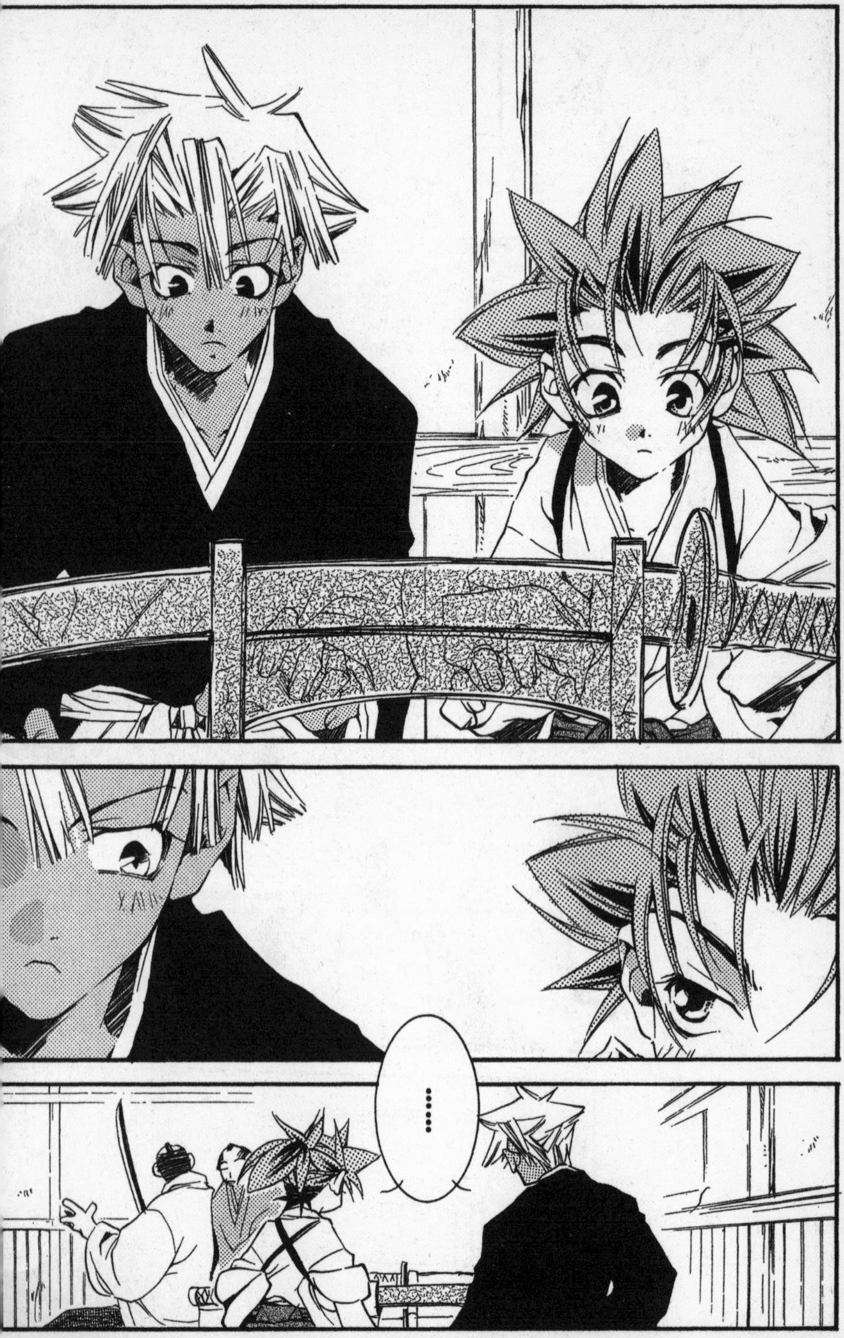
......

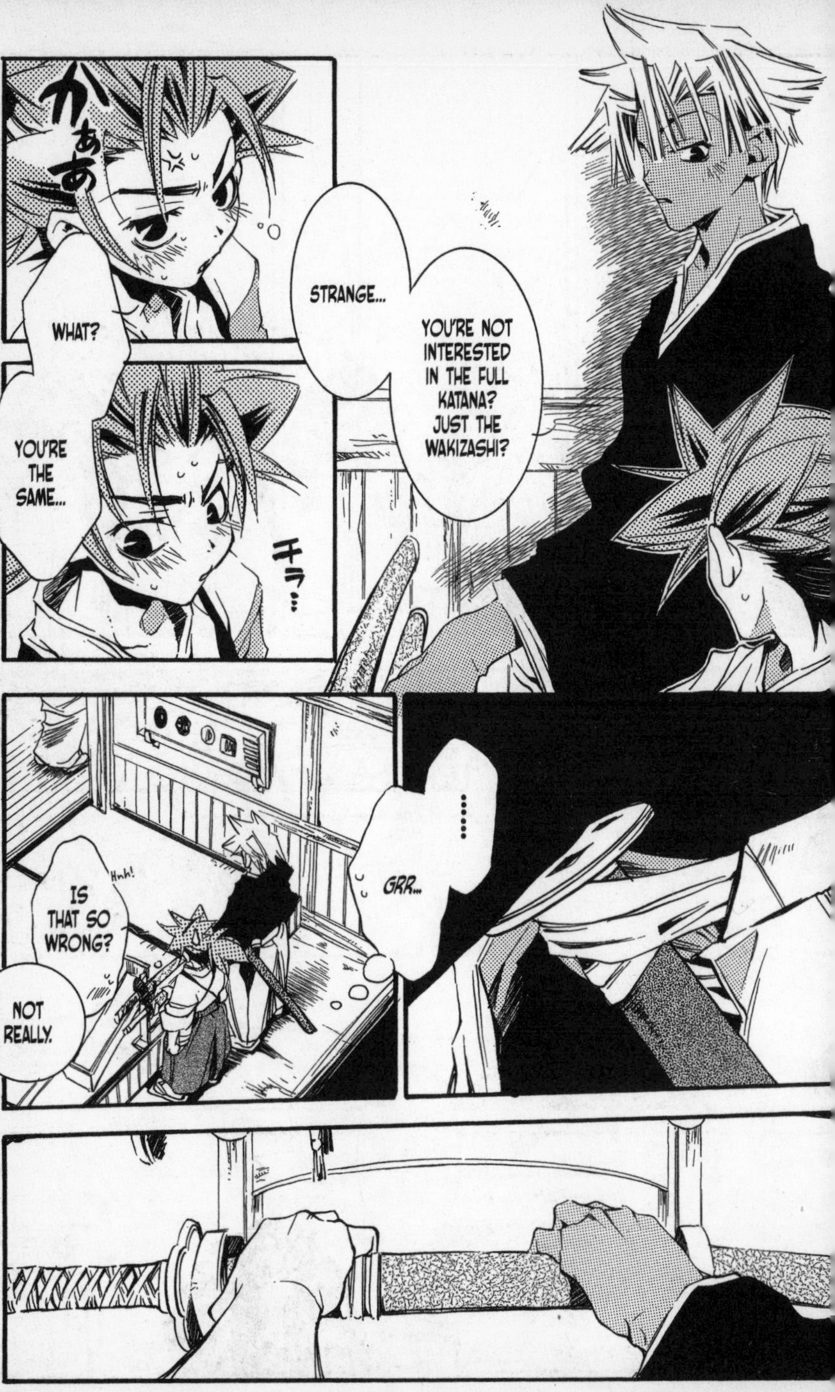
STRANGE...
YOU'RE NOT INTERESTED IN THE FULL KATANA? JUST THE WAKIZASHI?
かぁぁ
WHAT?
YOU'RE THE SAME...
チラ…
......
GRR...
Hnh!
IS THAT SO WRONG?
NOT REALLY.

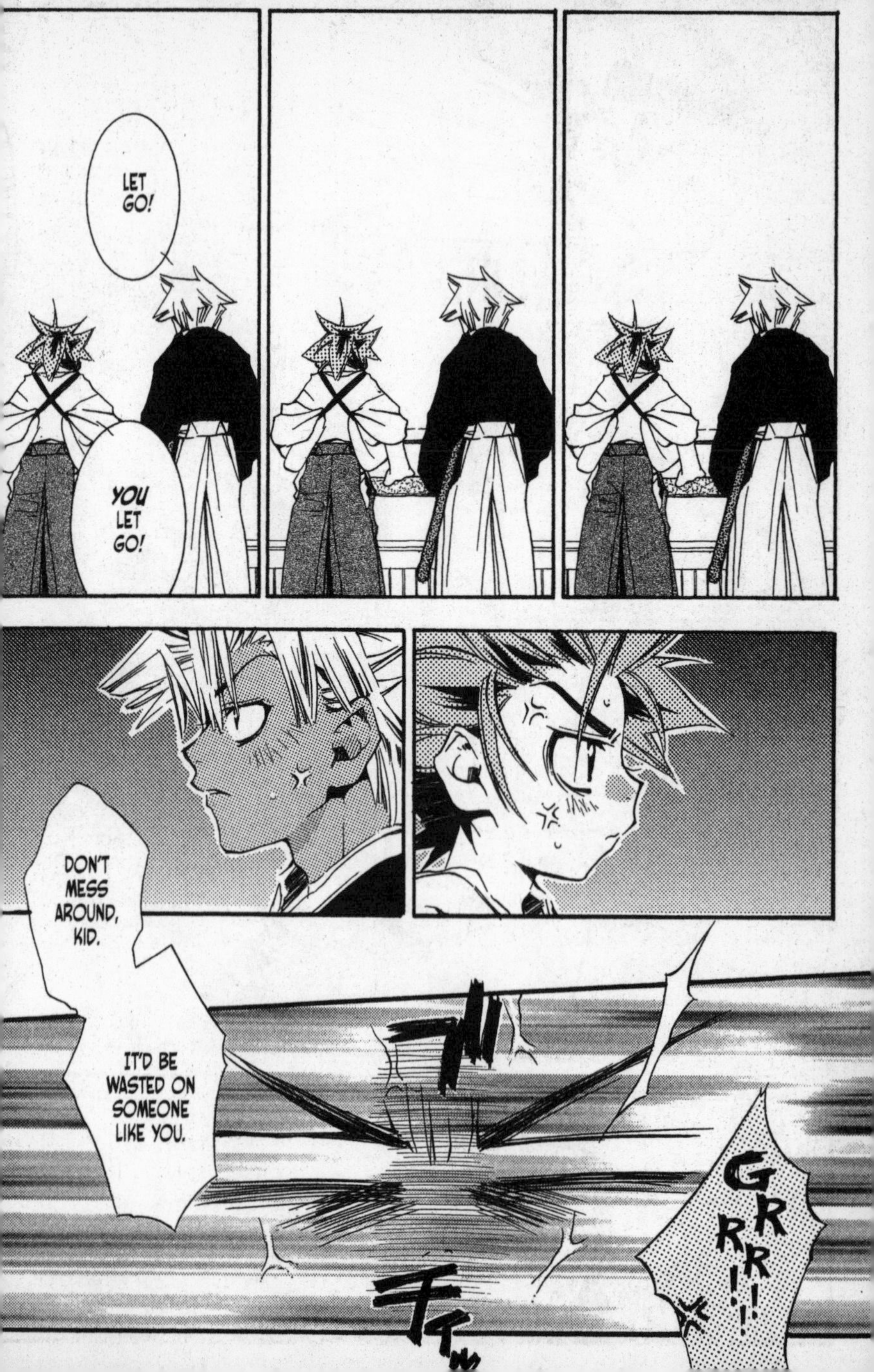
LET GO!
YOU LET GO!
DON'T MESS AROUND, KID.
IT'D BE WASTED ON SOMEONE LIKE YOU.
GRRR!!

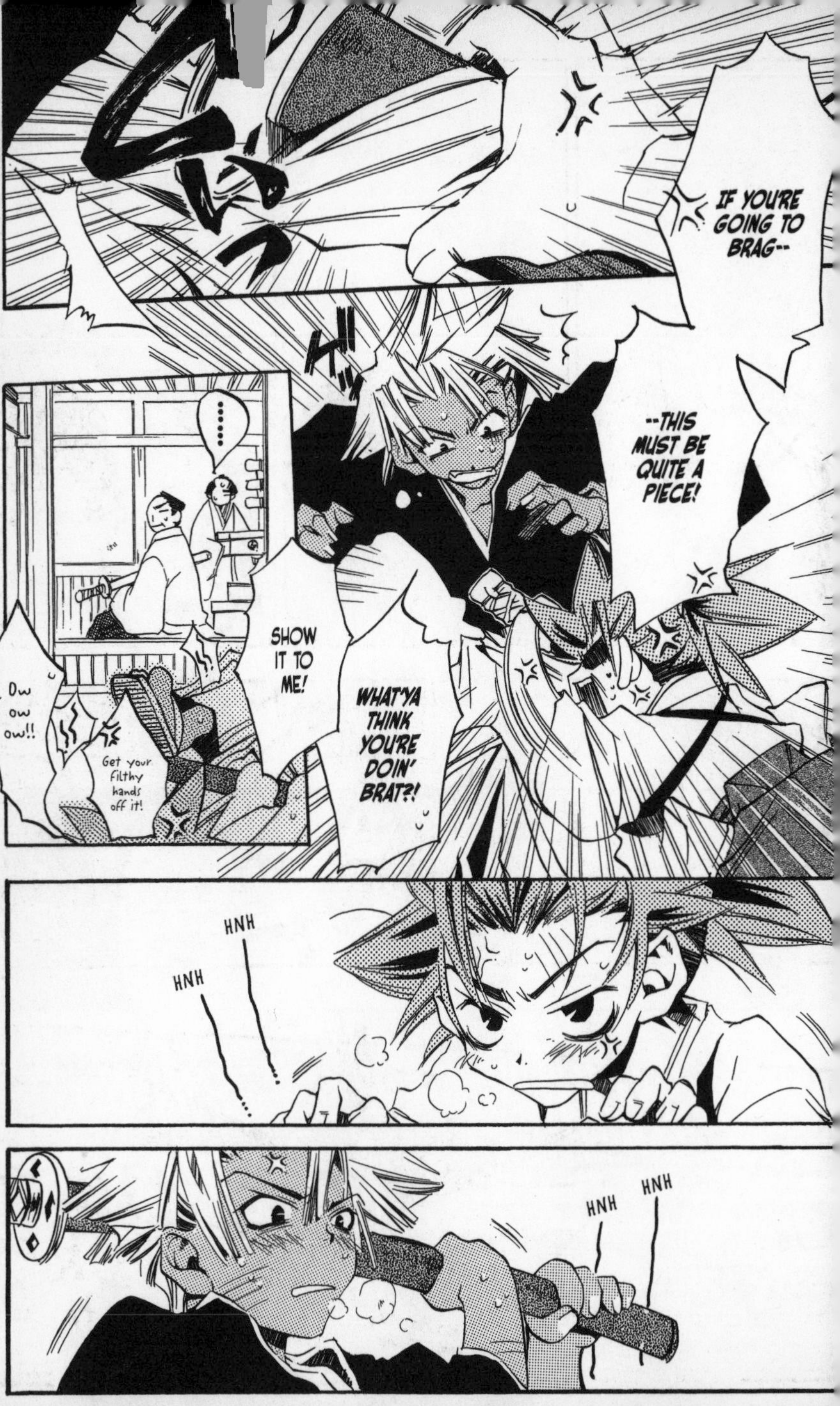

IF YOU'RE GOING TO BRAG--
--THIS MUST BE QUITE A PIECE!
SHOW IT TO ME!
WHAT'YA THINK YOU'RE DOIN' BRAT?!
......
Get your filthy hands off it!
Ow ow ow!!
HNH
HNH
HNH
HNH

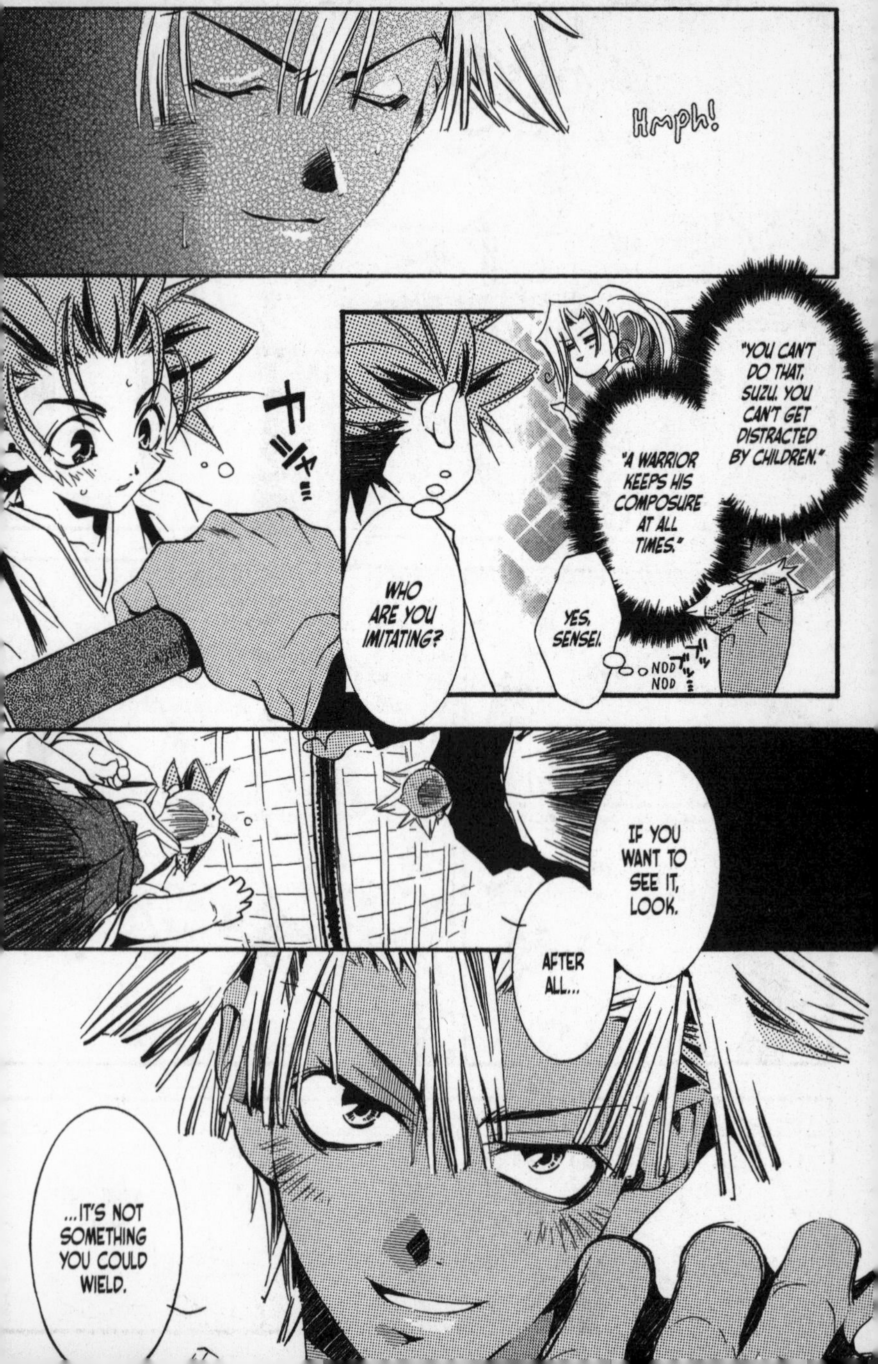
Hmph!
"YOU CAN'T DO THAT, SUZU. YOU CAN'T GET DISTRACTED BY CHILDREN."
"A WARRIOR KEEPS HIS COMPOSURE AT ALL TIMES."
YES, SENSEI.
NOD NOD
WHO ARE YOU IMITATING?
IF YOU WANT TO SEE IT, LOOK.
AFTER ALL...
...IT'S NOT SOMETHING YOU COULD WIELD.

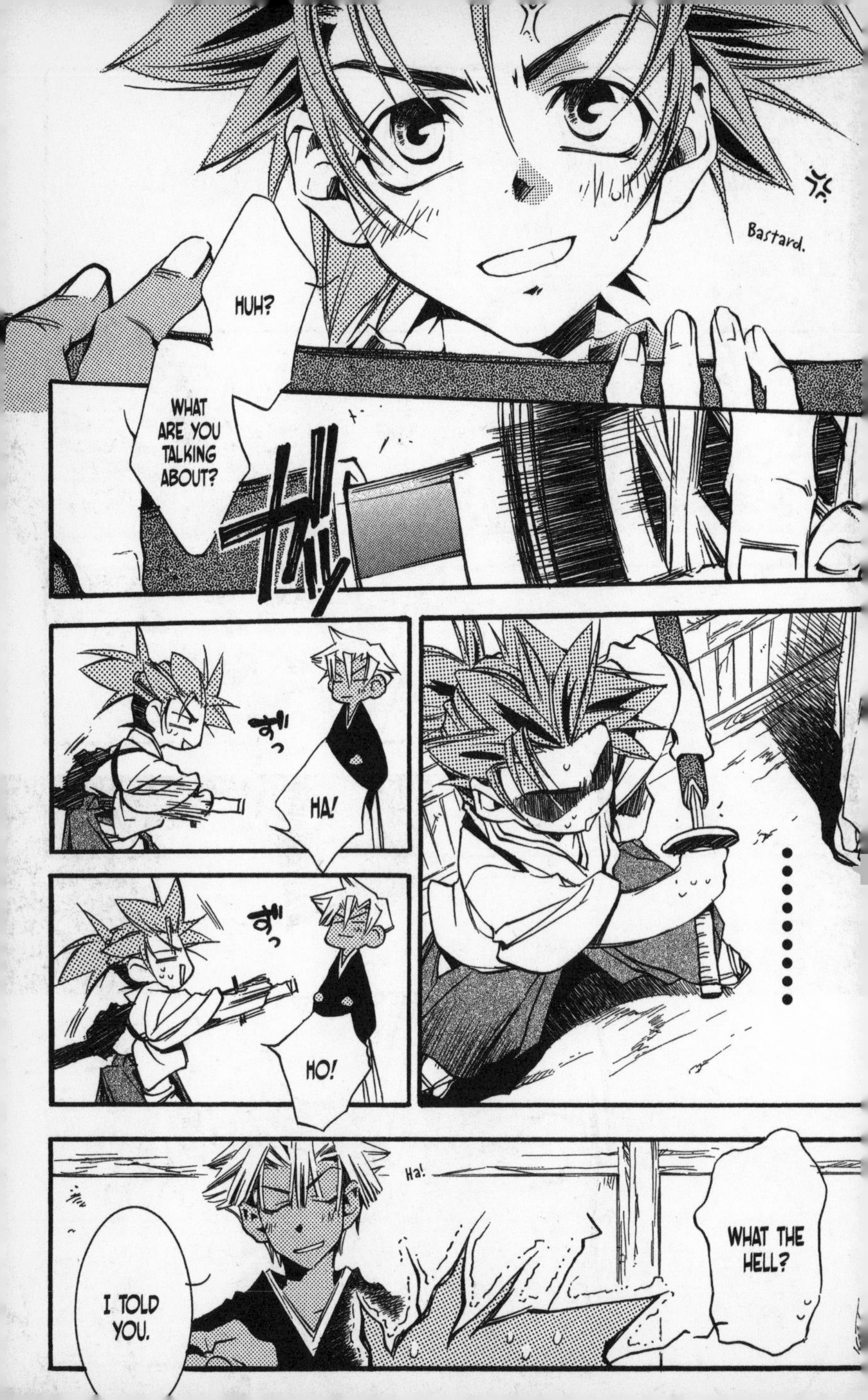
Bastard.
HUH?
WHAT ARE YOU TALKING ABOUT?
....
ずっ
HA!
ずっ
HO!
WHAT THE HELL?
Ha!
I TOLD YOU.

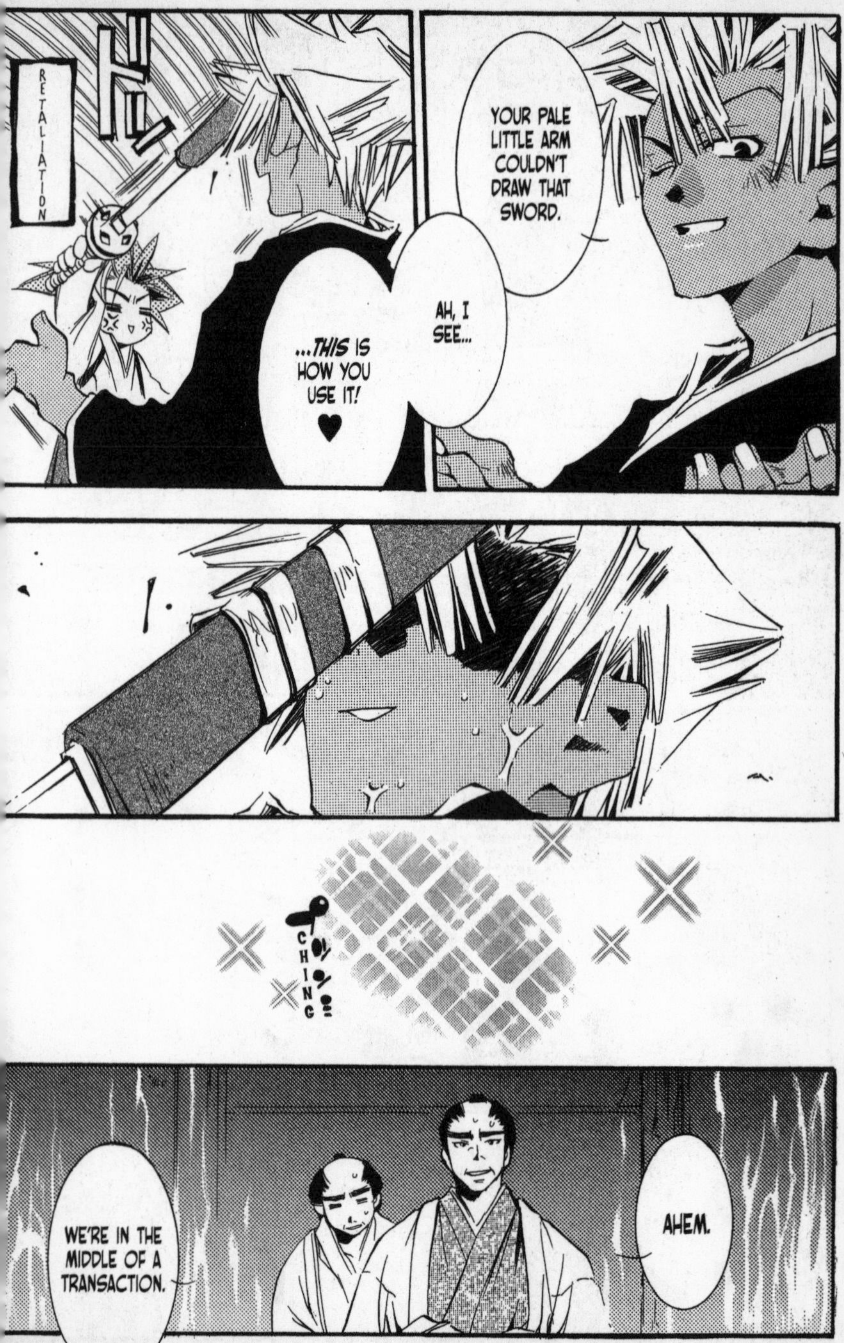
YOUR PALE LITTLE ARM COULDN'T DRAW THAT SWORD.
AH, I SEE...
...THIS IS HOW YOU USE IT! ♥
RETALIATION
CHING
AHEM.
WE'RE IN THE MIDDLE OF A TRANSACTION.

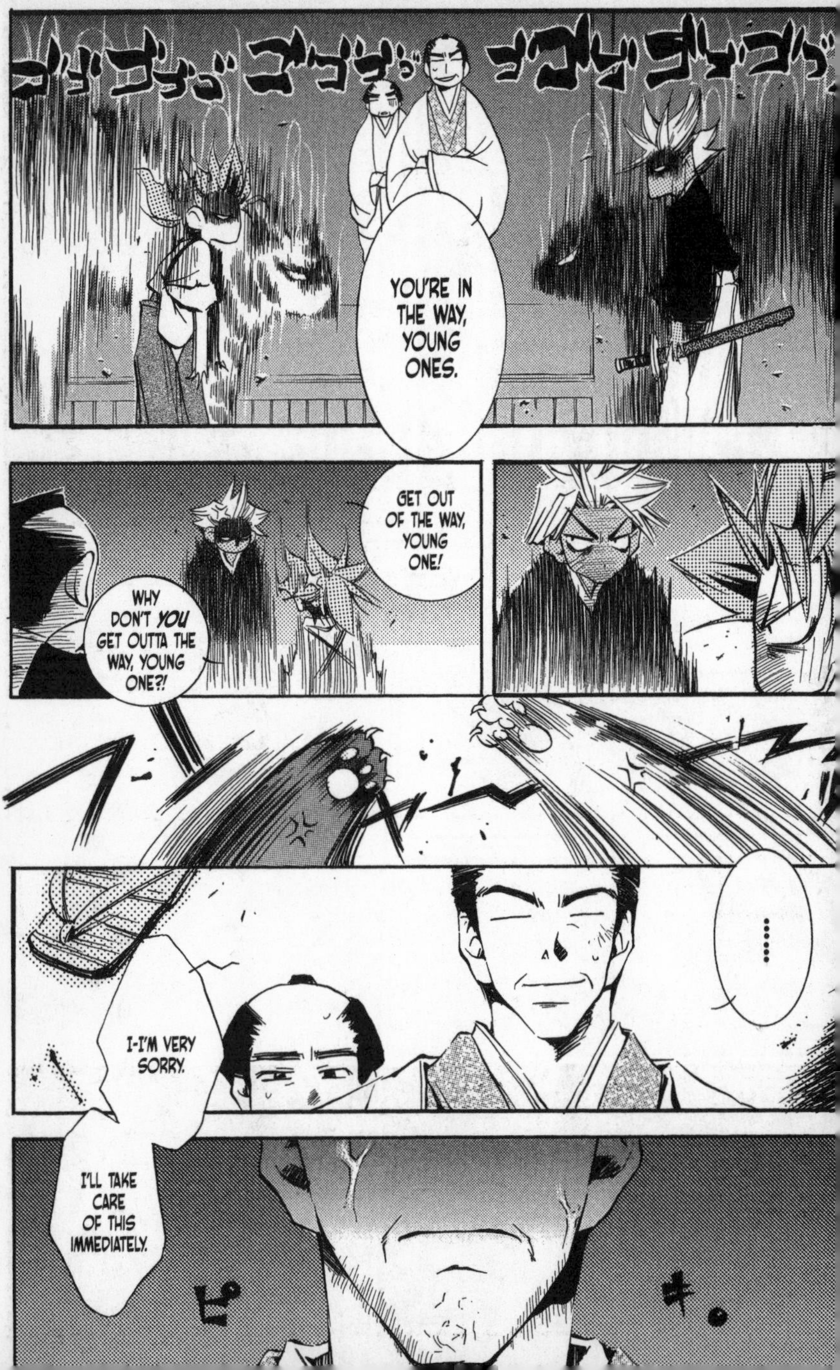
YOU'RE IN THE WAY, YOUNG ONES.
GET OUT OF THE WAY, YOUNG ONE!
WHY DON'T *YOU* GET OUTTA THE WAY, YOUNG ONE?!
......
I-I'M VERY SORRY.
I'LL TAKE CARE OF THIS IMMEDIATELY.
ピキ・

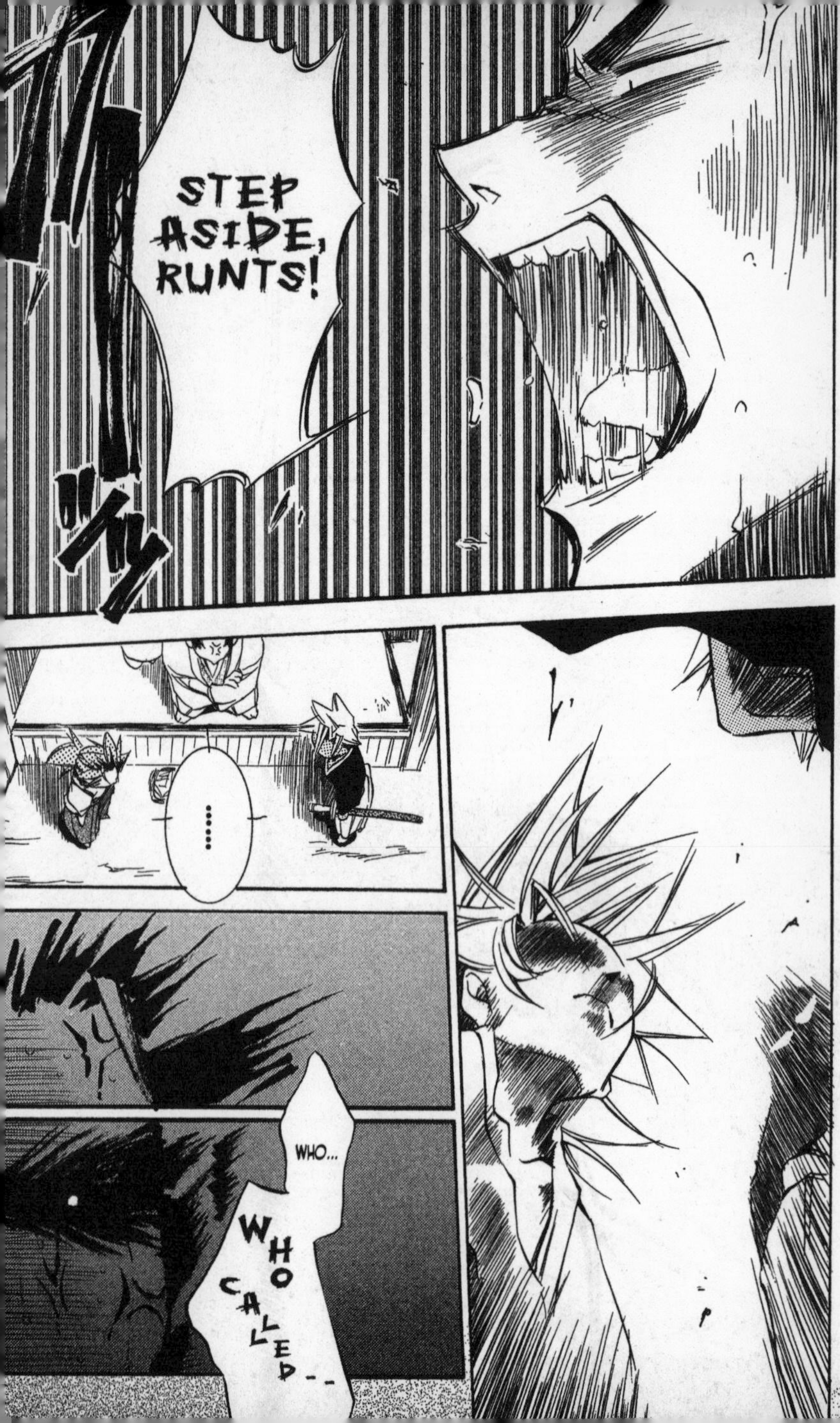
STEP ASIDE, RUNTS!
......
WHO...
WHO CALLED--

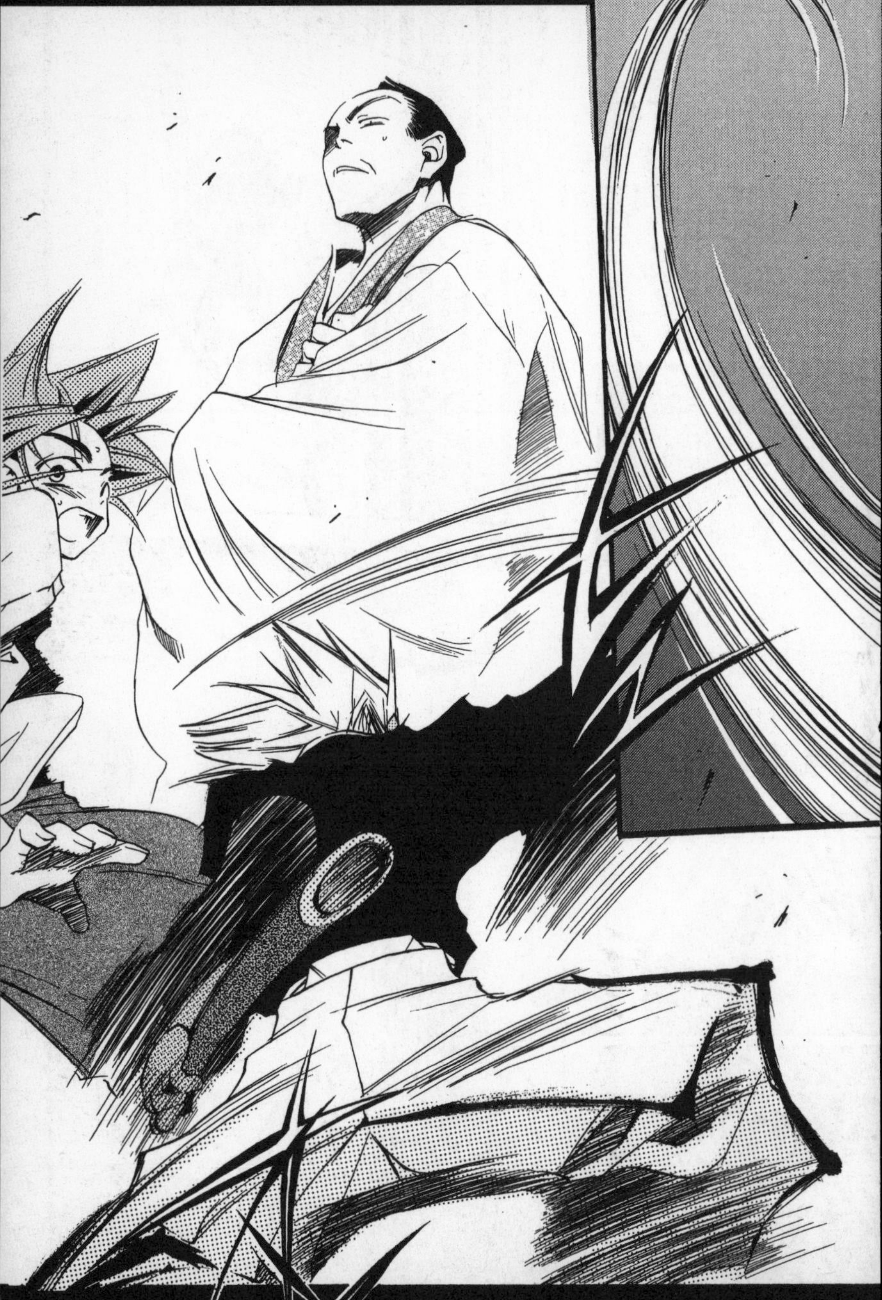

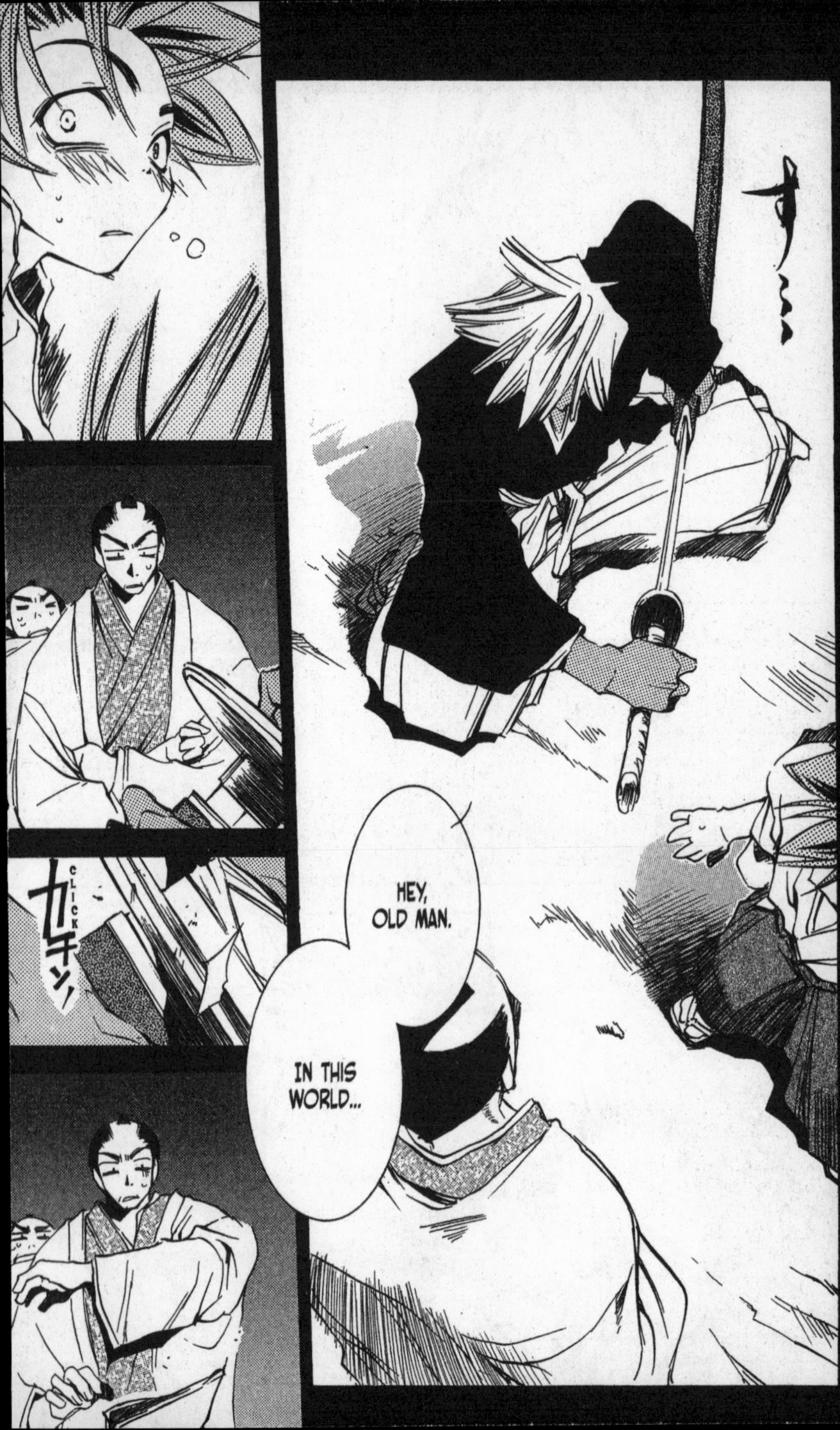
HEY, OLD MAN.
IN THIS WORLD...
CLICK

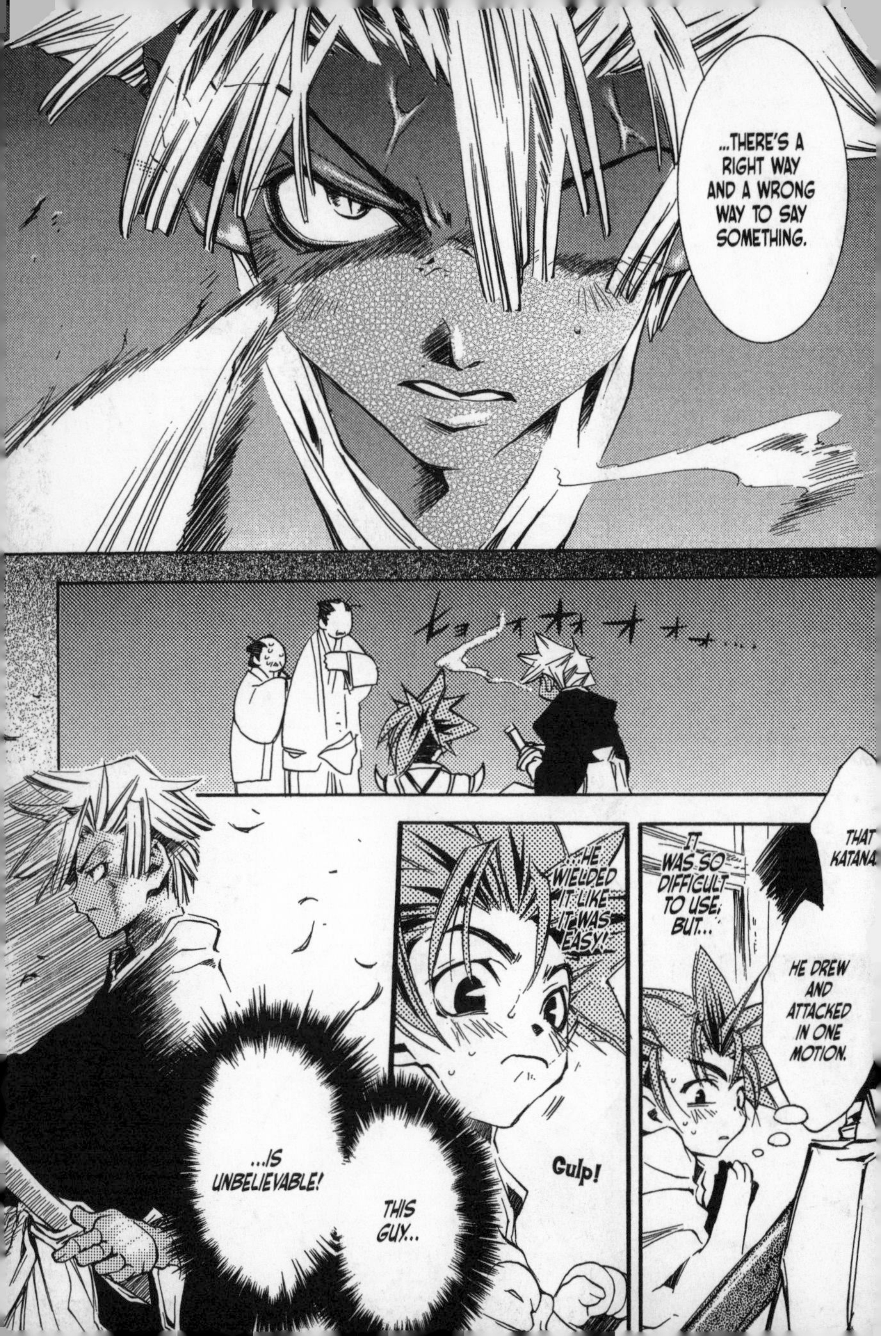
...THERE'S A RIGHT WAY AND A WRONG WAY TO SAY SOMETHING.
THAT KATANA...
IT WAS SO DIFFICULT TO USE, BUT...
HE DREW AND ATTACKED IN ONE MOTION.
HE WIELDED IT LIKE IT WAS EASY!
Gulp!
THIS GUY...
...IS UNBELIEVABLE!

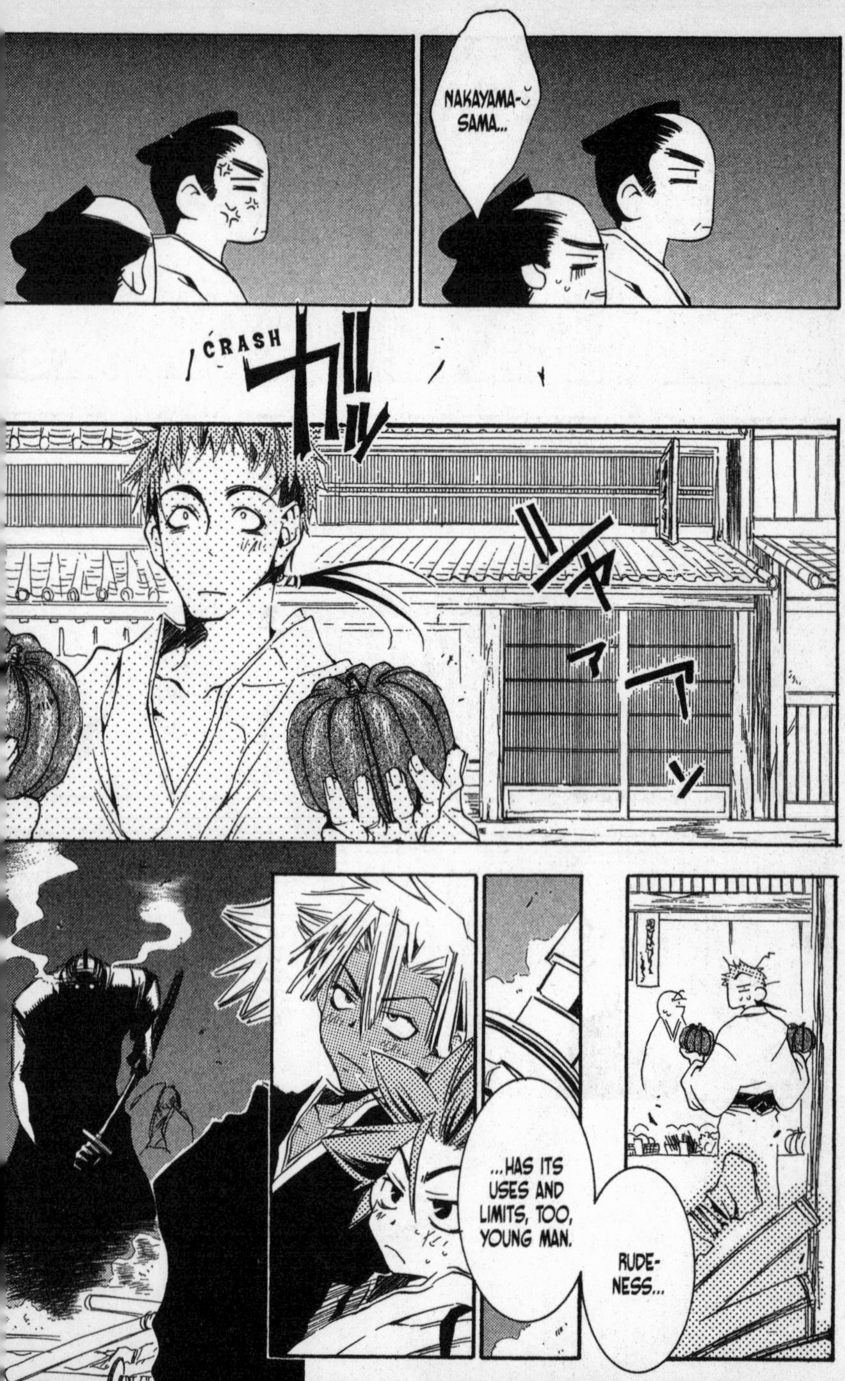
NAKAYAMA-SAMA...
CRASH
RUDE-NESS...
...HAS ITS USES AND LIMITS, TOO, YOUNG MAN.

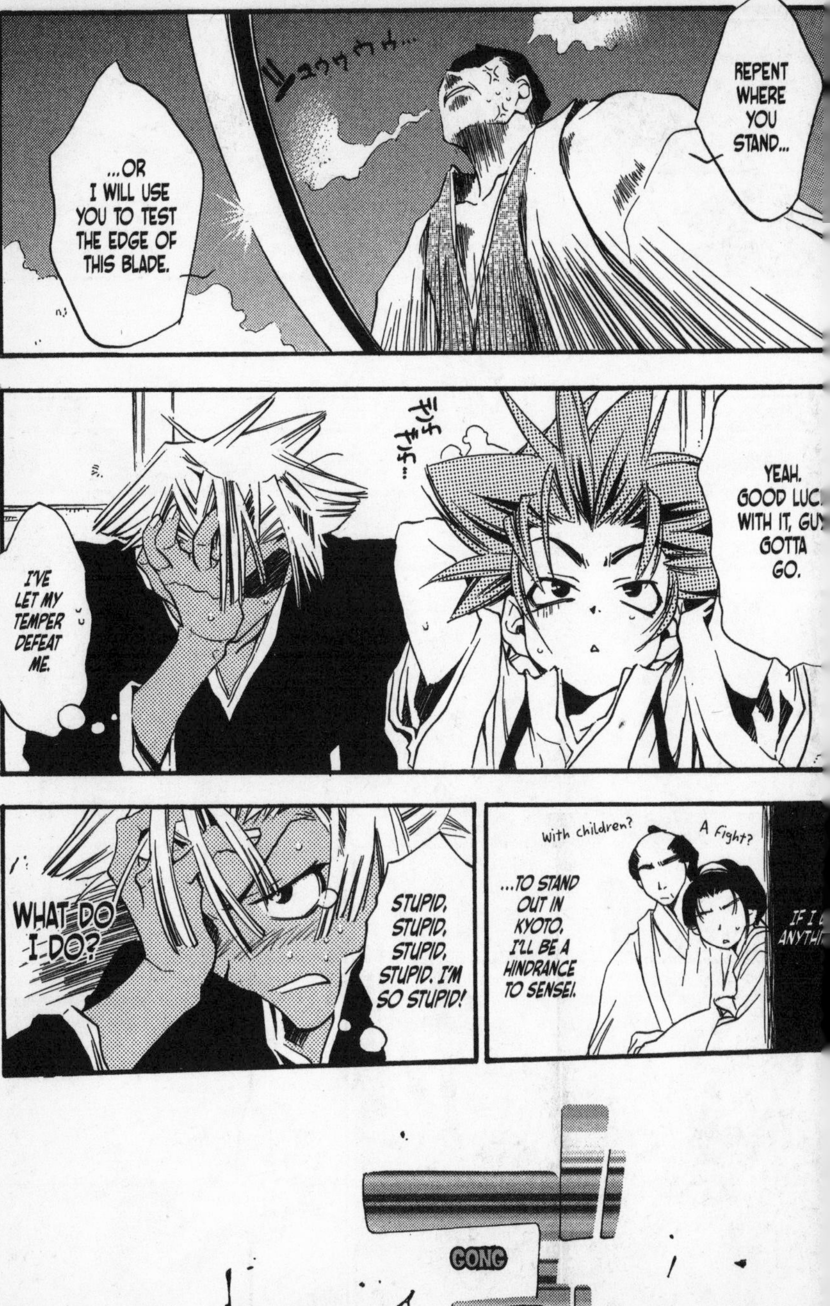
REPENT WHERE YOU STAND...
...OR I WILL USE YOU TO TEST THE EDGE OF THIS BLADE.
YEAH. GOOD LUC WITH IT, GUY GOTTA GO.
I'VE LET MY TEMPER DEFEAT ME.
IF I ANYTHI
A fight?
With children?
...TO STAND OUT IN KYOTO, I'LL BE A HINDRANCE TO SENSEI.
STUPID, STUPID, STUPID, STUPID. I'M SO STUPID!
WHAT DO I DO?
GONG

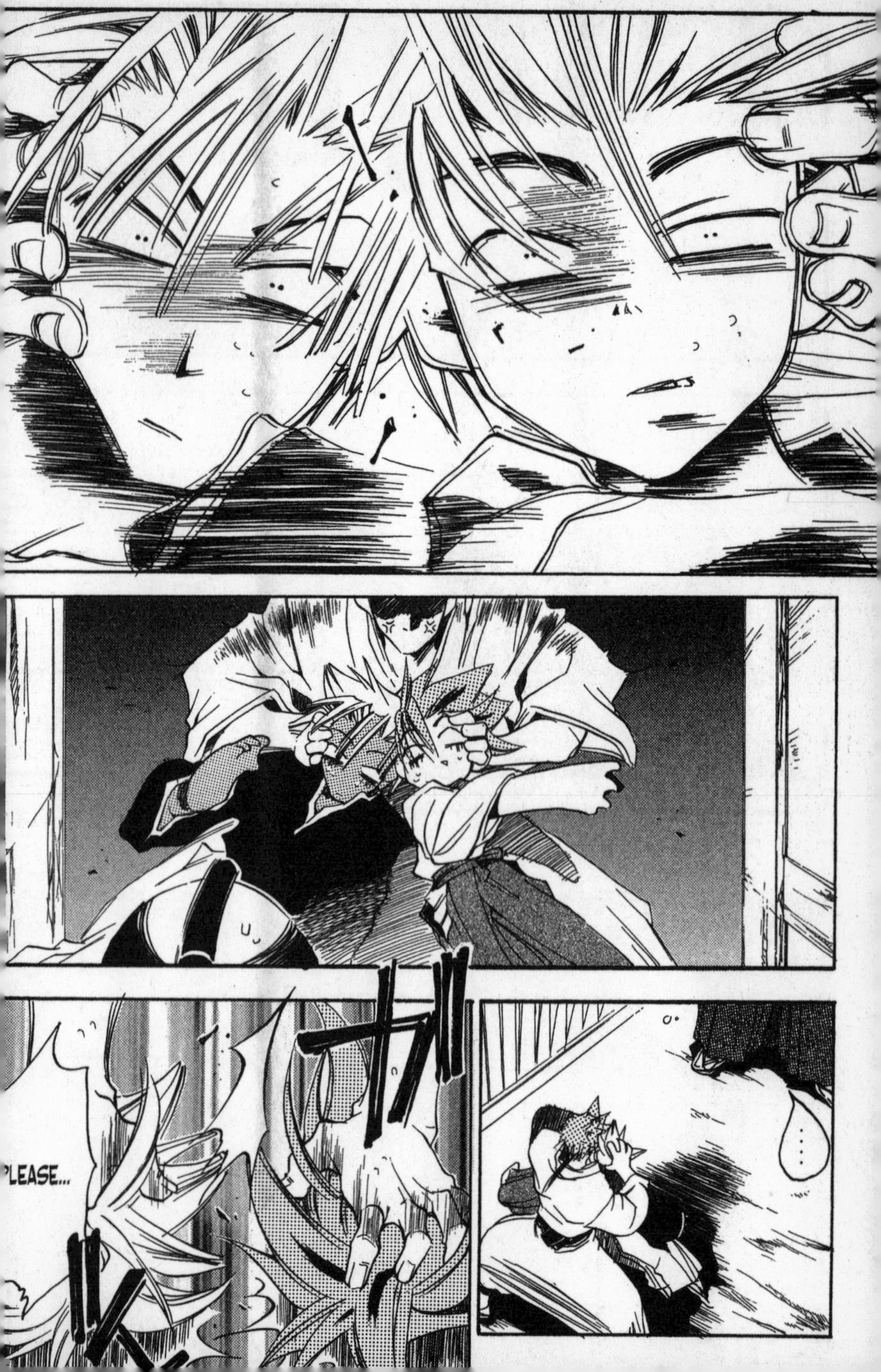
PLEASE...
...

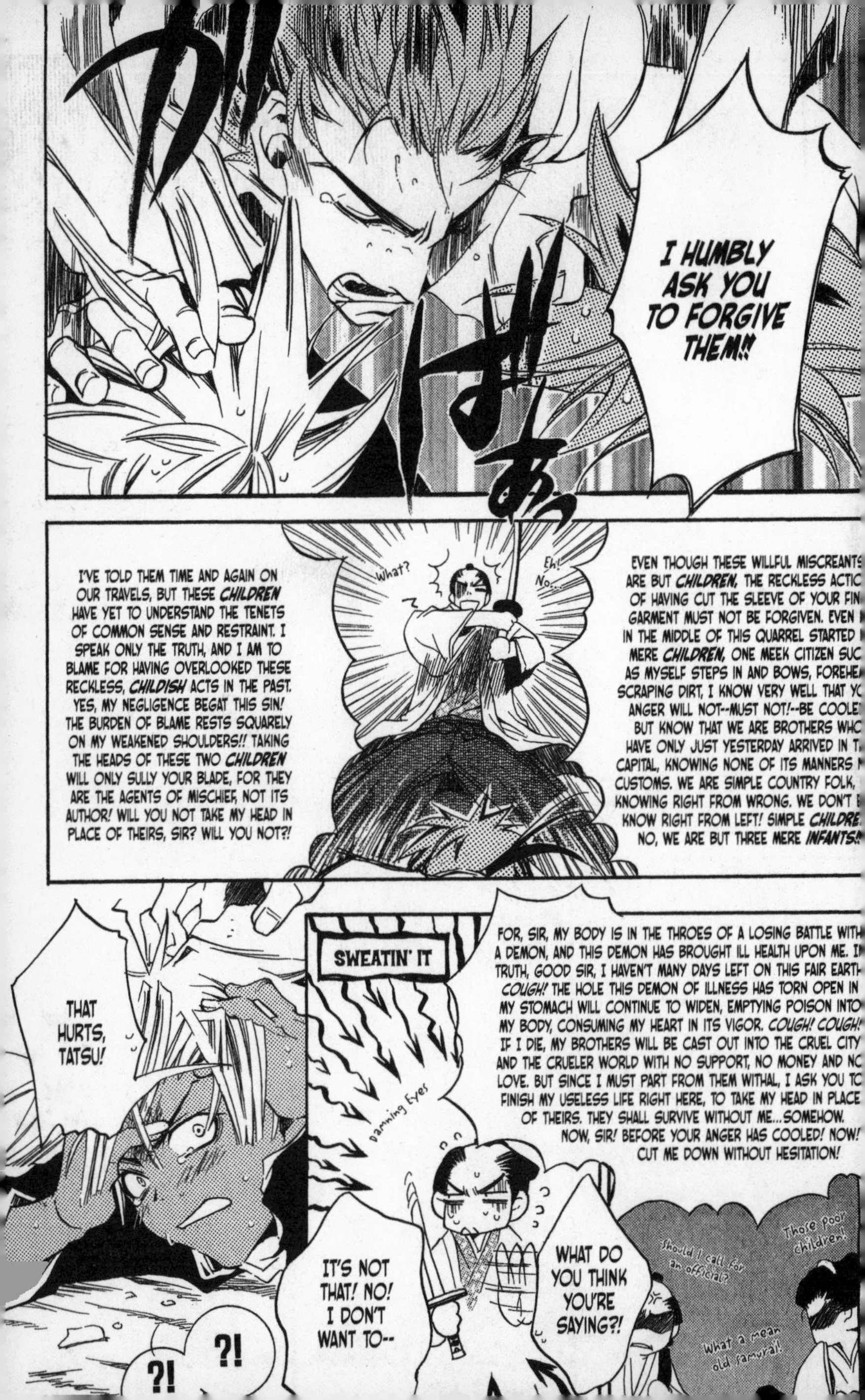

I HUMBLY ASK YOU TO FORGIVE THEM!!
EVEN THOUGH THESE WILLFUL MISCREANTS ARE BUT *CHILDREN,* THE RECKLESS ACTIO OF HAVING CUT THE SLEEVE OF YOUR FIN GARMENT MUST NOT BE FORGIVEN. EVEN I IN THE MIDDLE OF THIS QUARREL STARTED MERE *CHILDREN,* ONE MEEK CITIZEN SUC AS MYSELF STEPS IN AND BOWS, FOREHE SCRAPING DIRT, I KNOW VERY WELL THAT YO ANGER WILL NOT--MUST NOT!--BE COOLE BUT KNOW THAT WE ARE BROTHERS WHO HAVE ONLY JUST YESTERDAY ARRIVED IN T CAPITAL, KNOWING NONE OF ITS MANNERS CUSTOMS. WE ARE SIMPLE COUNTRY FOLK, KNOWING RIGHT FROM WRONG. WE DON'T KNOW RIGHT FROM LEFT! SIMPLE *CHILDRE* NO, WE ARE BUT THREE MERE *INFANTS!*
Eh! No...
What?
I'VE TOLD THEM TIME AND AGAIN ON OUR TRAVELS, BUT THESE *CHILDREN* HAVE YET TO UNDERSTAND THE TENETS OF COMMON SENSE AND RESTRAINT. I SPEAK ONLY THE TRUTH, AND I AM TO BLAME FOR HAVING OVERLOOKED THESE RECKLESS, *CHILDISH* ACTS IN THE PAST. YES, MY NEGLIGENCE BEGAT THIS SIN! THE BURDEN OF BLAME RESTS SQUARELY ON MY WEAKENED SHOULDERS!! TAKING THE HEADS OF THESE TWO *CHILDREN* WILL ONLY SULLY YOUR BLADE, FOR THEY ARE THE AGENTS OF MISCHIEF, NOT ITS AUTHOR! WILL YOU NOT TAKE MY HEAD IN PLACE OF THEIRS, SIR? WILL YOU NOT?!
FOR, SIR, MY BODY IS IN THE THROES OF A LOSING BATTLE WITH A DEMON, AND THIS DEMON HAS BROUGHT ILL HEALTH UPON ME. IN TRUTH, GOOD SIR, I HAVEN'T MANY DAYS LEFT ON THIS FAIR EARTH *COUGH!* THE HOLE THIS DEMON OF ILLNESS HAS TORN OPEN IN MY STOMACH WILL CONTINUE TO WIDEN, EMPTYING POISON INTO MY BODY, CONSUMING MY HEART IN ITS VIGOR. *COUGH! COUGH!* IF I DIE, MY BROTHERS WILL BE CAST OUT INTO THE CRUEL CITY AND THE CRUELER WORLD WITH NO SUPPORT, NO MONEY AND NO LOVE. BUT SINCE I MUST PART FROM THEM WITHAL, I ASK YOU TO FINISH MY USELESS LIFE RIGHT HERE, TO TAKE MY HEAD IN PLACE OF THEIRS. THEY SHALL SURVIVE WITHOUT ME...SOMEHOW. NOW, SIR! BEFORE YOUR ANGER HAS COOLED! NOW! CUT ME DOWN WITHOUT HESITATION!
SWEATIN' IT
Damning Eyes
Those poor children!
Should I call for an official?
WHAT DO YOU THINK YOU'RE SAYING?!
What a mean old samurai!
IT'S NOT THAT! NO! I DON'T WANT TO--
THAT HURTS, TATSU!
?!
?!

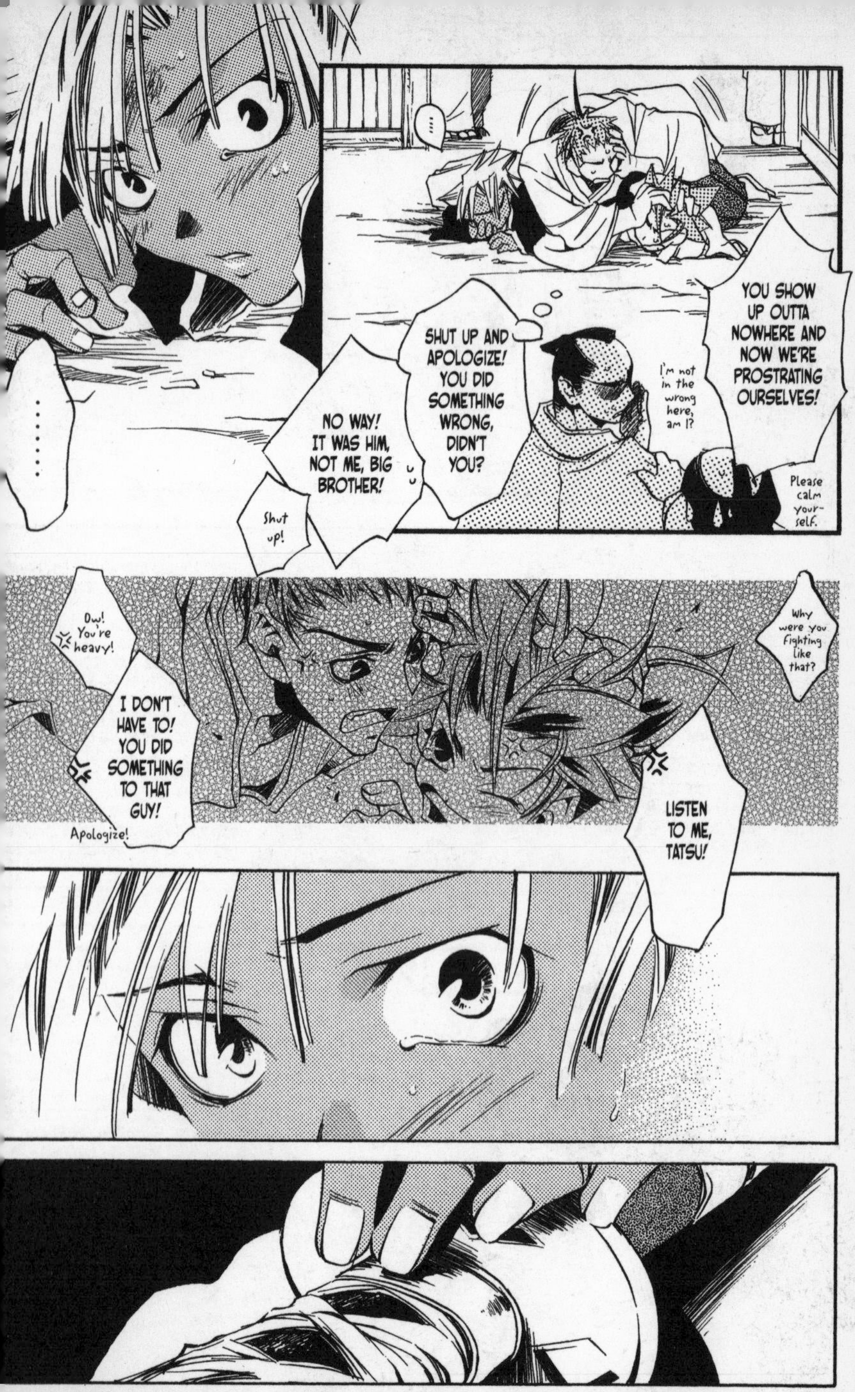
…
YOU SHOW UP OUTTA NOWHERE AND NOW WE'RE PROSTRATING OURSELVES!
Please calm your-self.
I'm not in the wrong here, am I?
SHUT UP AND APOLOGIZE! YOU DID SOMETHING WRONG, DIDN'T YOU?
NO WAY! IT WAS HIM, NOT ME, BIG BROTHER!
Shut up!
......
Why were you fighting like that?
LISTEN TO ME, TATSU!
I DON'T HAVE TO! YOU DID SOMETHING TO THAT GUY!
Ow! You're heavy!
Apologize!

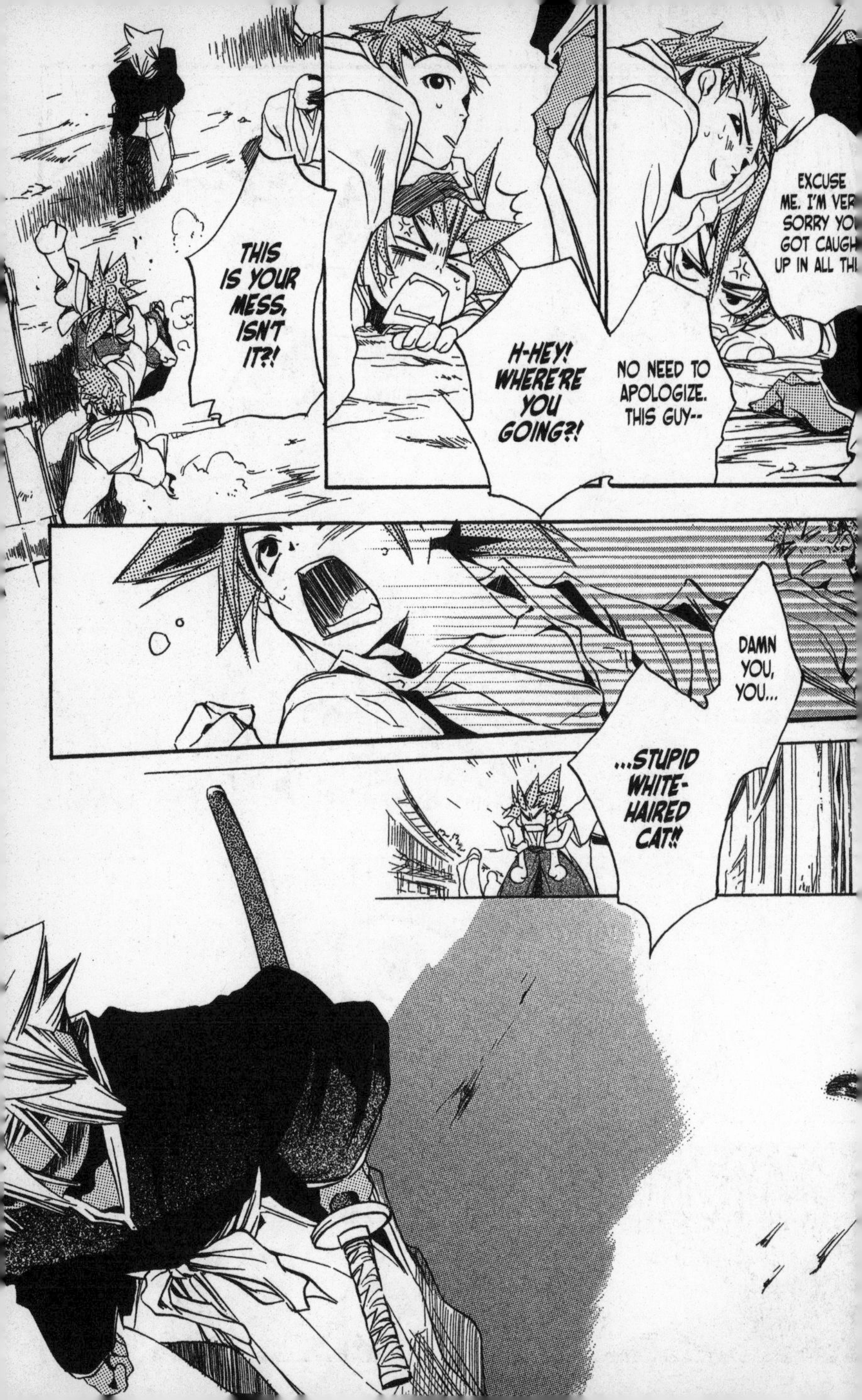
EXCUSE ME. I'M VER SORRY YO GOT CAUGH UP IN ALL TH
NO NEED TO APOLOGIZE. THIS GUY--
H-HEY! WHERE'RE YOU GOING?!
THIS IS YOUR MESS, ISN'T IT?!
DAMN YOU, YOU...
...STUPID WHITE-HAIRED CAT!!

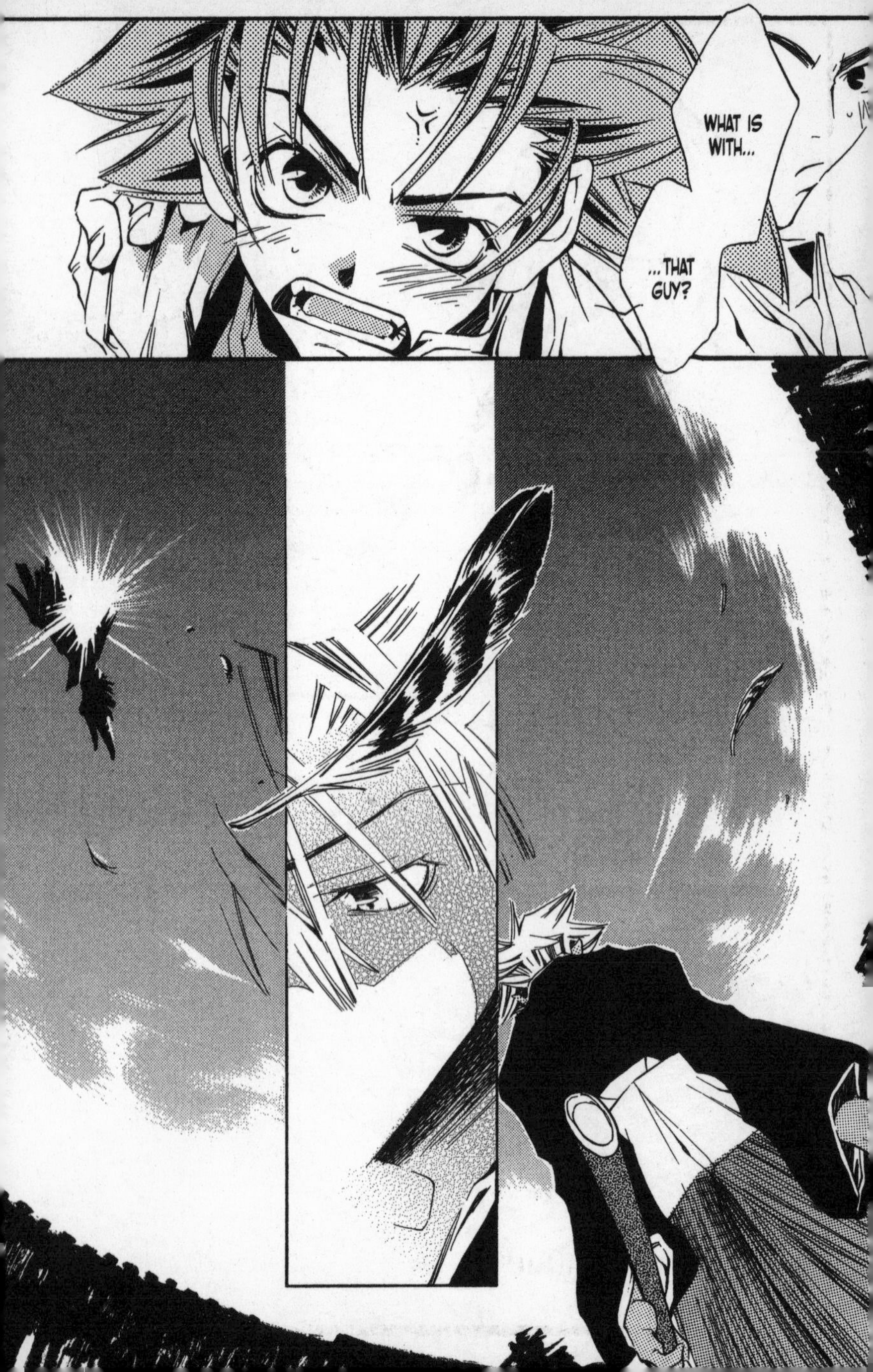
WHAT IS WITH...
...THAT GUY?

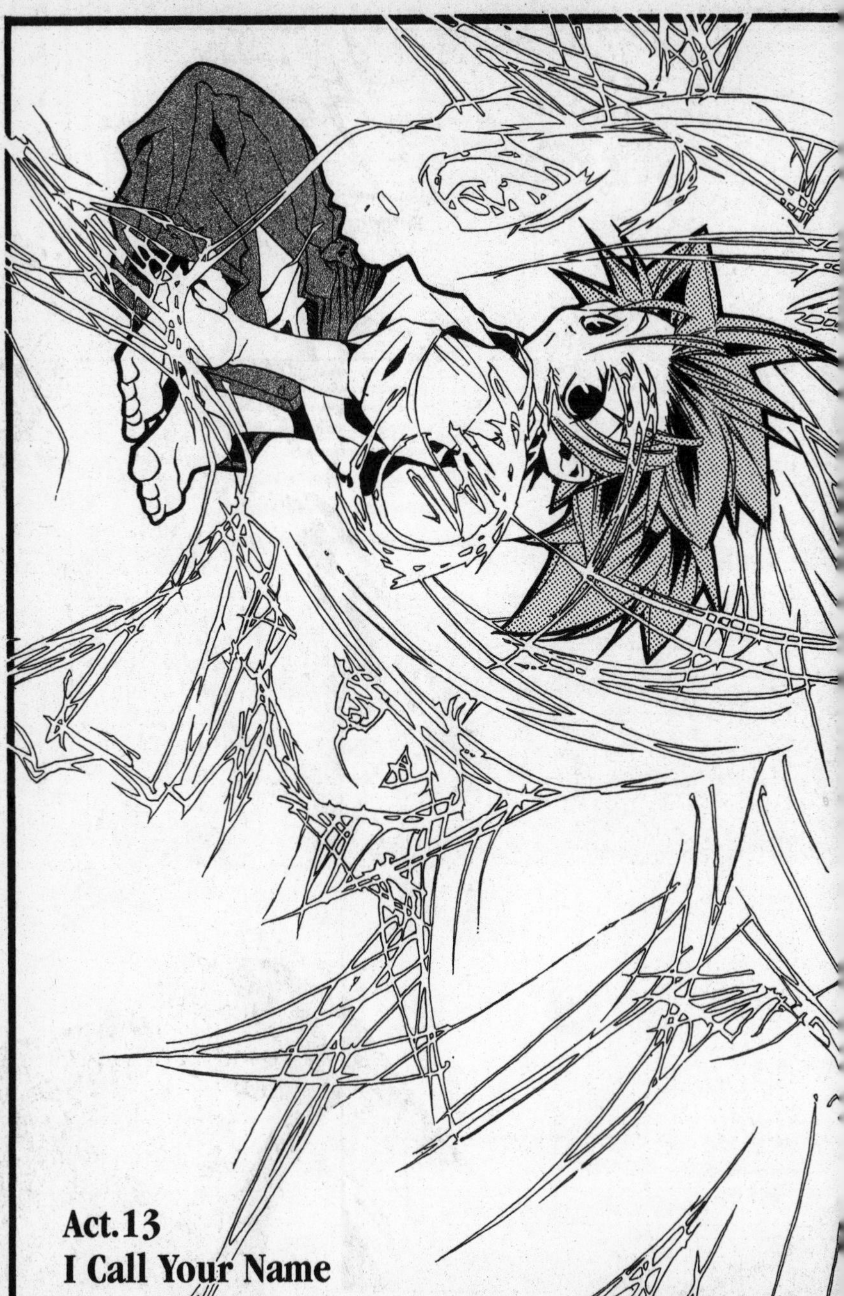

Act.13
I Call Your Name

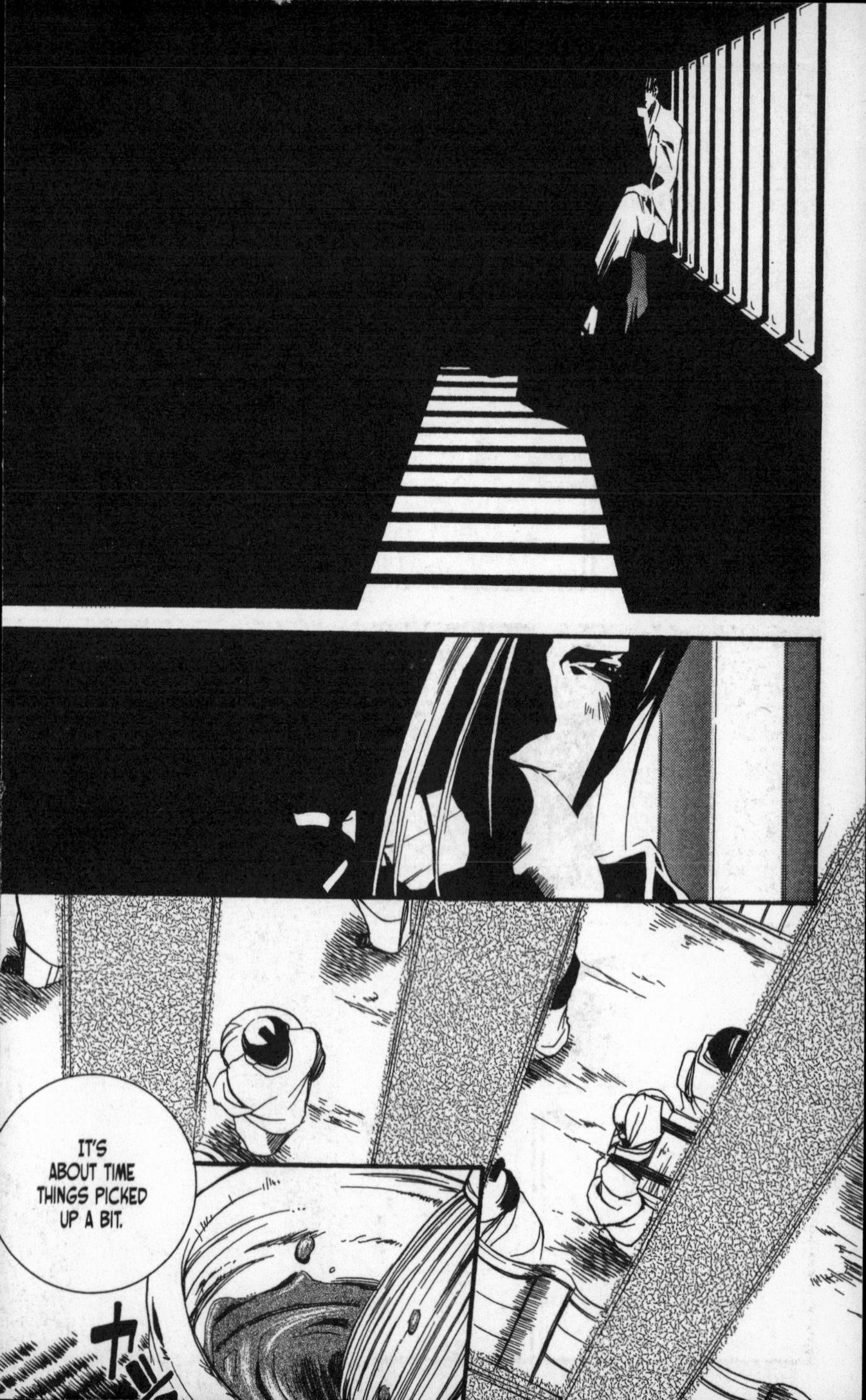
IT'S ABOUT TIME THINGS PICKED UP A BIT.
ガ

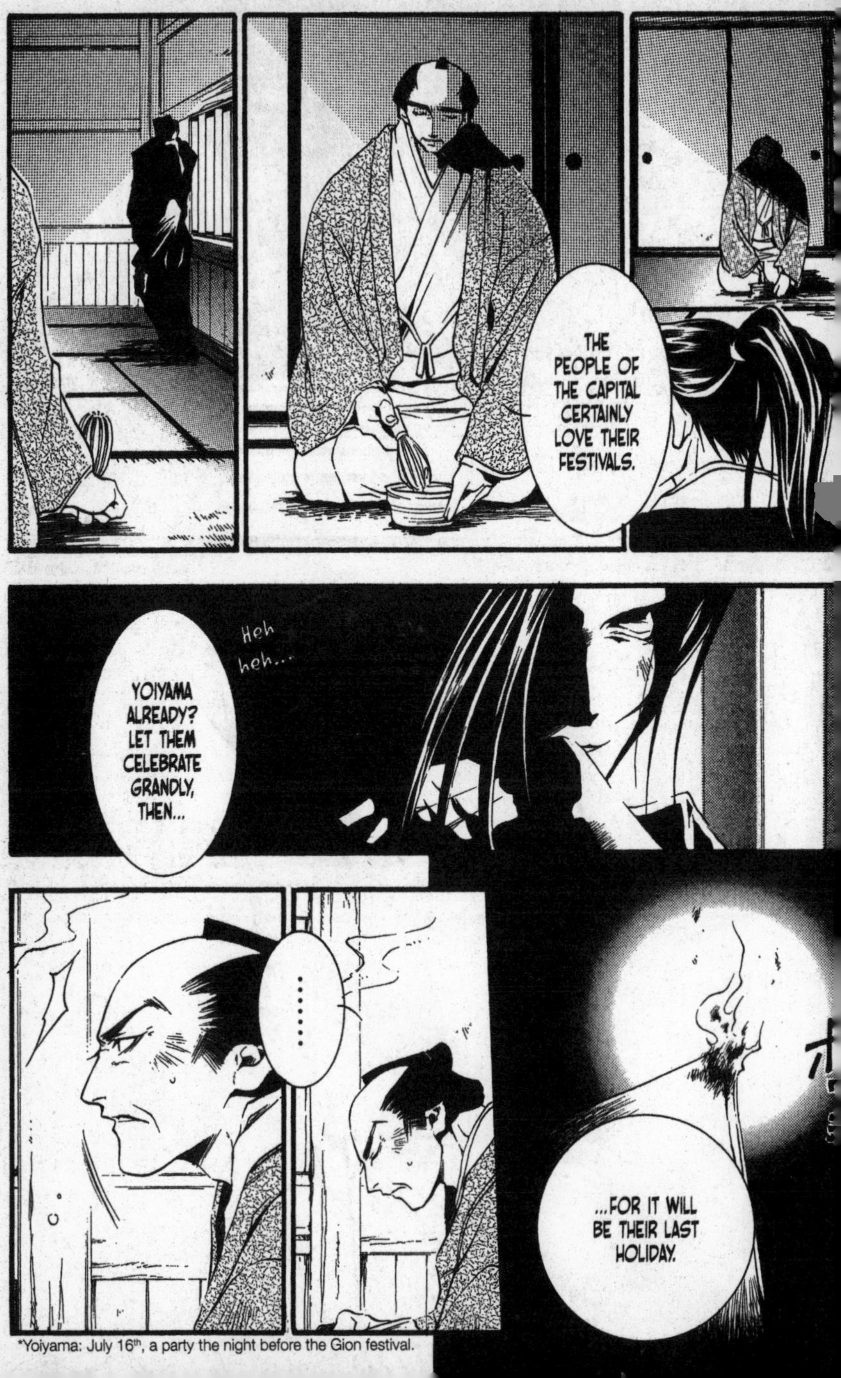
THE PEOPLE OF THE CAPITAL CERTAINLY LOVE THEIR FESTIVALS.
Heh heh...
YOIYAMA ALREADY? LET THEM CELEBRATE GRANDLY, THEN...
...FOR IT WILL BE THEIR LAST HOLIDAY.
......

*Yoiyama: July 16th, a party the night before the Gion festival.

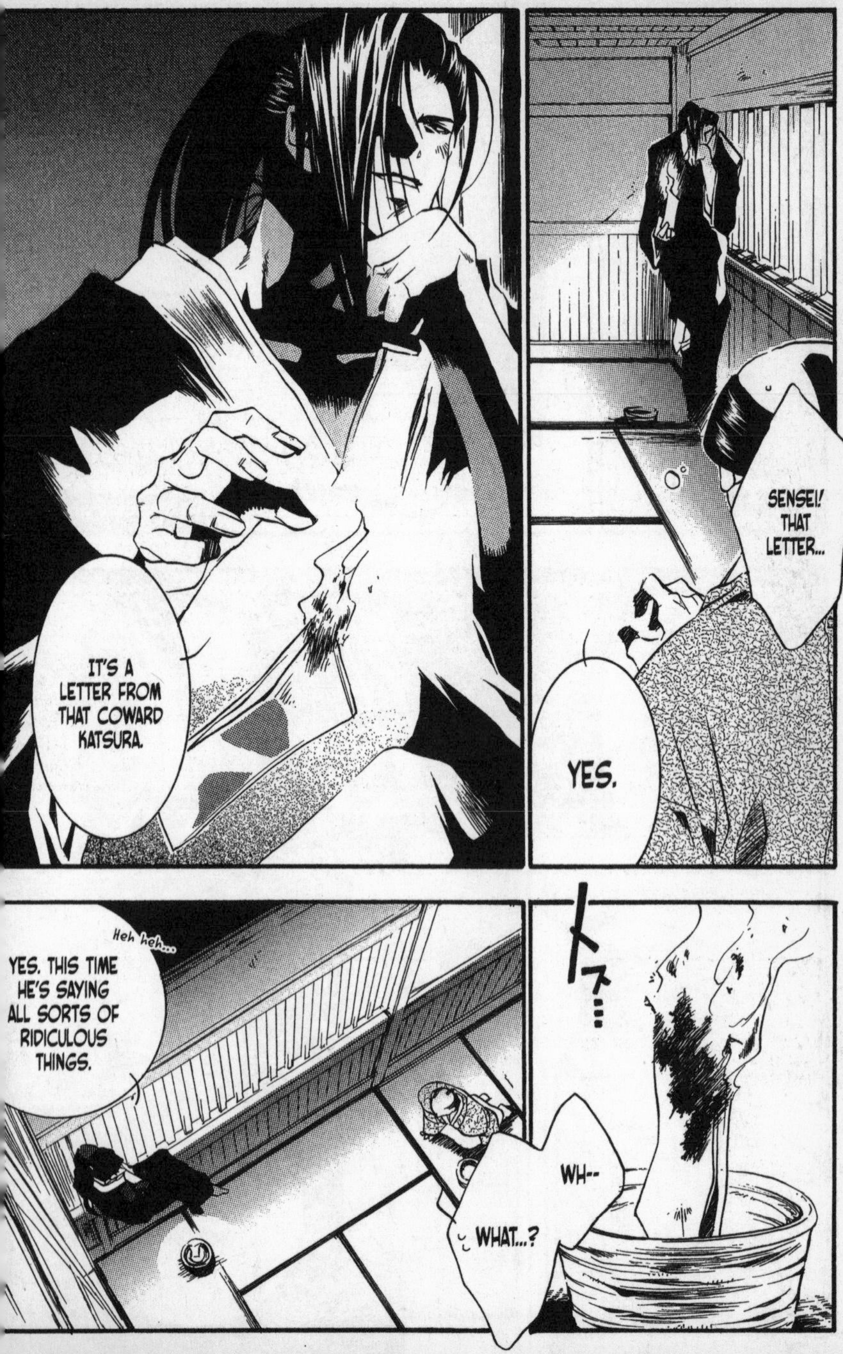
SENSEI! THAT LETTER...
YES.
IT'S A LETTER FROM THAT COWARD KATSURA.
トス...
WH--
WHAT...?
Heh heh...
YES. THIS TIME HE'S SAYING ALL SORTS OF RIDICULOUS THINGS.

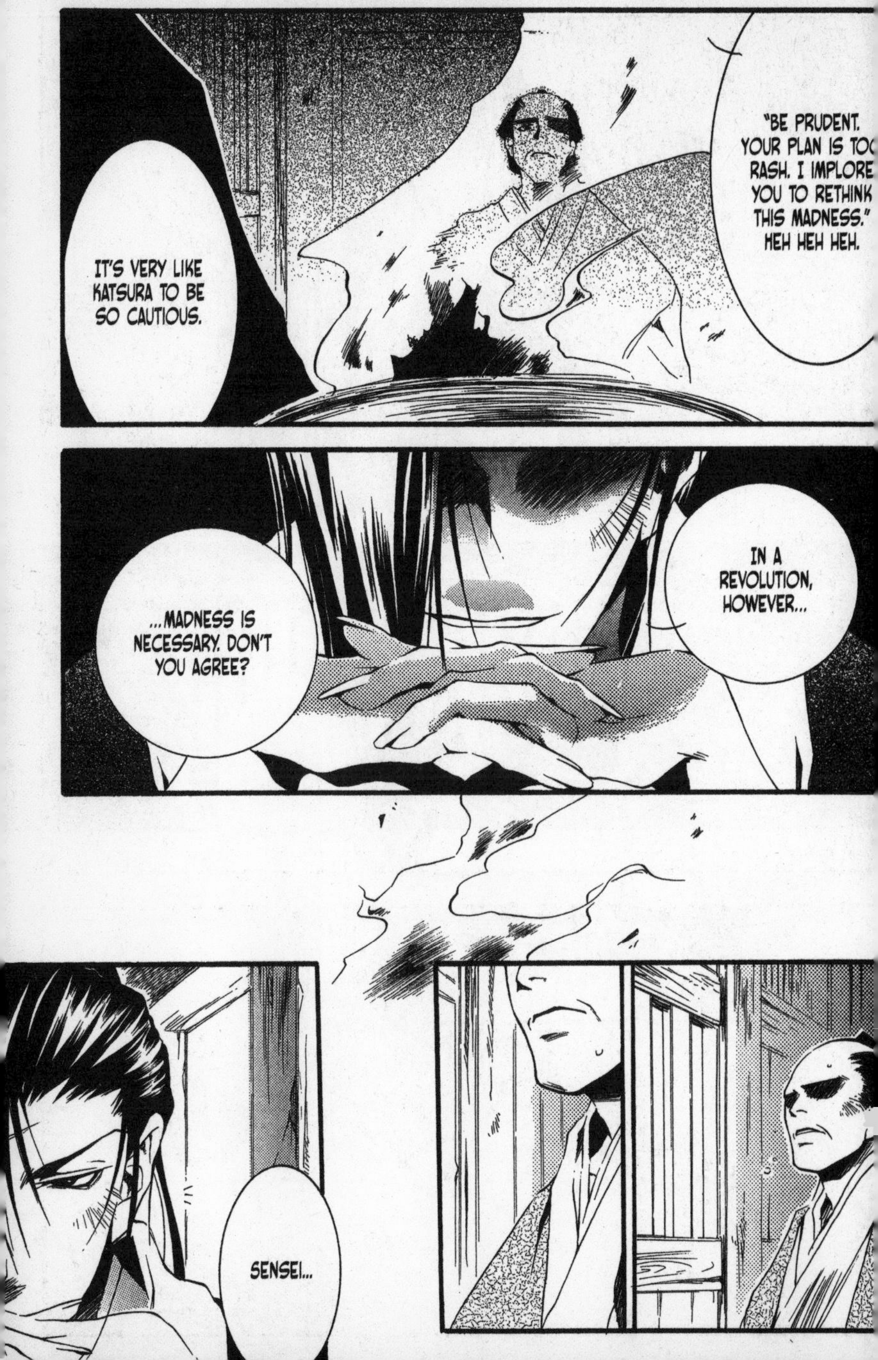
"BE PRUDENT. YOUR PLAN IS TOO RASH. I IMPLORE YOU TO RETHINK THIS MADNESS." HEH HEH HEH.
IT'S VERY LIKE KATSURA TO BE SO CAUTIOUS.
IN A REVOLUTION, HOWEVER...
...MADNESS IS NECESSARY. DON'T YOU AGREE?
SENSEI...

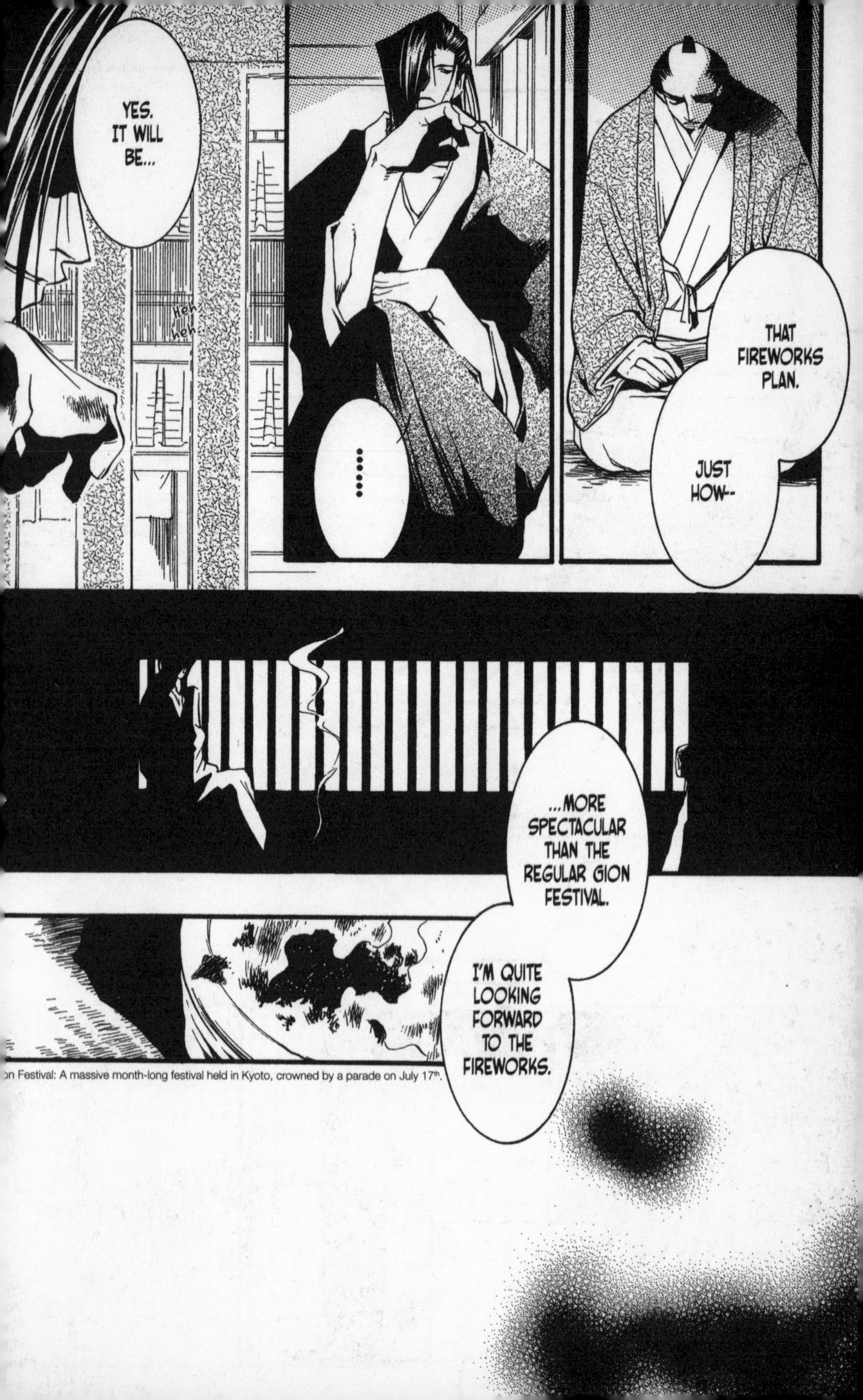
THAT FIREWORKS PLAN.
JUST HOW--
......
YES. IT WILL BE...
Heh heh
...MORE SPECTACULAR THAN THE REGULAR GION FESTIVAL.
I'M QUITE LOOKING FORWARD TO THE FIREWORKS.

on Festival: A massive month-long festival held in Kyoto, crowned by a parade on July 17th.

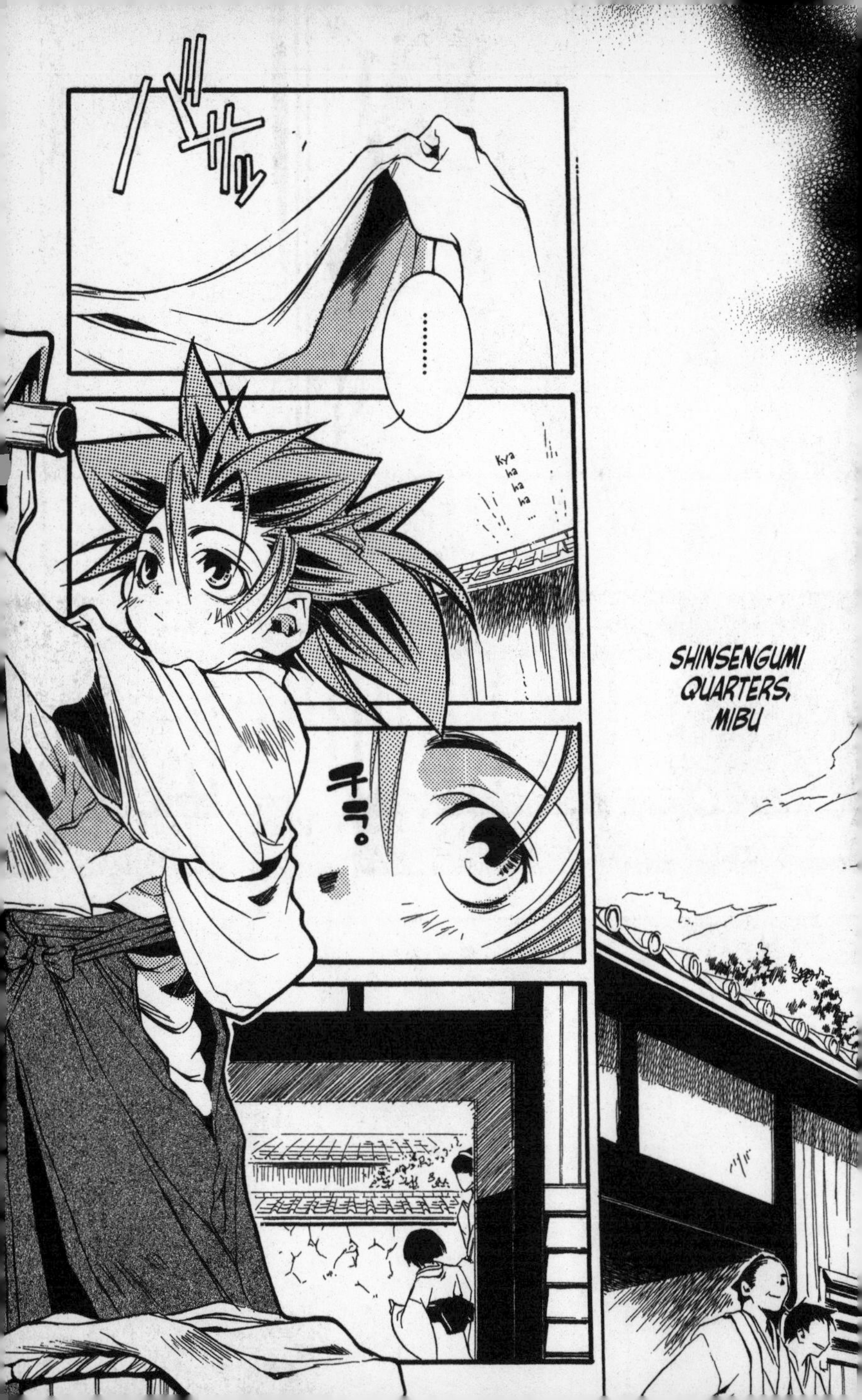
SHINSENGUMI QUARTERS, MIBU
バサッ
......
Kya ha ha ha...
チラ。

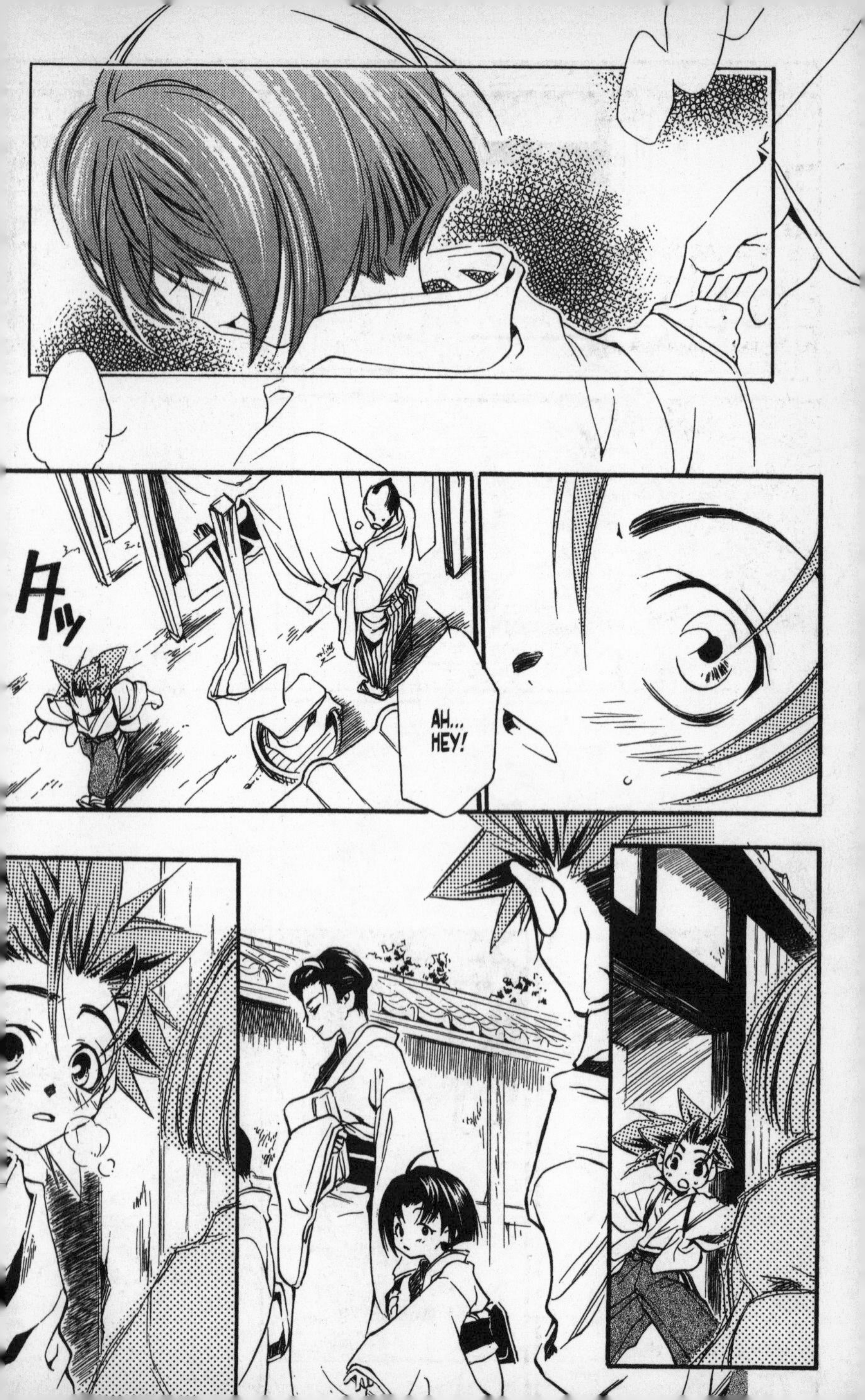
AH... HEY!
タッ

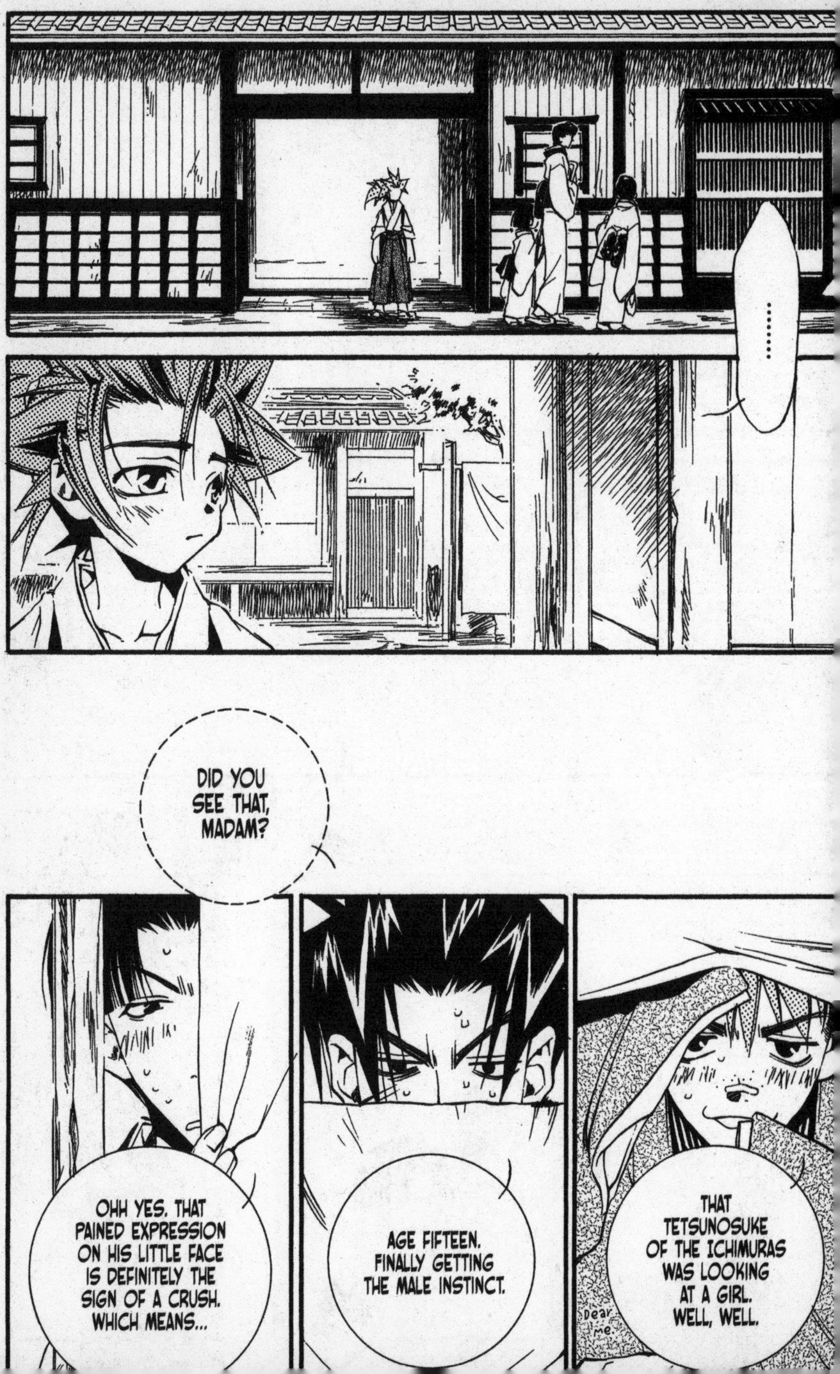
......
DID YOU SEE THAT, MADAM?
THAT TETSUNOSUKE OF THE ICHIMURAS WAS LOOKING AT A GIRL. WELL, WELL.
Dear me.
AGE FIFTEEN. FINALLY GETTING THE MALE INSTINCT.
OHH YES. THAT PAINED EXPRESSION ON HIS LITTLE FACE IS DEFINITELY THE SIGN OF A CRUSH. WHICH MEANS...

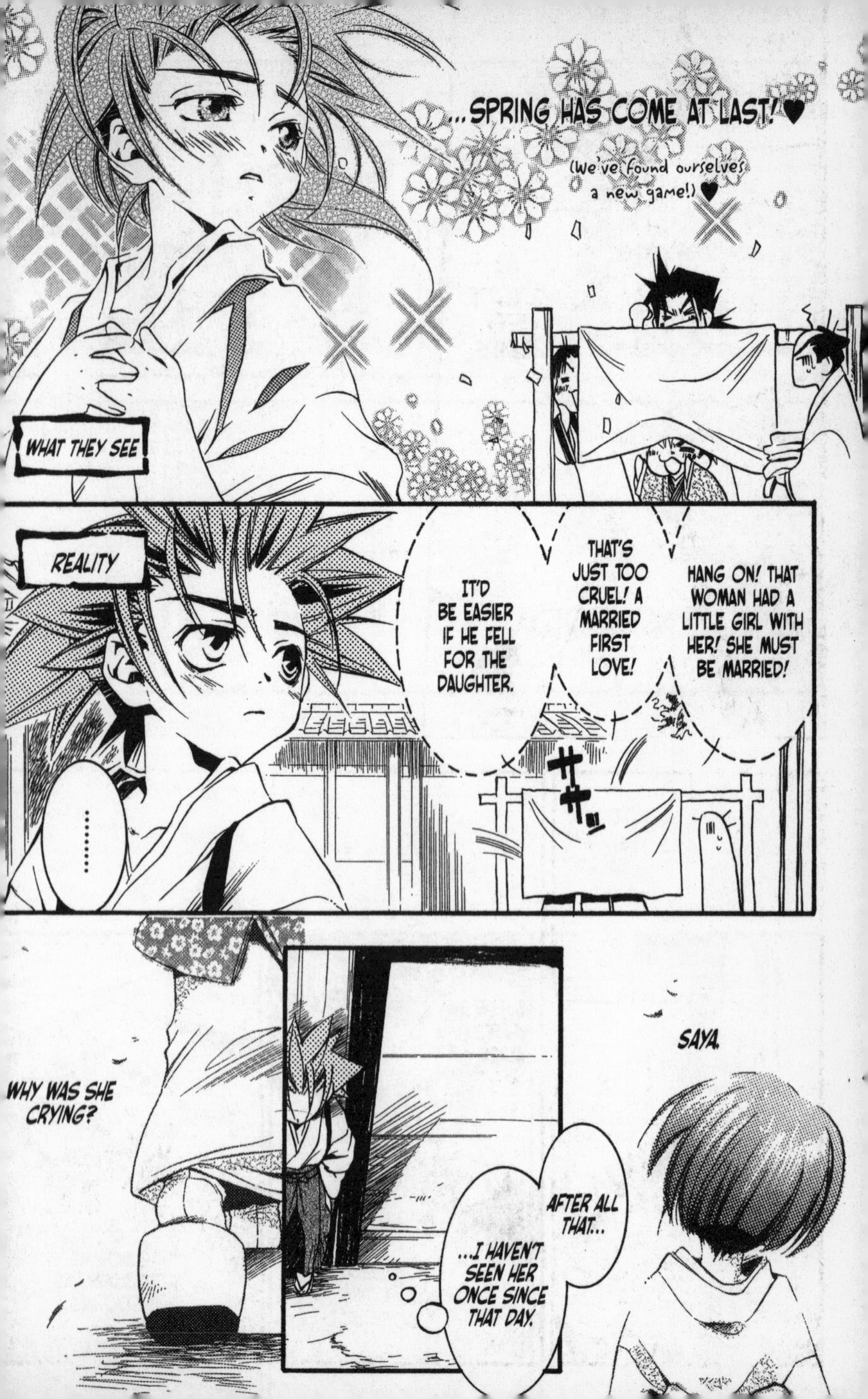
...SPRING HAS COME AT LAST! ♥
(We've found ourselves a new game!) ♥
WHAT THEY SEE
HANG ON! THAT WOMAN HAD A LITTLE GIRL WITH HER! SHE MUST BE MARRIED!
THAT'S JUST TOO CRUEL! A MARRIED FIRST LOVE!
IT'D BE EASIER IF HE FELL FOR THE DAUGHTER.
REALITY
......
SAYA.
AFTER ALL THAT...
...I HAVEN'T SEEN HER ONCE SINCE THAT DAY.
WHY WAS SHE CRYING?

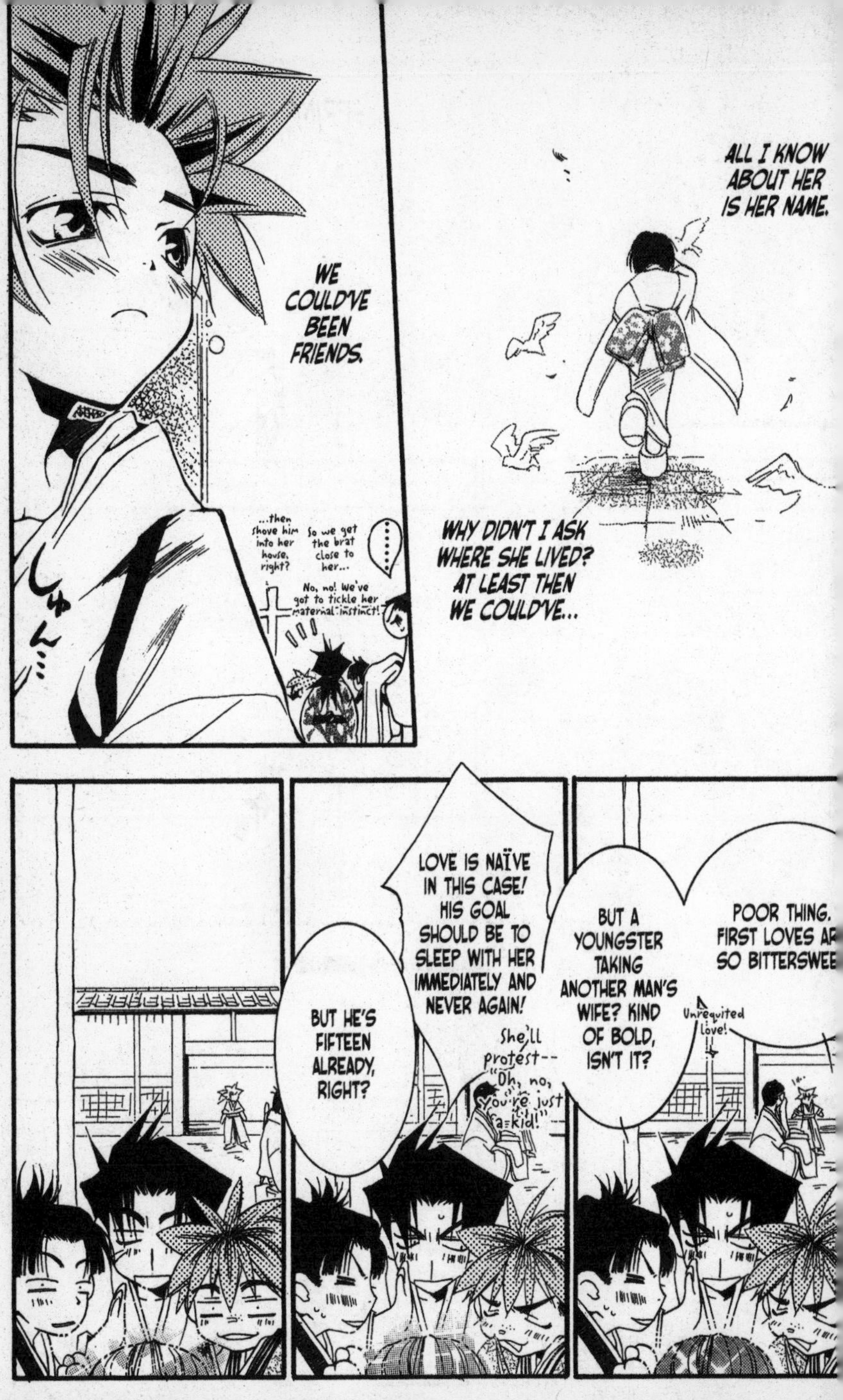
ALL I KNOW ABOUT HER IS HER NAME.
WHY DIDN'T I ASK WHERE SHE LIVED? AT LEAST THEN WE COULD'VE...
WE COULD'VE BEEN FRIENDS.
So we get the brat close to her...
...then shove him into her house, right?
No, no! We've got to tickle her material instinct!
しゅん…
POOR THING. FIRST LOVES AR SO BITTERSWEE
Unrequited love!
BUT A YOUNGSTER TAKING ANOTHER MAN'S WIFE? KIND OF BOLD, ISN'T IT?
LOVE IS NAÏVE IN THIS CASE! HIS GOAL SHOULD BE TO SLEEP WITH HER IMMEDIATELY AND NEVER AGAIN!
She'll protest-- "Oh, no, you're just a kid!"
BUT HE'S FIFTEEN ALREADY, RIGHT?

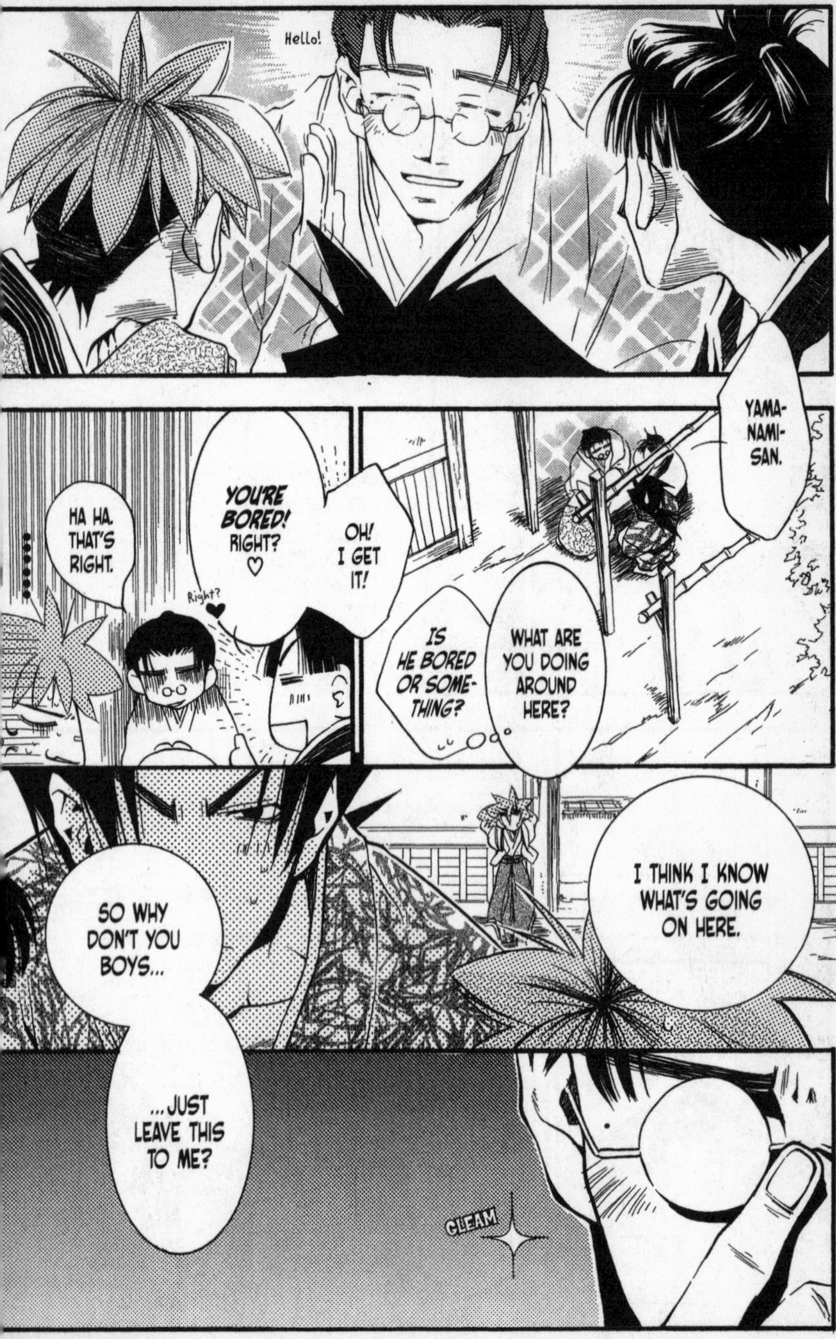
Hello!
YAMA-NAMI-SAN.
WHAT ARE YOU DOING AROUND HERE?
IS HE BORED OR SOME-THING?
OH! I GET IT!
YOU'RE BORED! RIGHT? ♡
Right? ♥
HA HA. THAT'S RIGHT.
I THINK I KNOW WHAT'S GOING ON HERE.
SO WHY DON'T YOU BOYS...
...JUST LEAVE THIS TO ME?
GLEAM

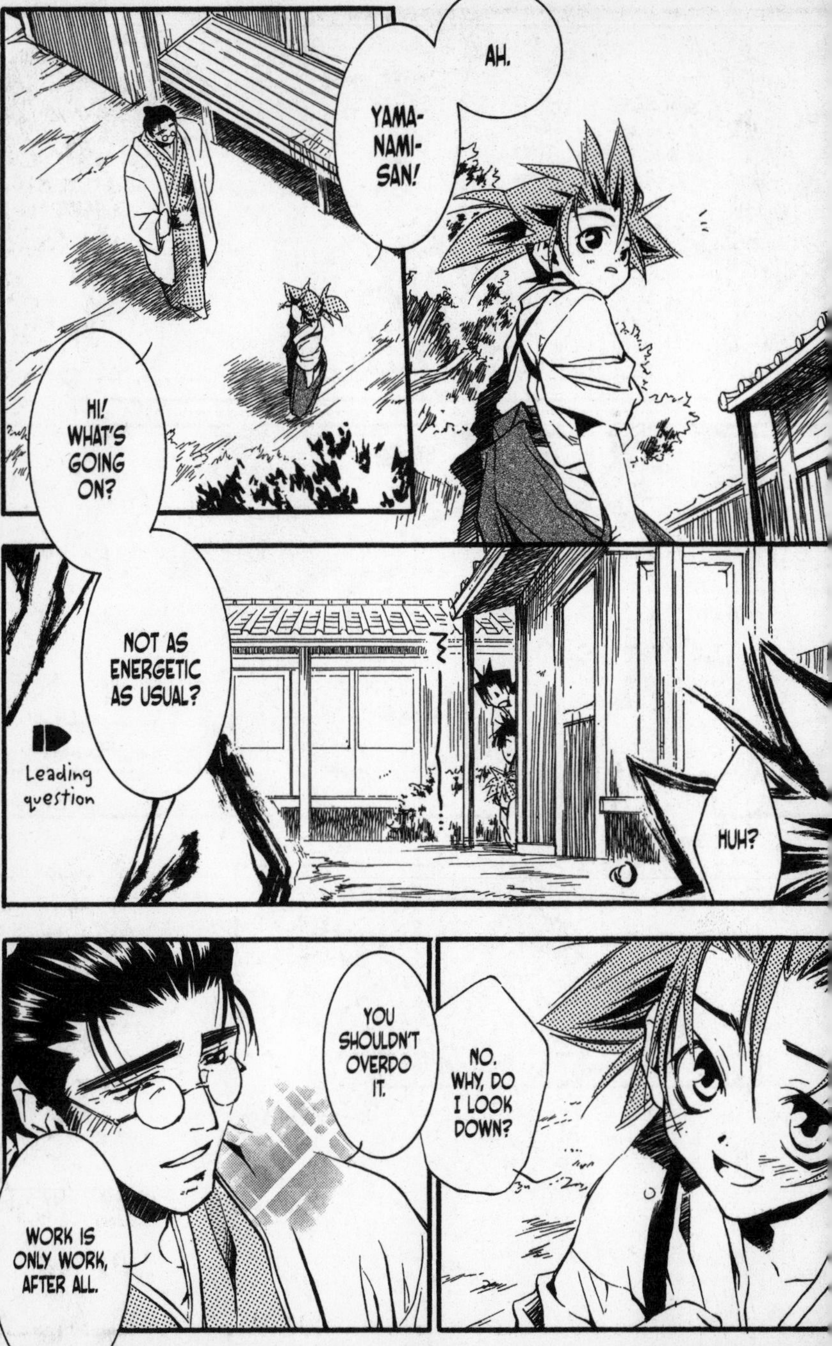
AH.
YAMA-NAMI-SAN!
HI! WHAT'S GOING ON?
NOT AS ENERGETIC AS USUAL?
Leading question
HUH?
NO. WHY, DO I LOOK DOWN?
YOU SHOULDN'T OVERDO IT.
WORK IS ONLY WORK, AFTER ALL.

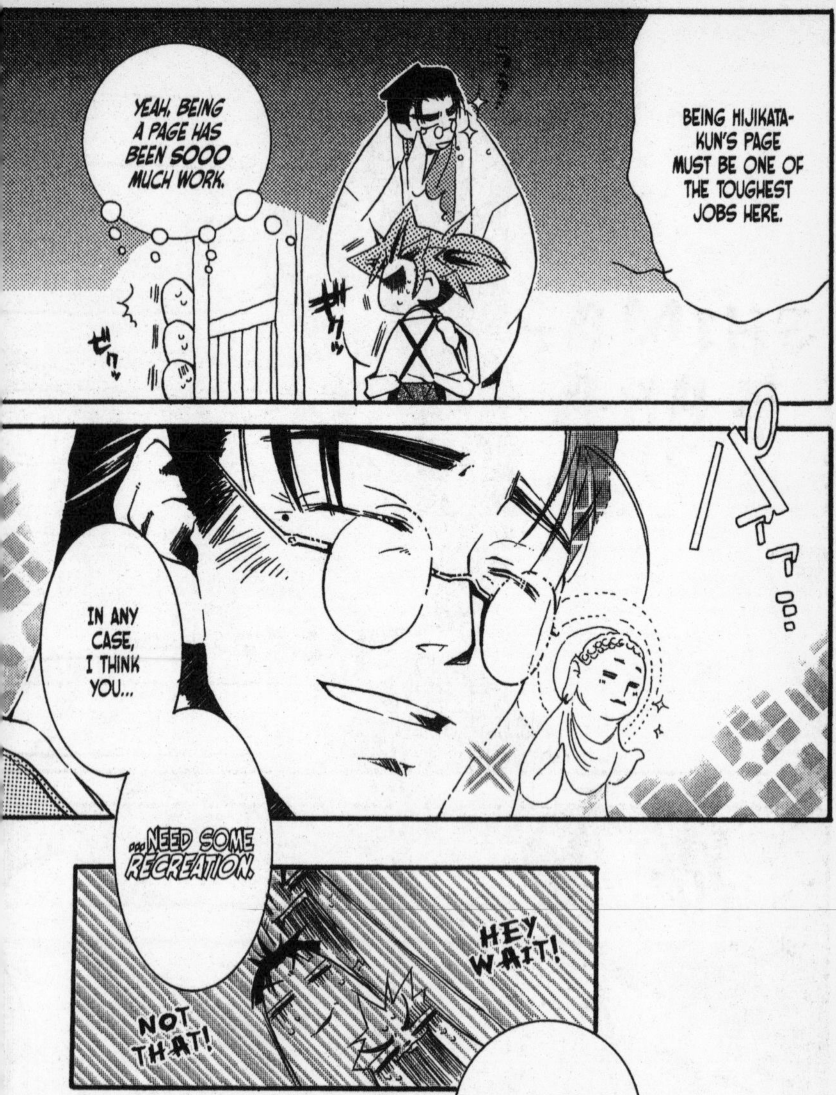
BEING HIJIKATA-KUN'S PAGE MUST BE ONE OF THE TOUGHEST JOBS HERE.
YEAH, BEING A PAGE HAS BEEN SOOO MUCH WORK.
IN ANY CASE, I THINK YOU...
...NEED SOME RECREATION.
HEY WAIT!
NOT THAT!
"RECREATION"?

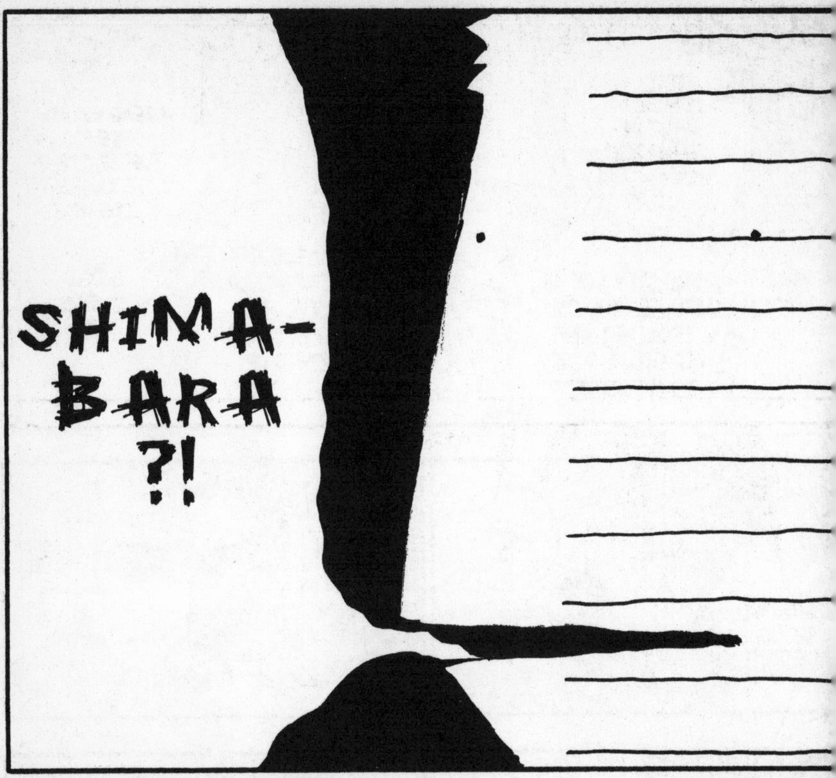
SHIMA-BARA ?!

*Shimabara: The pleasure district of Kyoto

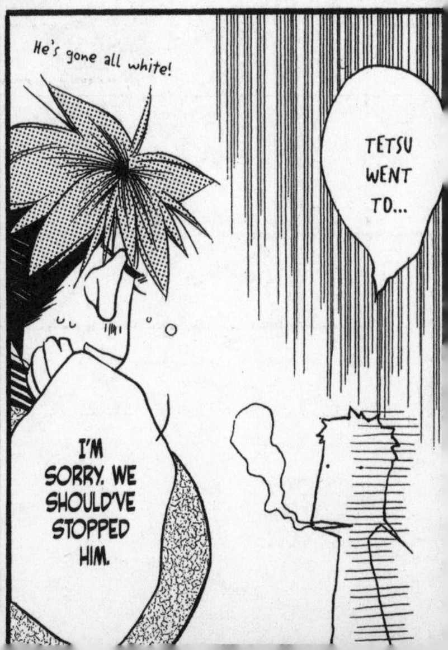
TETSU WENT TO...
He's gone all white!
I'M SORRY. WE SHOULD'VE STOPPED HIM.

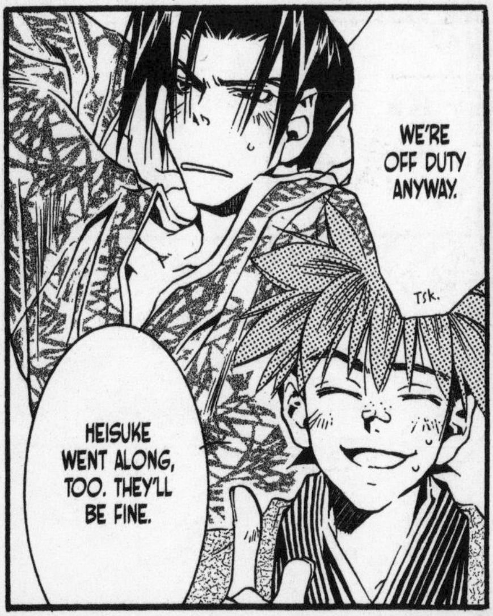
WE'RE OFF DUTY ANYWAY.
Tsk.
HEISUKE WENT ALONG, TOO. THEY'LL BE FINE.

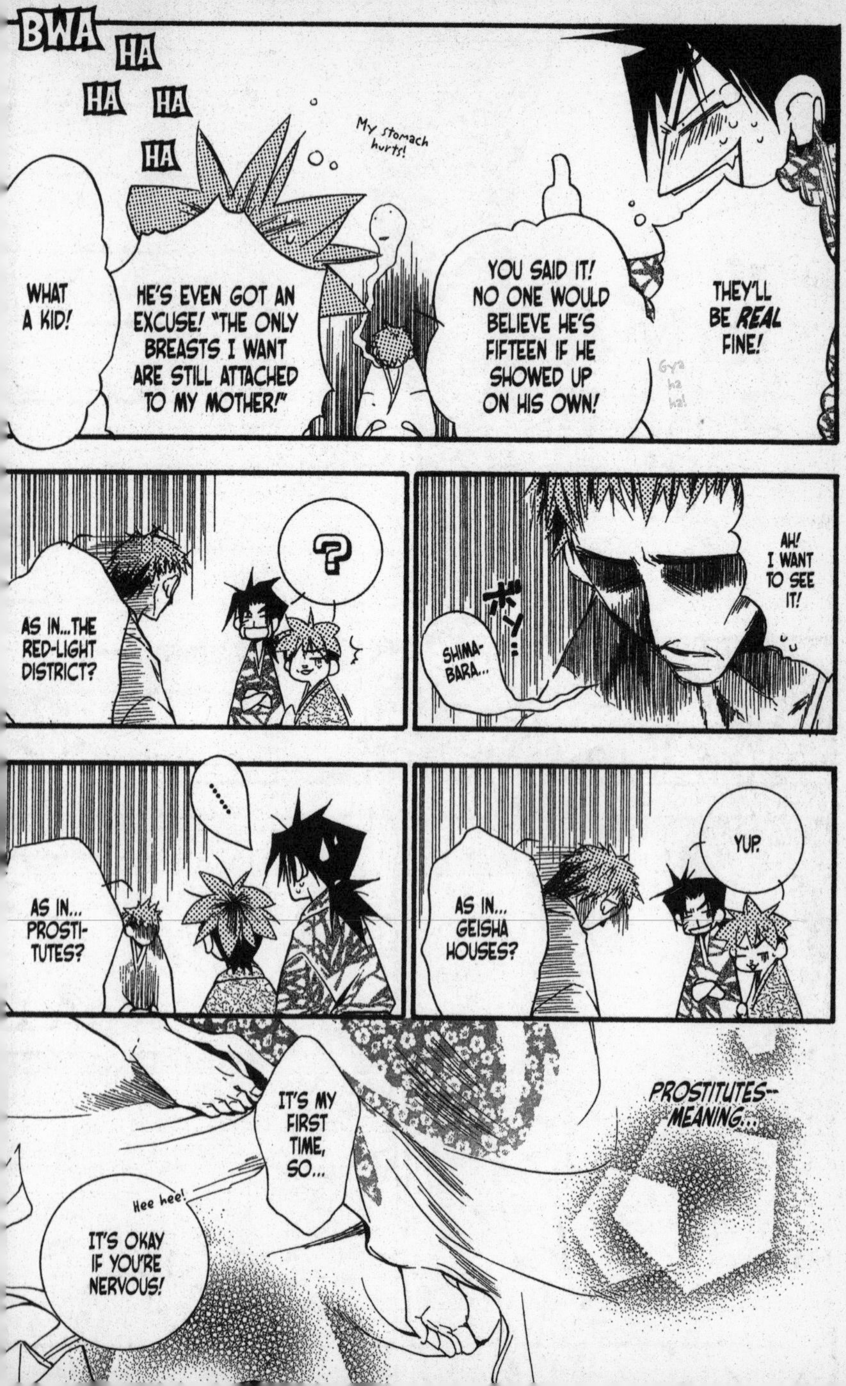
THEY'LL BE *REAL* FINE!
Gya ha ha!
YOU SAID IT! NO ONE WOULD BELIEVE HE'S FIFTEEN IF HE SHOWED UP ON HIS OWN!
My stomach hurts!
HE'S EVEN GOT AN EXCUSE! "THE ONLY BREASTS I WANT ARE STILL ATTACHED TO MY MOTHER!"
WHAT A KID!
BWA HA HA HA HA
AH! I WANT TO SEE IT!
SHIMA-BARA...
?
AS IN...THE RED-LIGHT DISTRICT?
YUP.
AS IN... GEISHA HOUSES?
......
AS IN... PROSTITUTES?
PROSTITUTES--MEANING...
IT'S MY FIRST TIME, SO...
Hee hee!
IT'S OKAY IF YOU'RE NERVOUS!

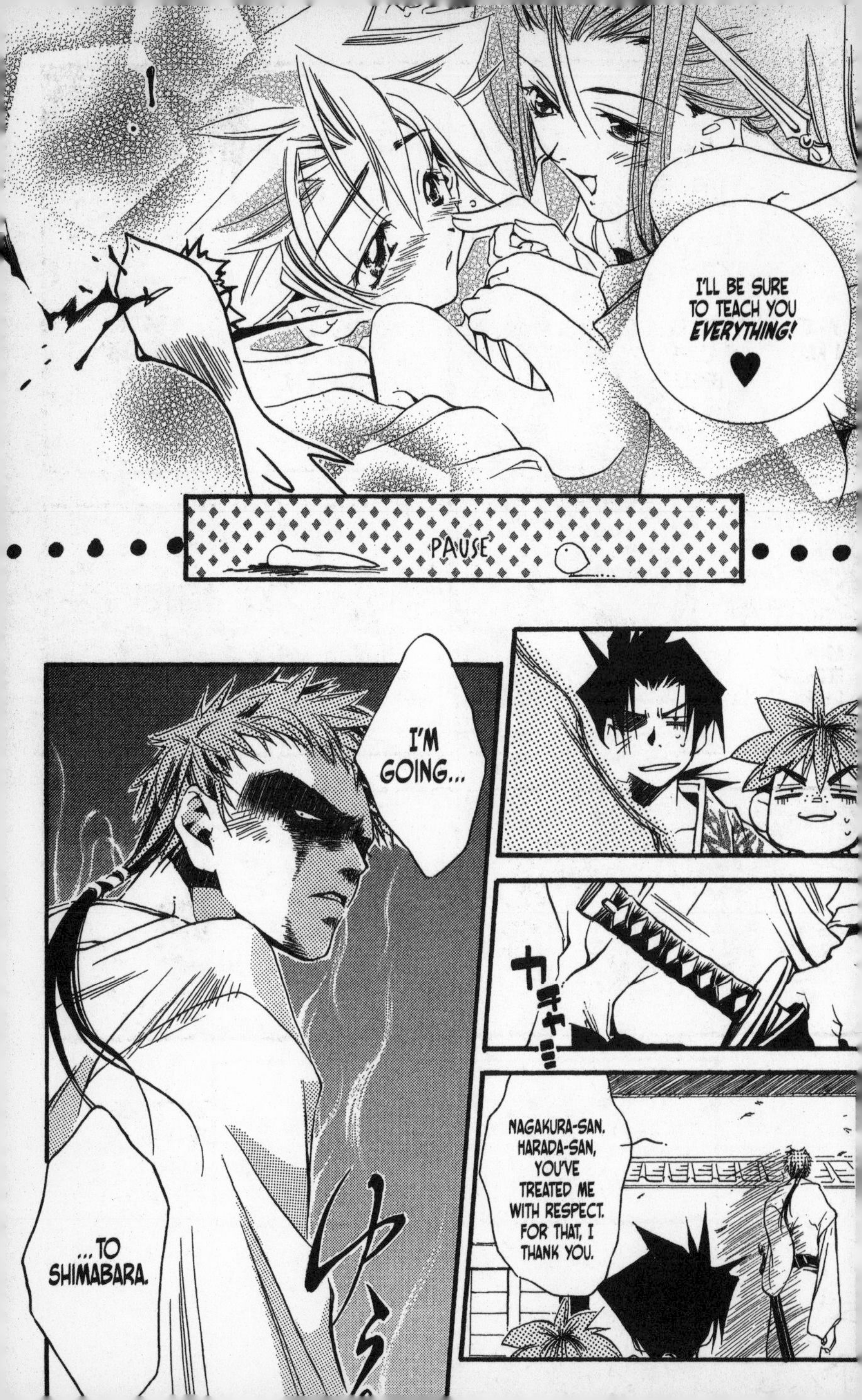
I'LL BE SURE TO TEACH YOU *EVERYTHING!* ♥
PAUSE
カチャ
NAGAKURA-SAN. HARADA-SAN, YOU'VE TREATED ME WITH RESPECT. FOR THAT, I THANK YOU.
I'M GOING...
...TO SHIMABARA.
ゆら

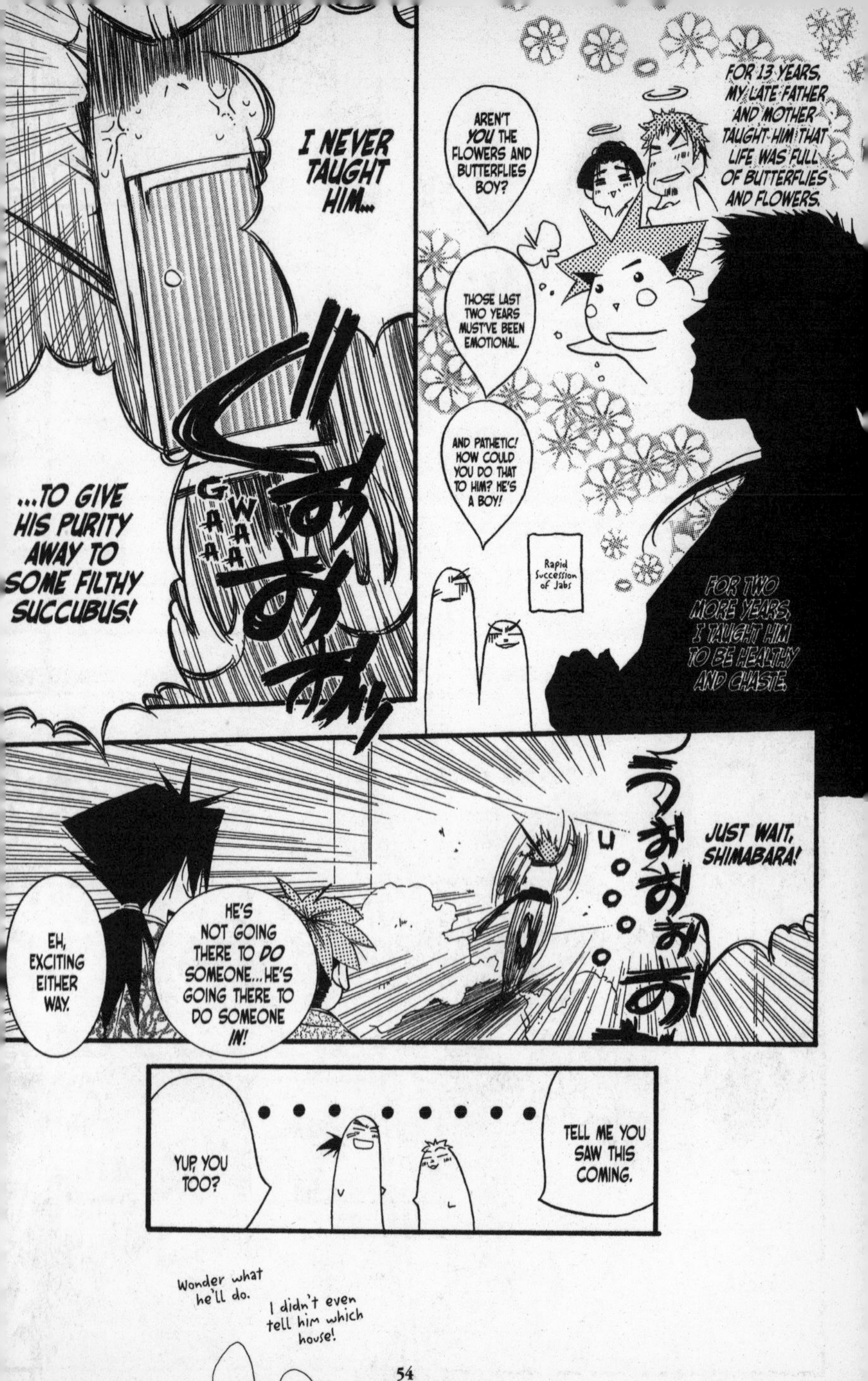
FOR 13 YEARS, MY LATE FATHER AND MOTHER TAUGHT HIM THAT LIFE WAS FULL OF BUTTERFLIES AND FLOWERS.
AREN'T YOU THE FLOWERS AND BUTTERFLIES BOY?
THOSE LAST TWO YEARS MUST'VE BEEN EMOTIONAL.
FOR TWO MORE YEARS, I TAUGHT HIM TO BE HEALTHY AND CHASTE.
AND PATHETIC! HOW COULD YOU DO THAT TO HIM? HE'S A BOY!
Rapid Succession of Jabs
I NEVER TAUGHT HIM...
...TO GIVE HIS PURITY AWAY TO SOME FILTHY SUCCUBUS!
GAAAA
WAAA
JUST WAIT, SHIMABARA!
UOOOO
HE'S NOT GOING THERE TO DO SOMEONE...HE'S GOING THERE TO DO SOMEONE IN!
EH, EXCITING EITHER WAY.
TELL ME YOU SAW THIS COMING.
• • • • • • • • •
YUP, YOU TOO?
I didn't even tell him which house!
Wonder what he'll do.

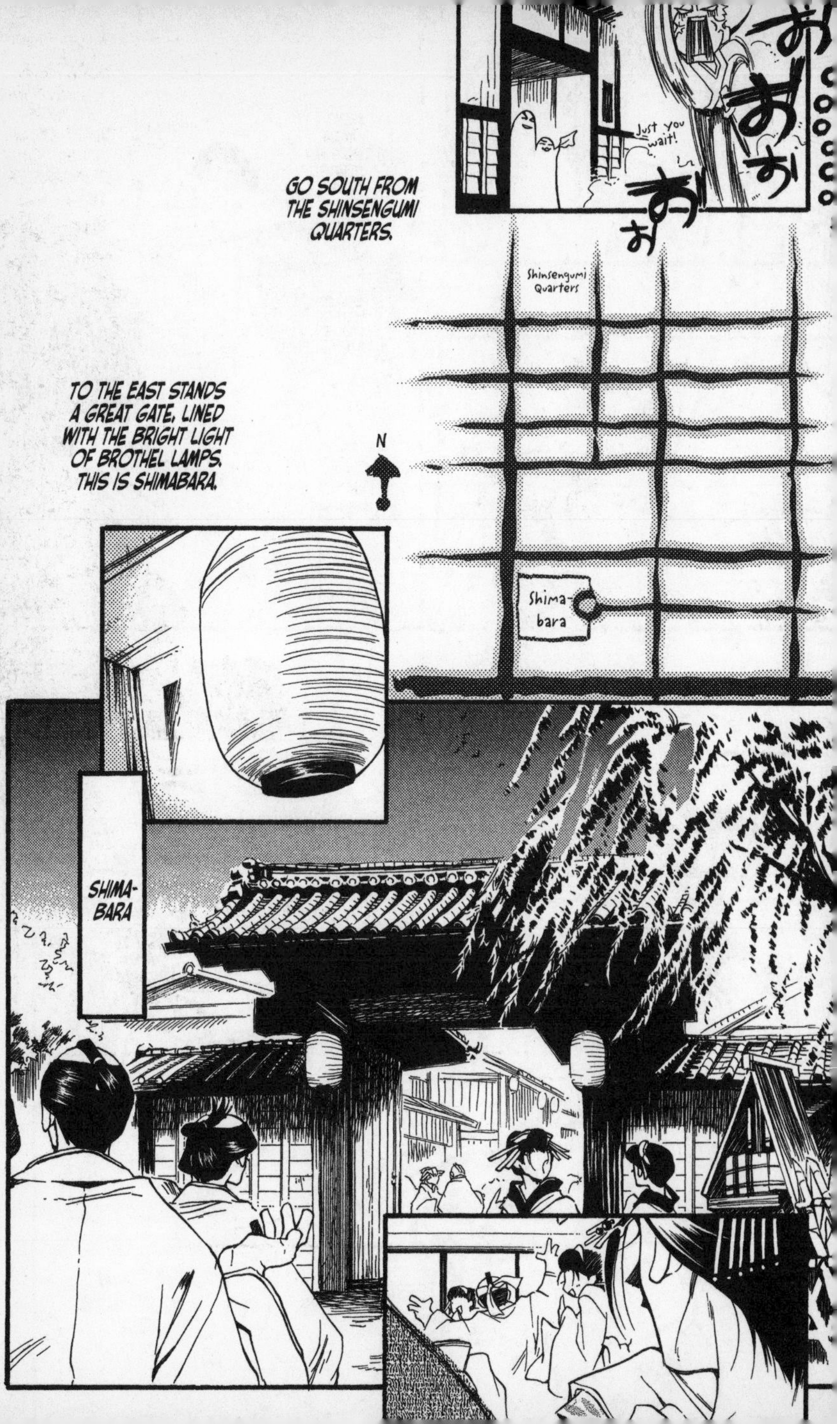

Just you wait!
GO SOUTH FROM THE SHINSENGUMI QUARTERS.
Shinsengumi Quarters
N
Shima-bara
TO THE EAST STANDS A GREAT GATE, LINED WITH THE BRIGHT LIGHT OF BROTHEL LAMPS. THIS IS SHIMABARA.
SHIMA-BARA

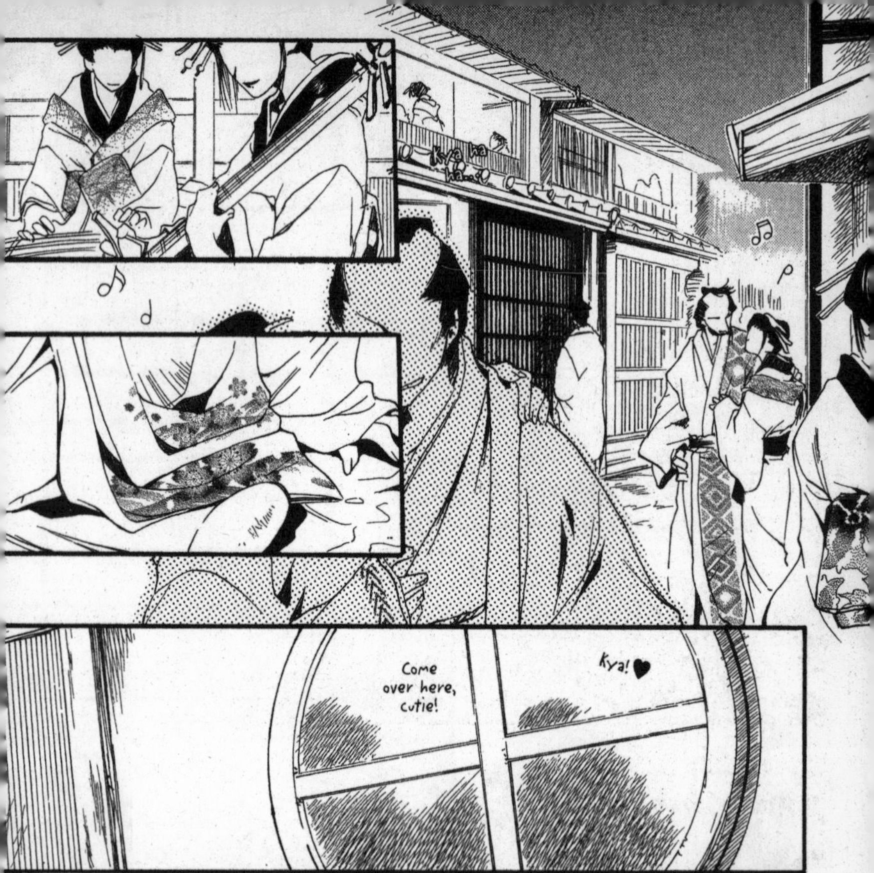
Kya ha ha...
Kya! ♥
Come over here, cutie!

an: The Kansai area version of the honorific -"san."

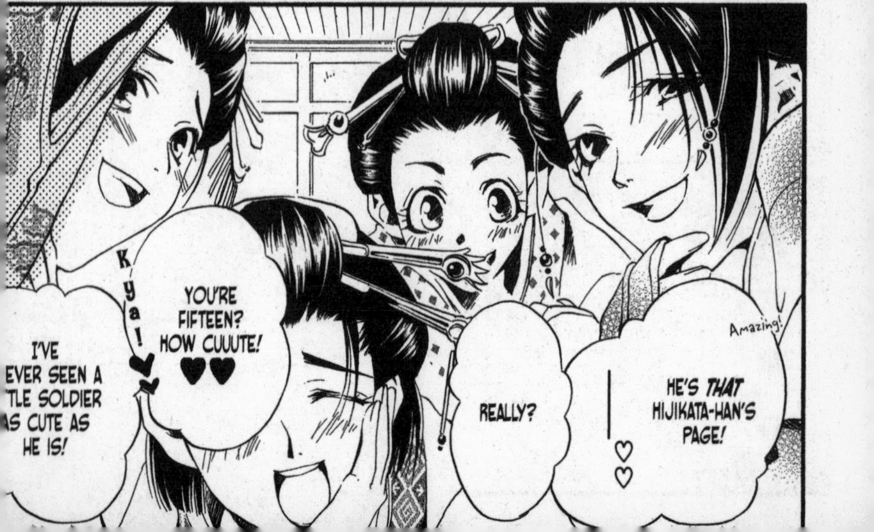
Amazing!
HE'S *THAT* HIJIKATA-HAN'S PAGE!
REALLY?
YOU'RE FIFTEEN? HOW CUUUTE! ♥♥
Kya!
I'VE EVER SEEN A TLE SOLDIER AS CUTE AS HE IS!

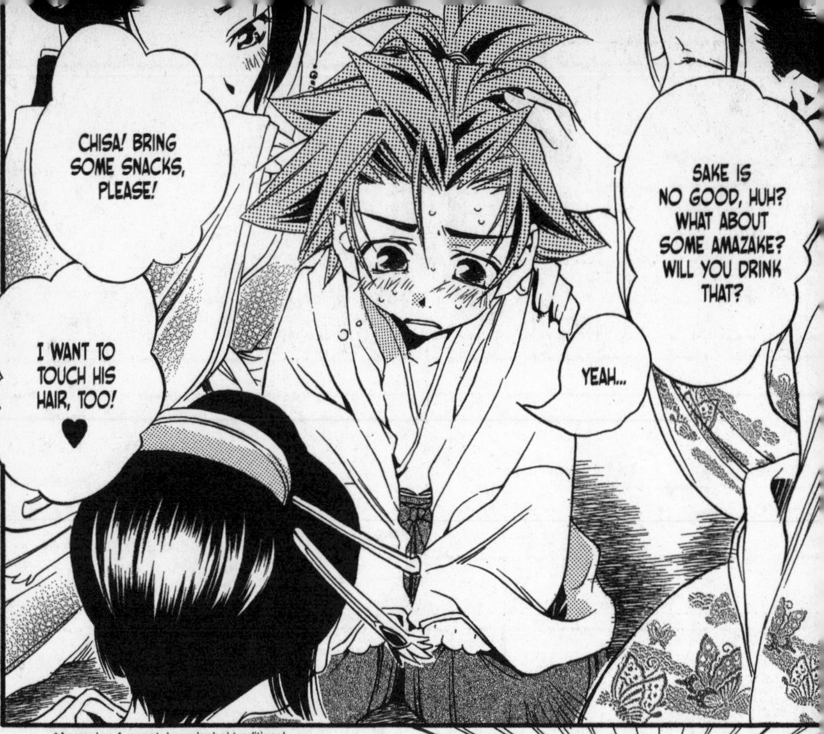
SAKE IS NO GOOD, HUH? WHAT ABOUT SOME AMAZAKE? WILL YOU DRINK THAT?
YEAH...
CHISA! BRING SOME SNACKS, PLEASE!
I WANT TO TOUCH HIS HAIR, TOO! ♥

*Amazake: A sweet, low-alcohol traditional beverage. Think white, milky champagne.

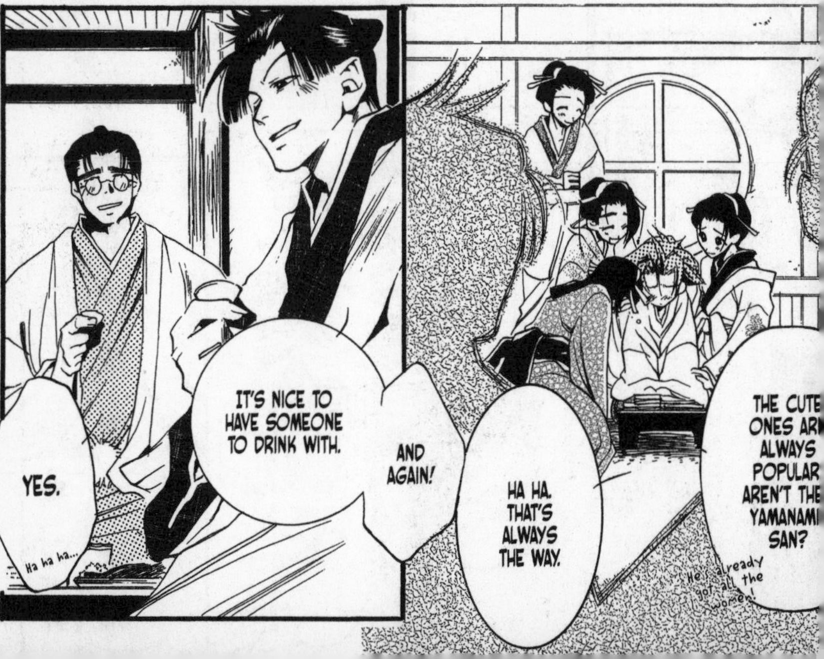
THE CUTE ONES AR ALWAYS POPULAR AREN'T THE YAMANAMI SAN?
He's already got all the women!
HA HA. THAT'S ALWAYS THE WAY.
AND AGAIN!
IT'S NICE TO HAVE SOMEONE TO DRINK WITH.
YES.
Ha ha ha...

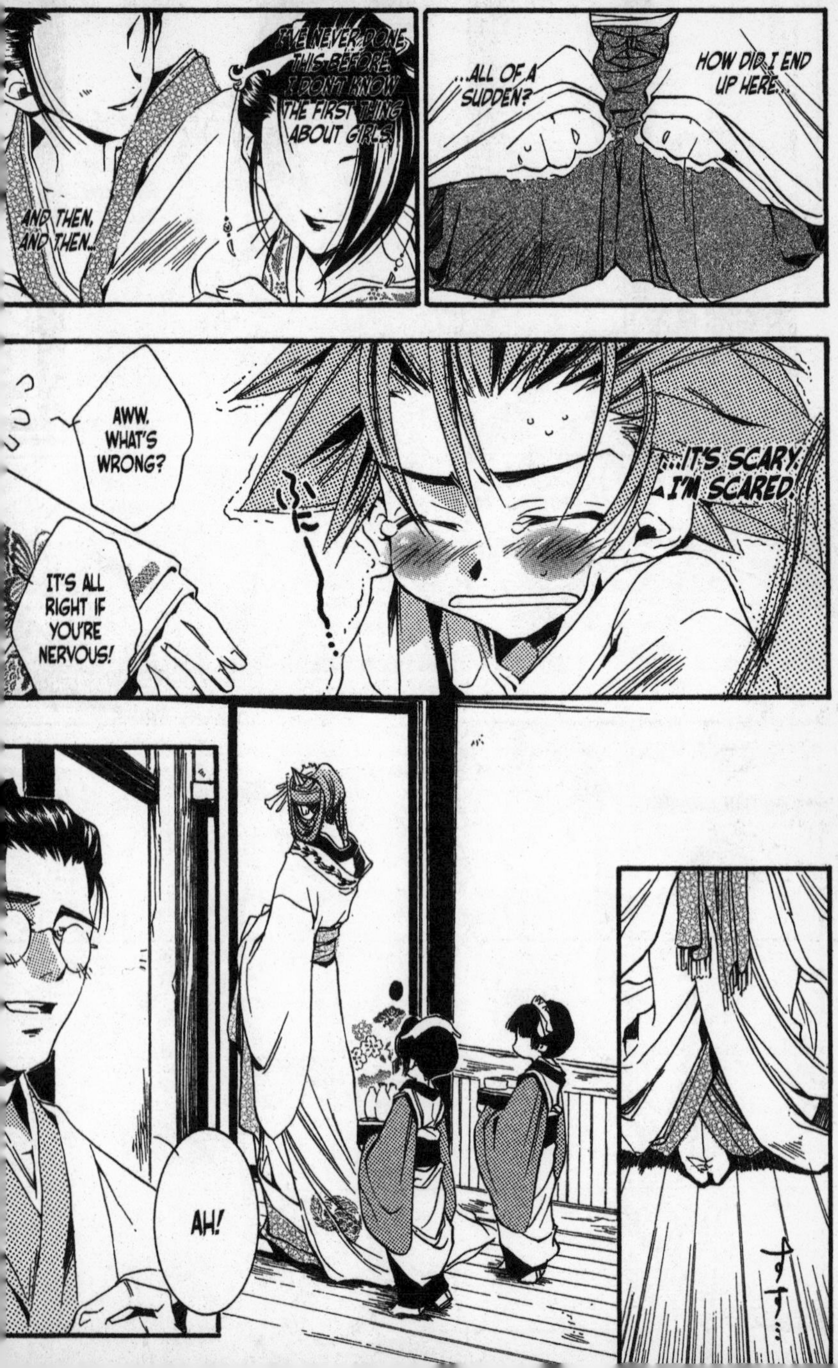
HOW DID I END UP HERE...
...ALL OF A SUDDEN?
I'VE NEVER DONE THIS BEFORE. I DON'T KNOW THE FIRST THING ABOUT GIRLS.
AND THEN, AND THEN...
...IT'S SCARY. I'M SCARED!
AWW. WHAT'S WRONG?
IT'S ALL RIGHT IF YOU'RE NERVOUS!
すす…
AH!

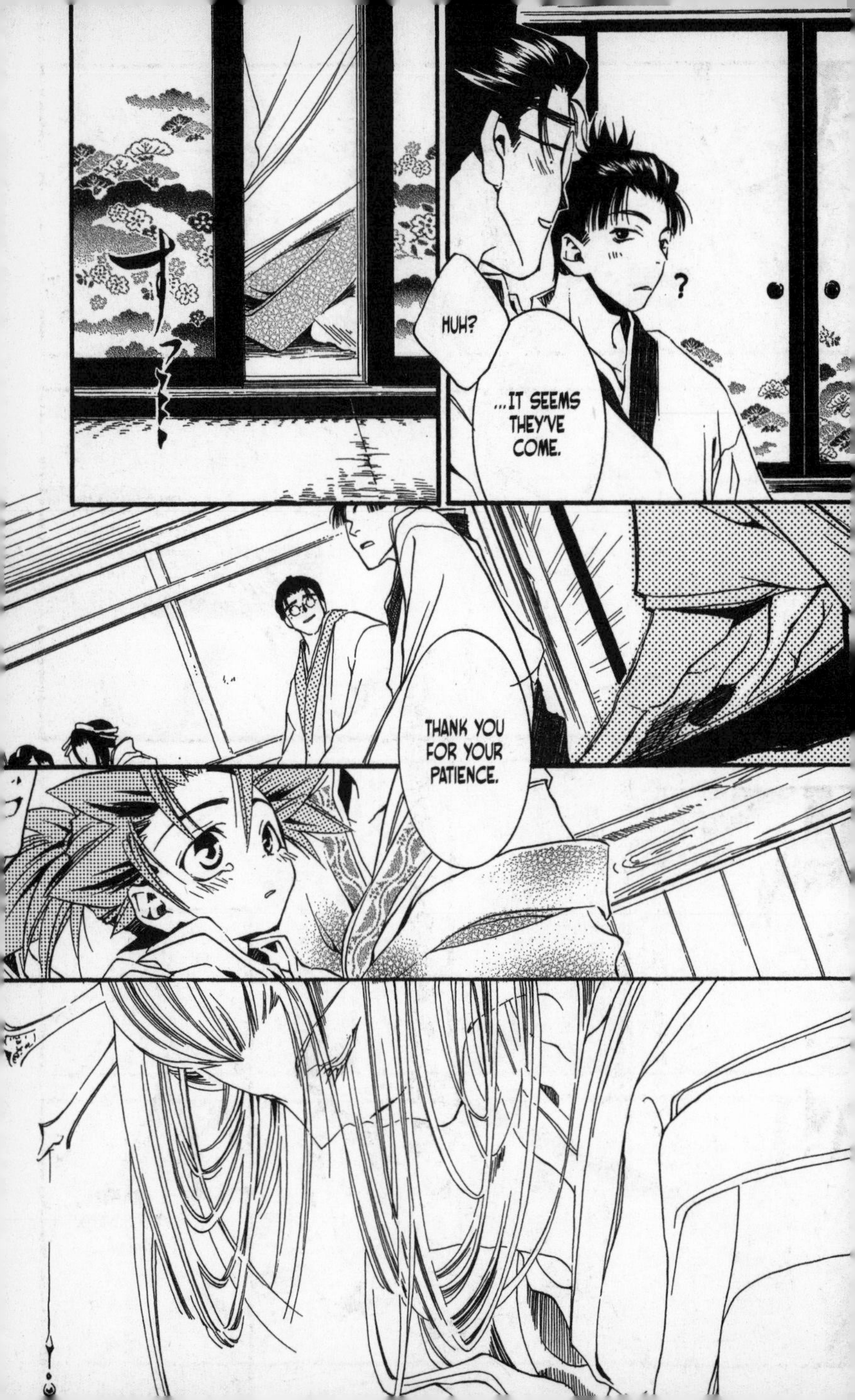
?
HUH?
...IT SEEMS THEY'VE COME.
THANK YOU FOR YOUR PATIENCE.

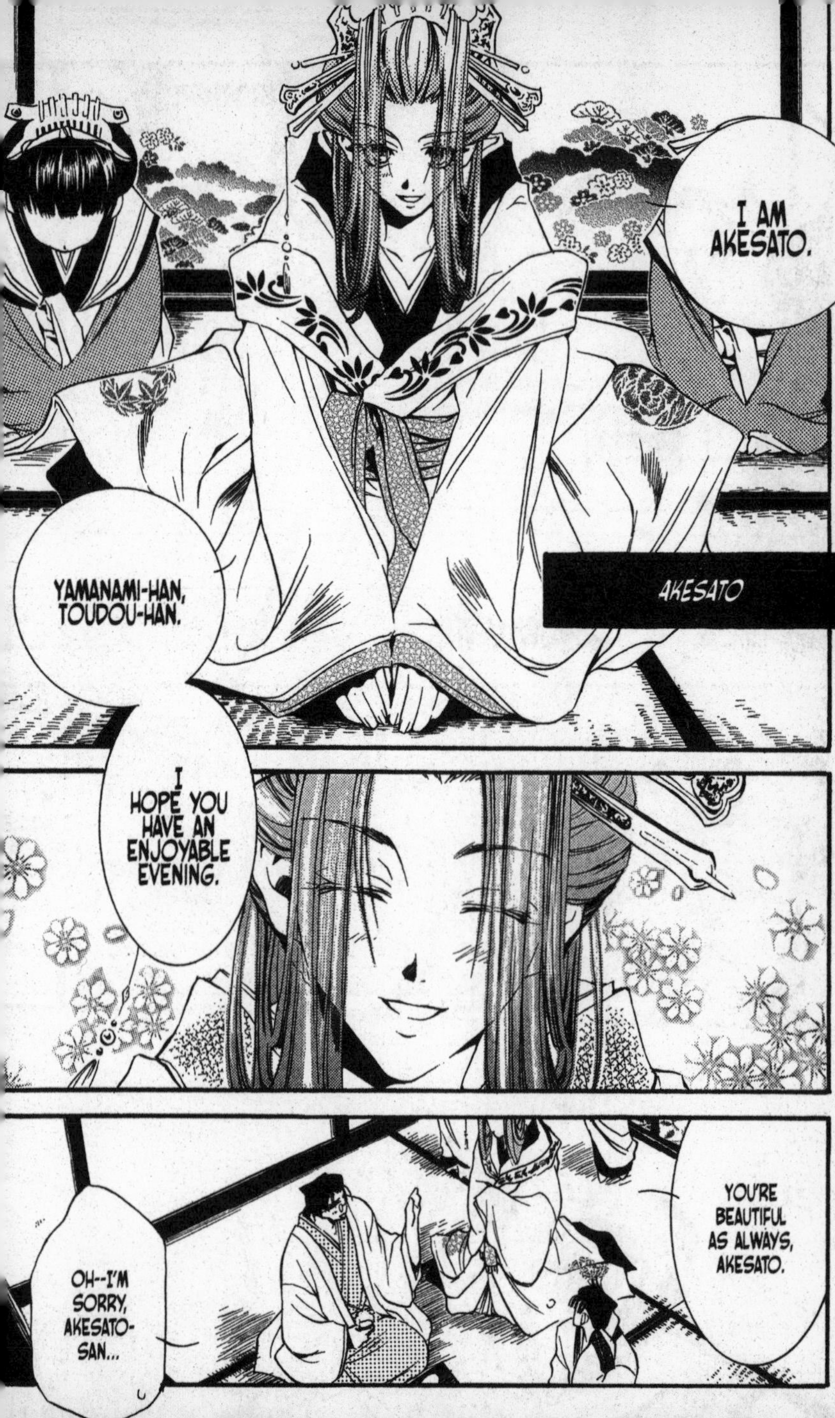
I AM AKESATO.
AKESATO
YAMANAMI-HAN, TOUDOU-HAN.
I HOPE YOU HAVE AN ENJOYABLE EVENING.
YOU'RE BEAUTIFUL AS ALWAYS, AKESATO.
OH--I'M SORRY, AKESATO-SAN...

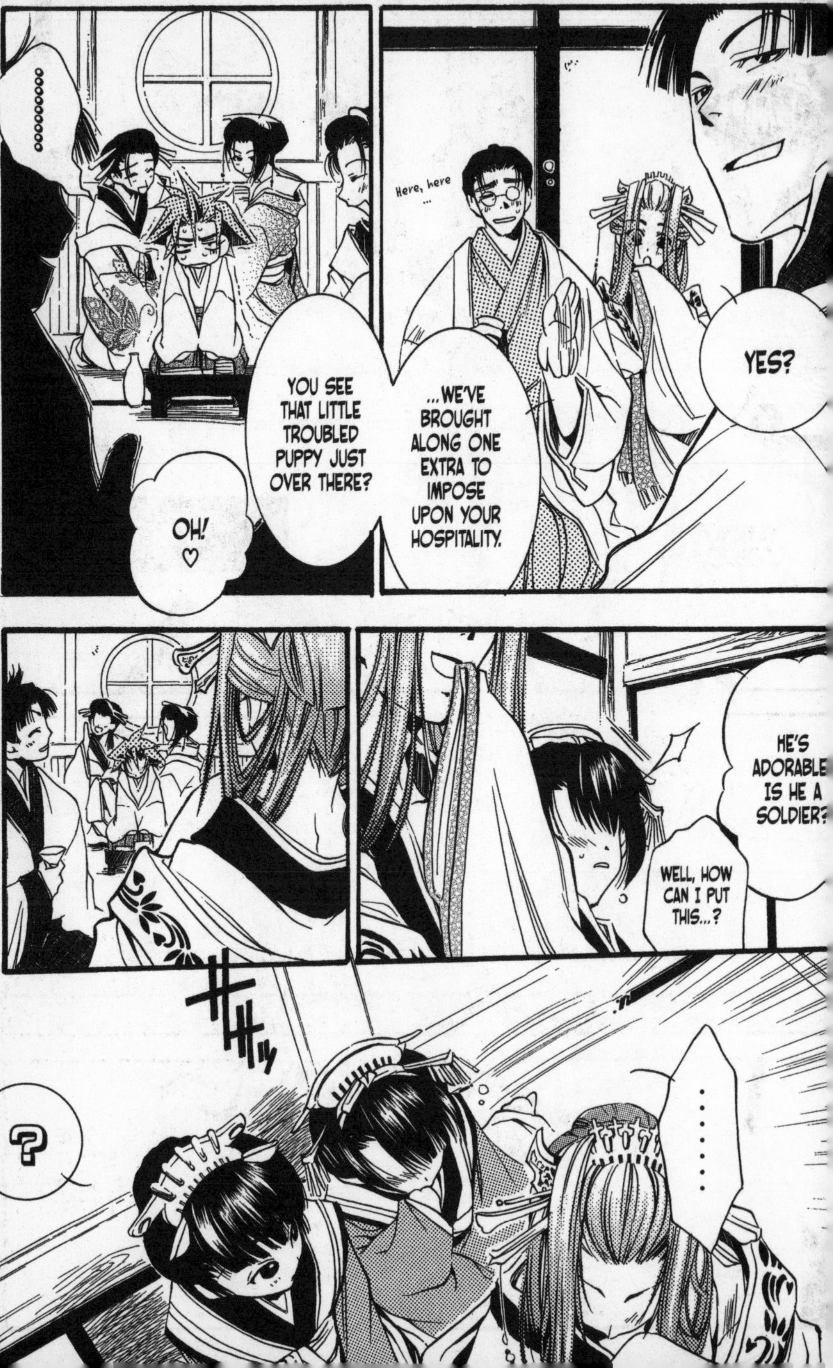
YES?
Here, here ...
...WE'VE BROUGHT ALONG ONE EXTRA TO IMPOSE UPON YOUR HOSPITALITY.
oooooooo
YOU SEE THAT LITTLE TROUBLED PUPPY JUST OVER THERE?
OH! ♡
HE'S ADORABLE IS HE A SOLDIER?
WELL, HOW CAN I PUT THIS...?
......
?

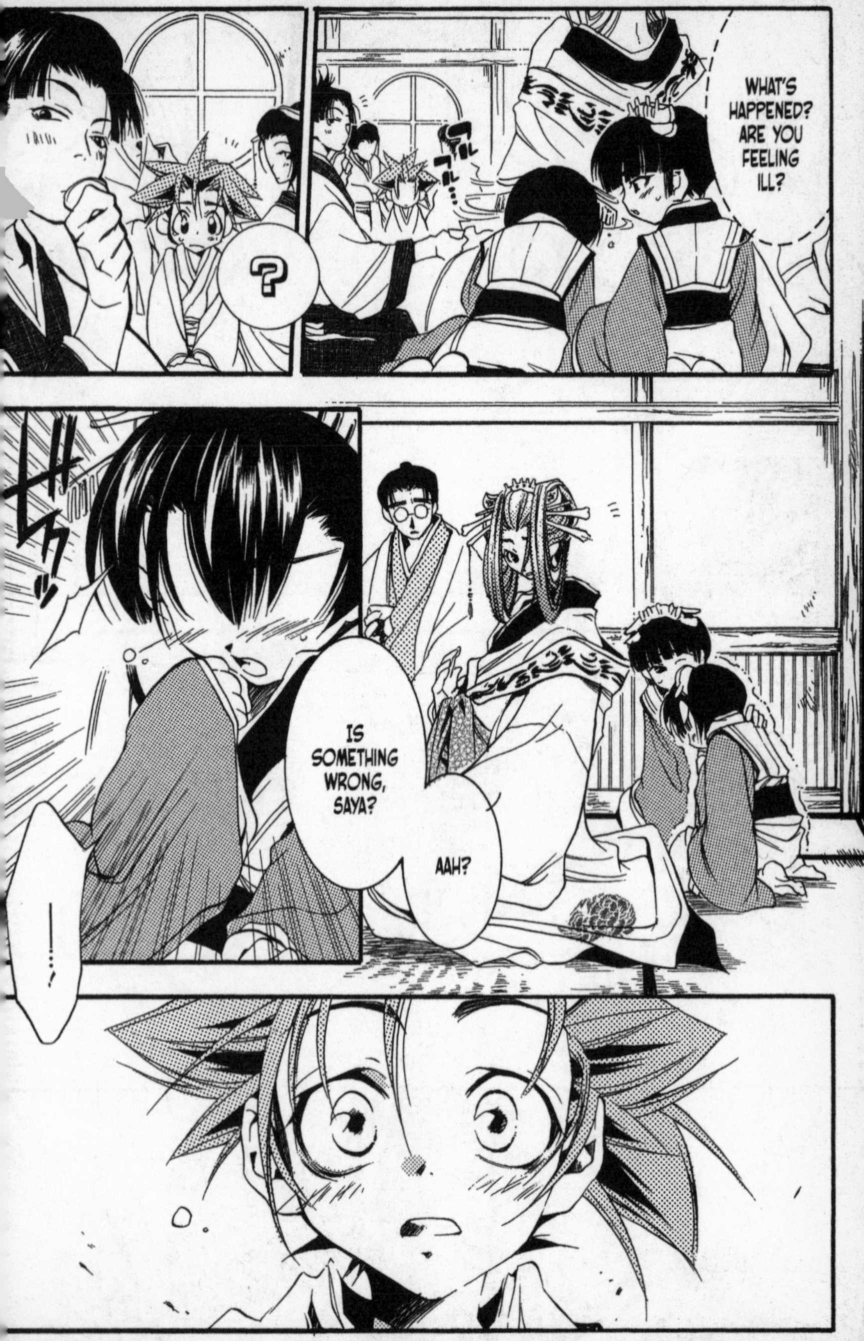

WHAT'S HAPPENED? ARE YOU FEELING ILL?
?
IS SOMETHING WRONG, SAYA?
AAH?
—...!

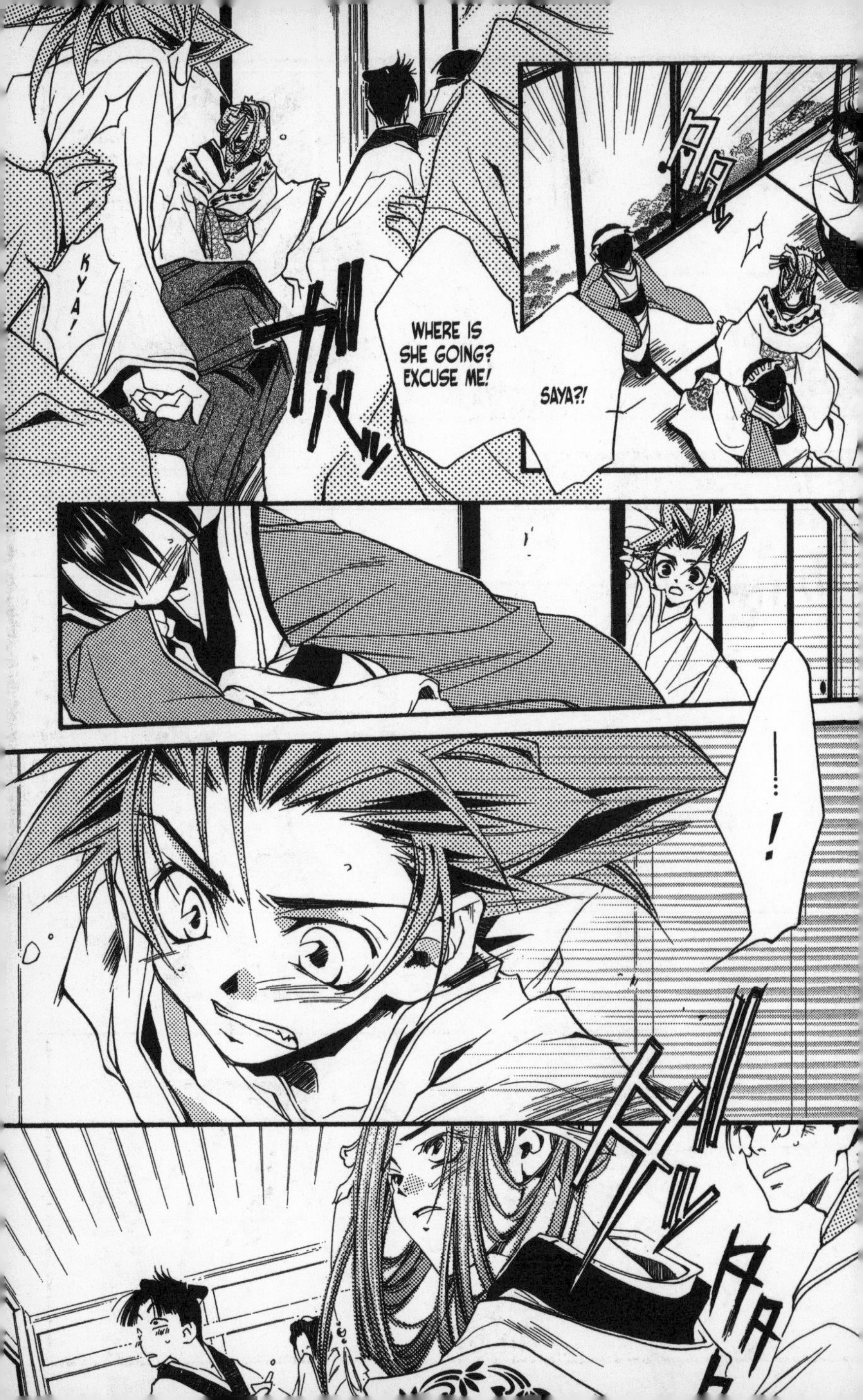
SAYA?!
WHERE IS SHE GOING? EXCUSE ME!
KYA!
......!

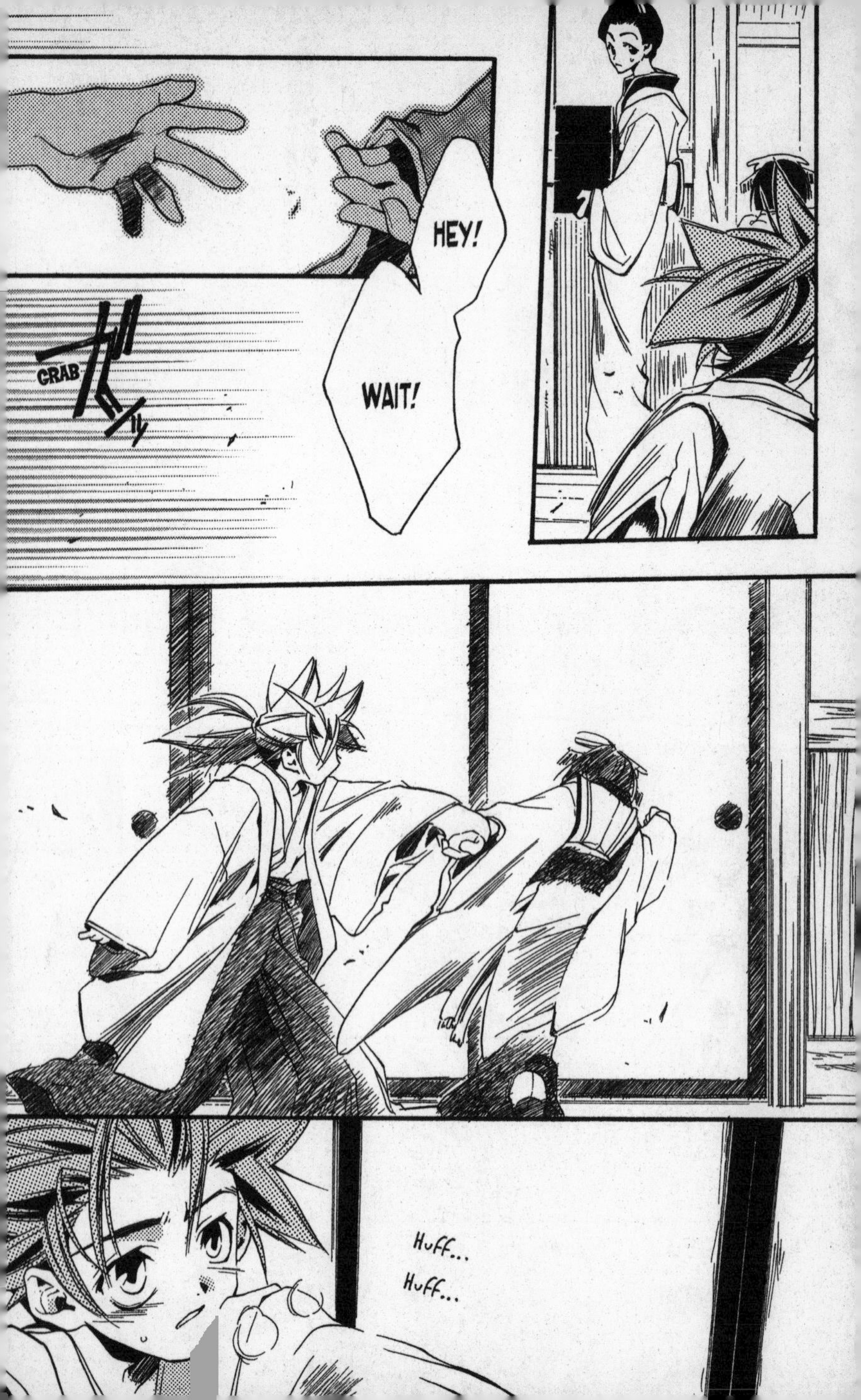
HEY!
WAIT!
GRAB
Huff... Huff...

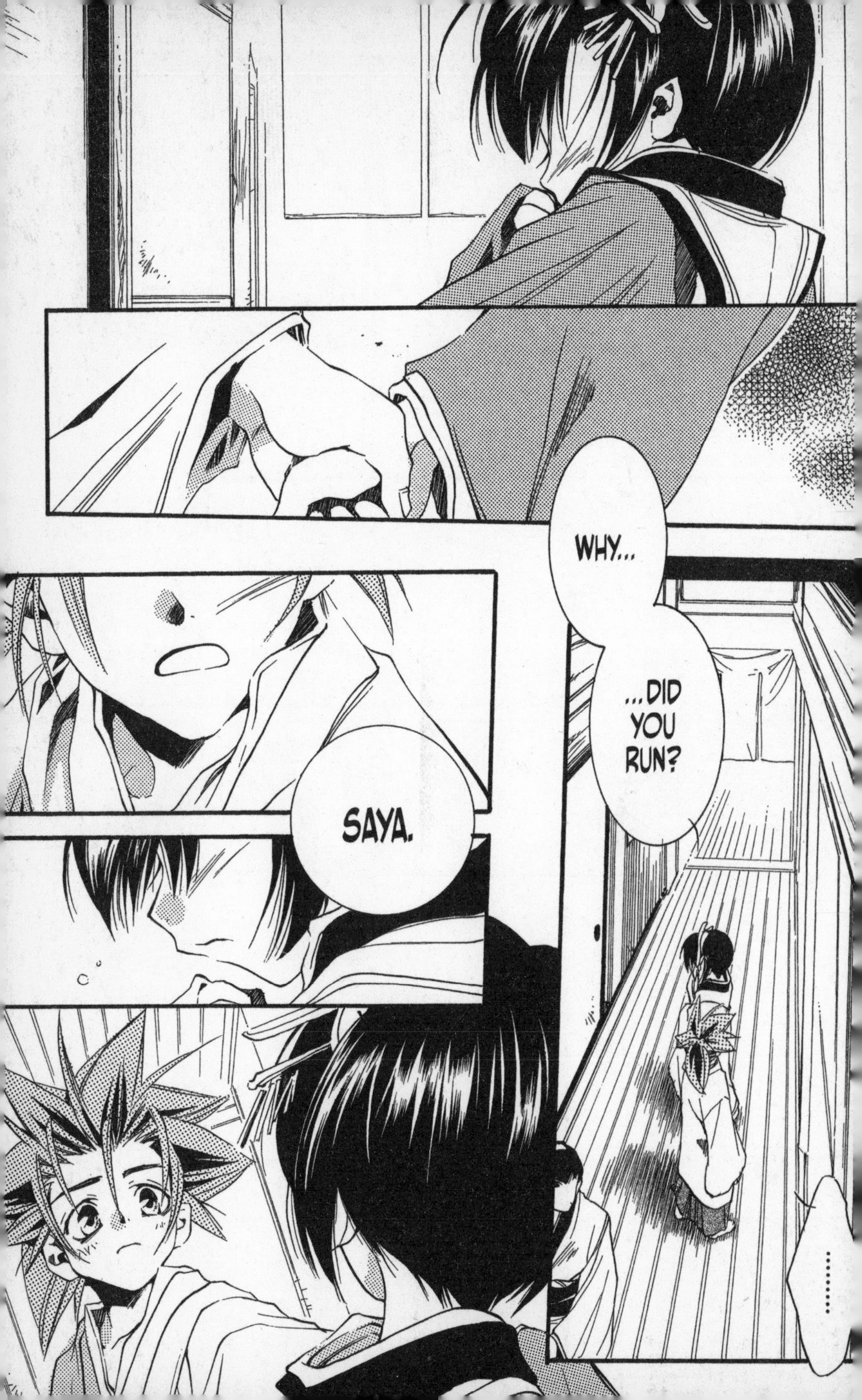
WHY...
...DID YOU RUN?
......
SAYA.

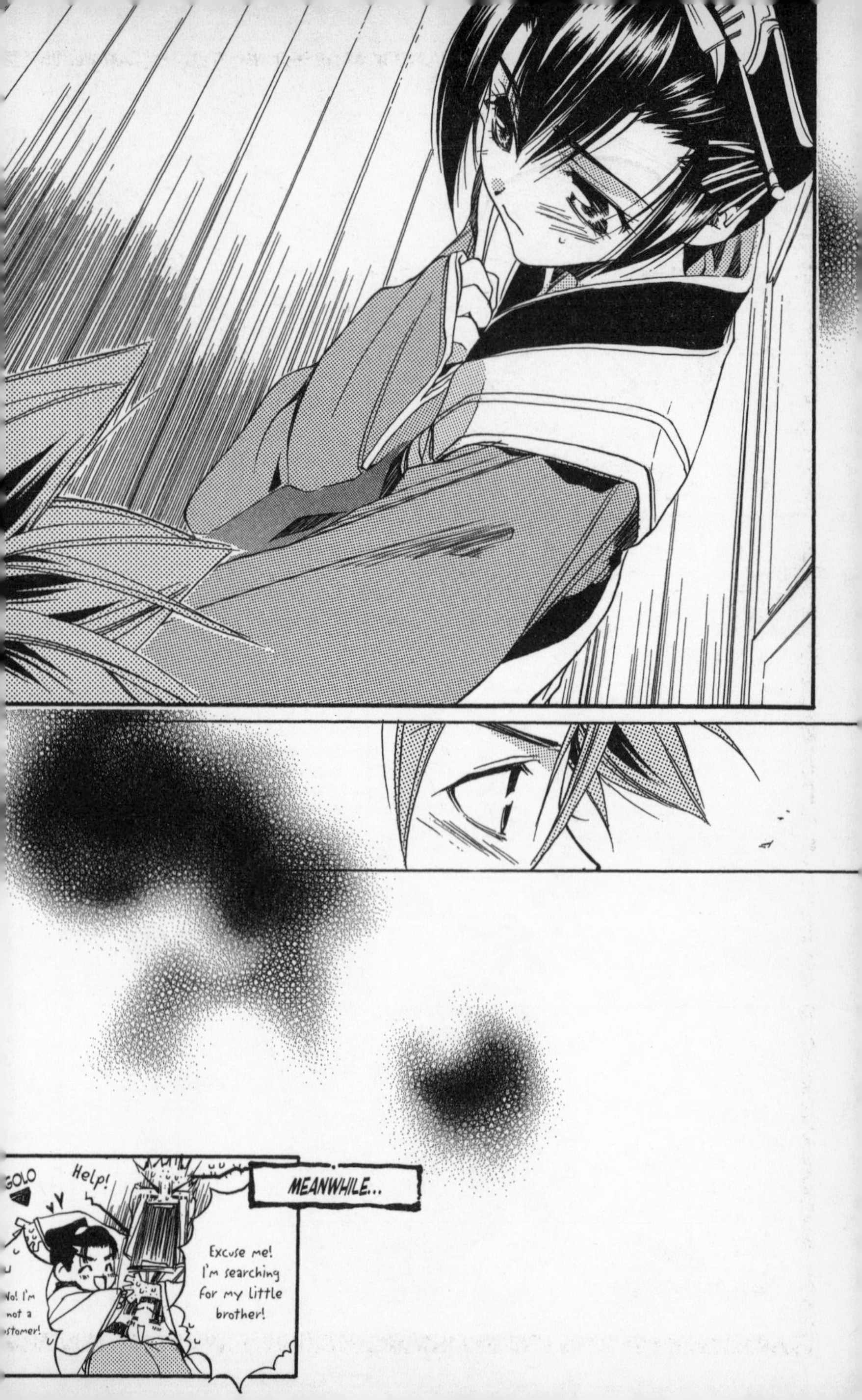
MEANWHILE...
Help!
GOLO
Excuse me! I'm searching for my little brother!
o! I'm not a stomer!

Act.14
Something

・・・・・・・

・・・・・・・

I'M SORRY.

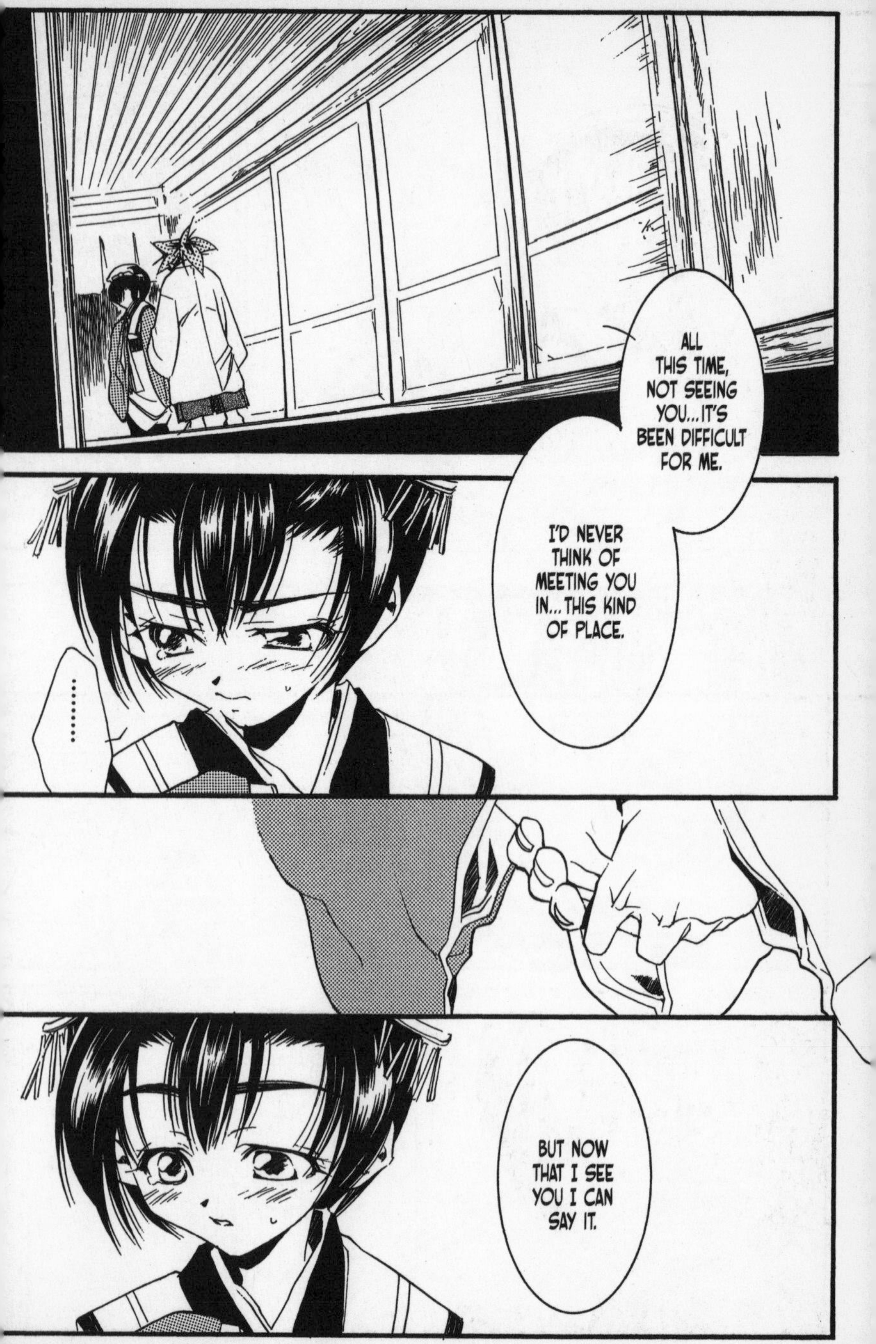
ALL THIS TIME, NOT SEEING YOU...IT'S BEEN DIFFICULT FOR ME.
I'D NEVER THINK OF MEETING YOU IN...THIS KIND OF PLACE.
....
BUT NOW THAT I SEE YOU I CAN SAY IT.

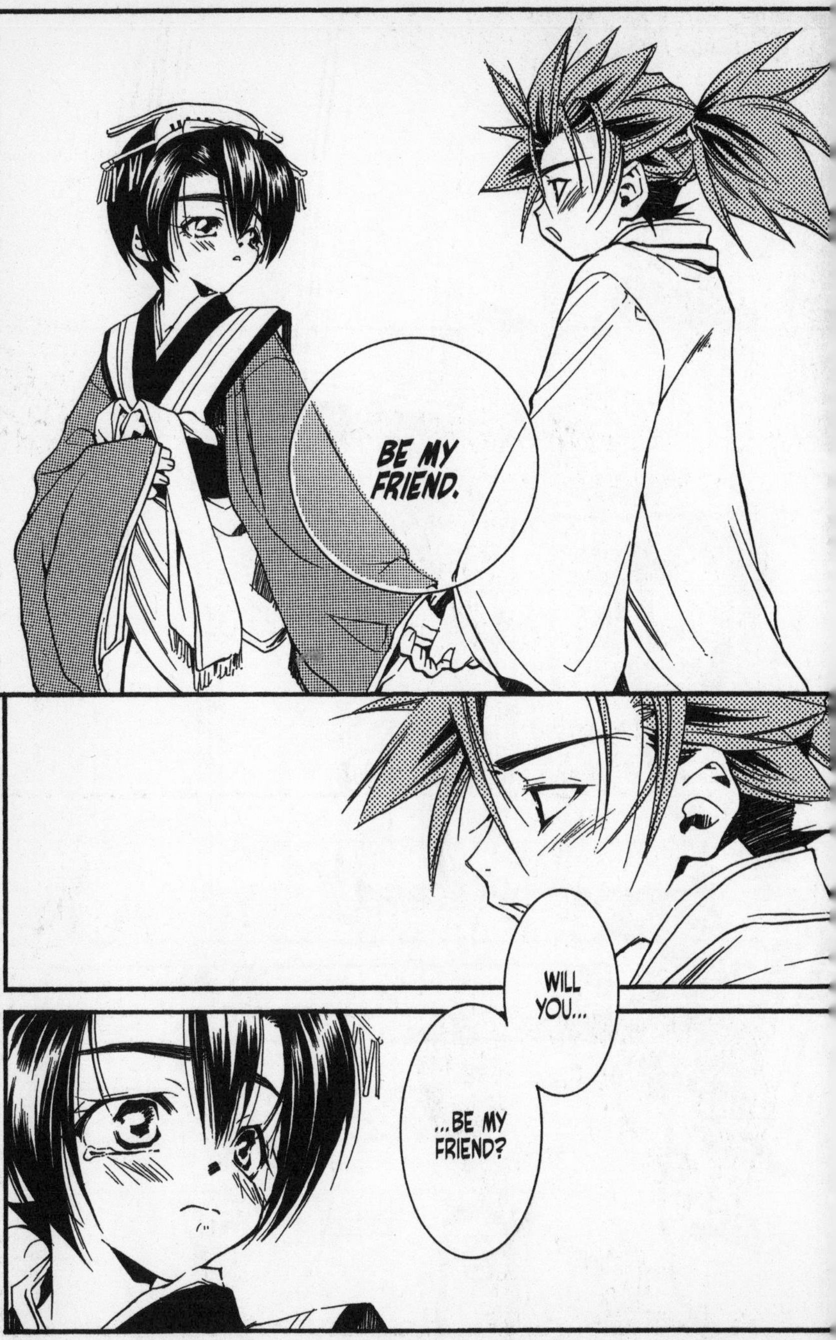
BE MY FRIEND.
WILL YOU...
...BE MY FRIEND?

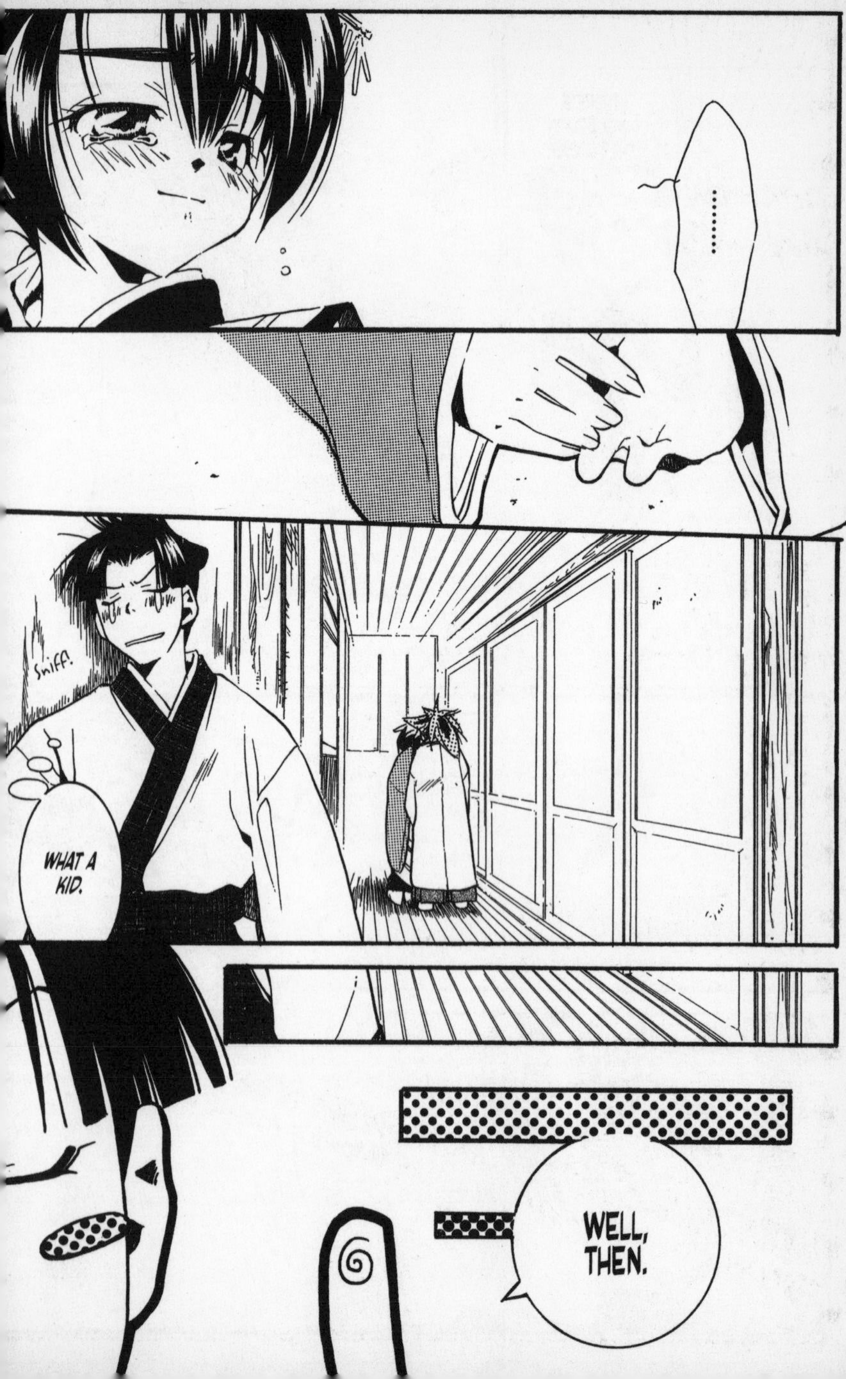
......
Sniff.
WHAT A KID.
WELL, THEN.

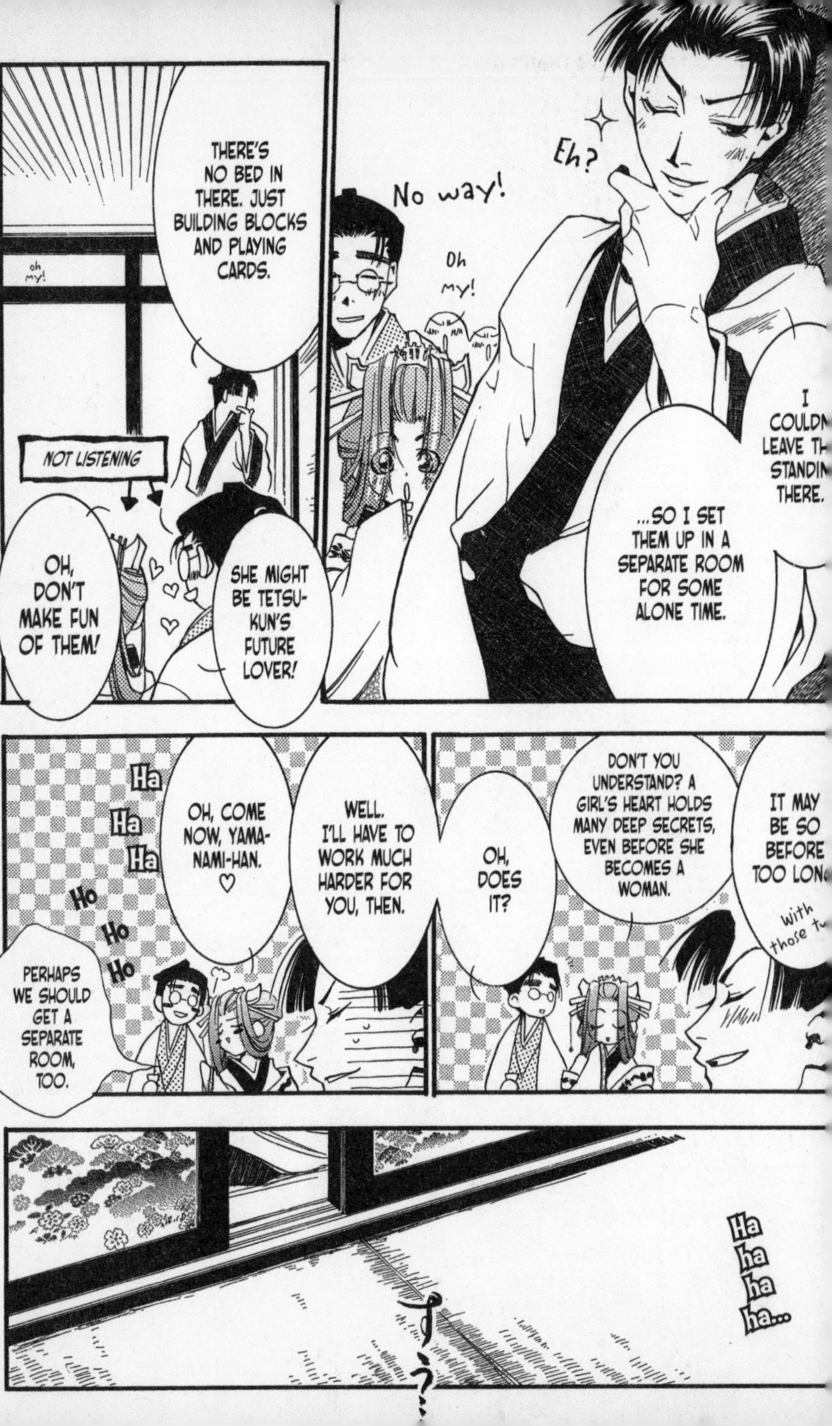
I COULDN LEAVE TH STANDIN THERE.
...SO I SET THEM UP IN A SEPARATE ROOM FOR SOME ALONE TIME.
Eh?
No way!
Oh my!
THERE'S NO BED IN THERE. JUST BUILDING BLOCKS AND PLAYING CARDS.
oh my!
NOT LISTENING
SHE MIGHT BE TETSU-KUN'S FUTURE LOVER!
OH, DON'T MAKE FUN OF THEM!
IT MAY BE SO BEFORE TOO LON
with those t
DON'T YOU UNDERSTAND? A GIRL'S HEART HOLDS MANY DEEP SECRETS, EVEN BEFORE SHE BECOMES A WOMAN.
OH, DOES IT?
WELL. I'LL HAVE TO WORK MUCH HARDER FOR YOU, THEN.
OH, COME NOW, YAMA-NAMI-HAN. ♡
Ha Ha Ha
Ho Ho Ho
PERHAPS WE SHOULD GET A SEPARATE ROOM, TOO.
Ha ha ha ha...
すぅ…

ster: "Nee-san;" a term of respect
n addressing a young woman.

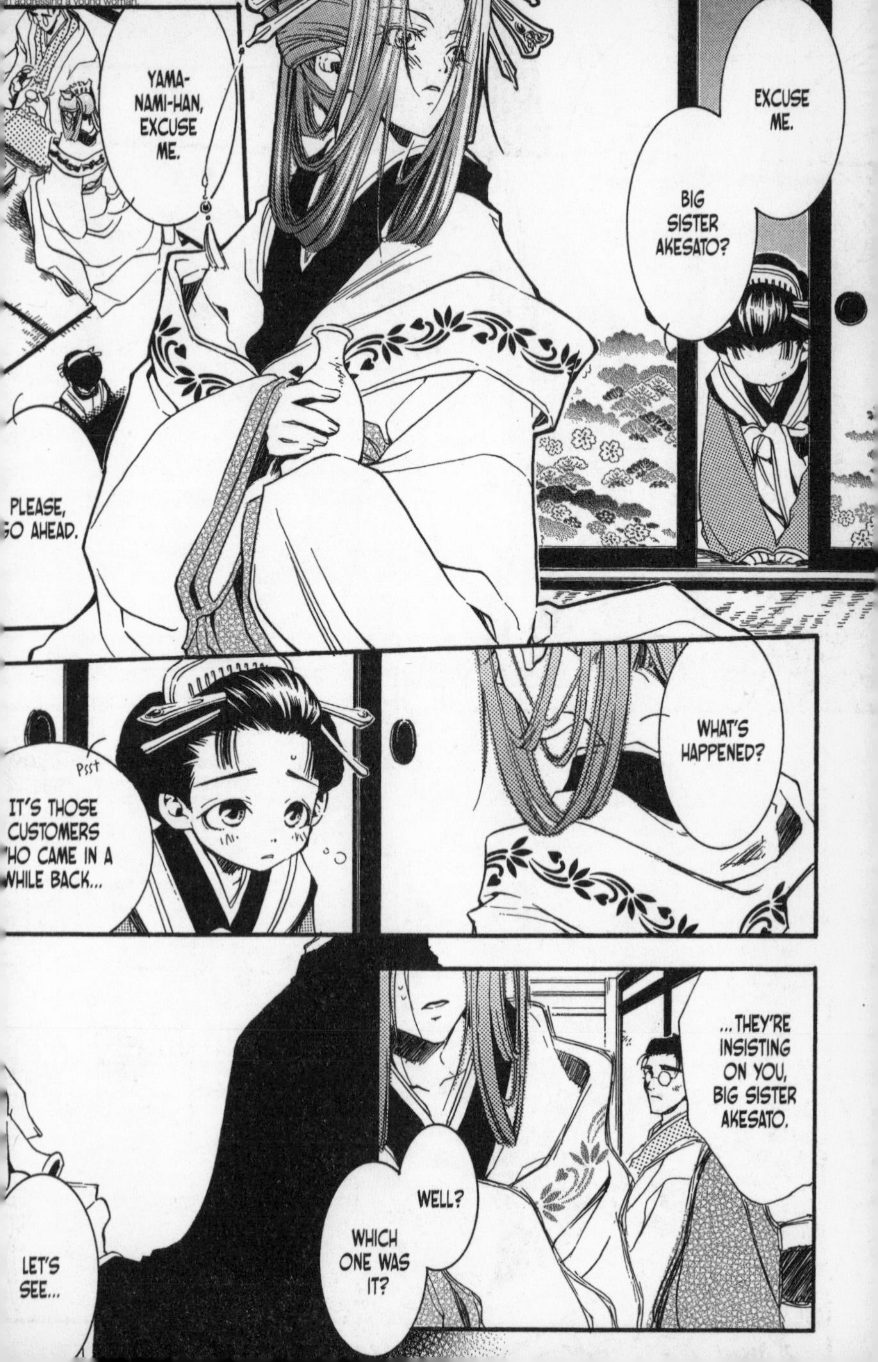

EXCUSE ME.
BIG SISTER AKESATO?
YAMA-NAMI-HAN, EXCUSE ME.
PLEASE, GO AHEAD.
WHAT'S HAPPENED?
Psst
IT'S THOSE CUSTOMERS HO CAME IN A HILE BACK...
...THEY'RE INSISTING ON YOU, BIG SISTER AKESATO.
WELL?
WHICH ONE WAS IT?
LET'S SEE...

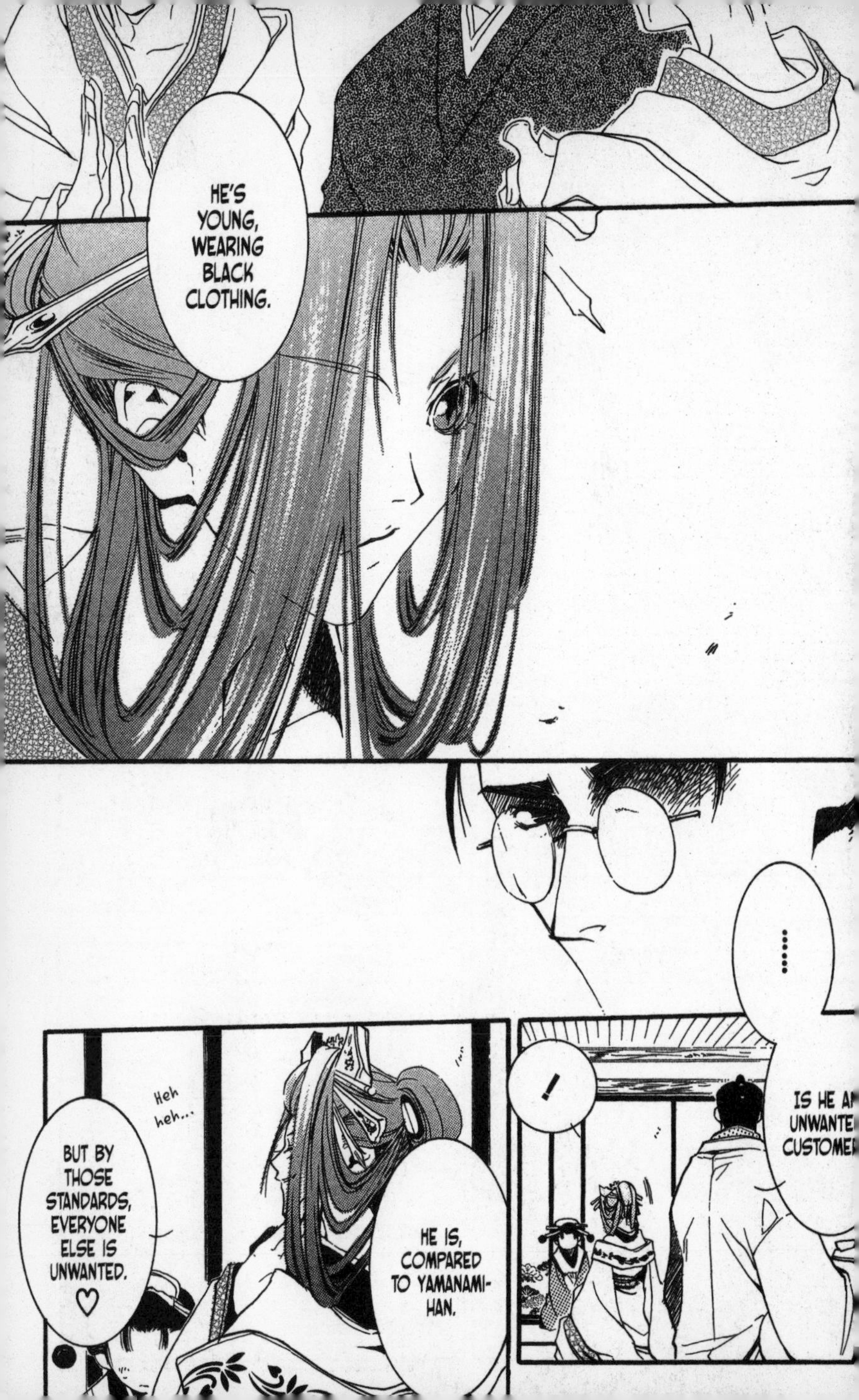
HE'S YOUNG, WEARING BLACK CLOTHING.
……
IS HE A UNWANTE CUSTOME
!
HE IS, COMPARED TO YAMANAMI-HAN.
Heh heh...
BUT BY THOSE STANDARDS, EVERYONE ELSE IS UNWANTED. ♡

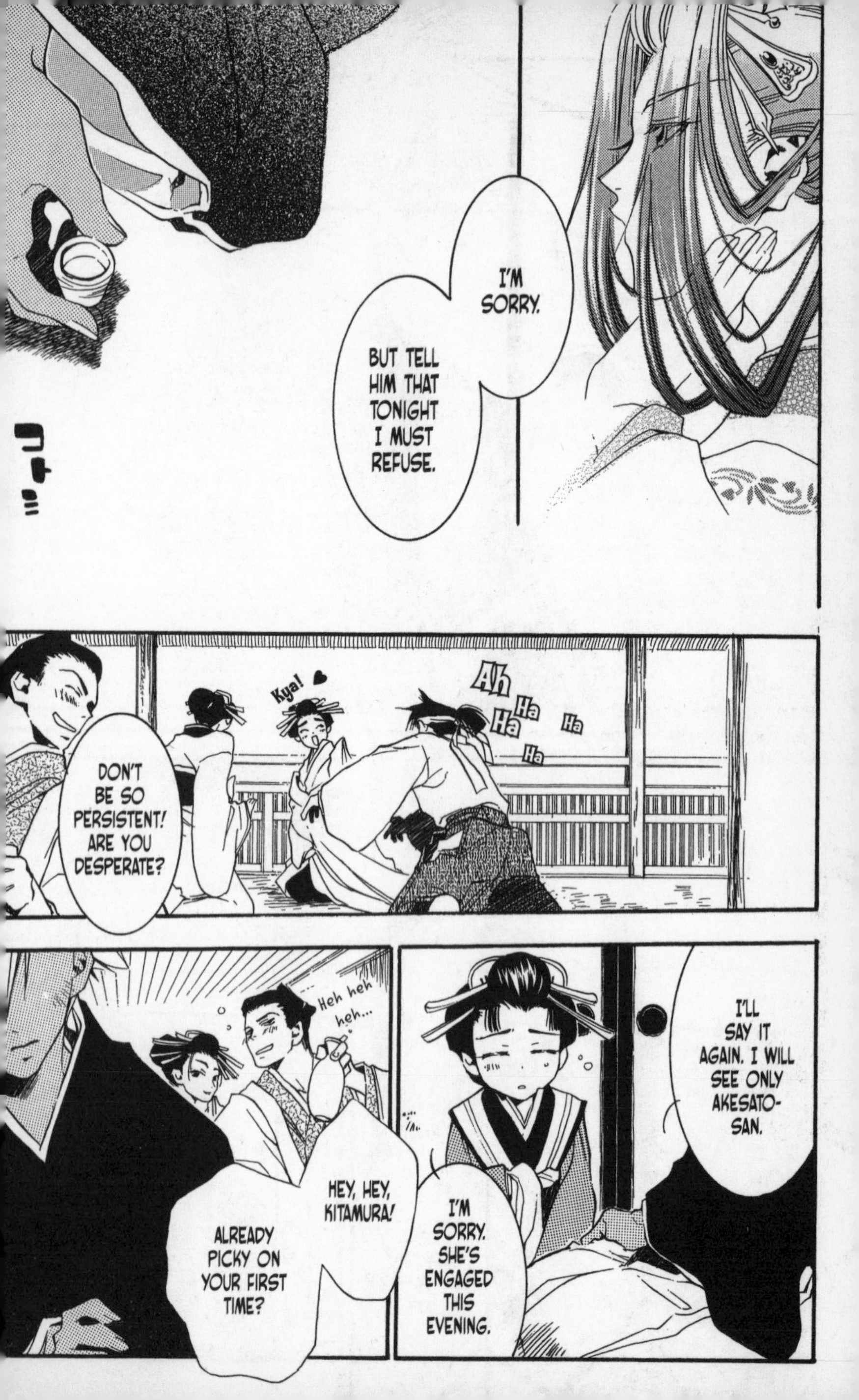
I'M SORRY.
BUT TELL HIM THAT TONIGHT I MUST REFUSE.
コト
Ah Ha Ha Ha Ha
Kya! ♥
DON'T BE SO PERSISTENT! ARE YOU DESPERATE?
I'LL SAY IT AGAIN. I WILL SEE ONLY AKESATO-SAN.
I'M SORRY. SHE'S ENGAGED THIS EVENING.
Heh heh heh...
HEY, HEY, KITAMURA!
ALREADY PICKY ON YOUR FIRST TIME?

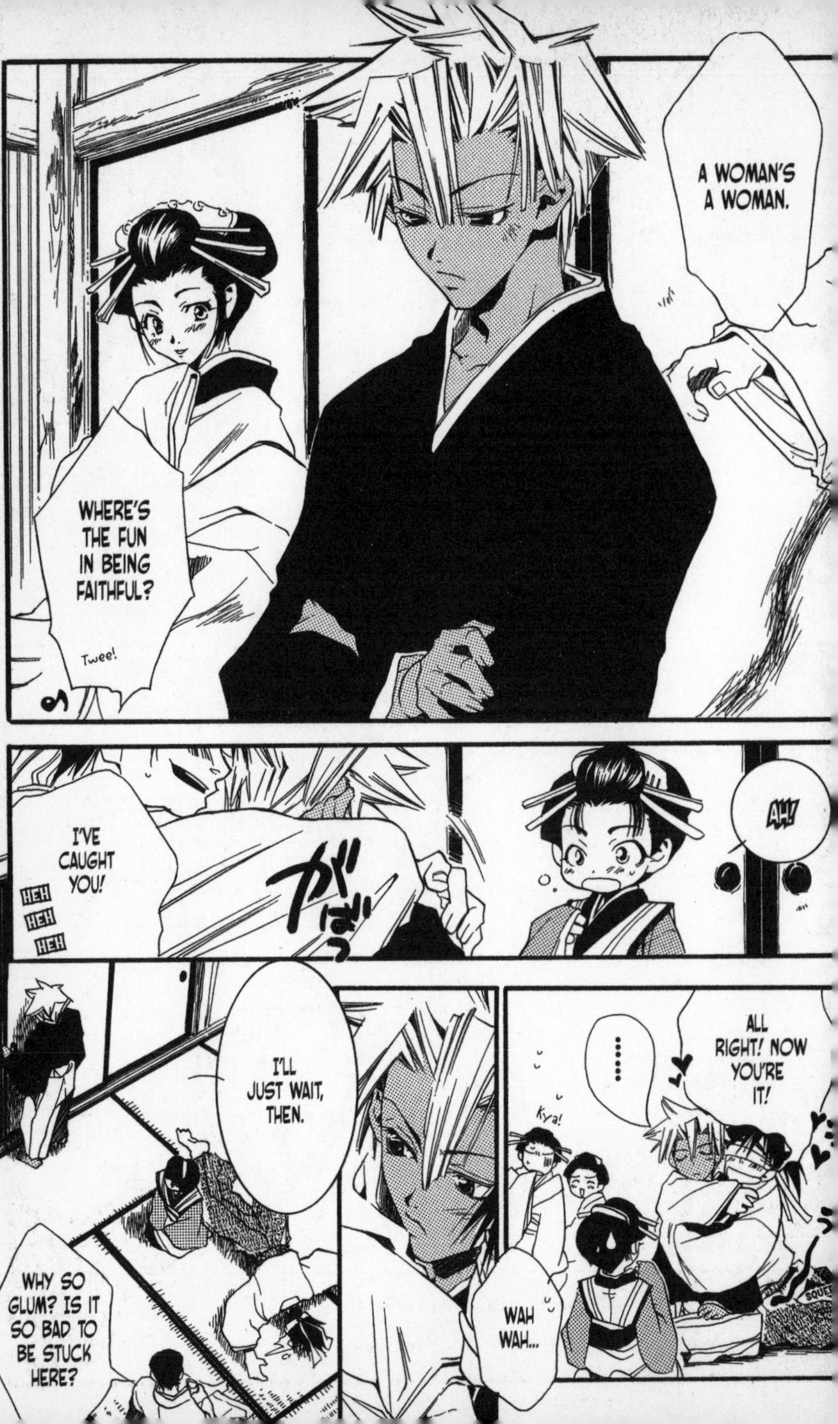
A WOMAN'S A WOMAN.
WHERE'S THE FUN IN BEING FAITHFUL?
Twee!
AH!
I'VE CAUGHT YOU!
HEH HEH HEH
がばっ
ALL RIGHT! NOW YOU'RE IT!
......
Kya!
WAH WAH...
I'LL JUST WAIT, THEN.
WHY SO GLUM? IS IT SO BAD TO BE STUCK HERE?

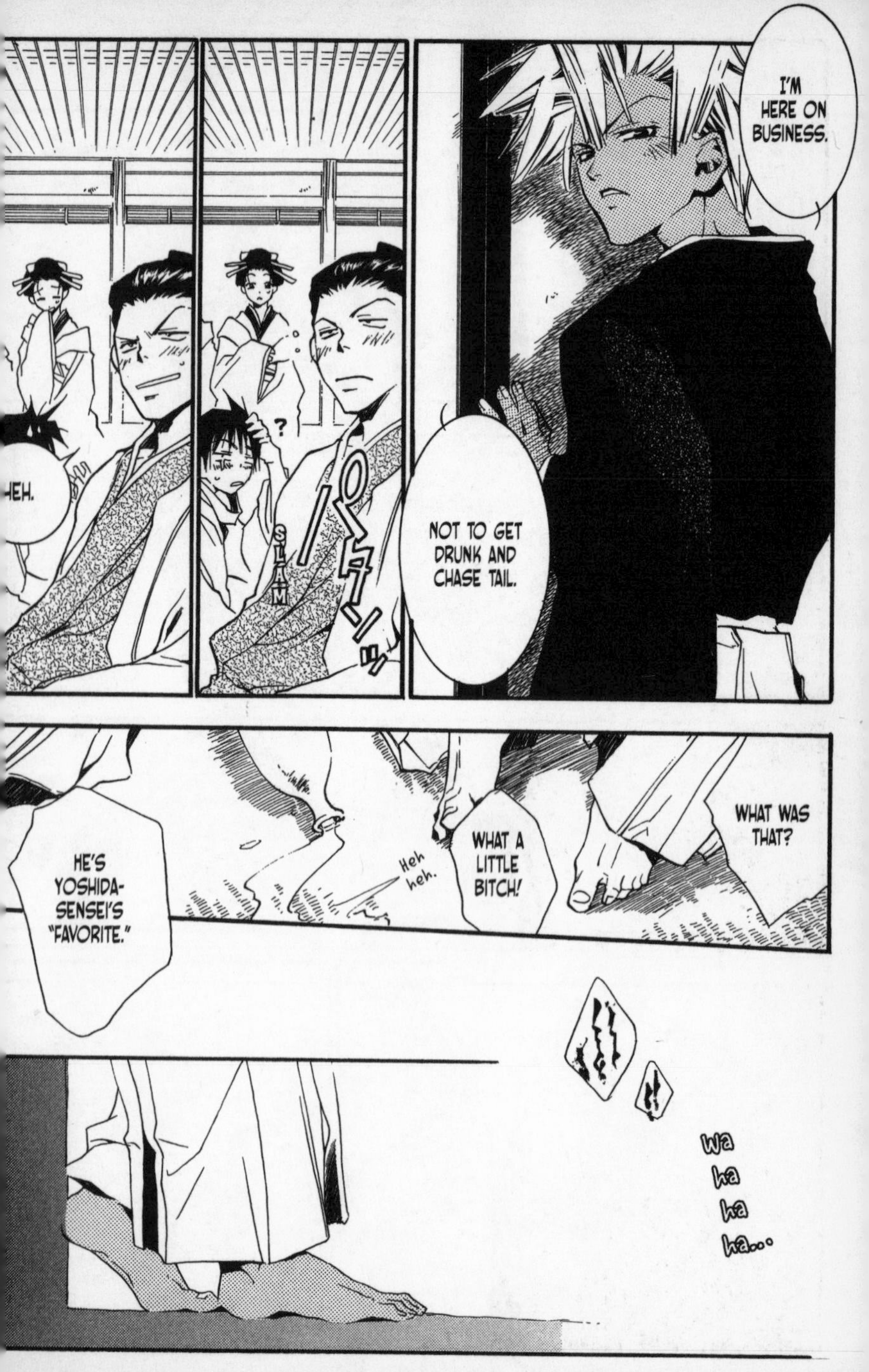
I'M HERE ON BUSINESS.
NOT TO GET DRUNK AND CHASE TAIL.
SLAM
?
HEH.
WHAT WAS THAT?
WHAT A LITTLE BITCH!
Heh heh.
HE'S YOSHIDA-SENSEI'S "FAVORITE."
Wa ha ha ha...

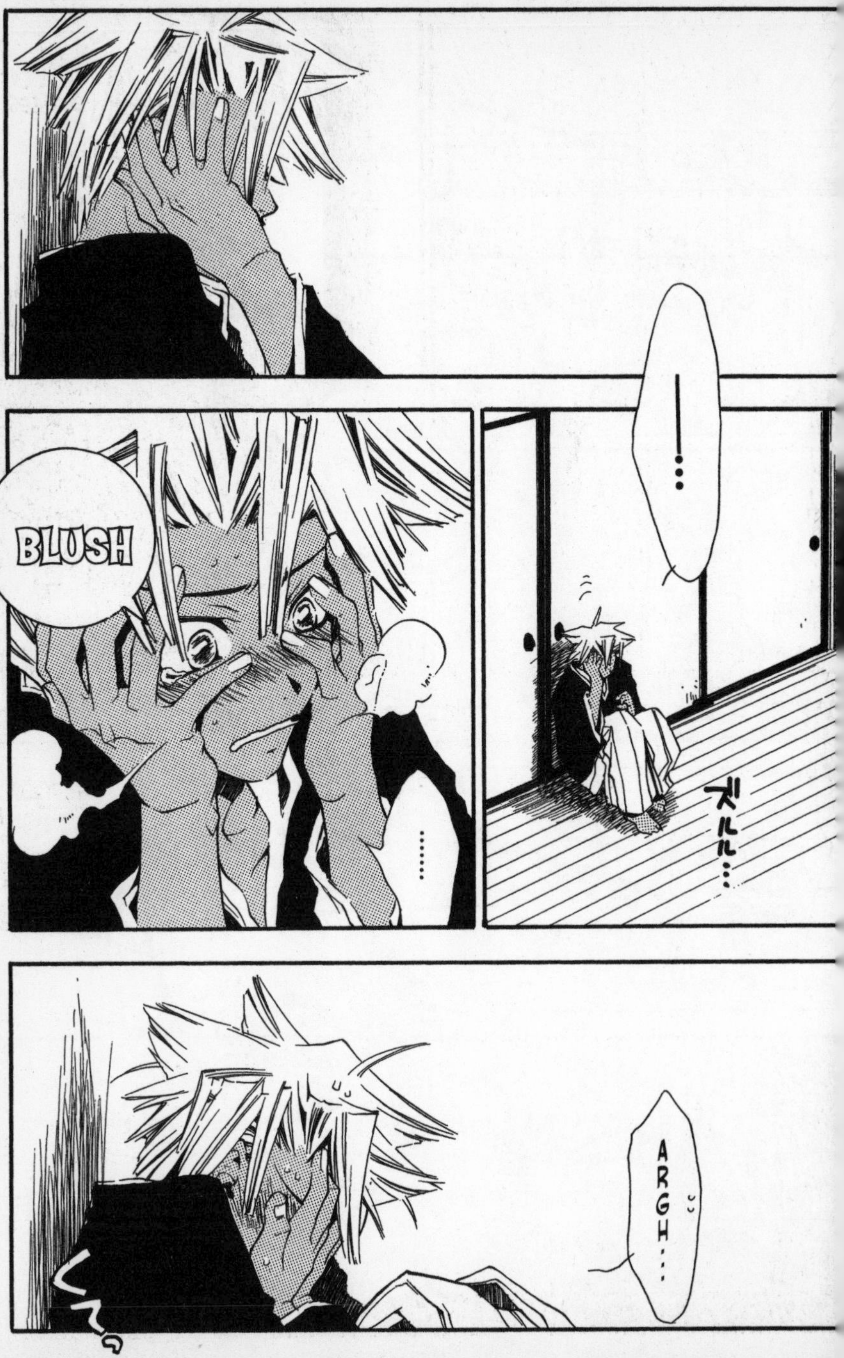
!...
ズルル…
BLUSH
......
ARGH...

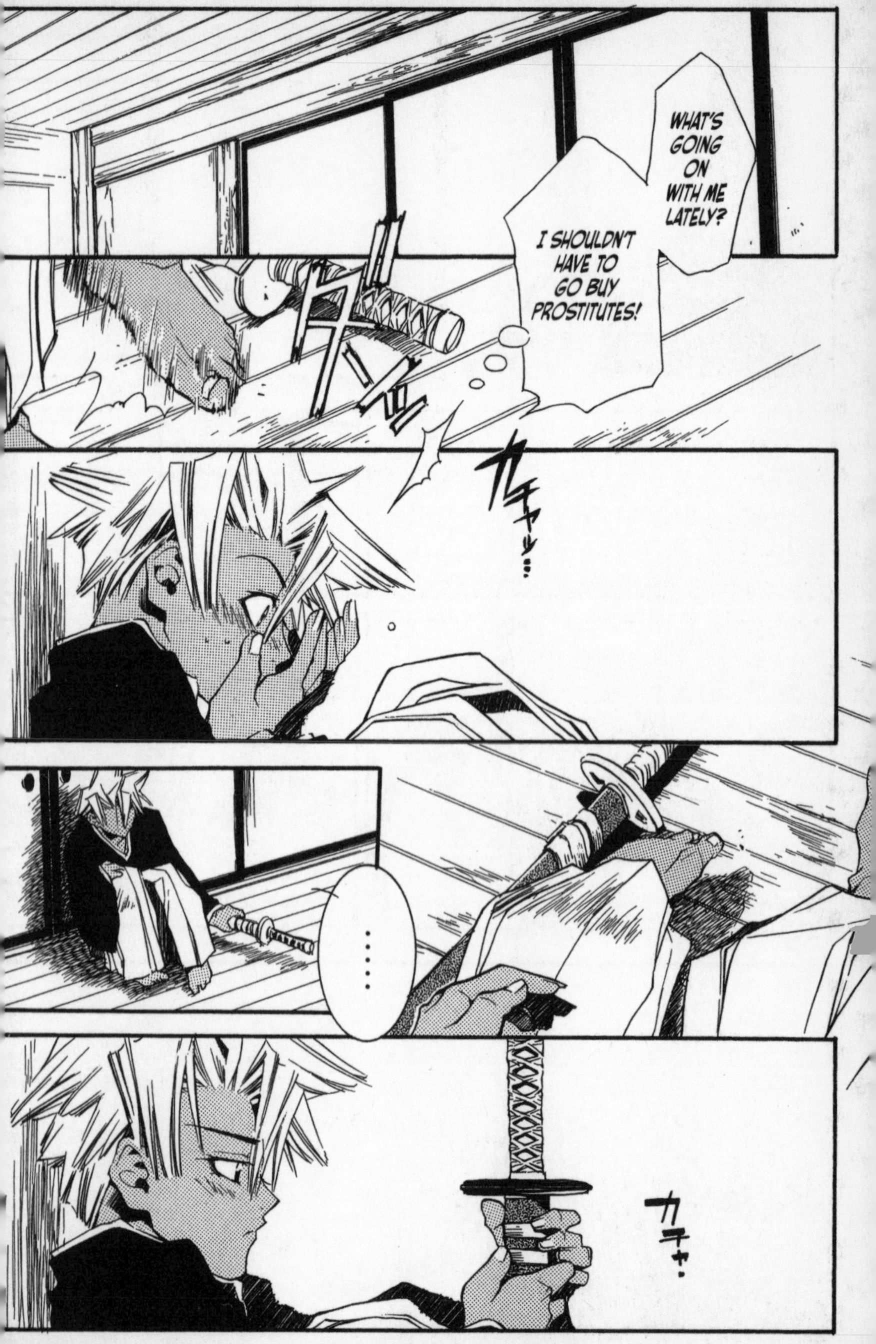
WHAT'S GOING ON WITH ME LATELY?
I SHOULDN'T HAVE TO GO BUY PROSTITUTES!
カチャッ…
……
カチャ・

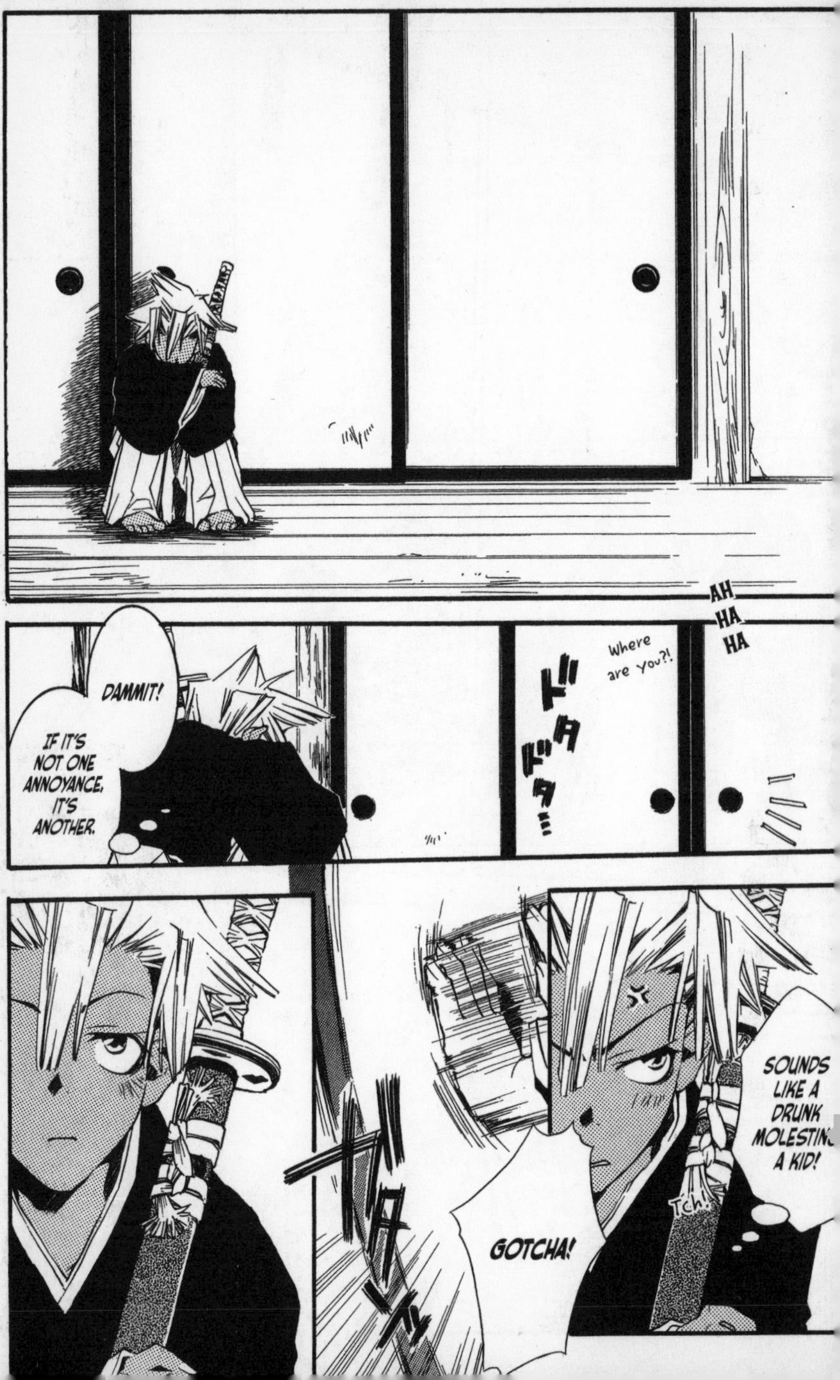
AH HA HA
Where are you?!
ドタドタ
DAMMIT!
IF IT'S NOT ONE ANNOYANCE, IT'S ANOTHER.
SOUNDS LIKE A DRUNK MOLESTING A KID!
Tch.
GOTCHA!

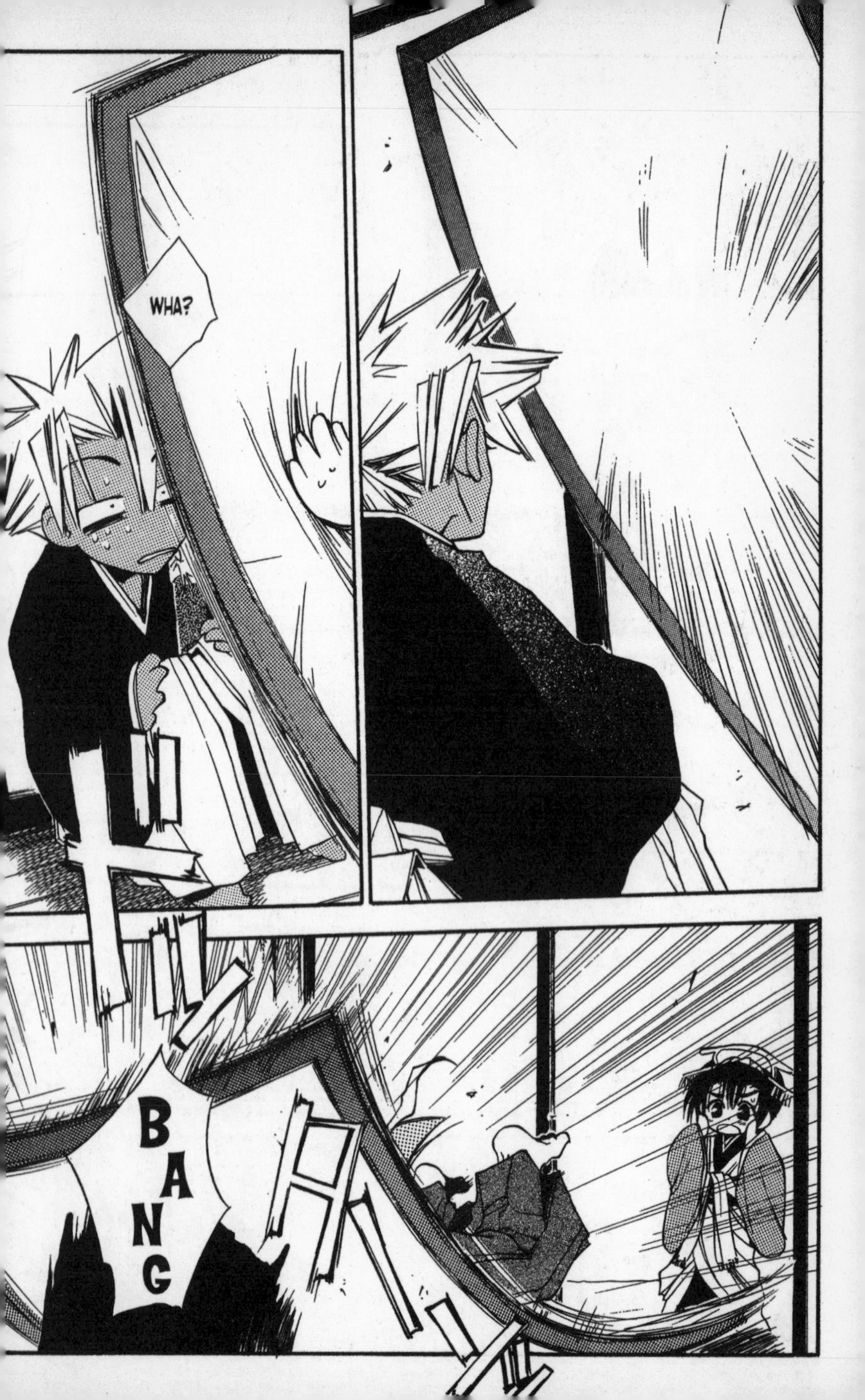
WHA?
BANG

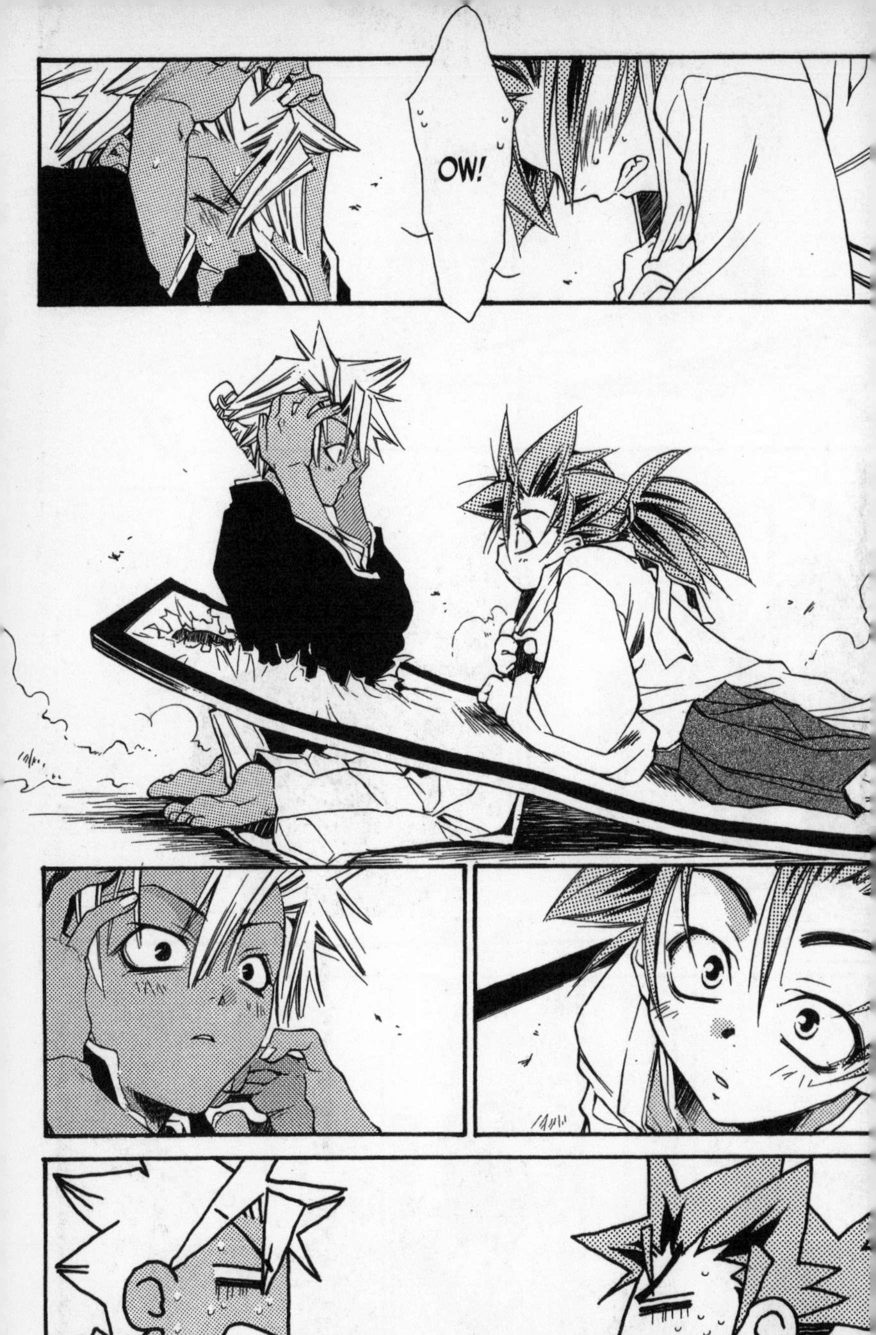
OW!

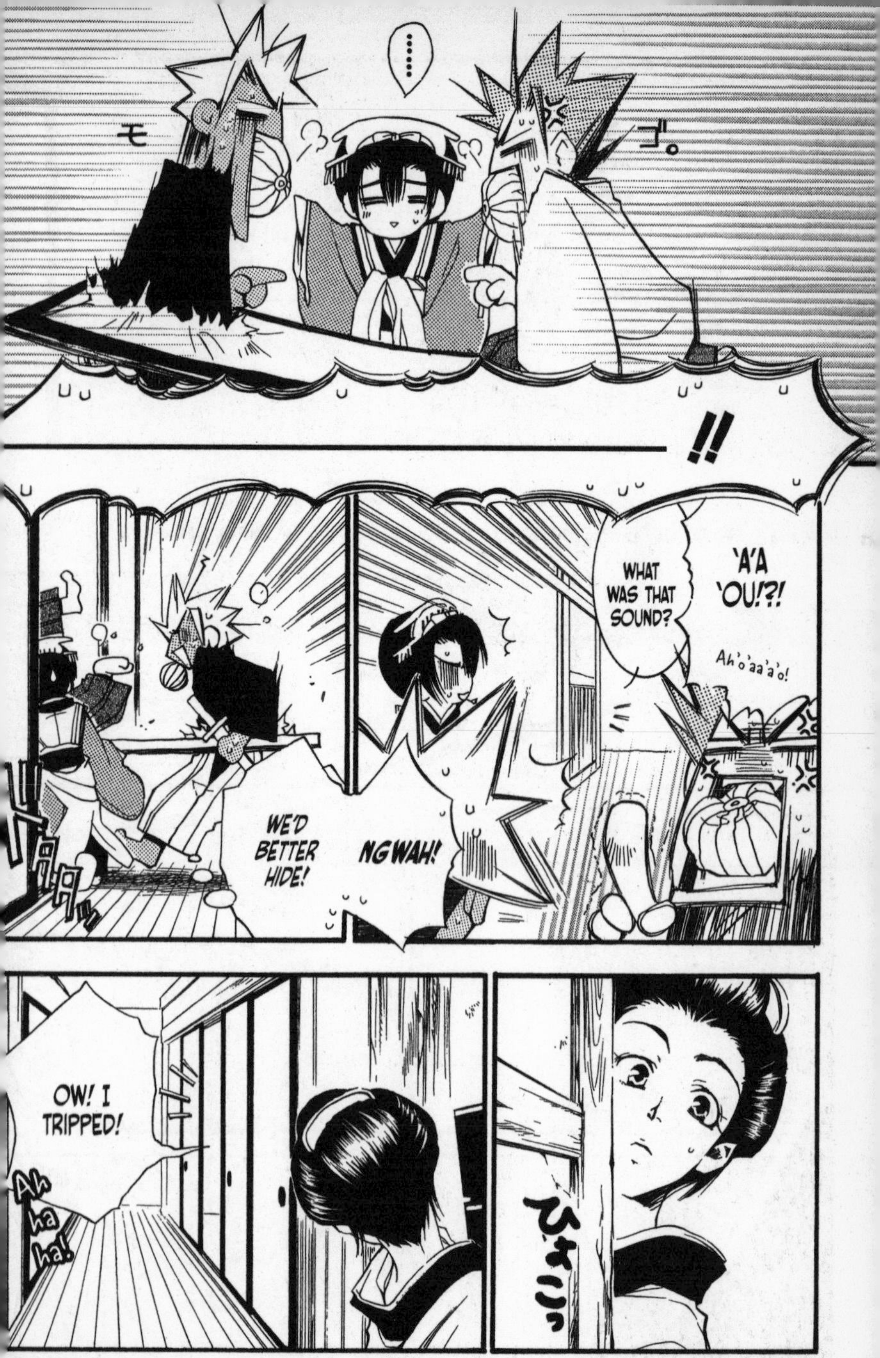
ゴ。
......
モ
!!
'A'A 'OU!?!
WHAT WAS THAT SOUND?
Ah'o'aa'a'o!
NGWAH!
WE'D BETTER HIDE!
ひょこっ
OW! I TRIPPED!
Ah ha ha!

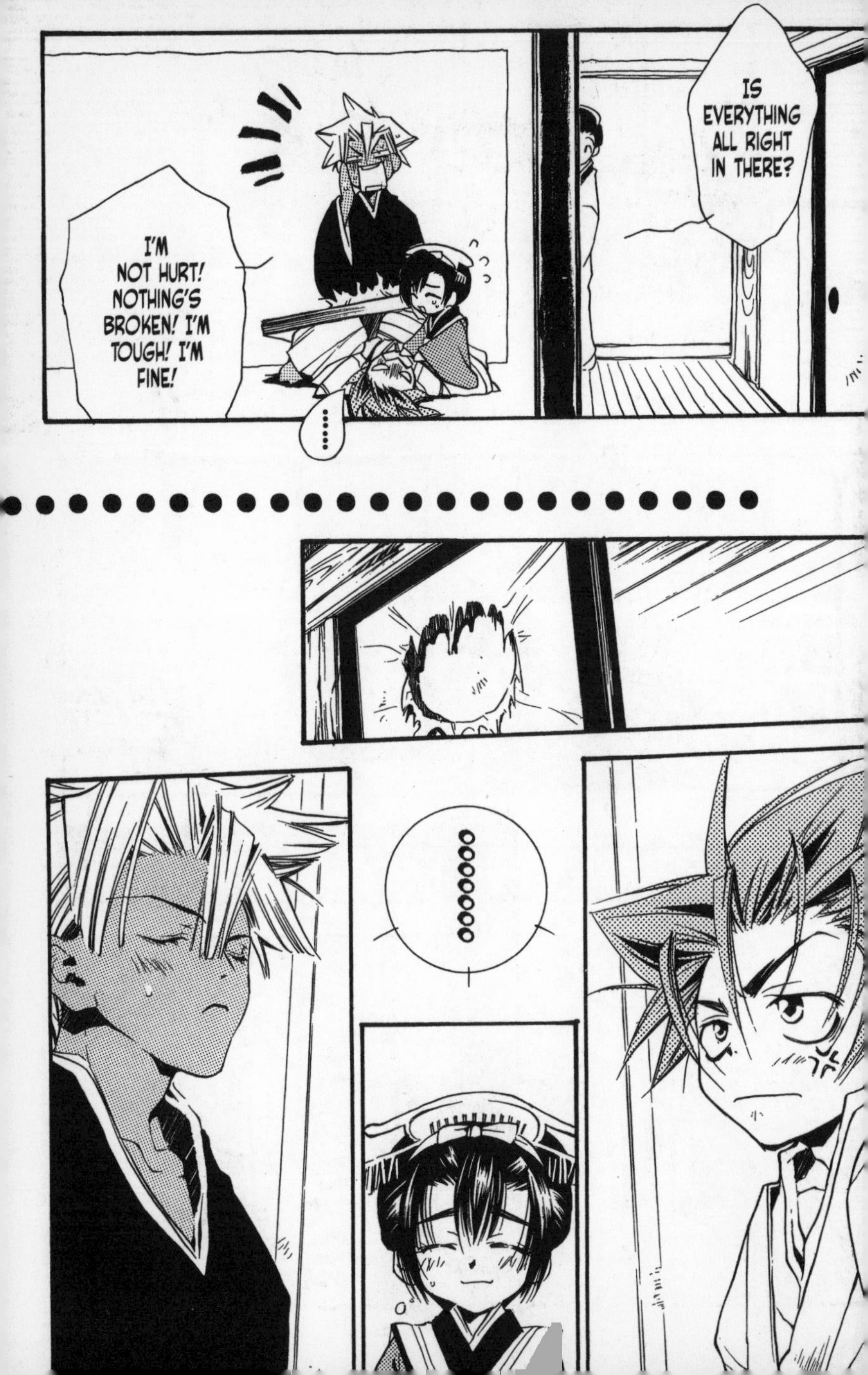
IS EVERYTHING ALL RIGHT IN THERE?
I'M NOT HURT! NOTHING'S BROKEN! I'M TOUGH! I'M FINE!
......
OOOOOOO

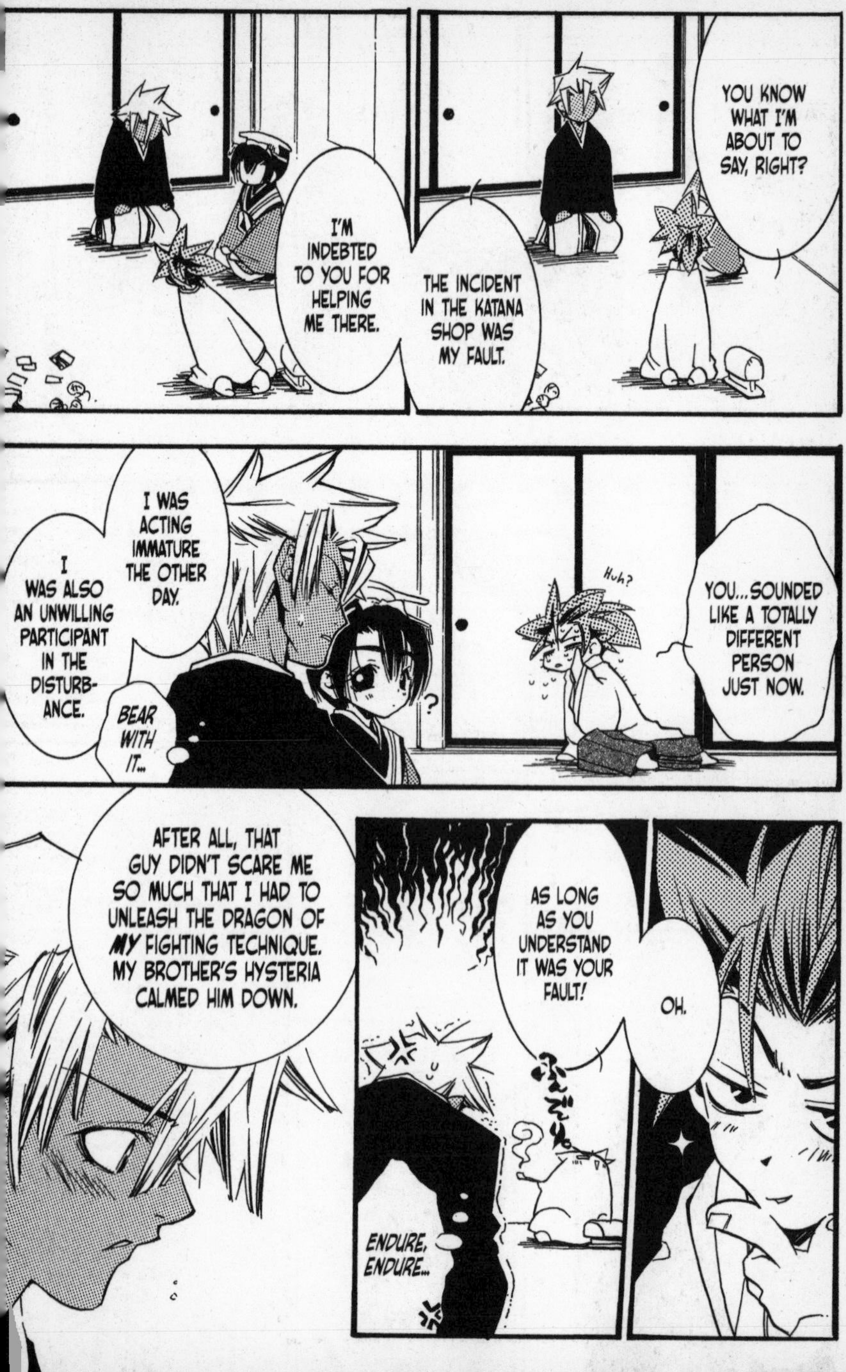
YOU KNOW WHAT I'M ABOUT TO SAY, RIGHT?
THE INCIDENT IN THE KATANA SHOP WAS MY FAULT.
I'M INDEBTED TO YOU FOR HELPING ME THERE.
YOU...SOUNDED LIKE A TOTALLY DIFFERENT PERSON JUST NOW.
Huh?
I WAS ACTING IMMATURE THE OTHER DAY.
I WAS ALSO AN UNWILLING PARTICIPANT IN THE DISTURB-ANCE.
BEAR WITH IT...
OH.
AS LONG AS YOU UNDERSTAND IT WAS YOUR FAULT!
ENDURE, ENDURE...
AFTER ALL, THAT GUY DIDN'T SCARE ME SO MUCH THAT I HAD TO UNLEASH THE DRAGON OF *MY* FIGHTING TECHNIQUE. MY BROTHER'S HYSTERIA CALMED HIM DOWN.

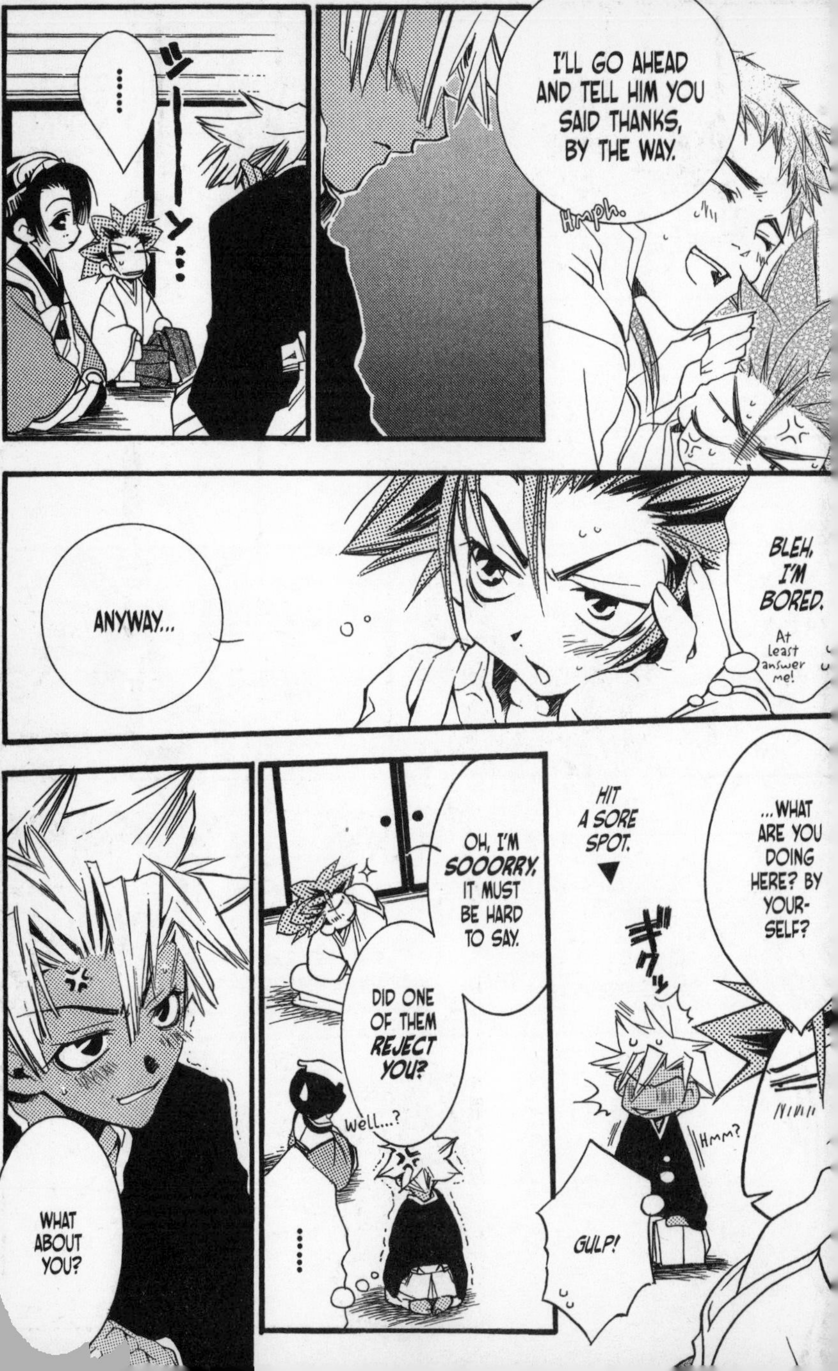
I'LL GO AHEAD AND TELL HIM YOU SAID THANKS, BY THE WAY.
Hmph.
......
ジーッ...
BLEH. I'M BORED.
At least answer me!
ANYWAY...
...WHAT ARE YOU DOING HERE? BY YOURSELF?
HIT A SORE SPOT.
ギクッ
Hmm?
GULP!
OH, I'M SOOORRY. IT MUST BE HARD TO SAY.
DID ONE OF THEM REJECT YOU?
Well...?
......
WHAT ABOUT YOU?

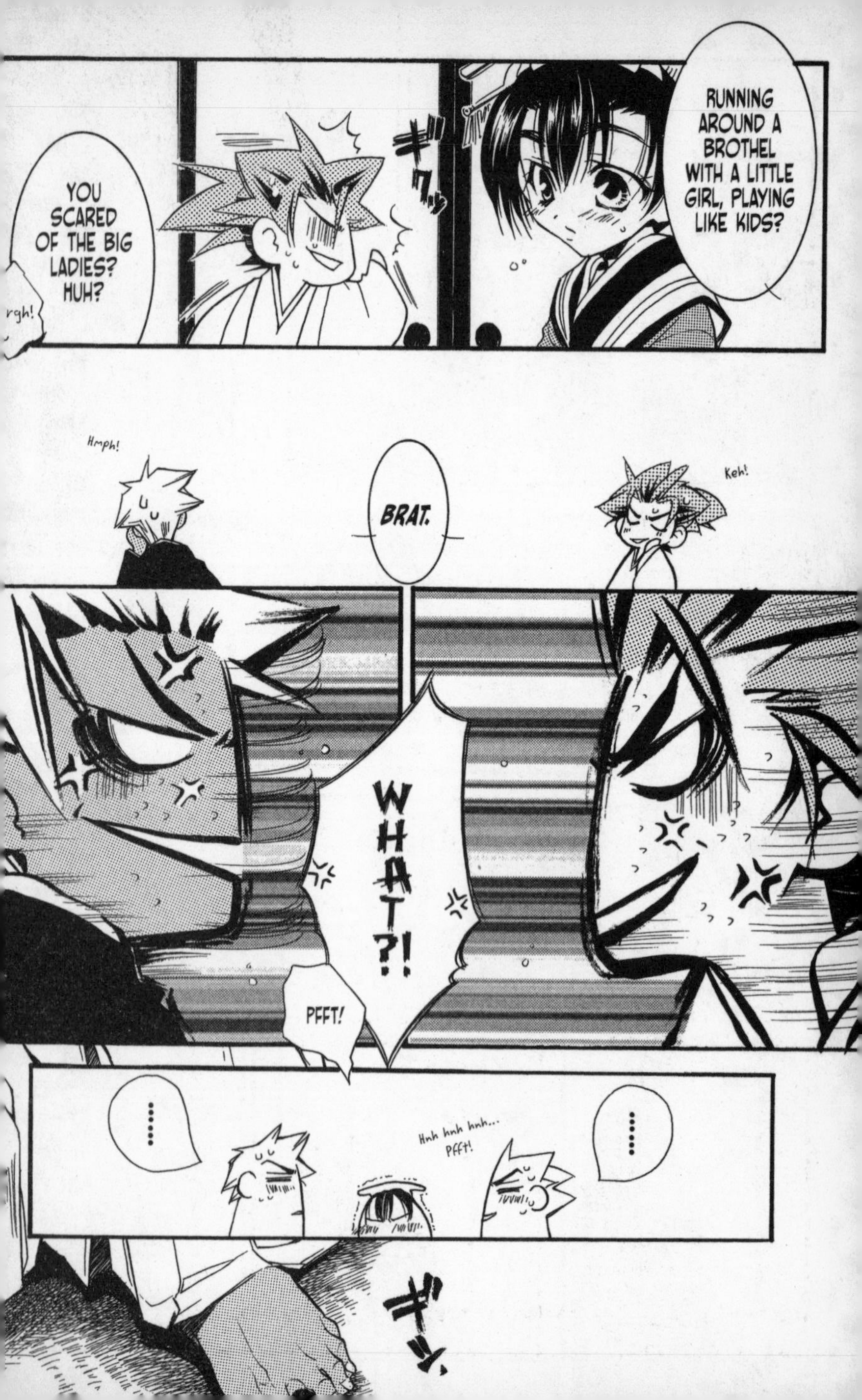
RUNNING AROUND A BROTHEL WITH A LITTLE GIRL, PLAYING LIKE KIDS?
YOU SCARED OF THE BIG LADIES? HUH?
rgh!
Keh!
BRAT.
Hmph!
WHAT?!
PFFT!
......
Hnh hnh hnh... Pfft!
......

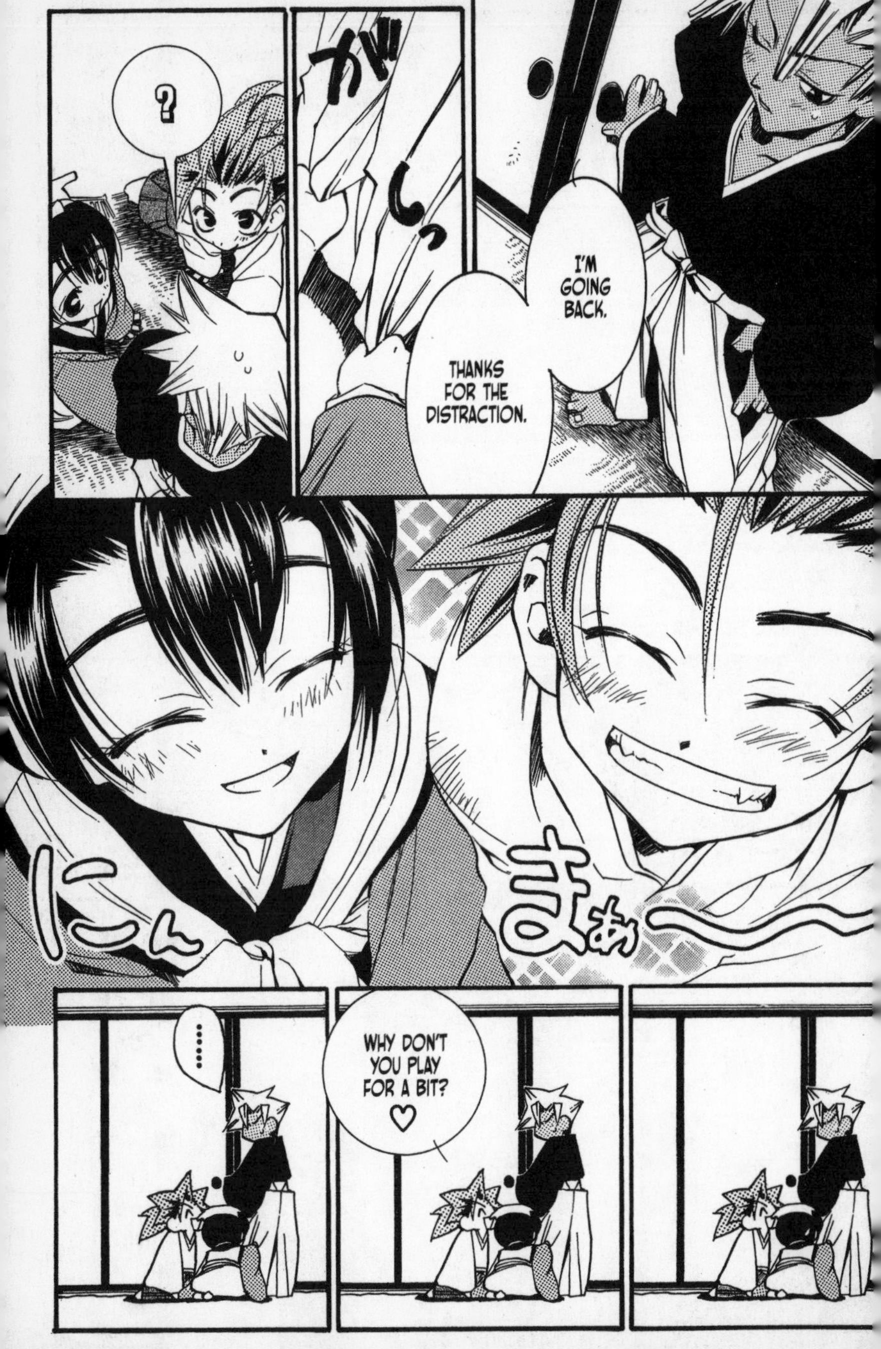

I'M GOING BACK.
THANKS FOR THE DISTRACTION.
しっ
?
まぁ〜〜
に〜ん
WHY DON'T YOU PLAY FOR A BIT? ♡
......

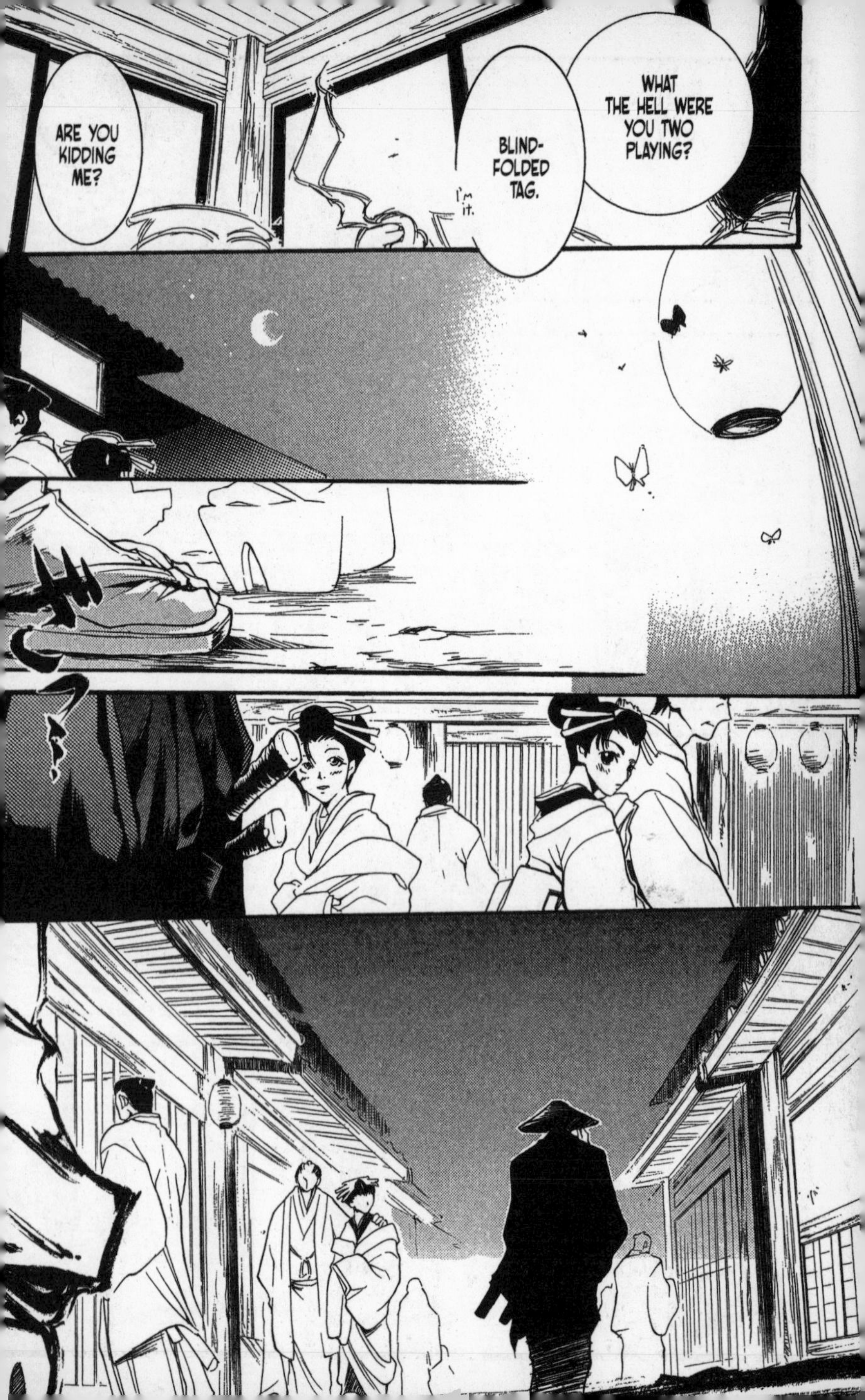
WHAT THE HELL WERE YOU TWO PLAYING?
BLIND-FOLDED TAG.
I'M IT.
ARE YOU KIDDING ME?

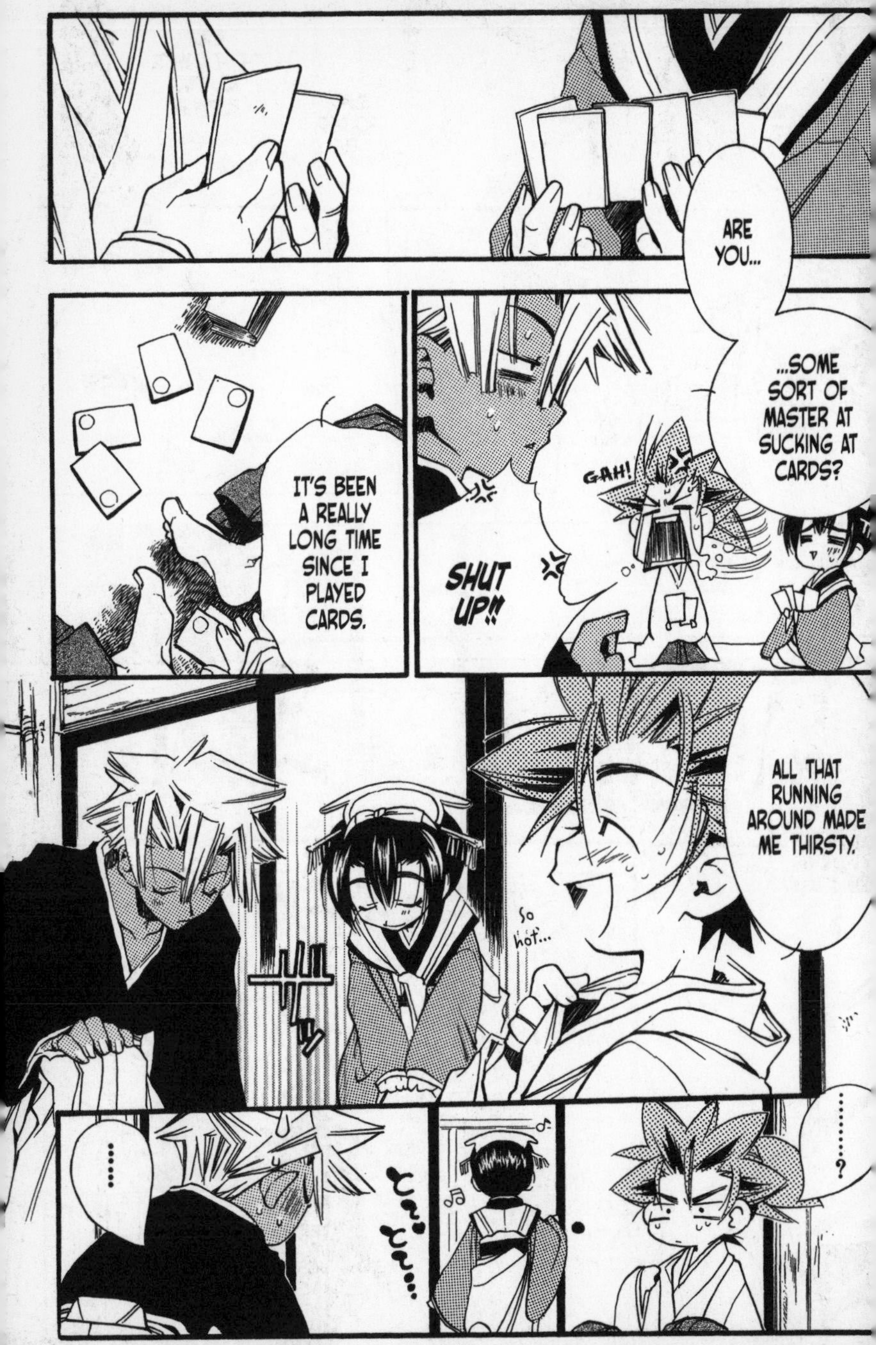
ARE YOU...
...SOME SORT OF MASTER AT SUCKING AT CARDS?
GAH!
SHUT UP!!
IT'S BEEN A REALLY LONG TIME SINCE I PLAYED CARDS.
ALL THAT RUNNING AROUND MADE ME THIRSTY.
So hot...
......?
......

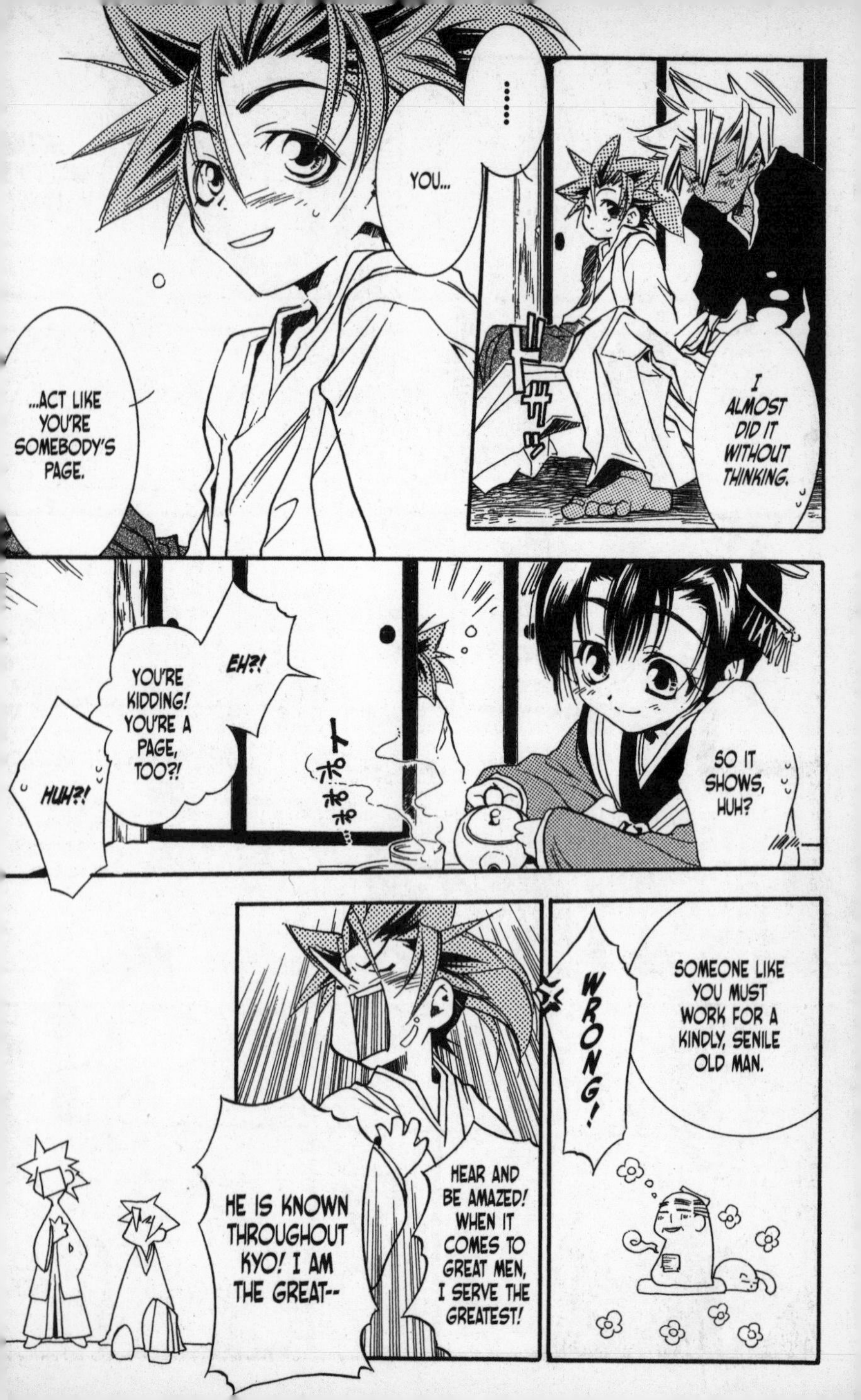
I ALMOST DID IT WITHOUT THINKING.
......
YOU...
...ACT LIKE YOU'RE SOMEBODY'S PAGE.
SO IT SHOWS, HUH?
トポポポ
EH?!
YOU'RE KIDDING! YOU'RE A PAGE, TOO?!
HUH?!
SOMEONE LIKE YOU MUST WORK FOR A KINDLY, SENILE OLD MAN.
WRONG!
HEAR AND BE AMAZED! WHEN IT COMES TO GREAT MEN, I SERVE THE GREATEST!
HE IS KNOWN THROUGHOUT KYO! I AM THE GREAT--

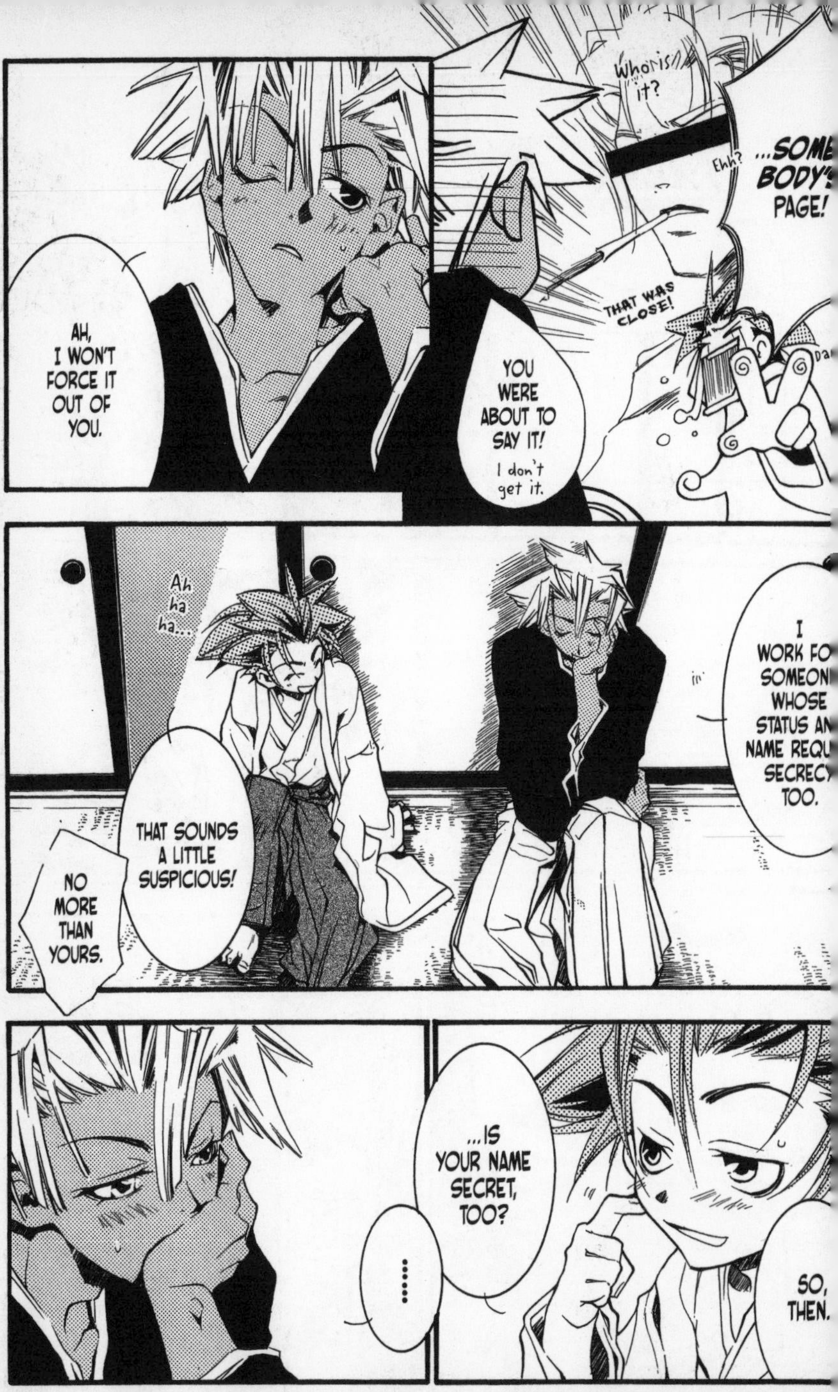
Who is it?
Ehh?
...SOMEBODY'S PAGE!
THAT WAS CLOSE!
YOU WERE ABOUT TO SAY IT!
I don't get it.
AH, I WON'T FORCE IT OUT OF YOU.
I WORK FO SOMEON WHOSE STATUS AN NAME REQU SECRECY TOO.
Ah ha ha...
THAT SOUNDS A LITTLE SUSPICIOUS!
NO MORE THAN YOURS.
SO, THEN.
...IS YOUR NAME SECRET, TOO?
......

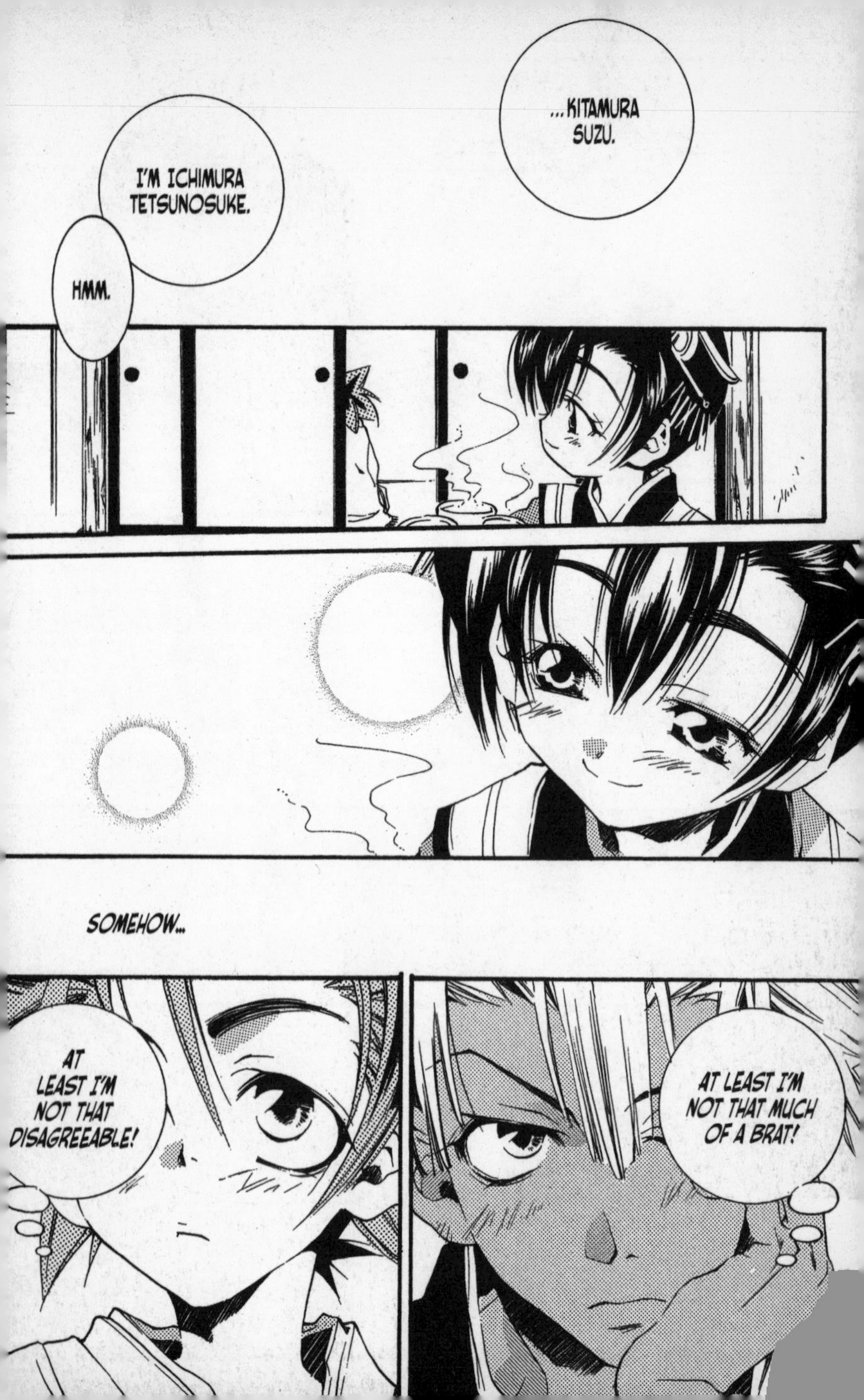
...KITAMURA SUZU.
I'M ICHIMURA TETSUNOSUKE.
HMM.
SOMEHOW...
AT LEAST I'M NOT THAT MUCH OF A BRAT!
AT LEAST I'M NOT THAT DISAGREEABLE!

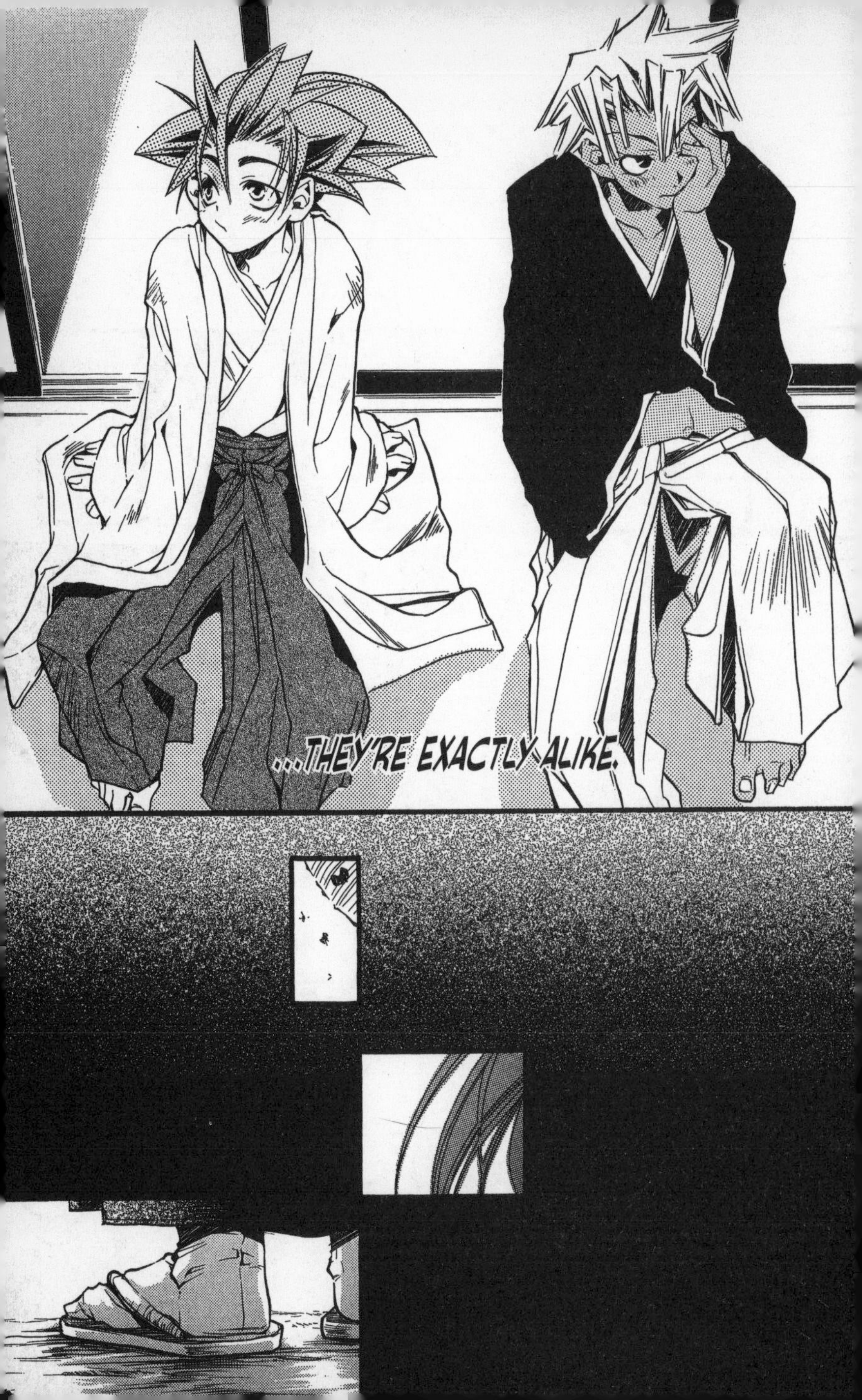
...THEY'RE EXACTLY ALIKE.

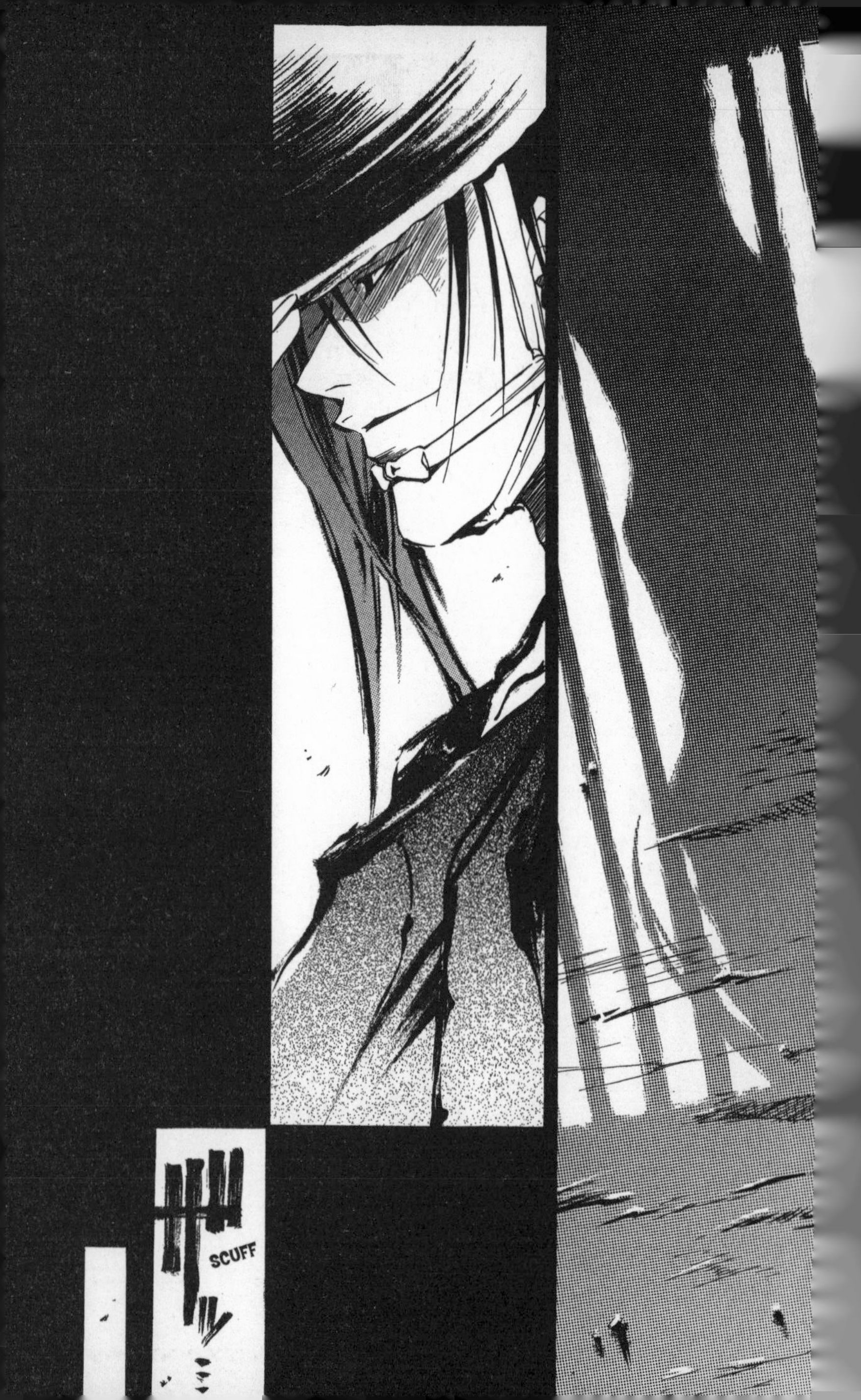
SCUFF

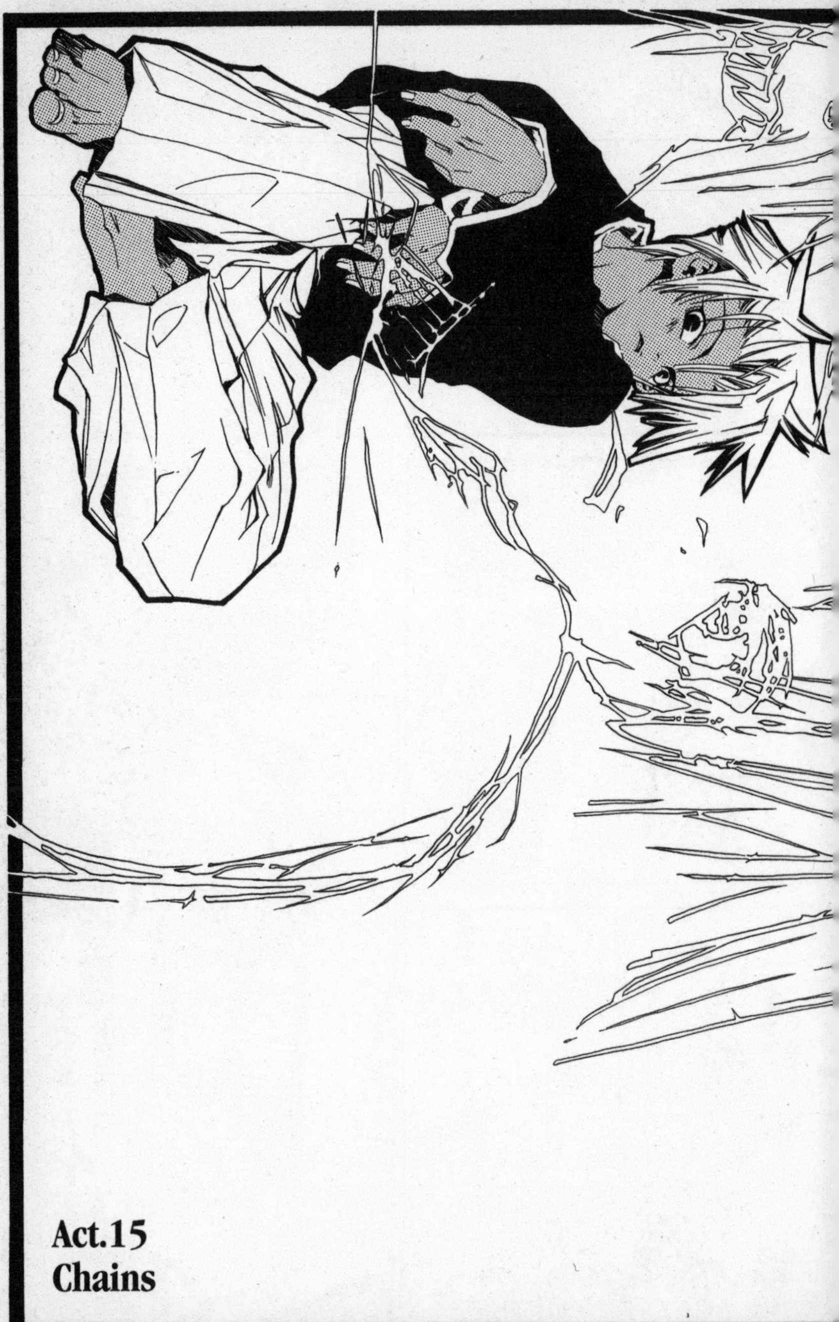

Act.15
Chains

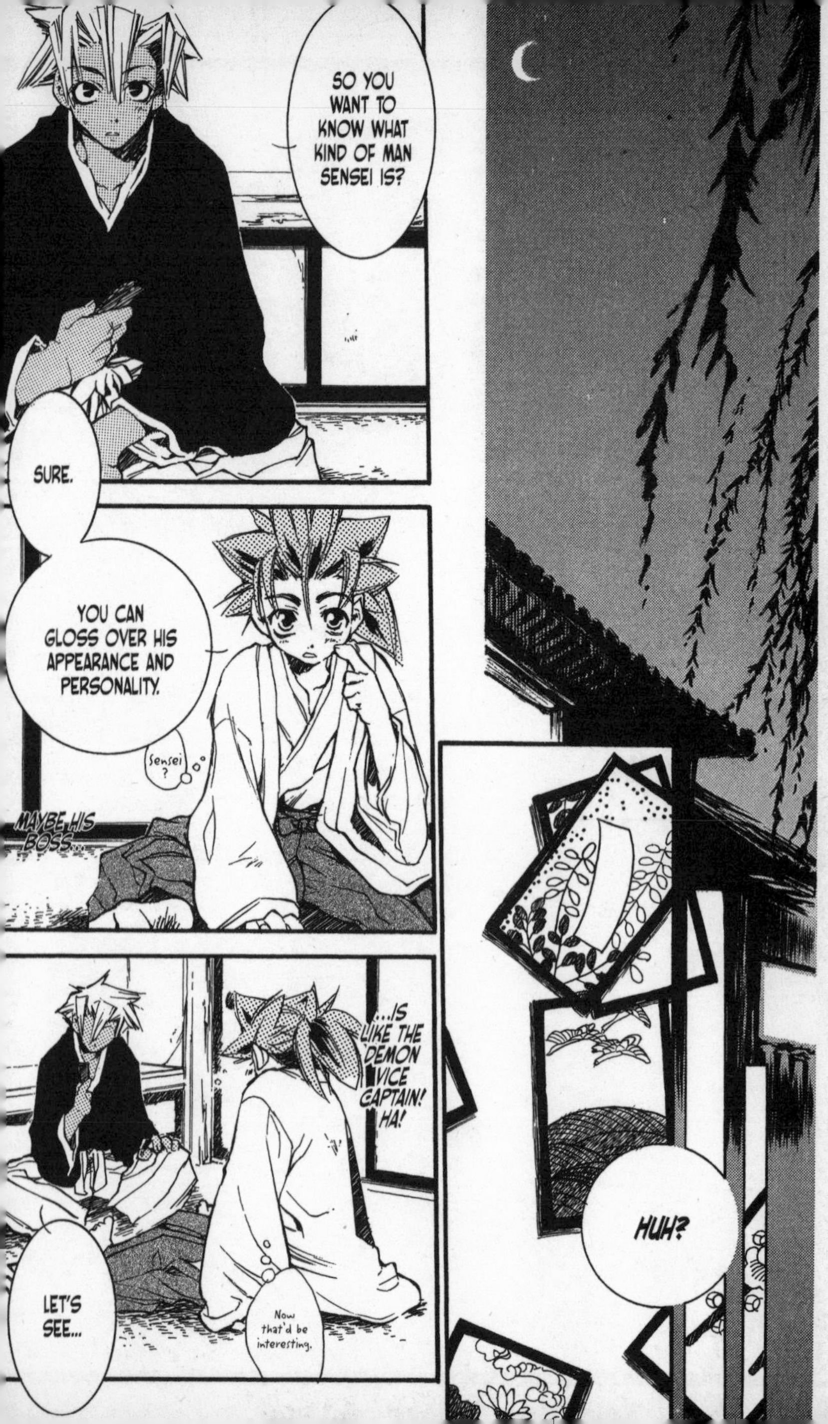
HUH?
SO YOU WANT TO KNOW WHAT KIND OF MAN SENSEI IS?
SURE.
YOU CAN GLOSS OVER HIS APPEARANCE AND PERSONALITY.
Sensei?
MAYBE HIS BOSS...
...IS LIKE THE DEMON VICE CAPTAIN! HA!
Now that'd be interesting.
LET'S SEE...

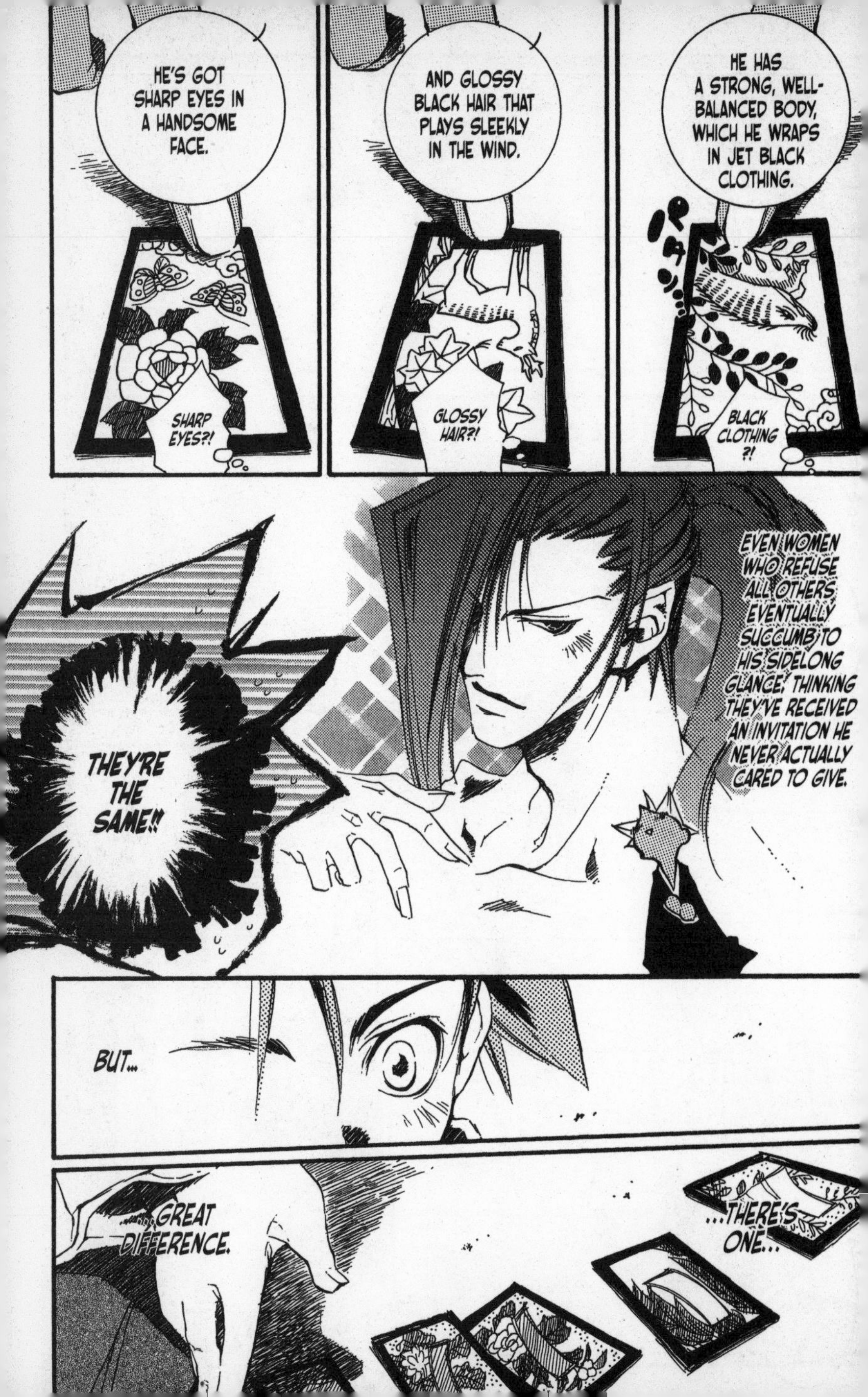
HE HAS A STRONG, WELL-BALANCED BODY, WHICH HE WRAPS IN JET BLACK CLOTHING.
BLACK CLOTHING ?!
AND GLOSSY BLACK HAIR THAT PLAYS SLEEKLY IN THE WIND.
GLOSSY HAIR?!
HE'S GOT SHARP EYES IN A HANDSOME FACE.
SHARP EYES?!
EVEN WOMEN WHO REFUSE ALL OTHERS EVENTUALLY SUCCUMB TO HIS SIDELONG GLANCE, THINKING THEY'VE RECEIVED AN INVITATION HE NEVER ACTUALLY CARED TO GIVE.
THEY'RE THE SAME!!
BUT...
...THERE'S ONE...
...GREAT DIFFERENCE.

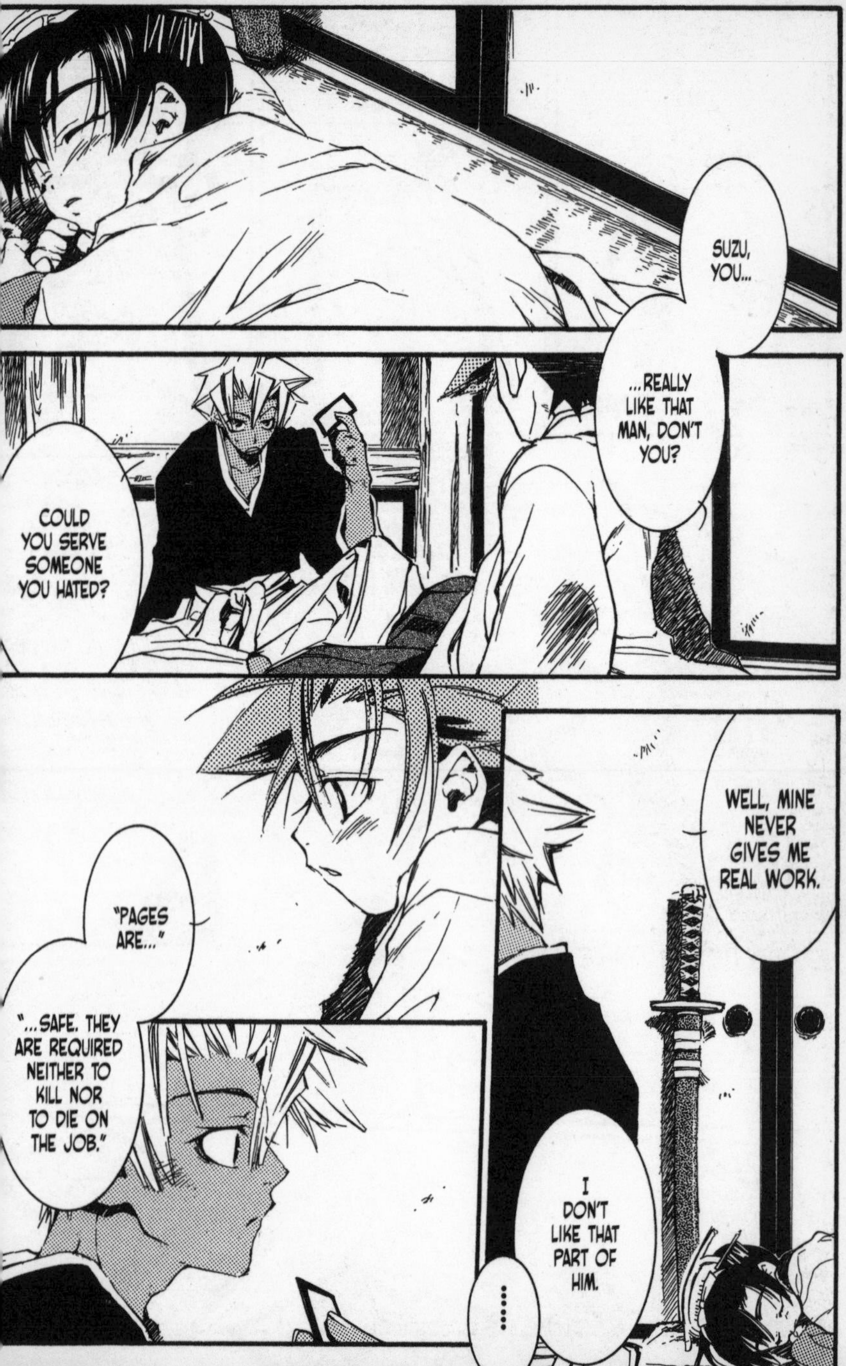
SUZU, YOU...
...REALLY LIKE THAT MAN, DON'T YOU?
COULD YOU SERVE SOMEONE YOU HATED?
WELL, MINE NEVER GIVES ME REAL WORK.
"PAGES ARE..."
"...SAFE. THEY ARE REQUIRED NEITHER TO KILL NOR TO DIE ON THE JOB."
I DON'T LIKE THAT PART OF HIM.
......

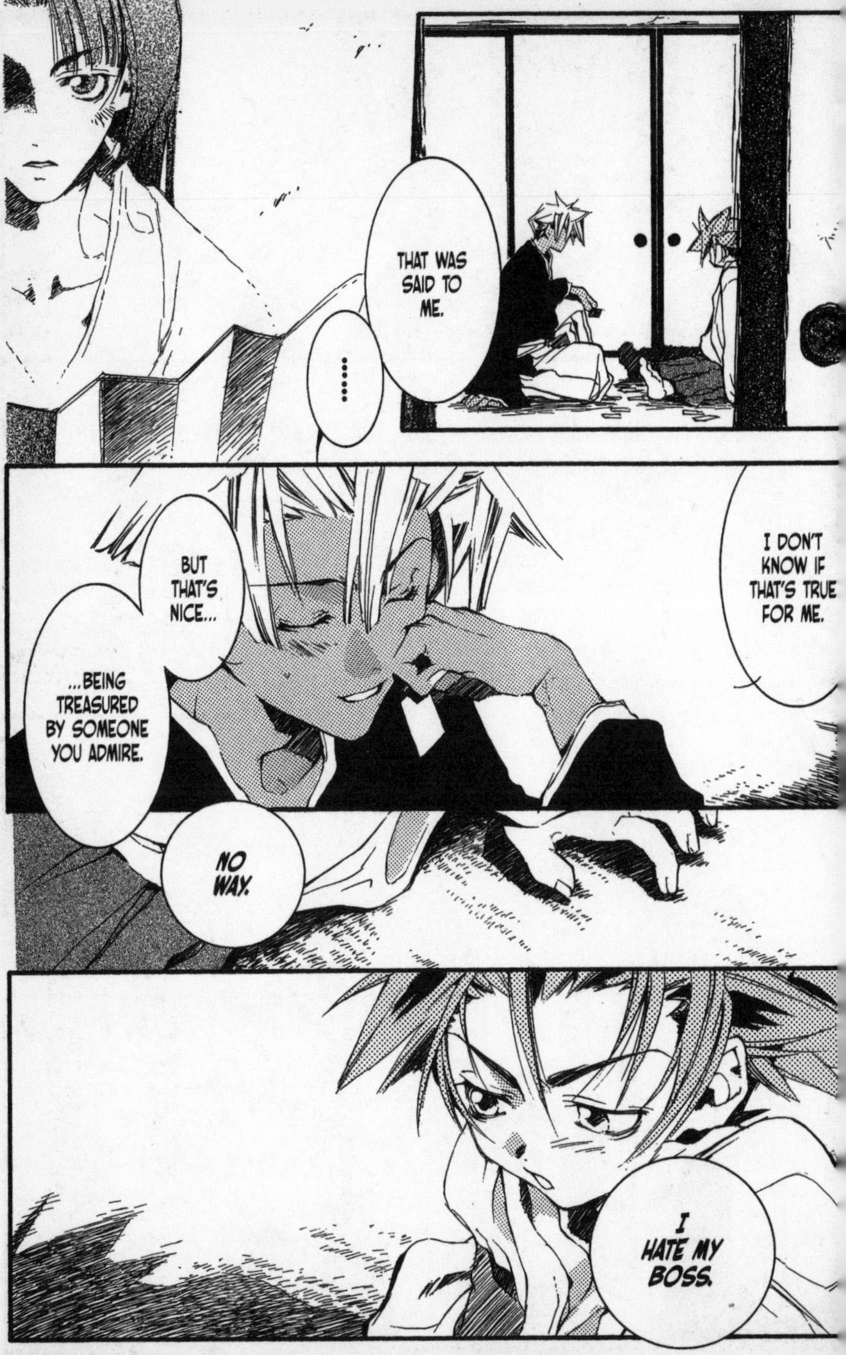
THAT WAS SAID TO ME.
......
I DON'T KNOW IF THAT'S TRUE FOR ME.
BUT THAT'S NICE...
...BEING TREASURED BY SOMEONE YOU ADMIRE.
NO WAY.
I HATE MY BOSS.

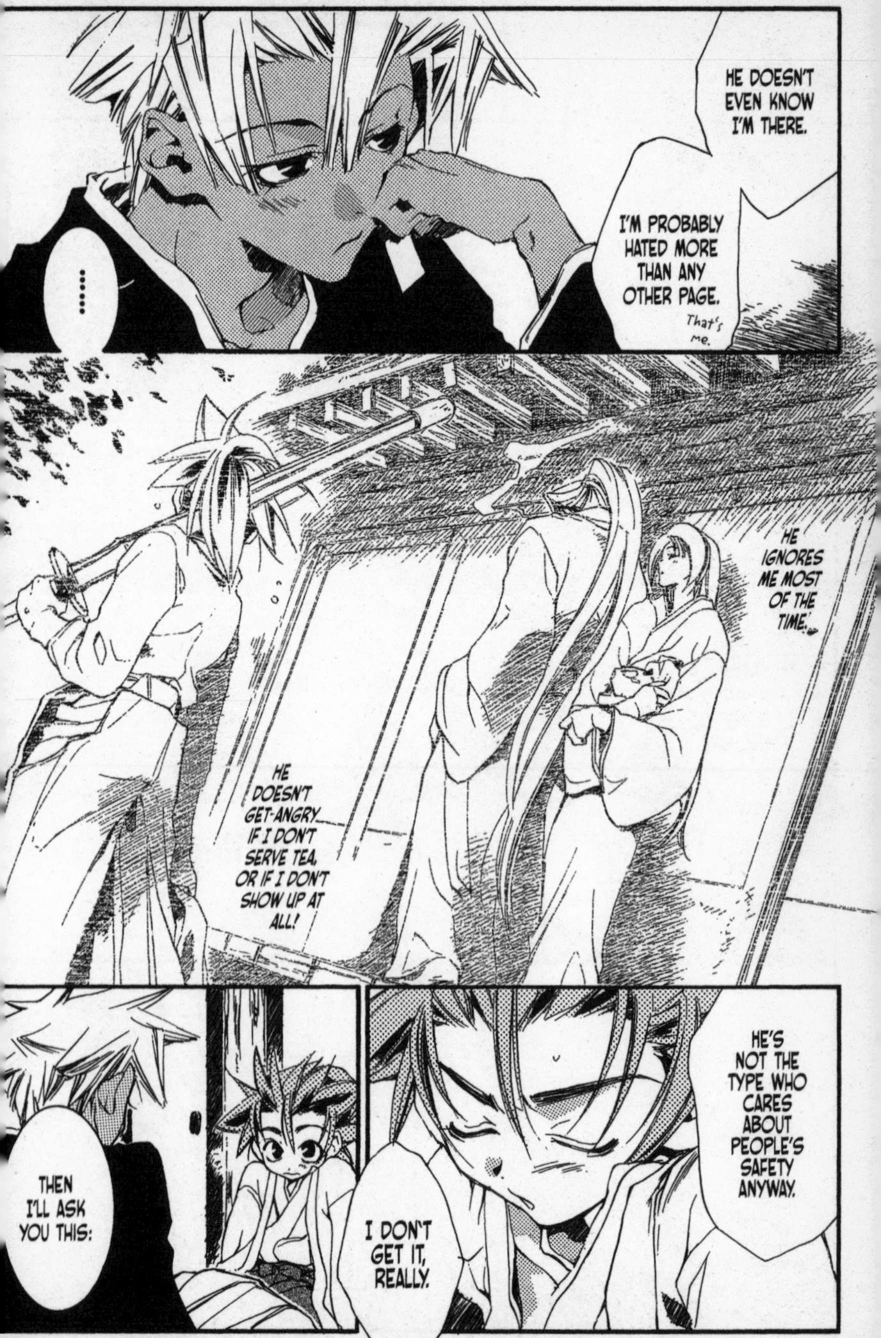
HE DOESN'T EVEN KNOW I'M THERE.
I'M PROBABLY HATED MORE THAN ANY OTHER PAGE.
That's me.
......
HE IGNORES ME MOST OF THE TIME...
HE DOESN'T GET ANGRY IF I DON'T SERVE TEA, OR IF I DON'T SHOW UP AT ALL!
HE'S NOT THE TYPE WHO CARES ABOUT PEOPLE'S SAFETY ANYWAY.
I DON'T GET IT, REALLY.
THEN I'LL ASK YOU THIS:

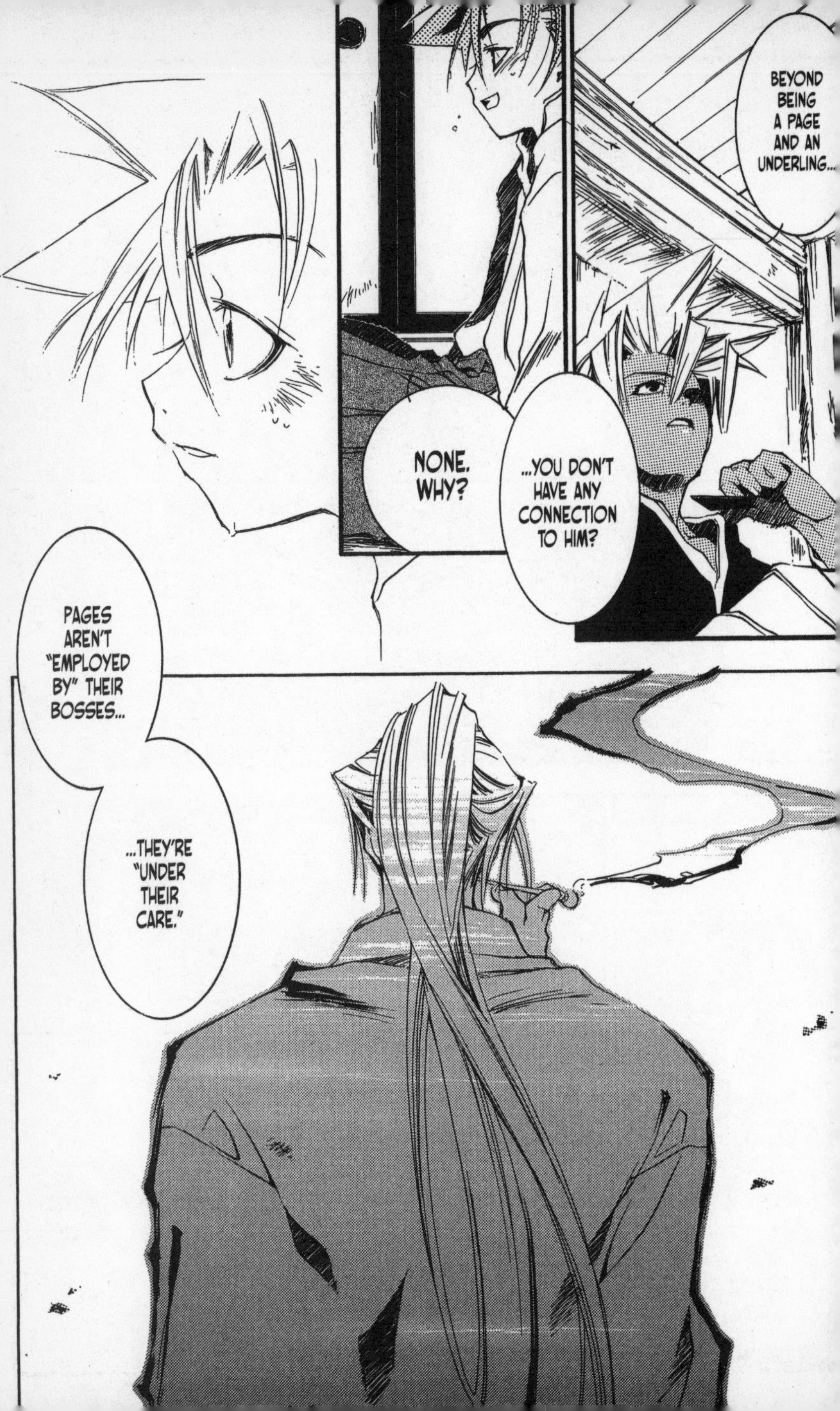
BEYOND BEING A PAGE AND AN UNDERLING...
...YOU DON'T HAVE ANY CONNECTION TO HIM?
NONE. WHY?
PAGES AREN'T "EMPLOYED BY" THEIR BOSSES...
...THEY'RE "UNDER THEIR CARE."

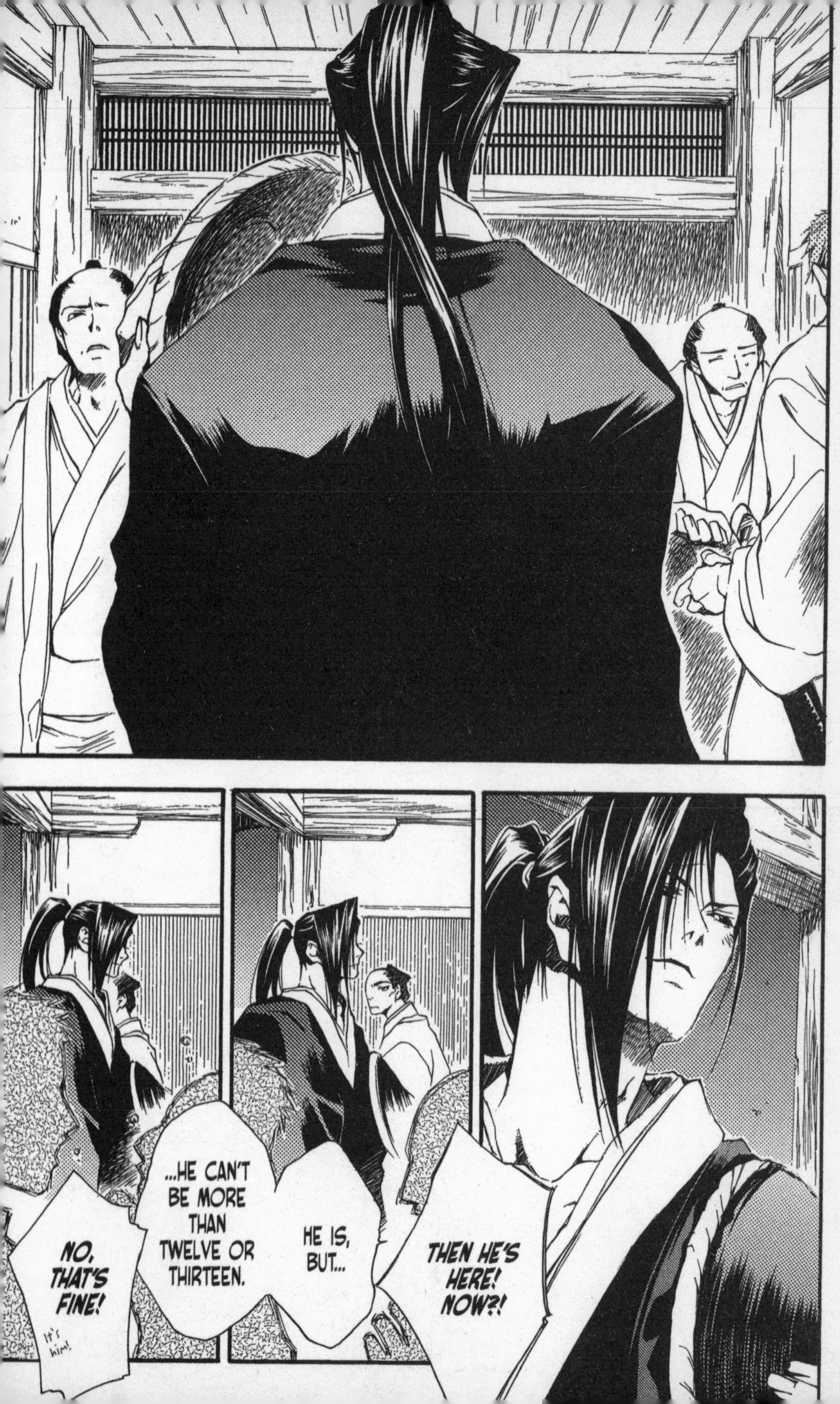
THEN HE'S HERE! NOW?!
HE IS, BUT...
...HE CAN'T BE MORE THAN TWELVE OR THIRTEEN.
NO, THAT'S FINE!
It's him!

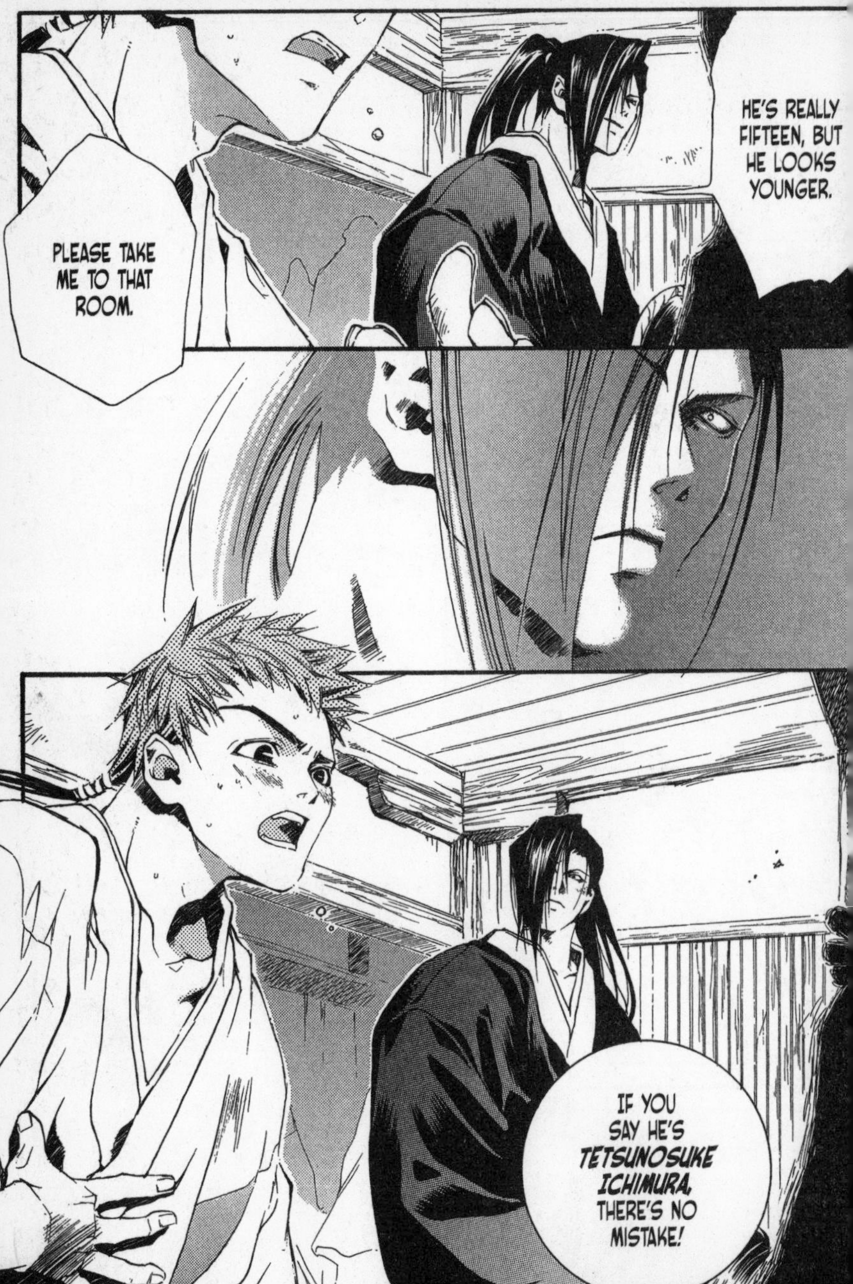
HE'S REALLY FIFTEEN, BUT HE LOOKS YOUNGER.
PLEASE TAKE ME TO THAT ROOM.
IF YOU SAY HE'S *TETSUNOSUKE ICHIMURA,* THERE'S NO MISTAKE!

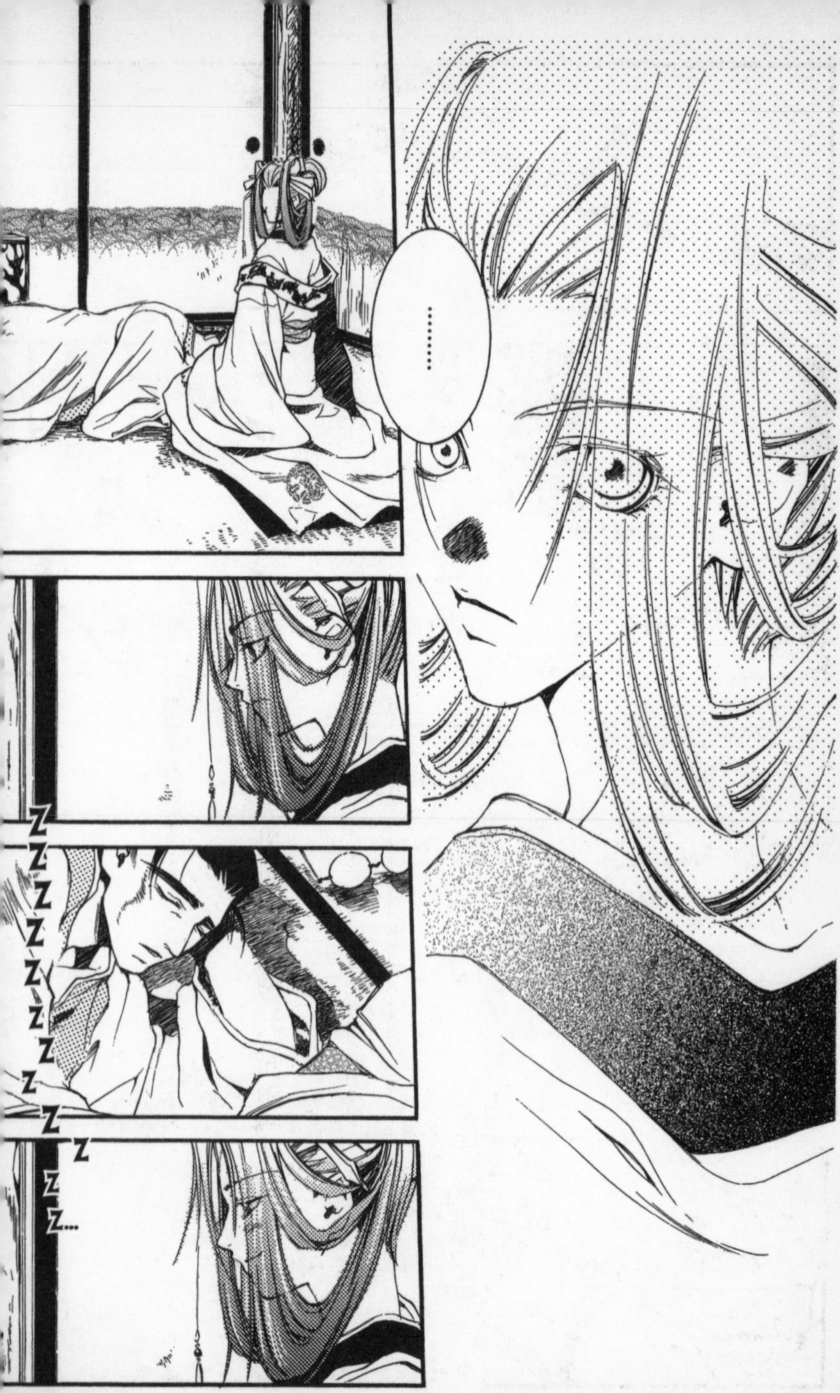
......
ZZZZZZZZZZZZ...

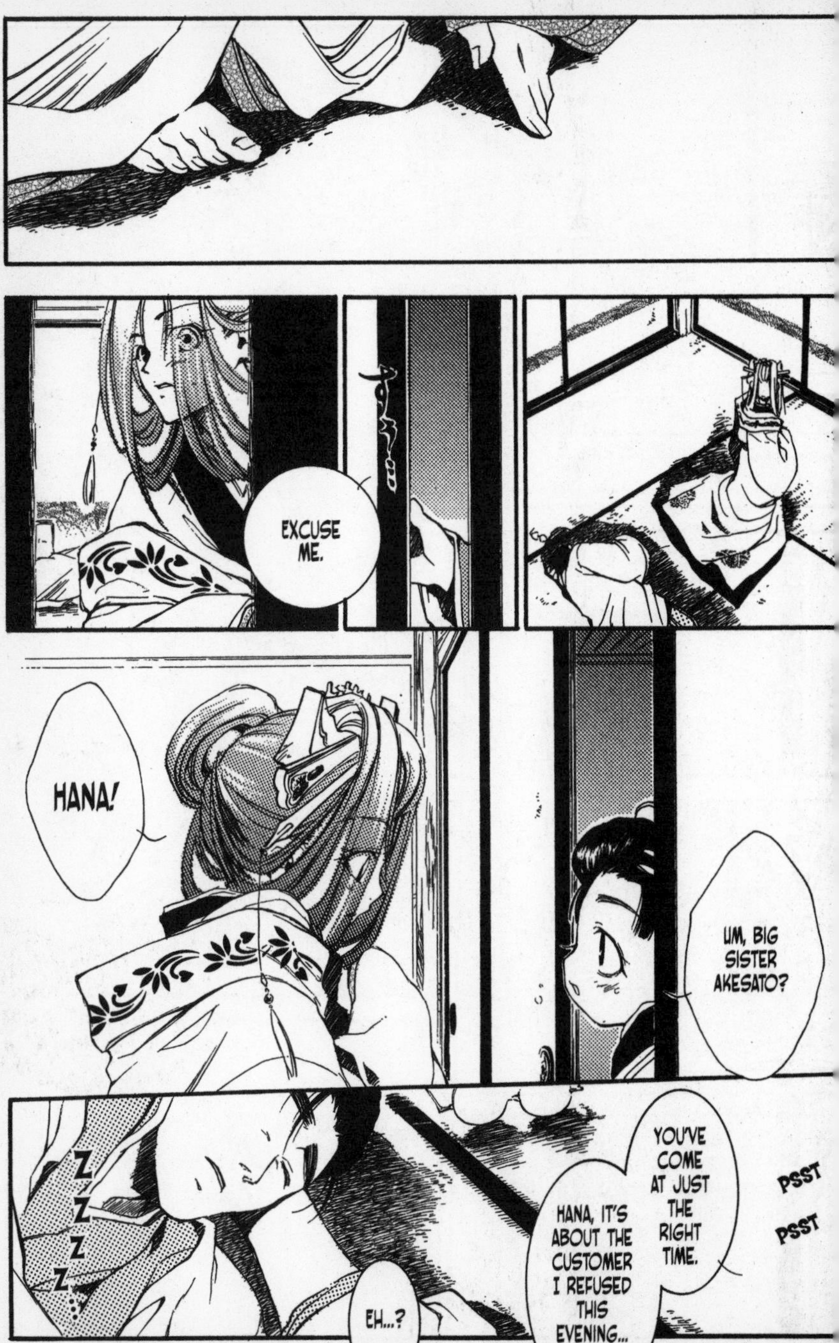
EXCUSE ME.
UM, BIG SISTER AKESATO?
HANA!
PSST
PSST
YOU'VE COME AT JUST THE RIGHT TIME.
HANA, IT'S ABOUT THE CUSTOMER I REFUSED THIS EVENING...
EH...?
ZZZZ...

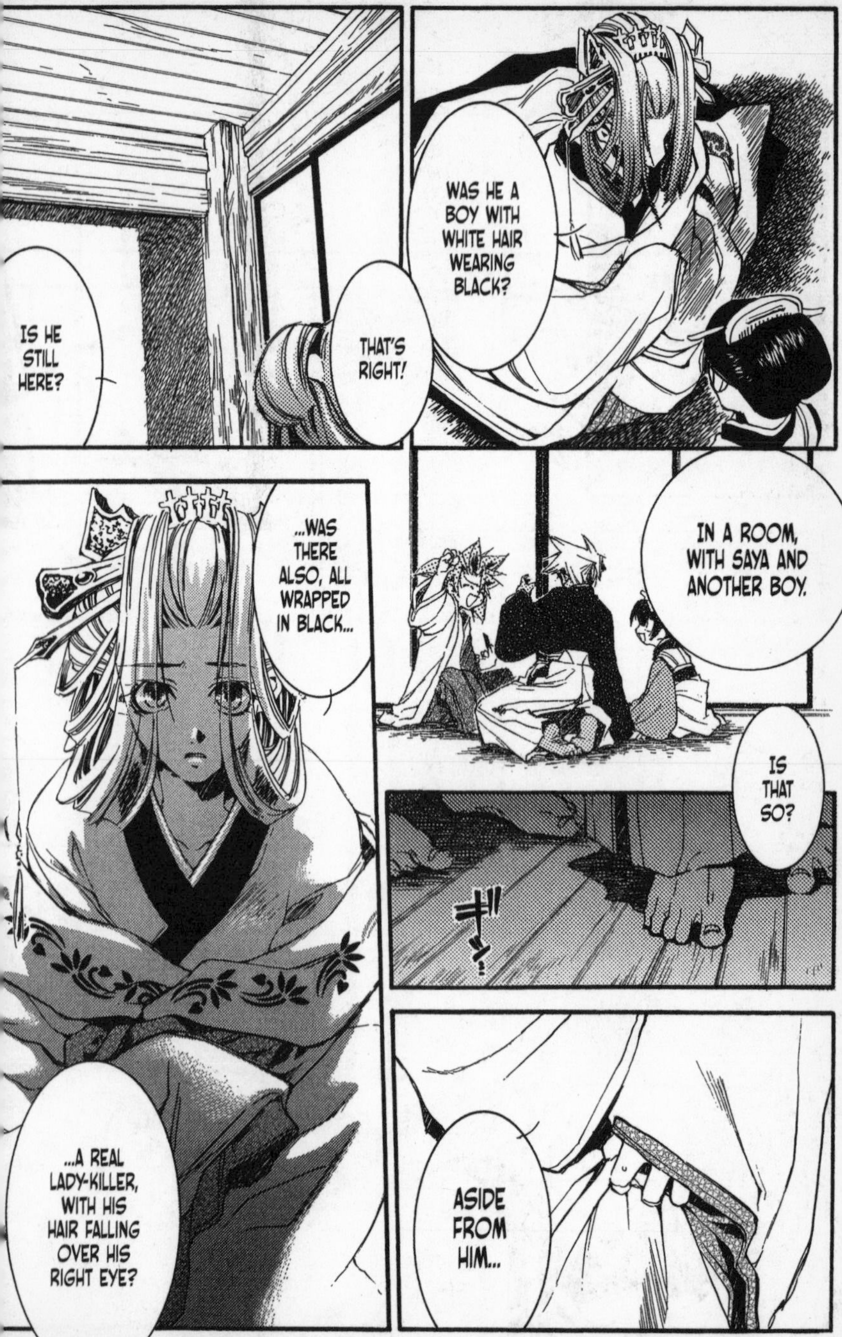
WAS HE A BOY WITH WHITE HAIR WEARING BLACK?
THAT'S RIGHT!
IS HE STILL HERE?
IN A ROOM, WITH SAYA AND ANOTHER BOY.
IS THAT SO?
ASIDE FROM HIM...
...WAS THERE ALSO, ALL WRAPPED IN BLACK...
...A REAL LADY-KILLER, WITH HIS HAIR FALLING OVER HIS RIGHT EYE?

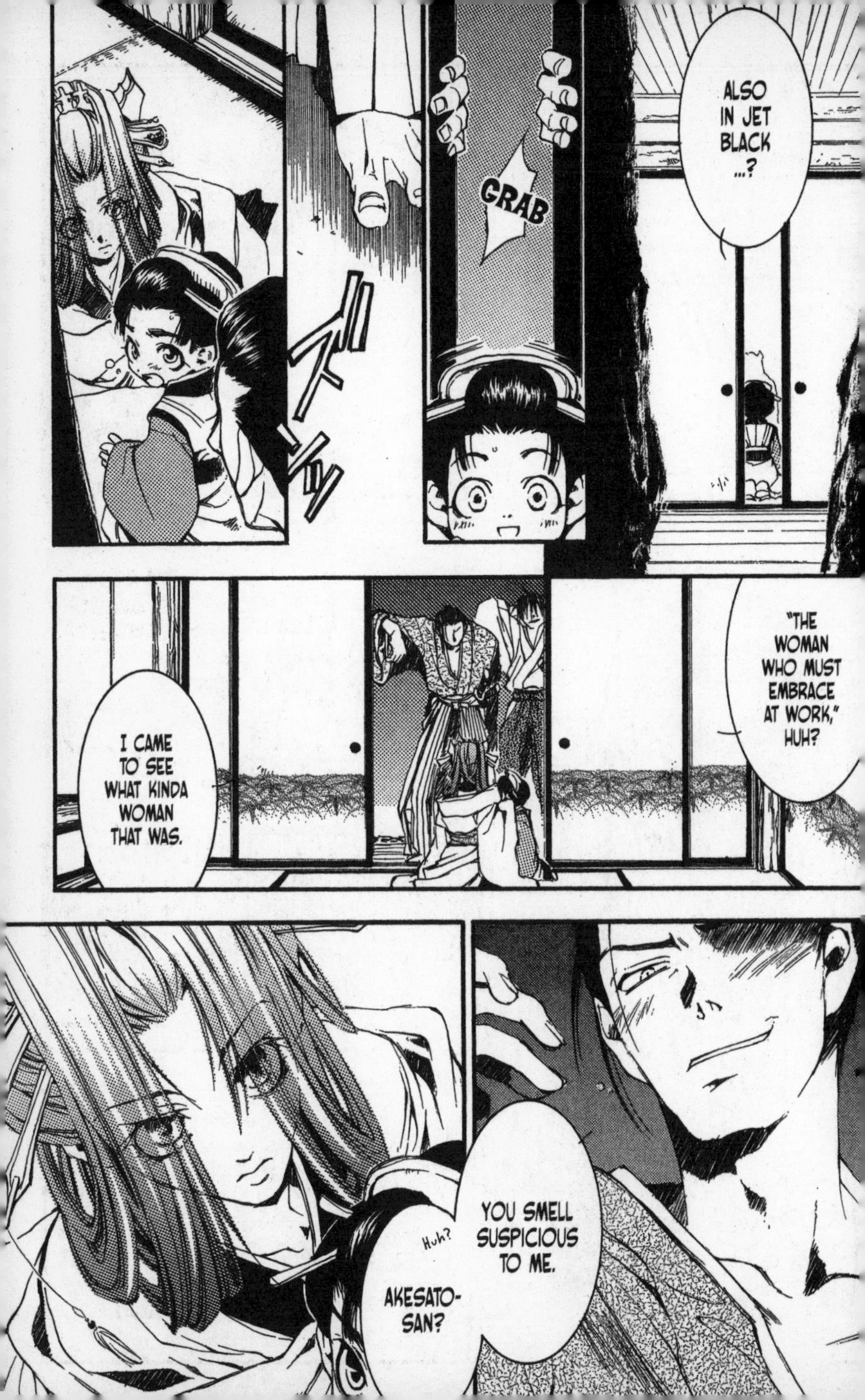
ALSO IN JET BLACK ...?
GRAB
"THE WOMAN WHO MUST EMBRACE AT WORK," HUH?
I CAME TO SEE WHAT KINDA WOMAN THAT WAS.
YOU SMELL SUSPICIOUS TO ME.
Huh?
AKESATO-SAN?

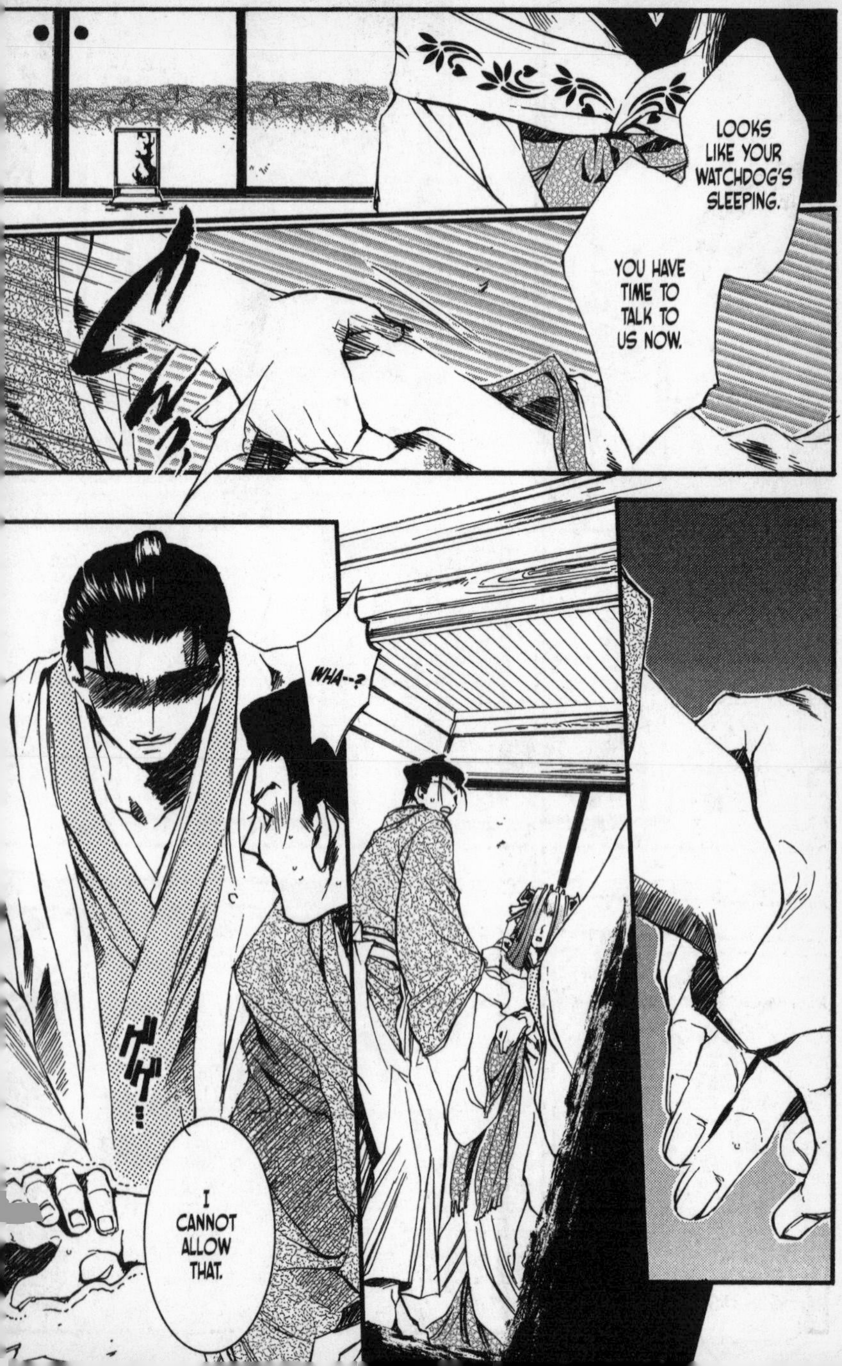
LOOKS LIKE YOUR WATCHDOG'S SLEEPING.
YOU HAVE TIME TO TALK TO US NOW.
WHA--?
I CANNOT ALLOW THAT.

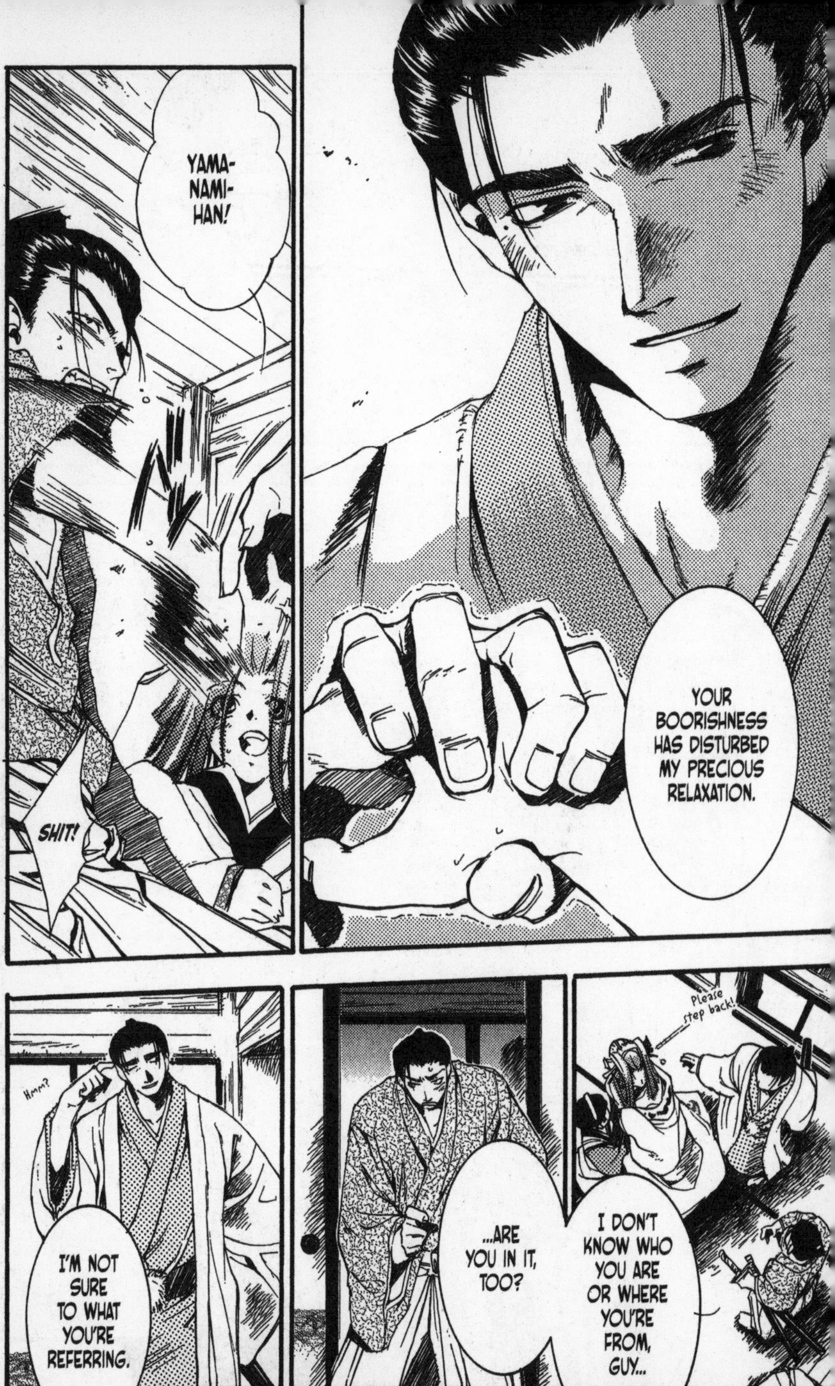
YOUR BOORISHNESS HAS DISTURBED MY PRECIOUS RELAXATION.
YAMA-NAMI-HAN!
SHIT!
Please step back!
I DON'T KNOW WHO YOU ARE OR WHERE YOU'RE FROM, GUY...
...ARE YOU IN IT, TOO?
Hmm?
I'M NOT SURE TO WHAT YOU'RE REFERRING.

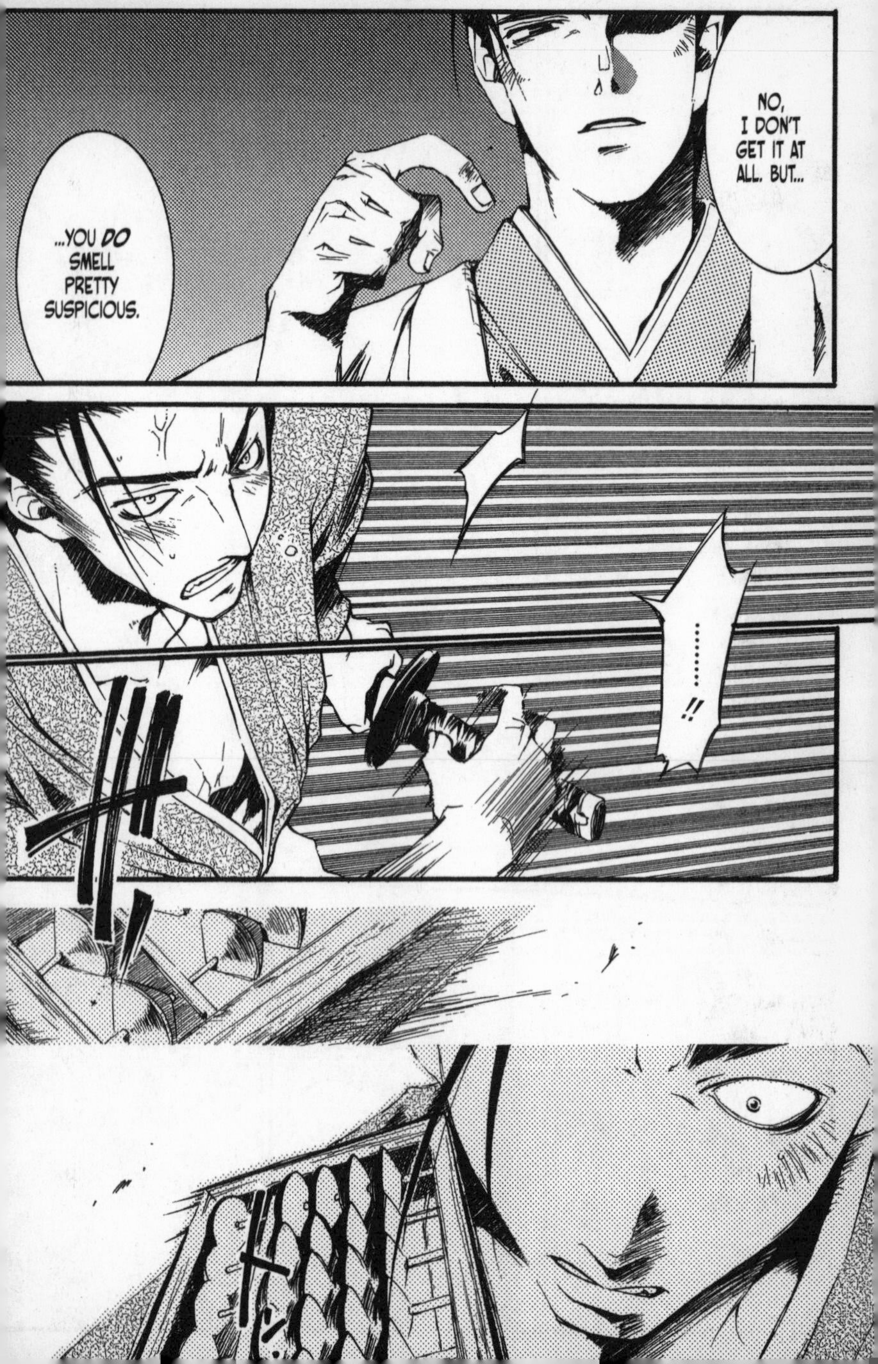
NO, I DON'T GET IT AT ALL. BUT...
...YOU DO SMELL PRETTY SUSPICIOUS.
......!!

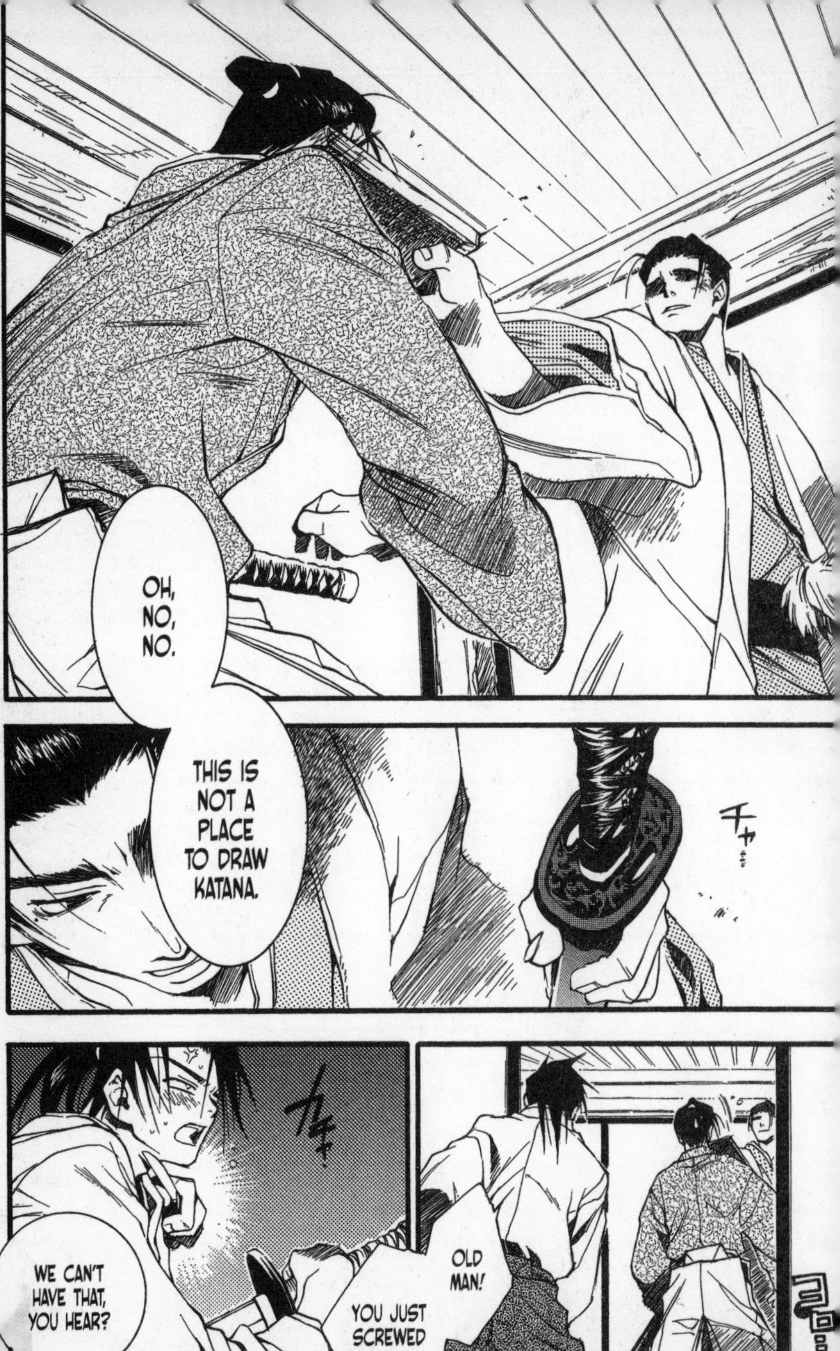
OH, NO, NO.
THIS IS NOT A PLACE TO DRAW KATANA.
チャ
OLD MAN!
YOU JUST SCREWED UP BIG!
WE CAN'T HAVE THAT, YOU HEAR?

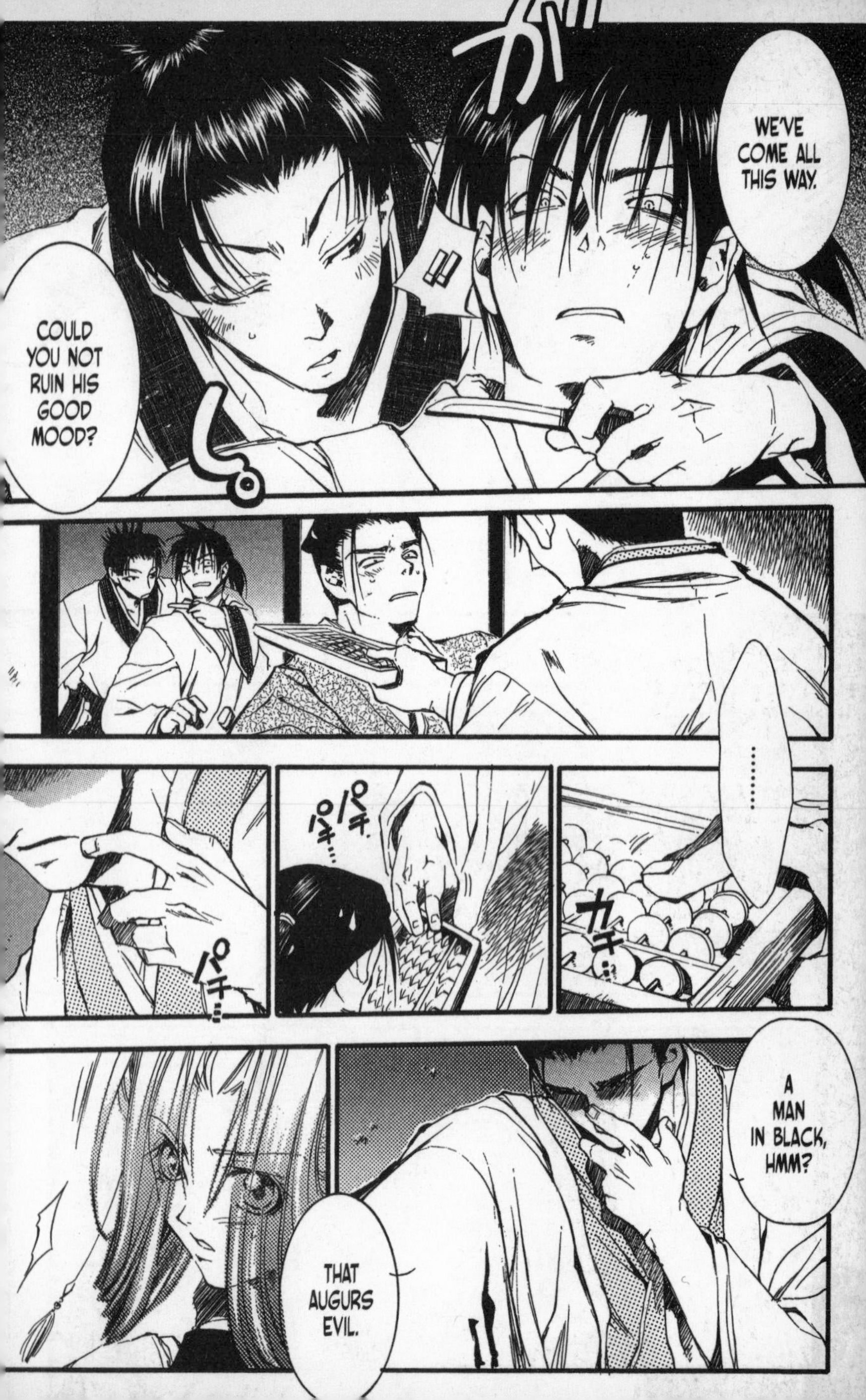

WE'VE COME ALL THIS WAY.
が
!!
COULD YOU NOT RUIN HIS GOOD MOOD?
......
カチ…
パチ、
パチ…
パチ…
A MAN IN BLACK, HMM?
THAT AUGURS EVIL.

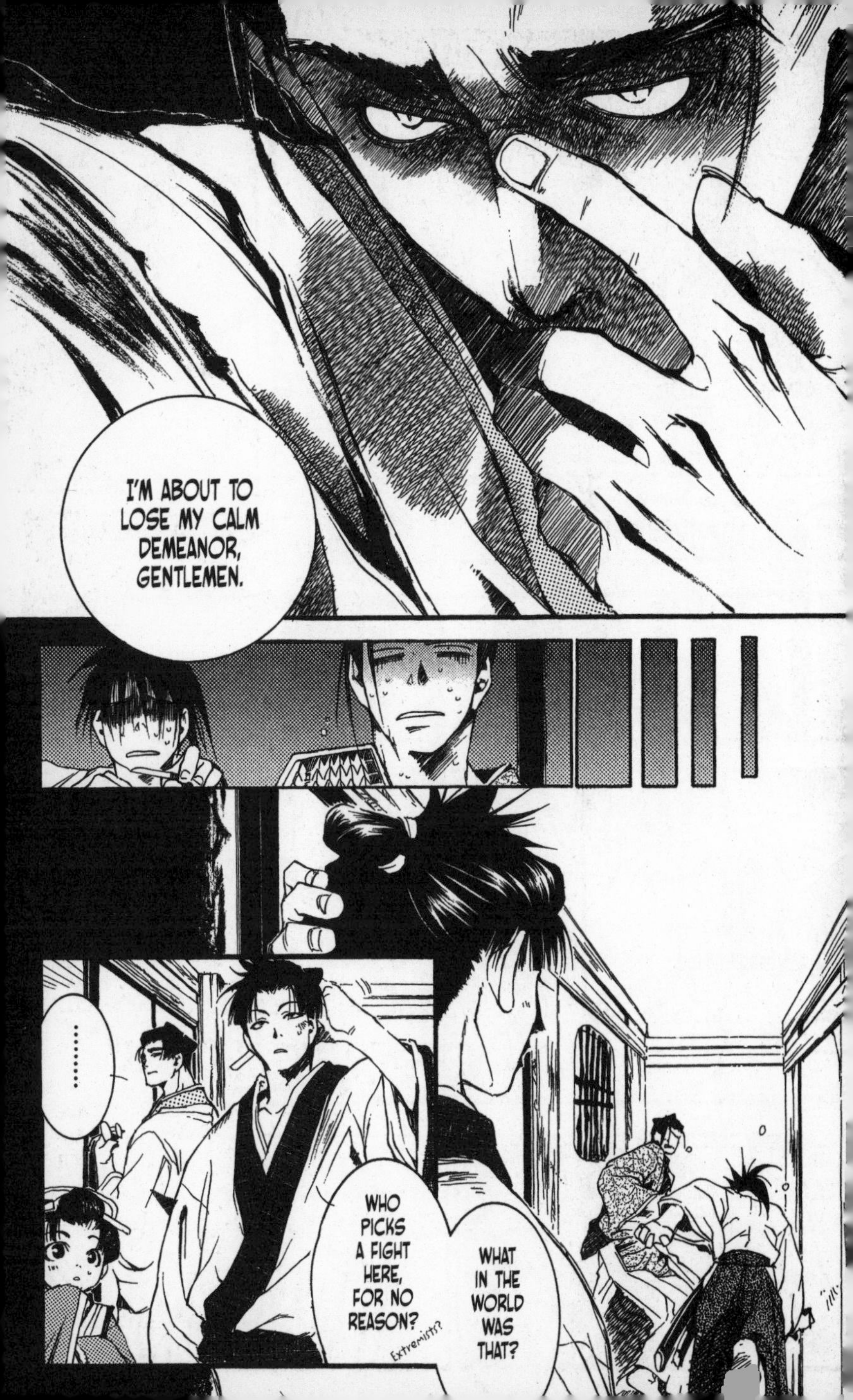
I'M ABOUT TO LOSE MY CALM DEMEANOR, GENTLEMEN.
WHAT IN THE WORLD WAS THAT?
WHO PICKS A FIGHT HERE, FOR NO REASON?
Extremists?
....

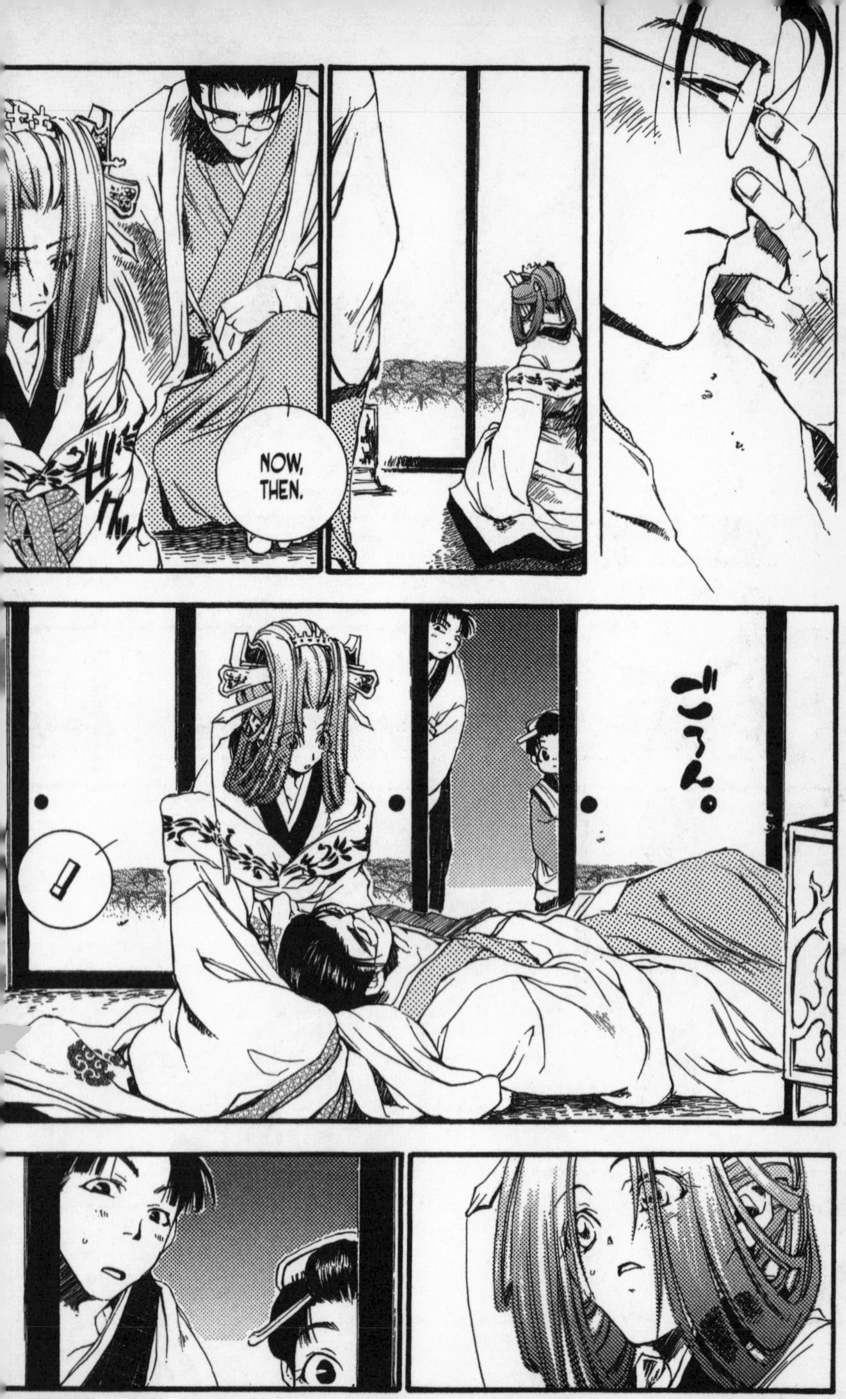
NOW, THEN.
!
ごろん。

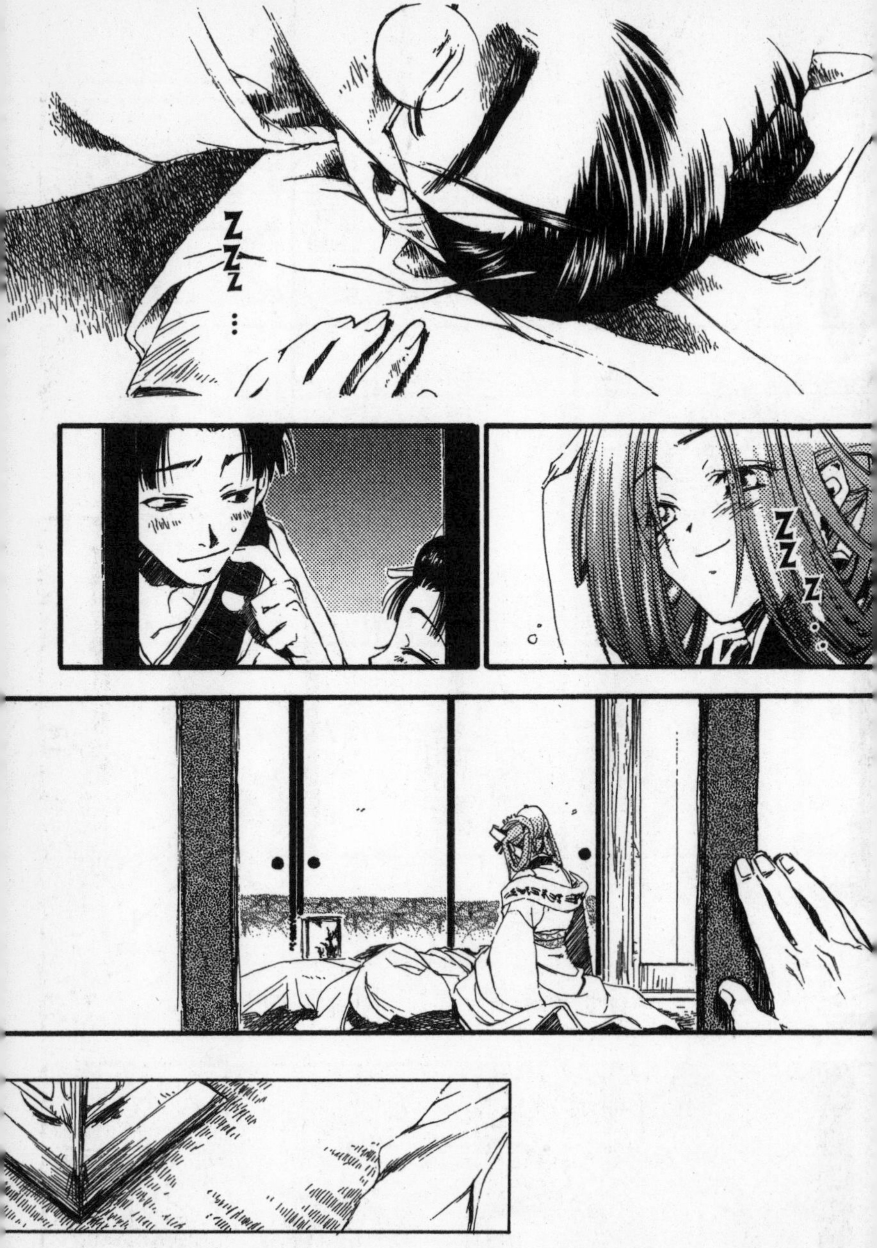
ZZZ...
ZZZ

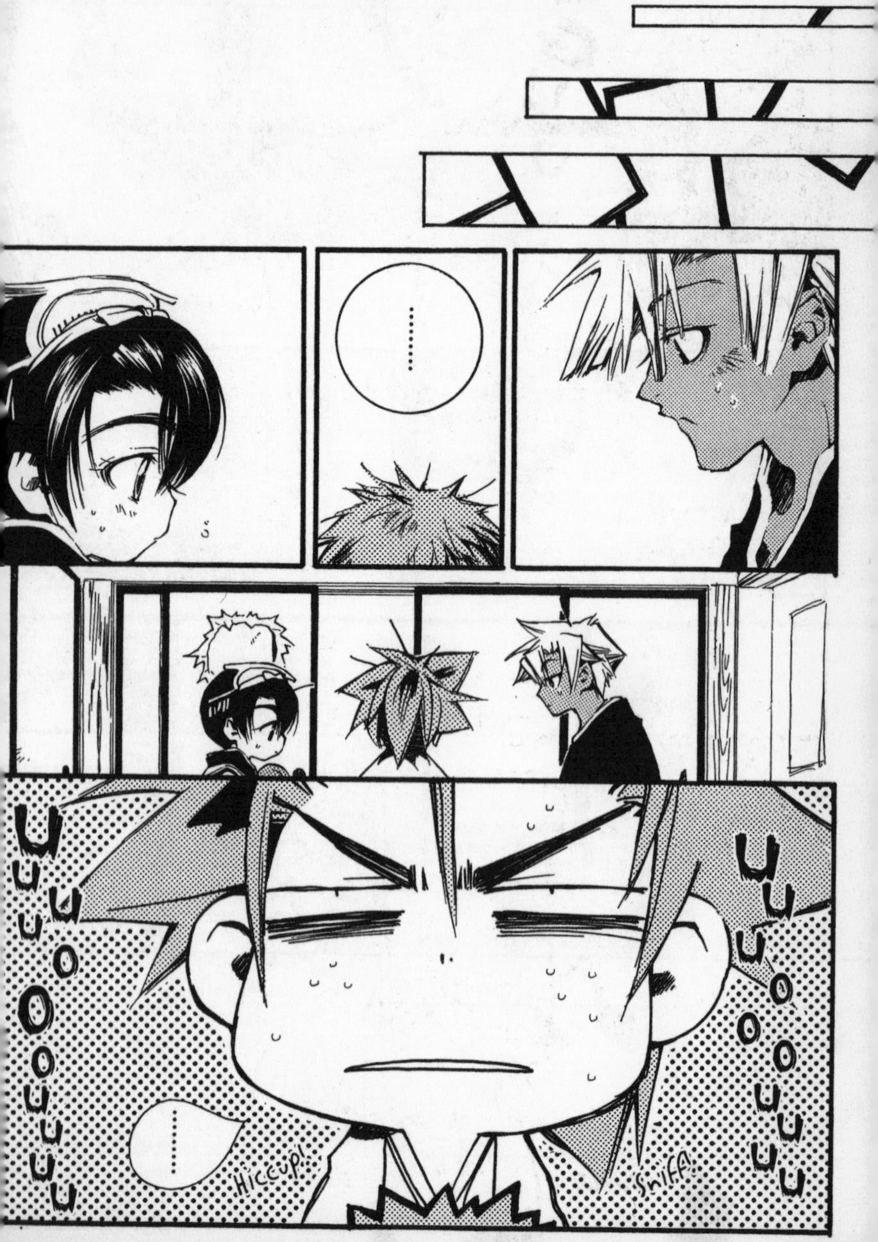
......
UUUUOOOUUUU
Sniff!
UUUUOOOUUUUU
......
Hiccup!

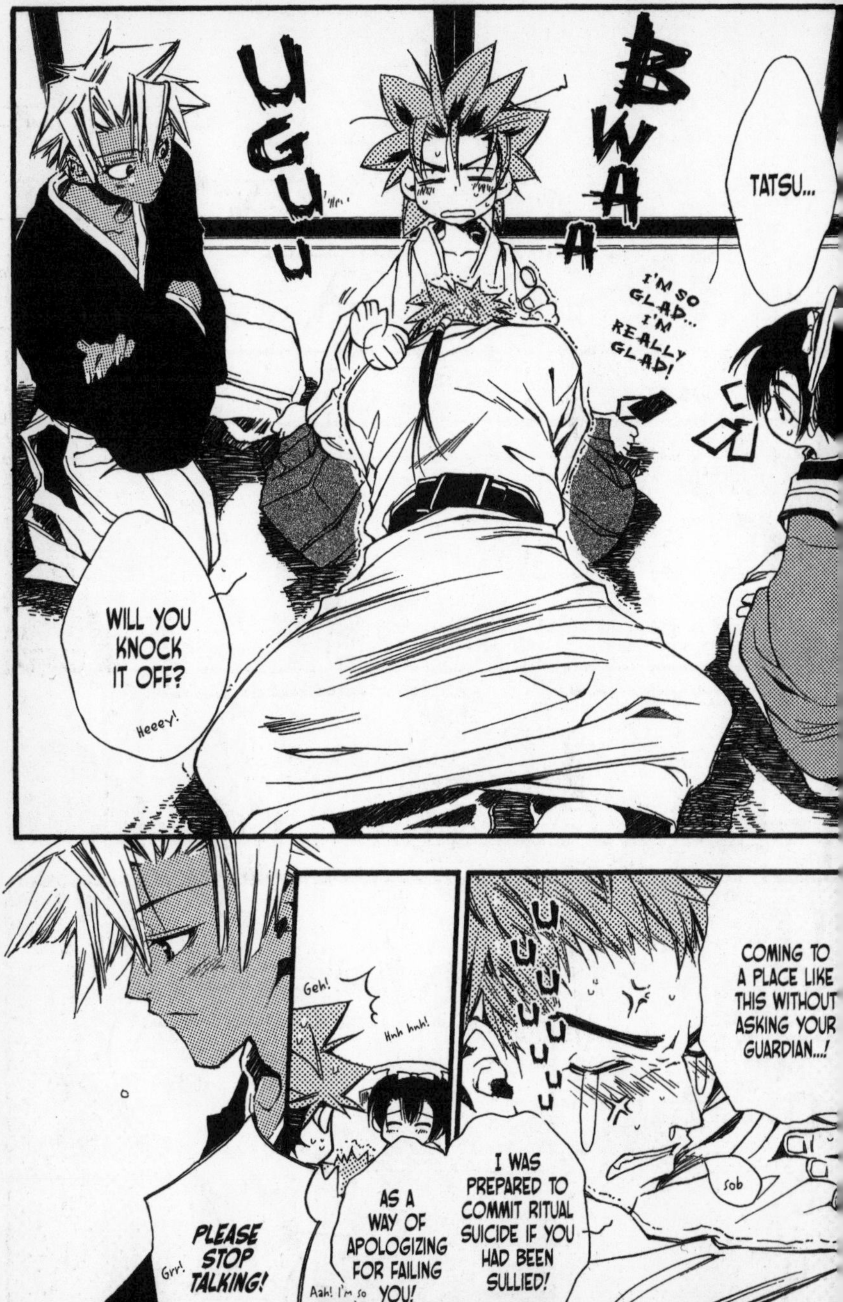
TATSU...
BWA A
I'M SO GLAD... I'M REALLY GLAD!
UGUU
WILL YOU KNOCK IT OFF?
Heeey!
COMING TO A PLACE LIKE THIS WITHOUT ASKING YOUR GUARDIAN...!
UUUUUUUUU
sob
I WAS PREPARED TO COMMIT RITUAL SUICIDE IF YOU HAD BEEN SULLIED!
AS A WAY OF APOLOGIZING FOR FAILING YOU!
Hnh hnh!
Geh!
Aah! I'm so glad you're still a child!
PLEASE STOP TALKING!
Grr!

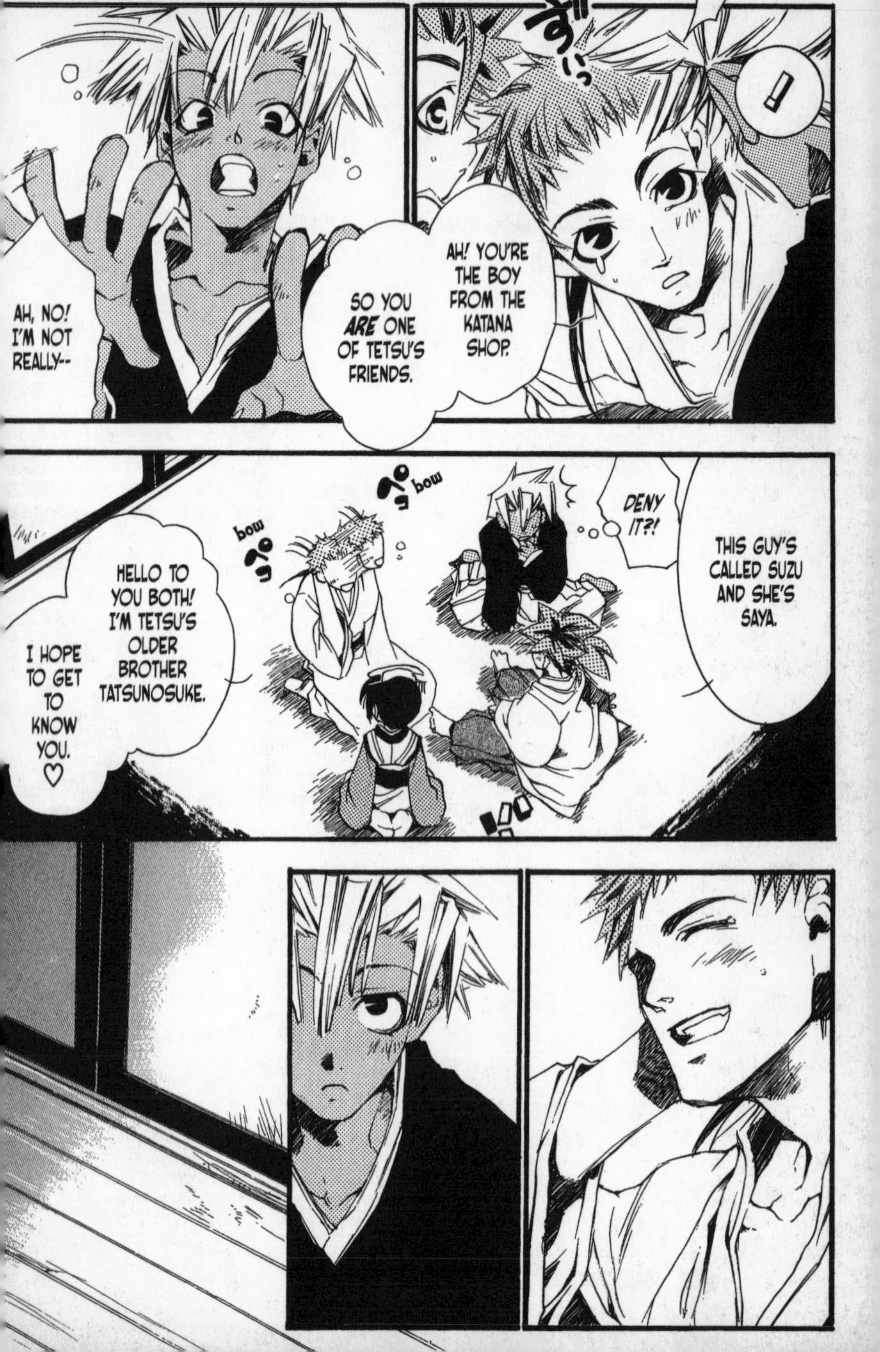
ずいっ
!
AH! YOU'RE THE BOY FROM THE KATANA SHOP.
SO YOU *ARE* ONE OF TETSU'S FRIENDS.
AH, NO! I'M NOT REALLY--
THIS GUY'S CALLED SUZU AND SHE'S SAYA.
DENY IT?!
ぺこ bow
ぺこ bow
HELLO TO YOU BOTH! I'M TETSU'S OLDER BROTHER TATSUNOSUKE.
I HOPE TO GET TO KNOW YOU. ♡

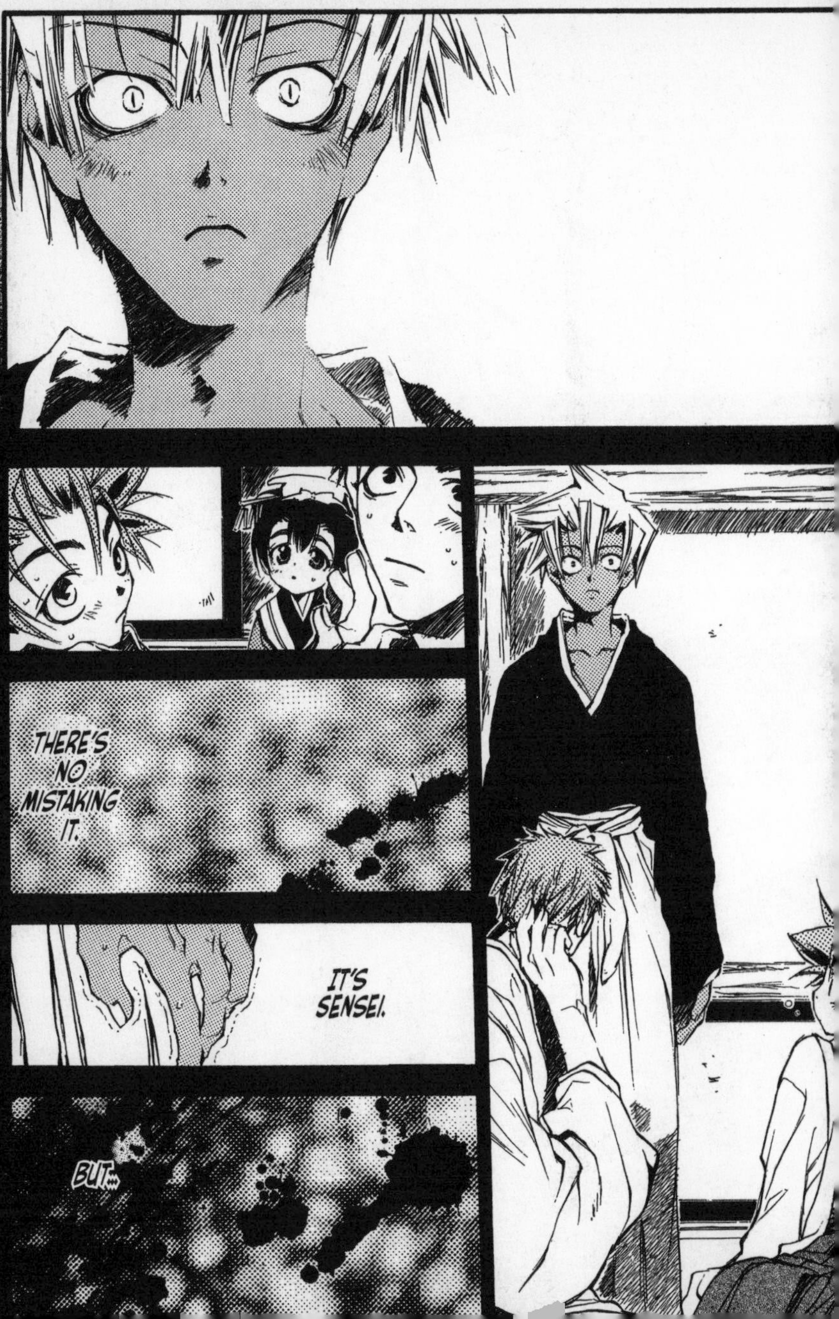
THERE'S NO MISTAKING IT.
IT'S SENSEI.
BUT...

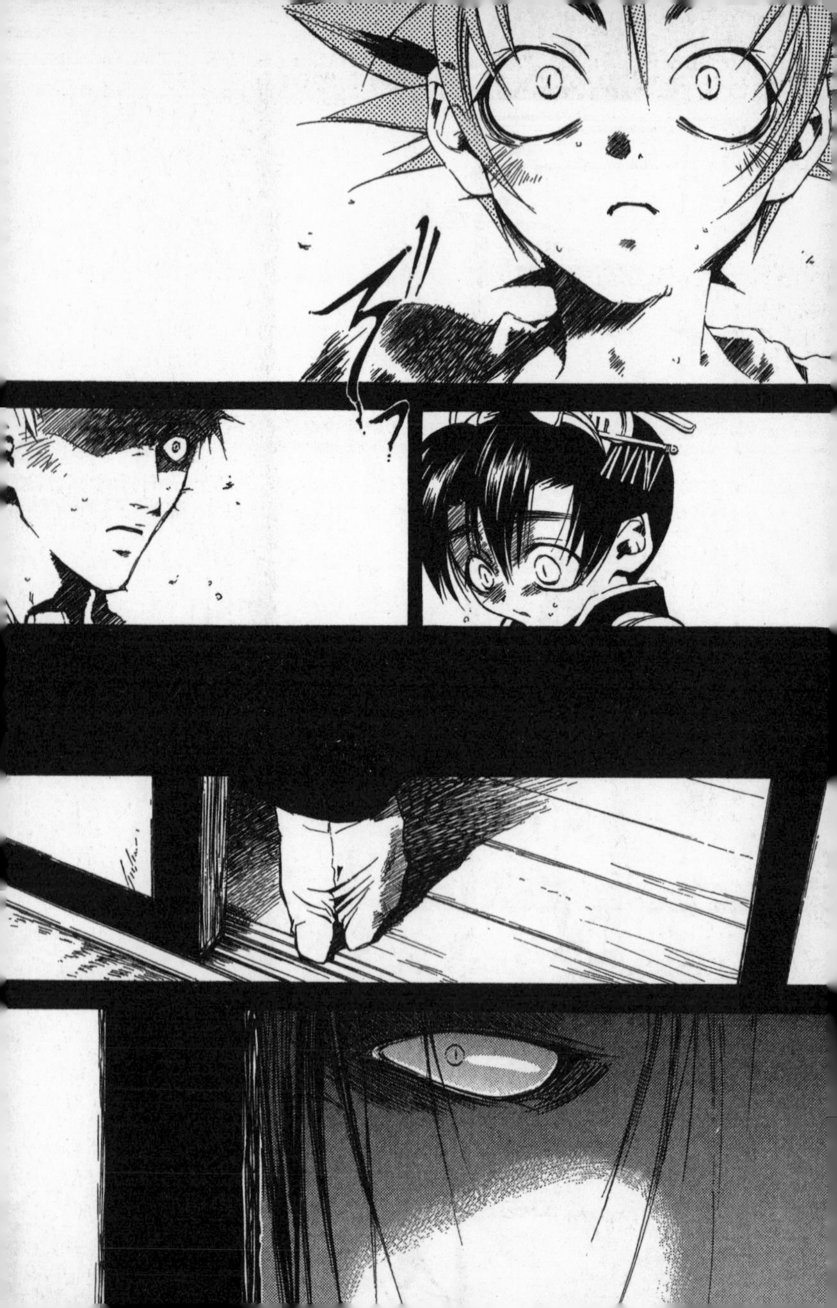

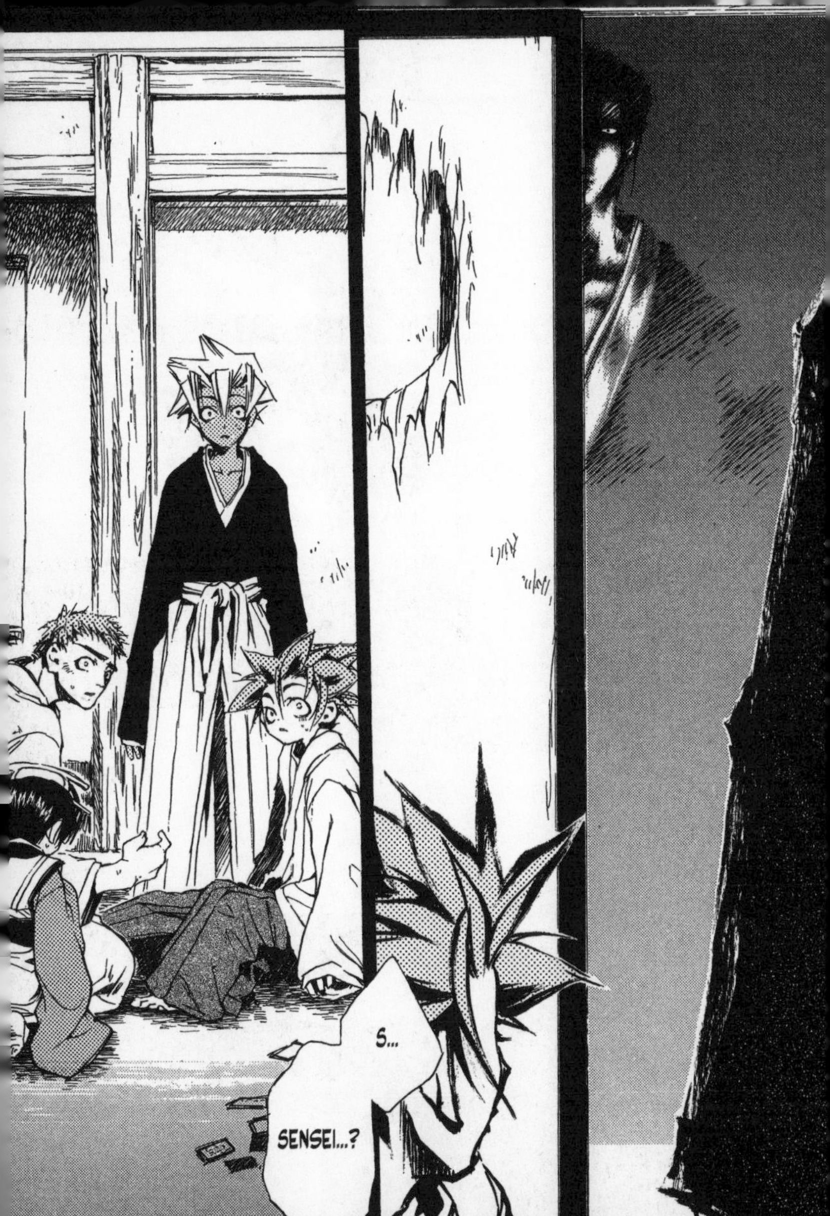
S...
SENSEI...?

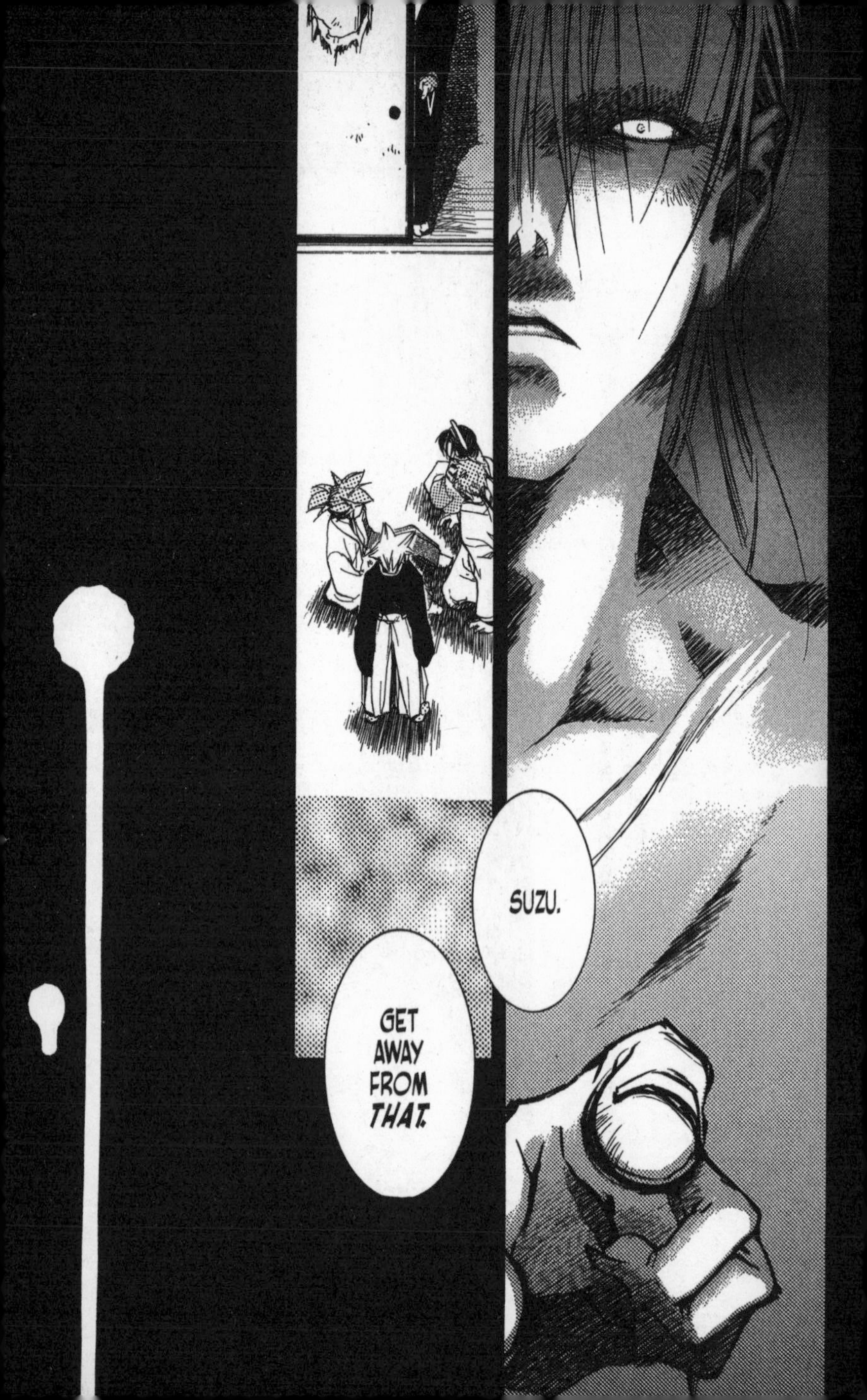
SUZU.
GET AWAY FROM *THAT.*

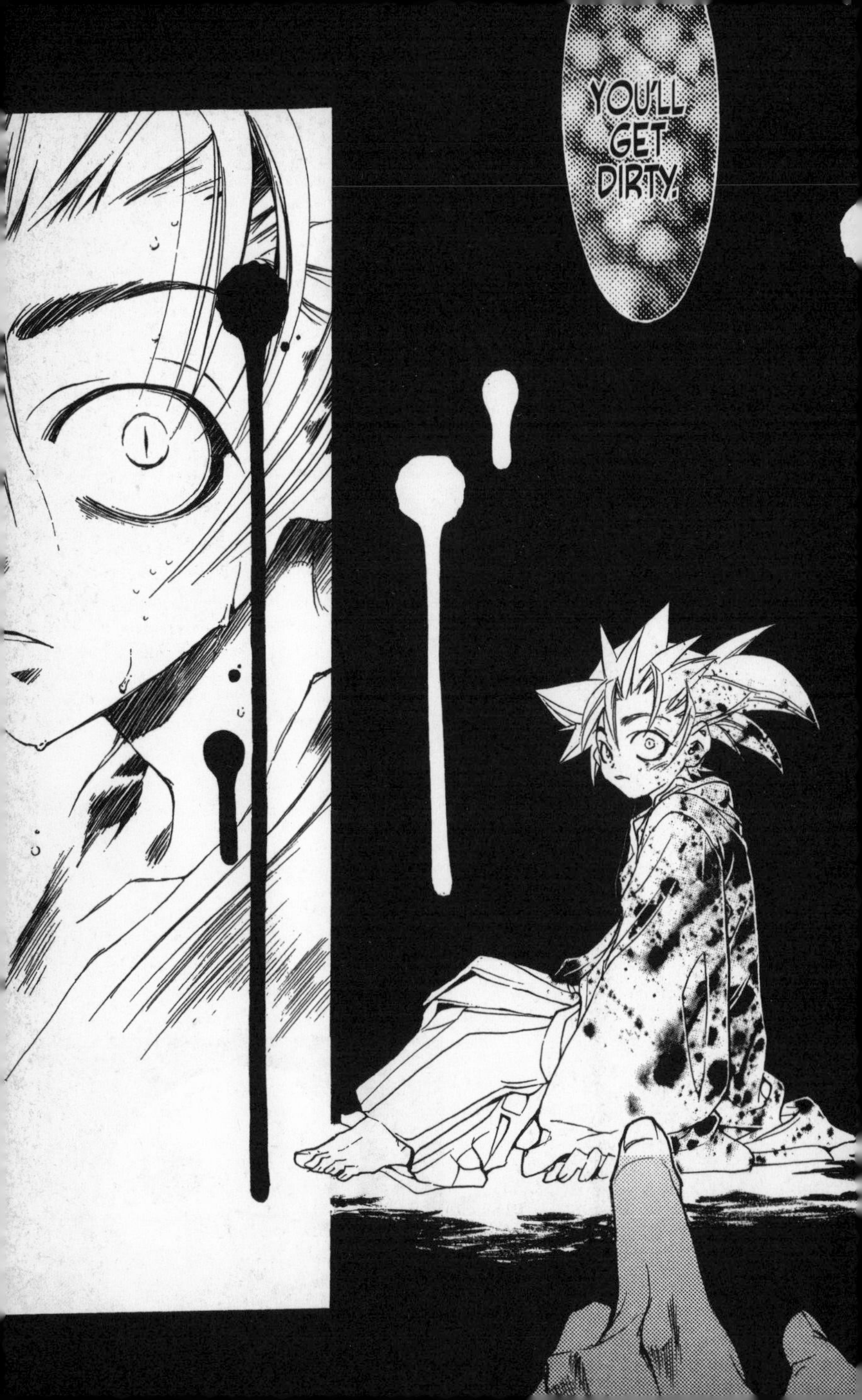
YOU'LL GET DIRTY.

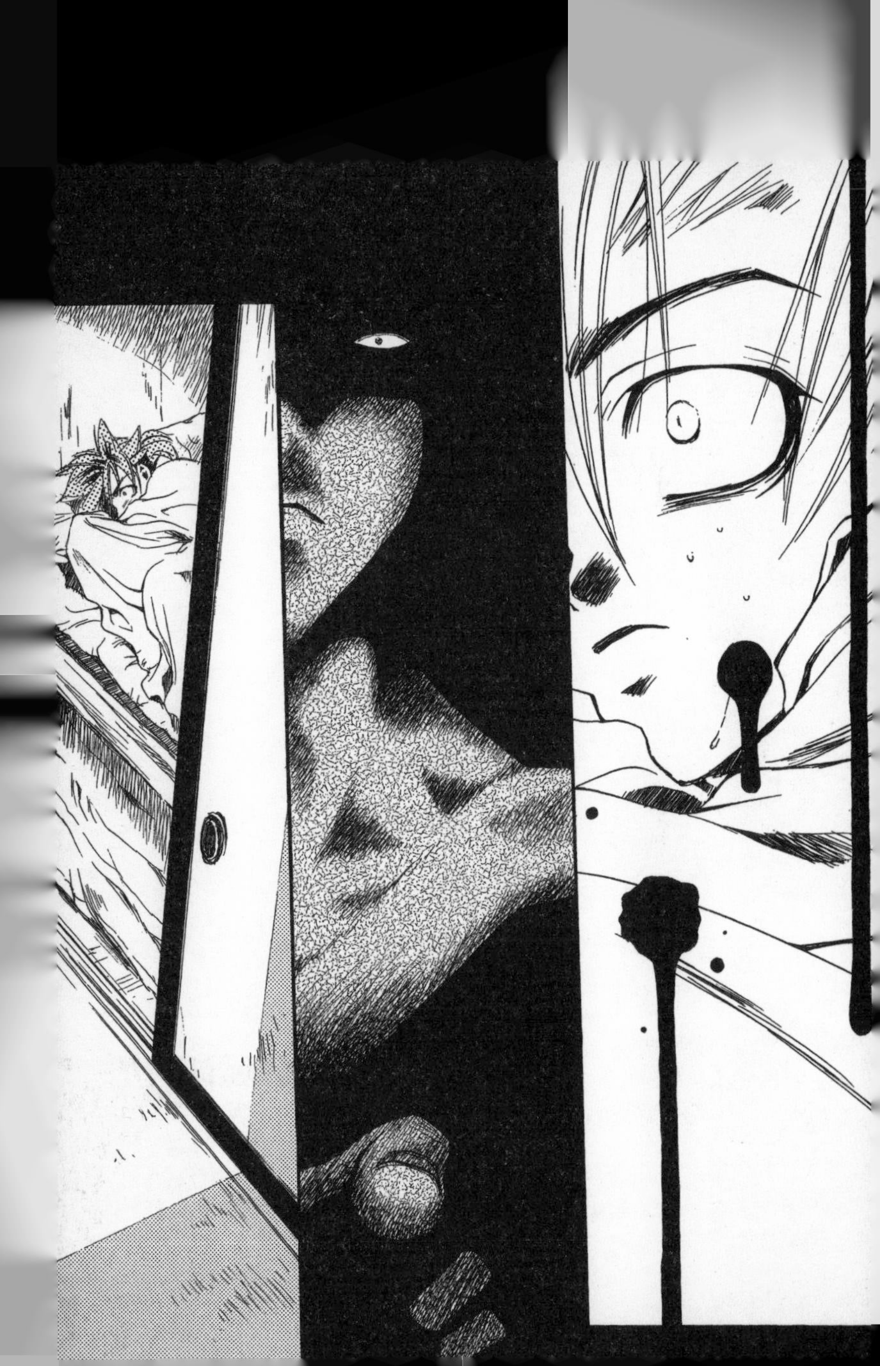

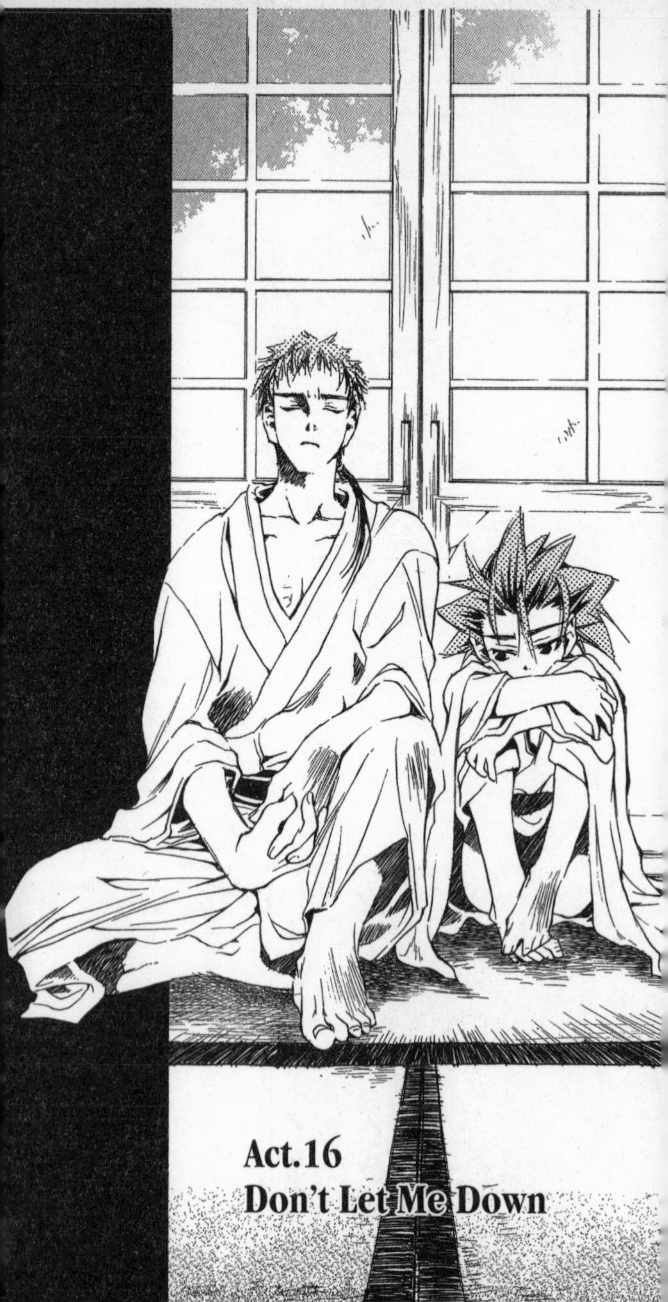
Act.16
Don't Let Me Down

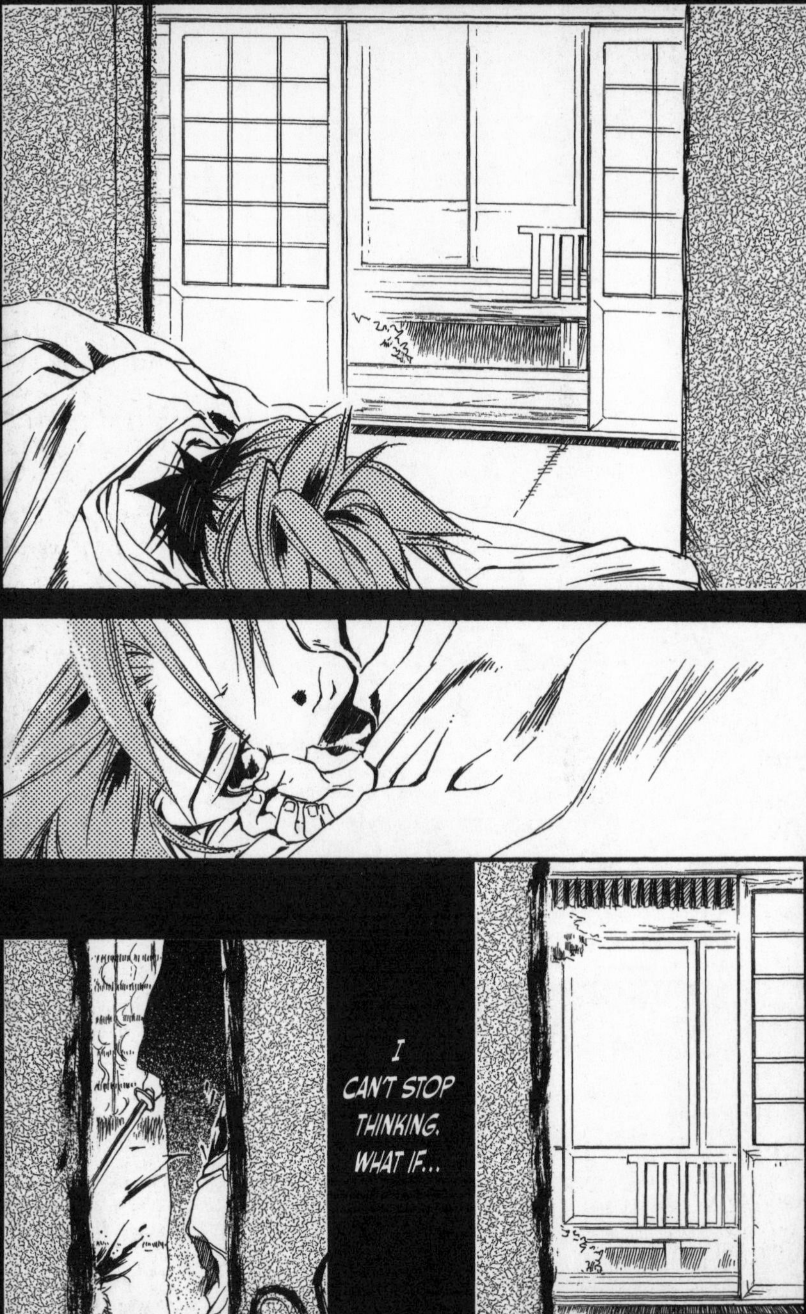
I CAN'T STOP THINKING. WHAT IF...

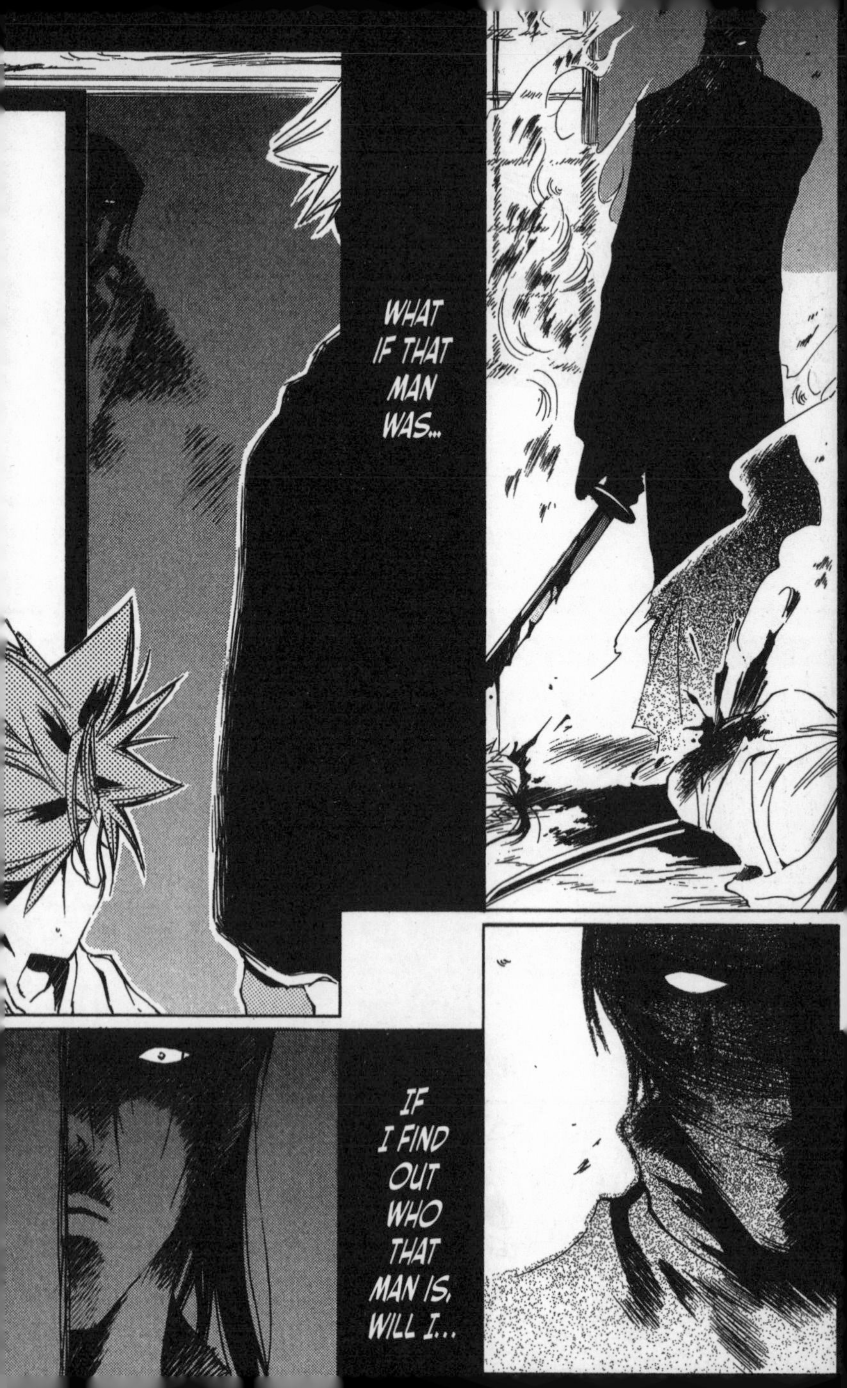
WHAT IF THAT MAN WAS...
IF I FIND OUT WHO THAT MAN IS, WILL I...

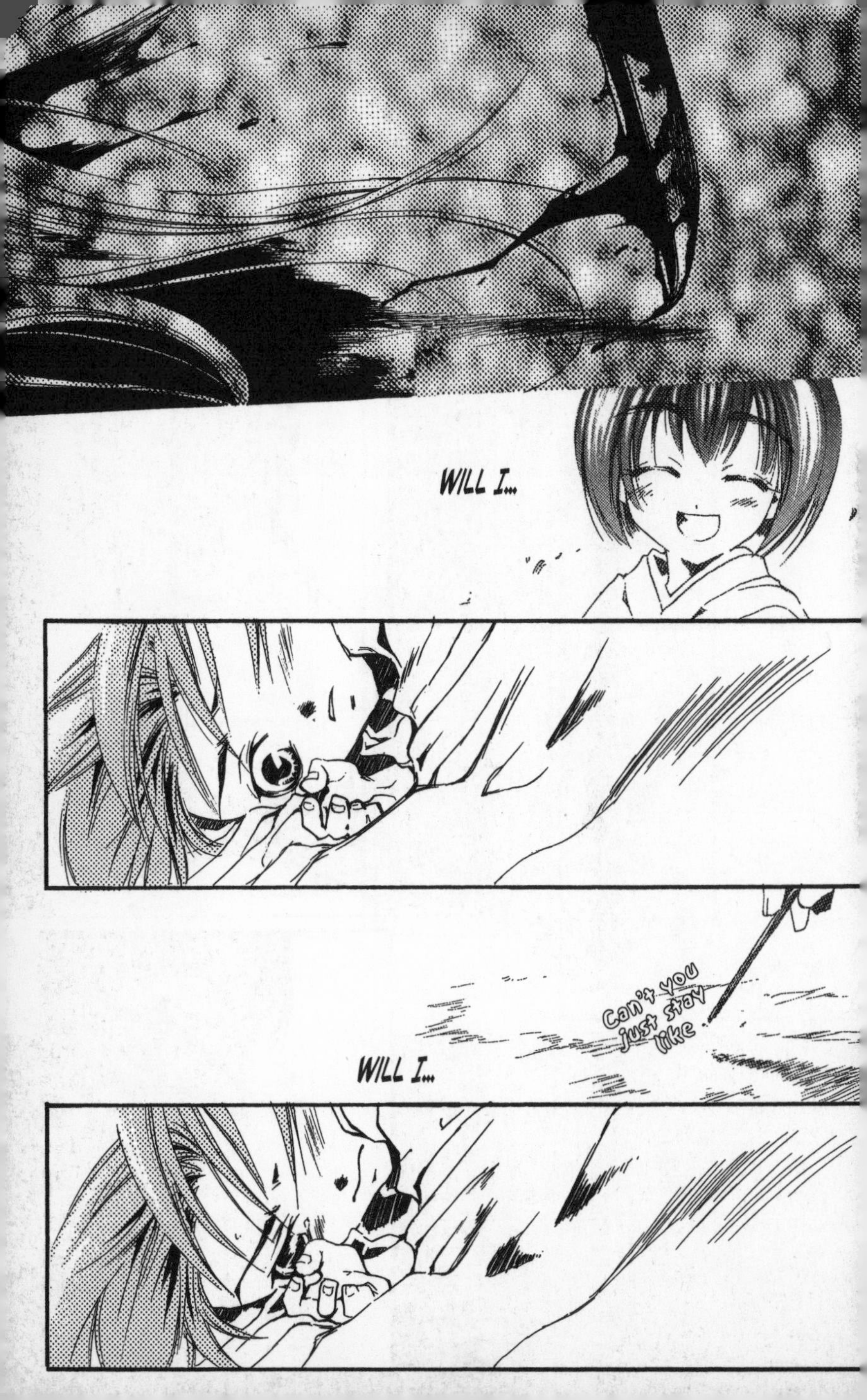
WILL I...
Can't you just stay like
WILL I...

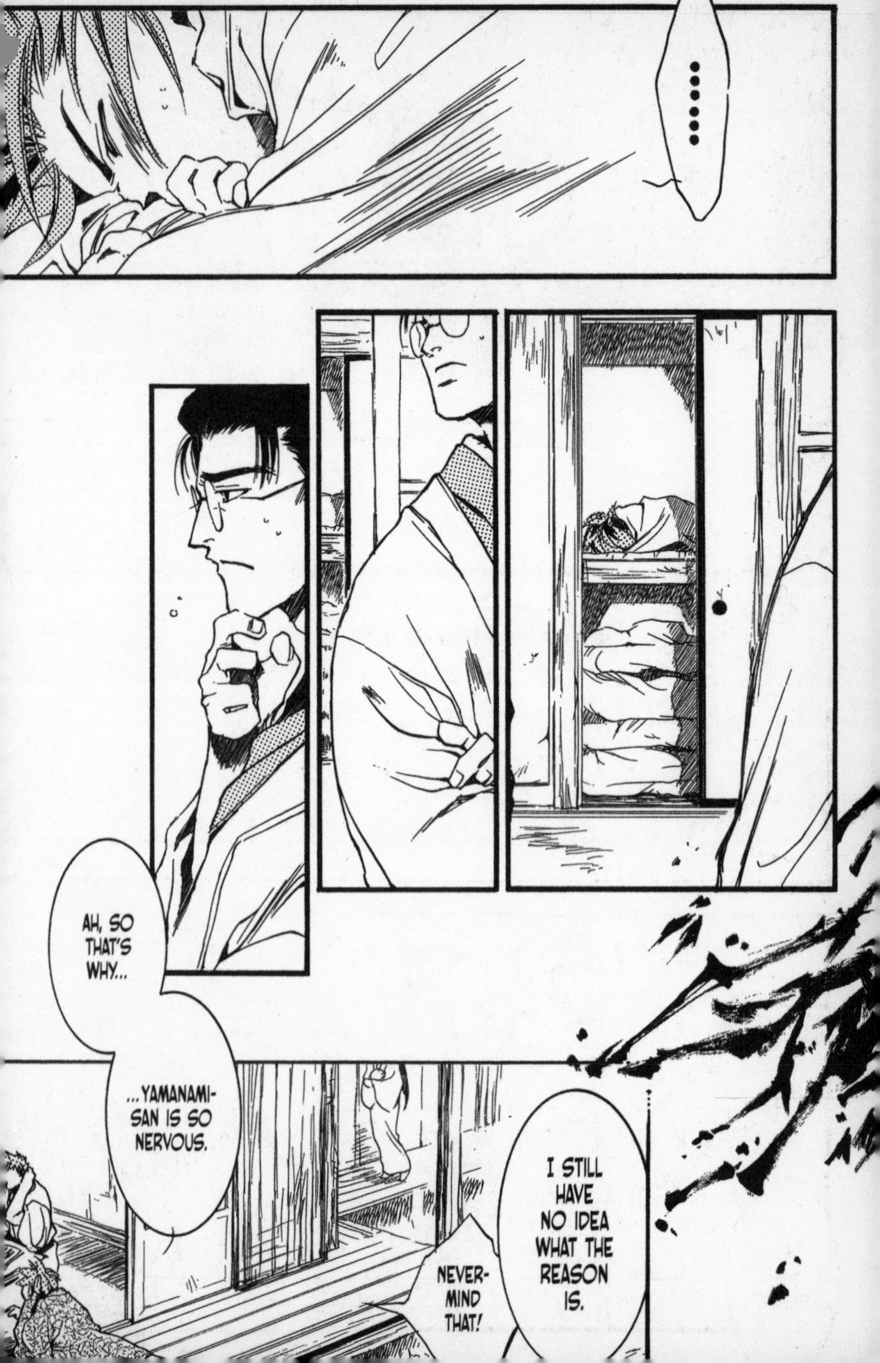
......
AH, SO THAT'S WHY...
...YAMANAMI-SAN IS SO NERVOUS.
I STILL HAVE NO IDEA WHAT THE REASON IS.
NEVER-MIND THAT!

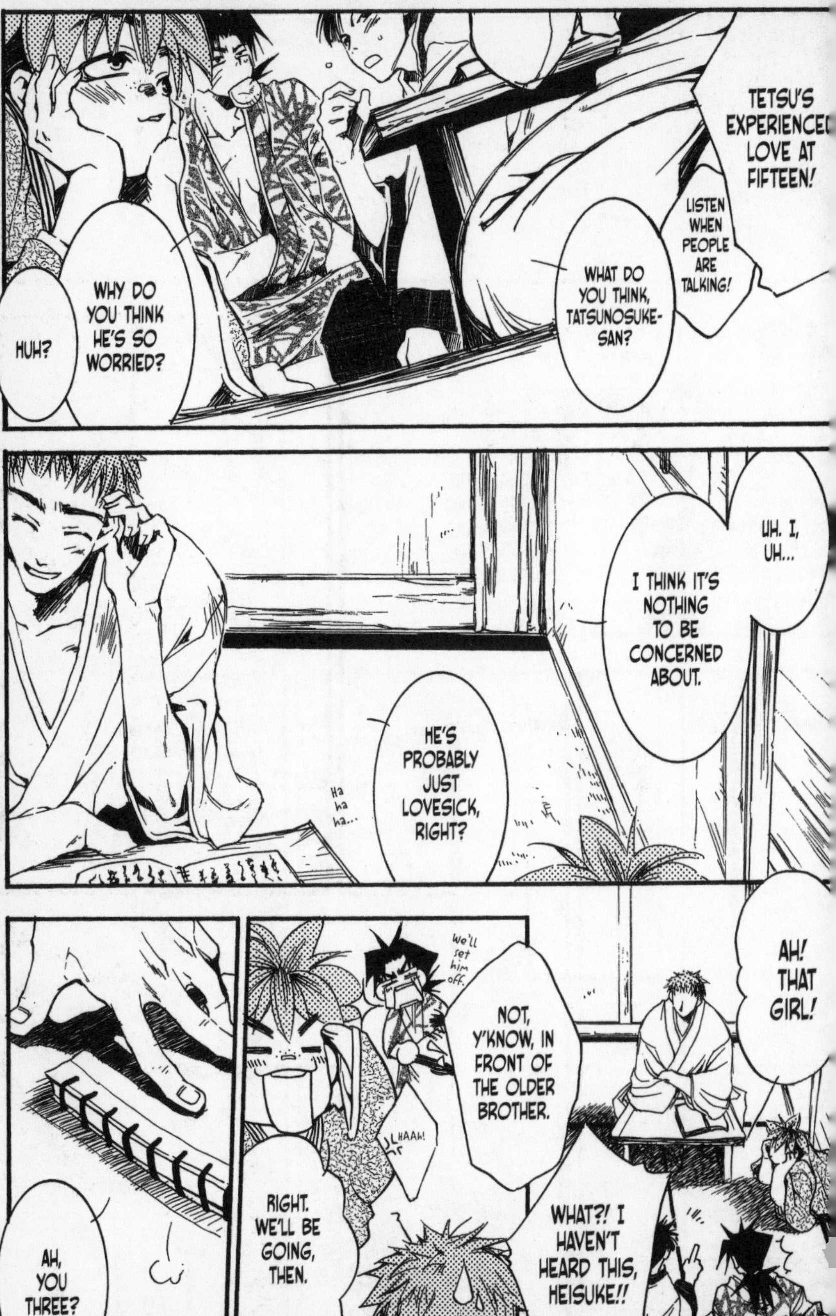
TETSU'S EXPERIENCED LOVE AT FIFTEEN!
LISTEN WHEN PEOPLE ARE TALKING!
WHAT DO YOU THINK, TATSUNOSUKE-SAN?
WHY DO YOU THINK HE'S SO WORRIED?
HUH?
UH. I, UH...
I THINK IT'S NOTHING TO BE CONCERNED ABOUT.
HE'S PROBABLY JUST LOVESICK, RIGHT?
Ha ha ha...
AH! THAT GIRL!
WHAT?! I HAVEN'T HEARD THIS, HEISUKE!!
NOT, Y'KNOW, IN FRONT OF THE OLDER BROTHER.
We'll set him off.
HAAH!
RIGHT. WE'LL BE GOING, THEN.
AH, YOU THREE?

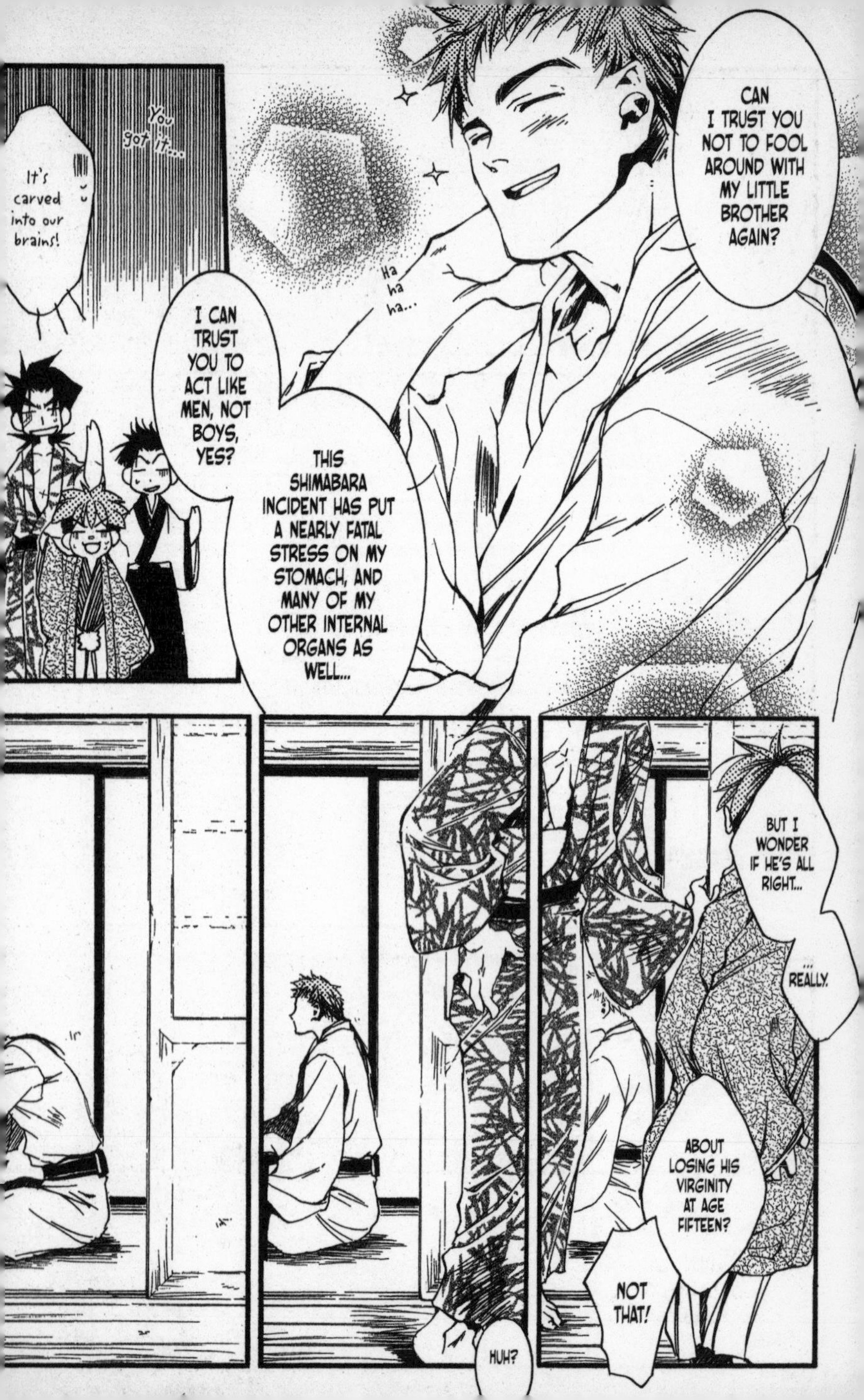
CAN I TRUST YOU NOT TO FOOL AROUND WITH MY LITTLE BROTHER AGAIN?
Ha ha ha...
THIS SHIMABARA INCIDENT HAS PUT A NEARLY FATAL STRESS ON MY STOMACH, AND MANY OF MY OTHER INTERNAL ORGANS AS WELL...
I CAN TRUST YOU TO ACT LIKE MEN, NOT BOYS, YES?
You got it...
It's carved into our brains!
BUT I WONDER IF HE'S ALL RIGHT...
...REALLY.
ABOUT LOSING HIS VIRGINITY AT AGE FIFTEEN?
NOT THAT!
HUH?

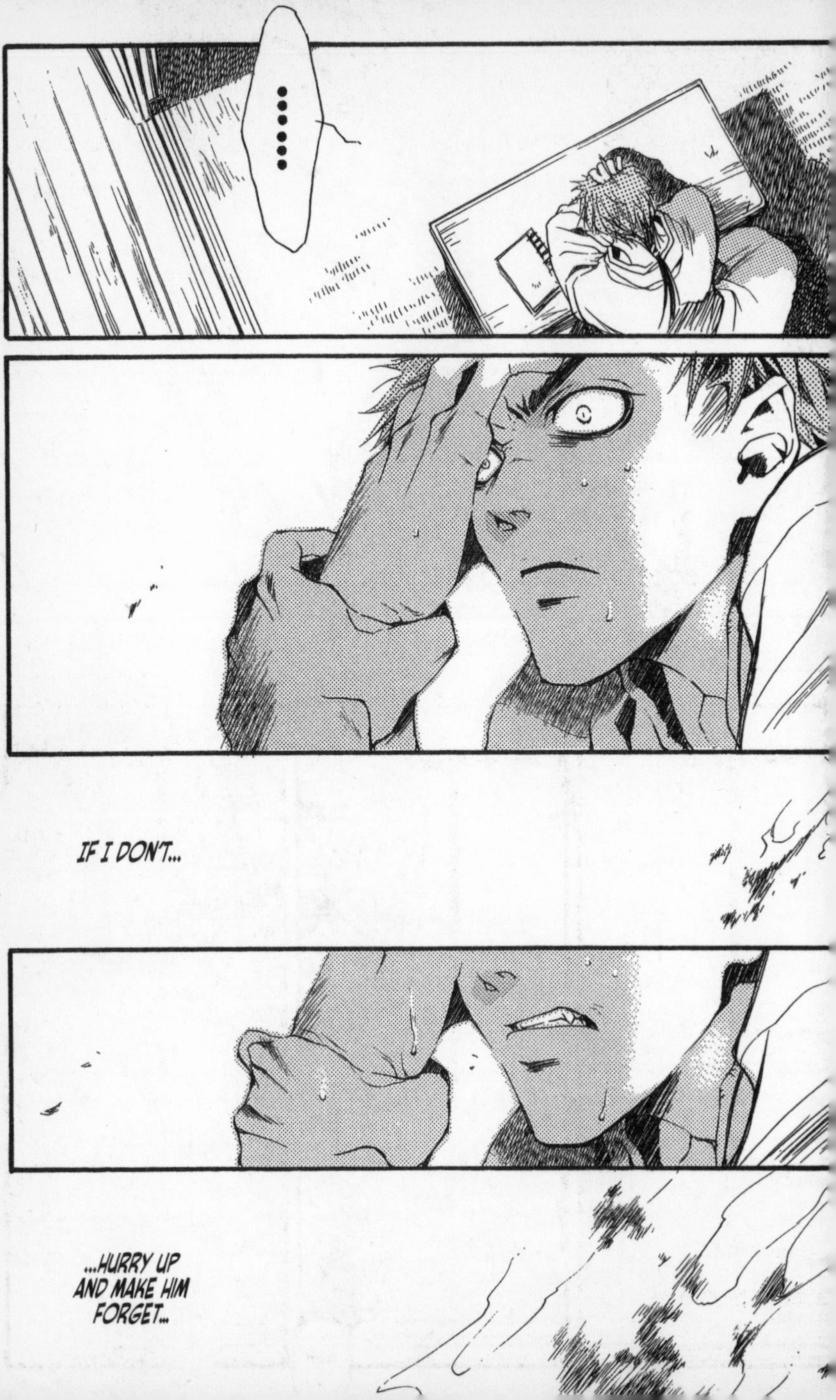
......
IF I DON'T...
...HURRY UP AND MAKE HIM FORGET...

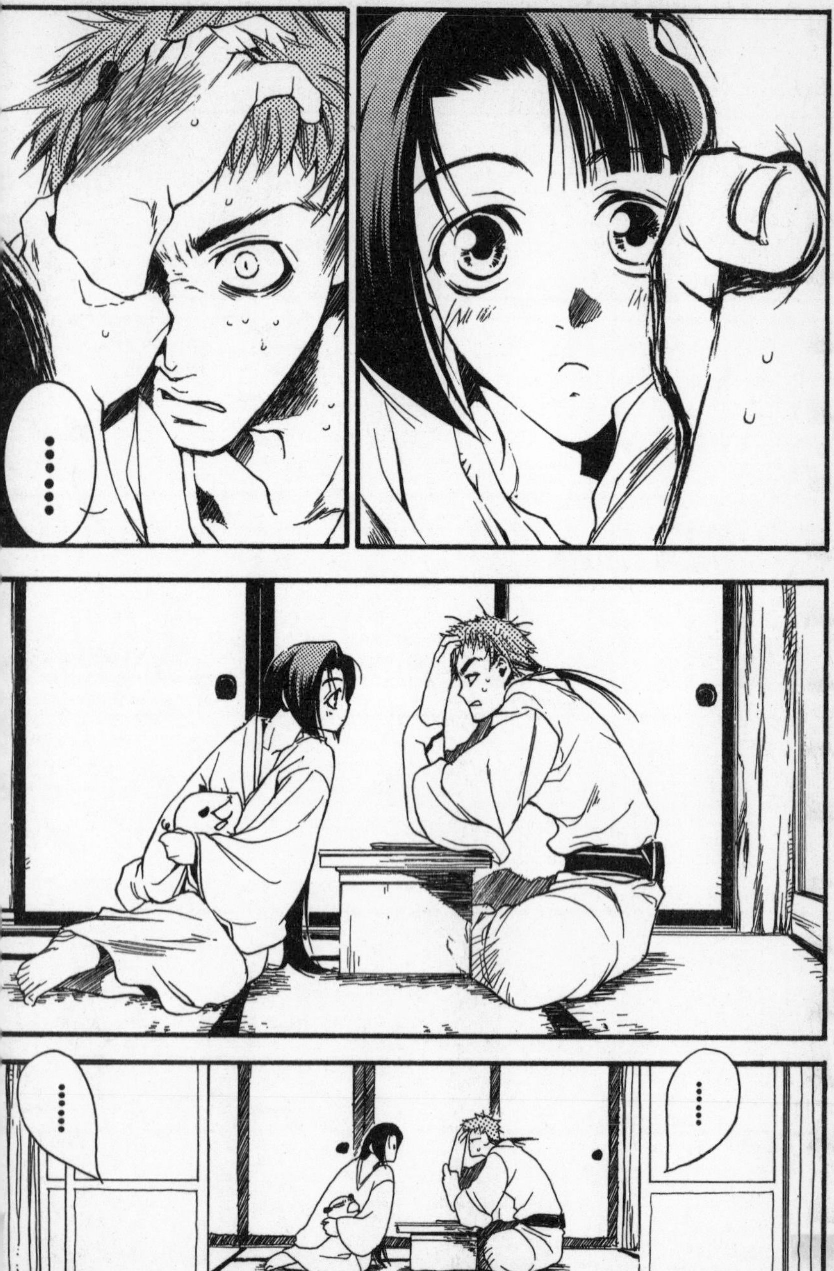
……
……
……

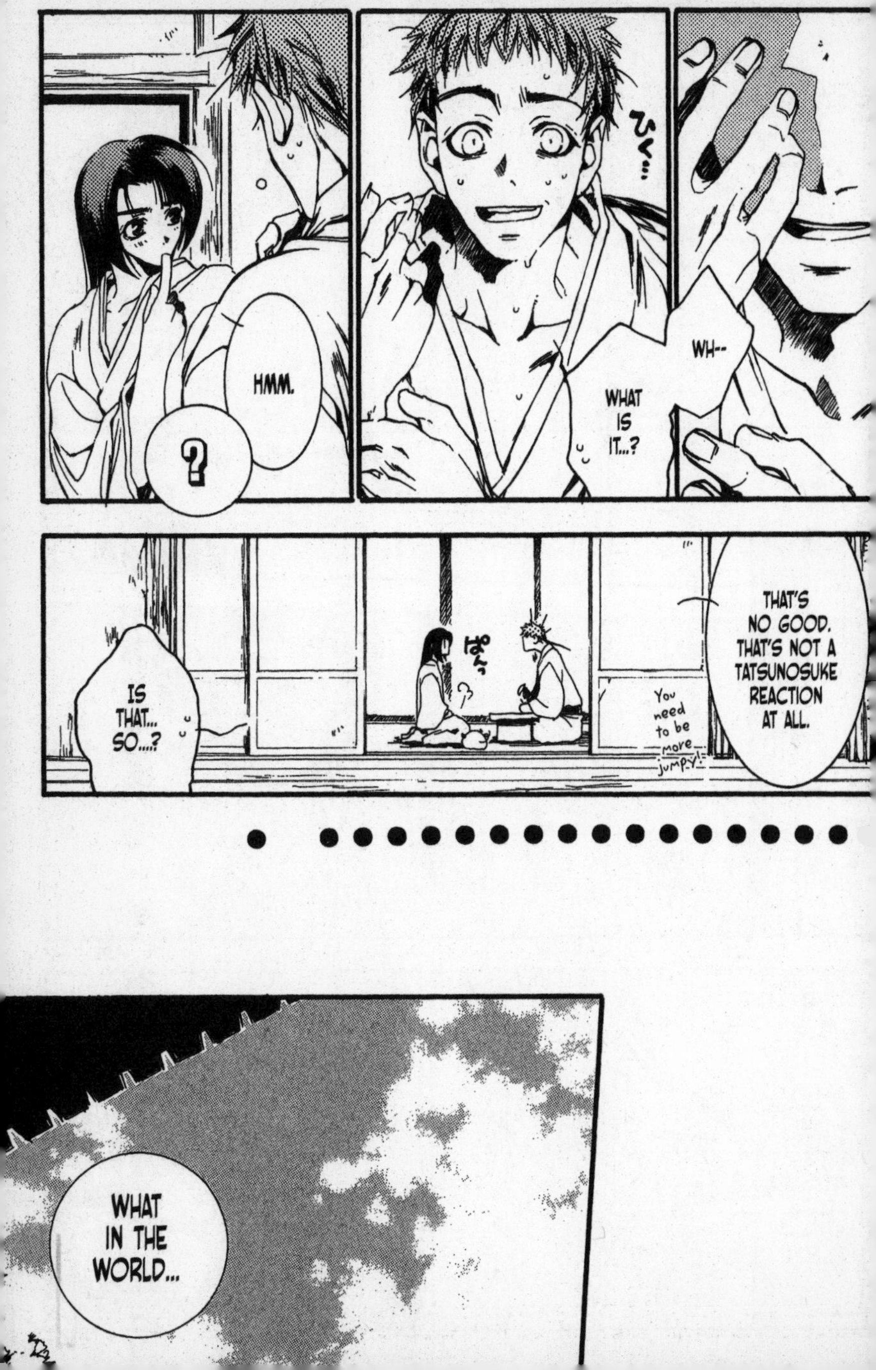
WH--
ぴく...
WHAT IS IT...?
HMM.
?
THAT'S NO GOOD. THAT'S NOT A TATSUNOSUKE REACTION AT ALL.
You need to be more jumpy!
ぱんっ
IS THAT... SO...?
WHAT IN THE WORLD...

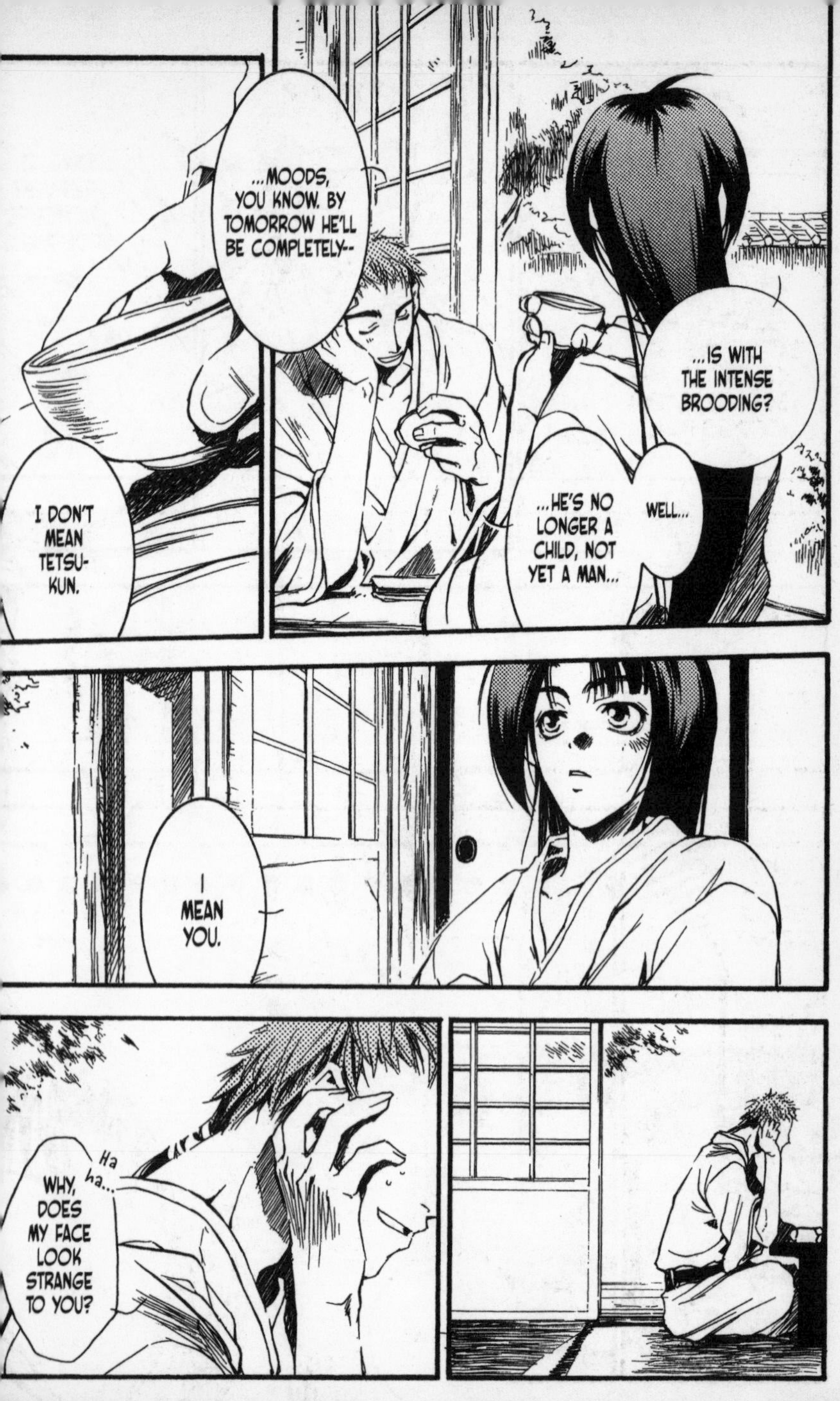
...IS WITH THE INTENSE BROODING?
WELL...
...HE'S NO LONGER A CHILD, NOT YET A MAN...
...MOODS, YOU KNOW. BY TOMORROW HE'LL BE COMPLETELY--
I DON'T MEAN TETSU-KUN.
I MEAN YOU.
Ha ha...
WHY, DOES MY FACE LOOK STRANGE TO YOU?

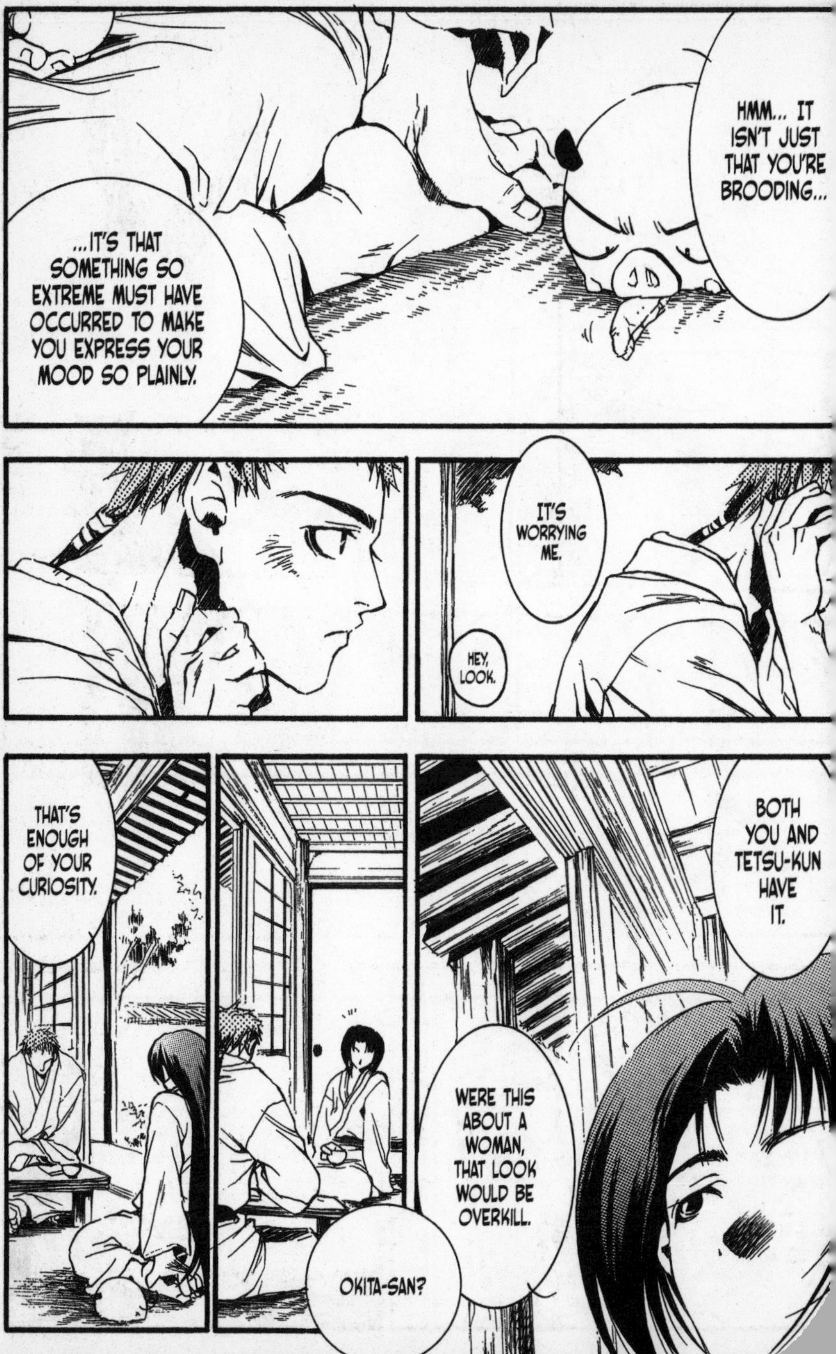
HMM... IT ISN'T JUST THAT YOU'RE BROODING...
...IT'S THAT SOMETHING SO EXTREME MUST HAVE OCCURRED TO MAKE YOU EXPRESS YOUR MOOD SO PLAINLY.
IT'S WORRYING ME.
HEY, LOOK.
BOTH YOU AND TETSU-KUN HAVE IT.
WERE THIS ABOUT A WOMAN, THAT LOOK WOULD BE OVERKILL.
OKITA-SAN?
THAT'S ENOUGH OF YOUR CURIOSITY.

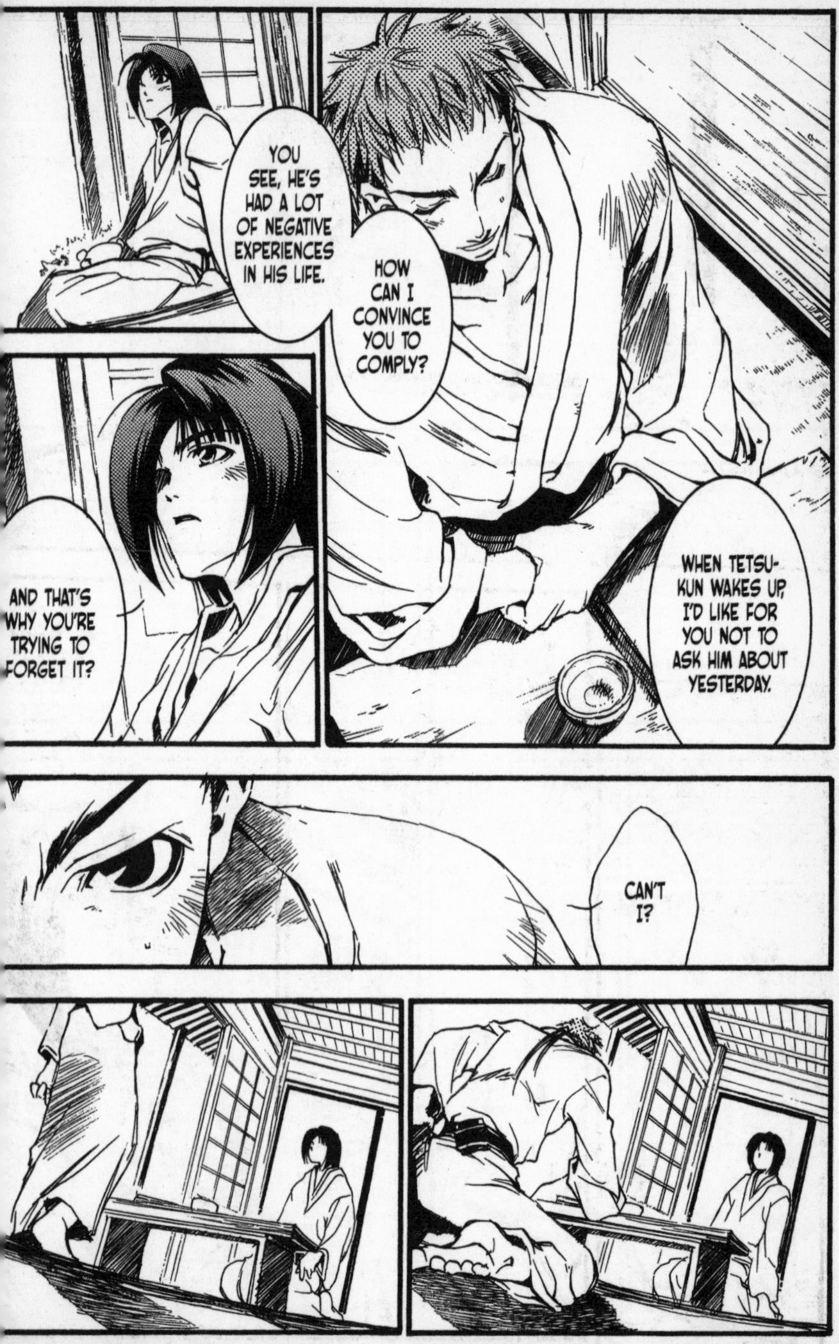
WHEN TETSU-KUN WAKES UP, I'D LIKE FOR YOU NOT TO ASK HIM ABOUT YESTERDAY.
YOU SEE, HE'S HAD A LOT OF NEGATIVE EXPERIENCES IN HIS LIFE.
AND THAT'S WHY YOU'RE TRYING TO FORGET IT?
HOW CAN I CONVINCE YOU TO COMPLY?
CAN'T I?

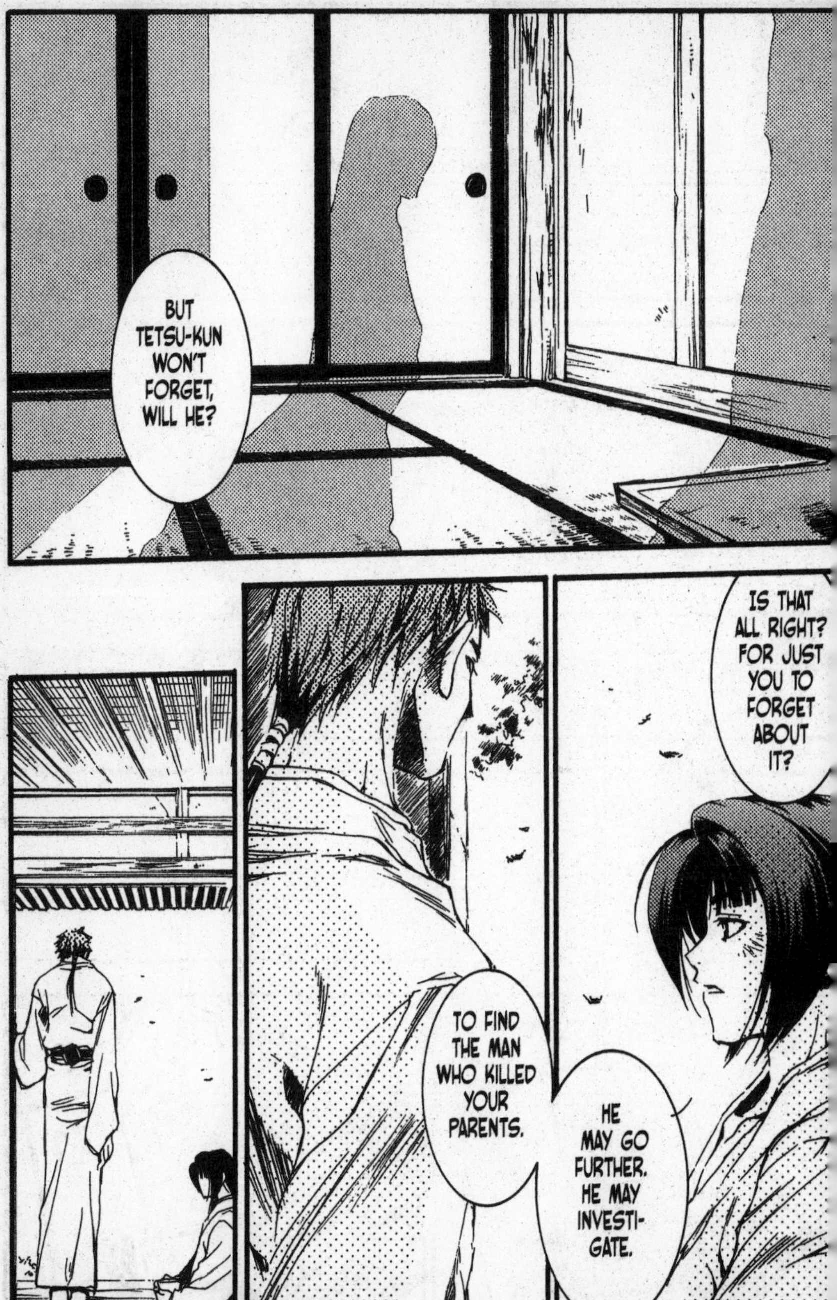
BUT TETSU-KUN WON'T FORGET, WILL HE?
IS THAT ALL RIGHT? FOR JUST YOU TO FORGET ABOUT IT?
HE MAY GO FURTHER. HE MAY INVESTI-GATE.
TO FIND THE MAN WHO KILLED YOUR PARENTS.

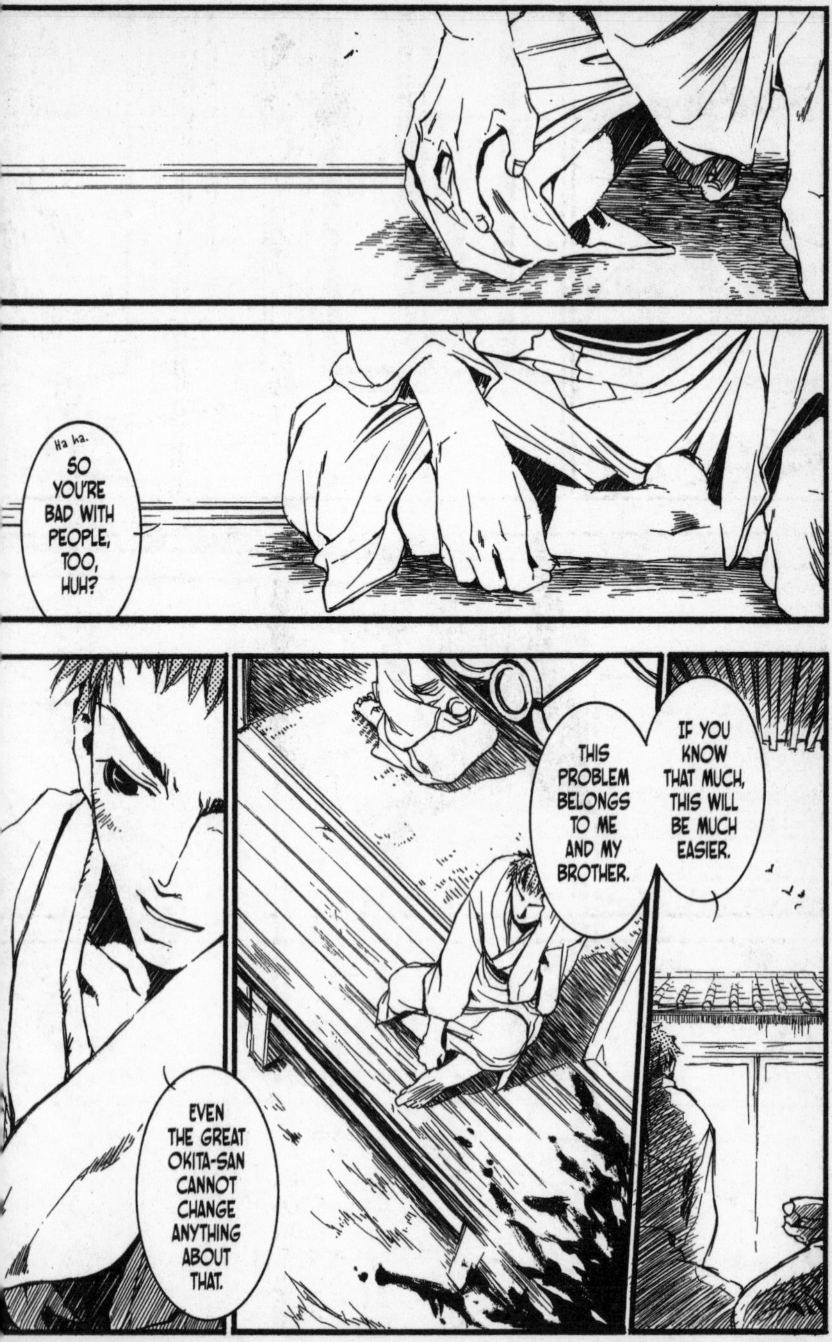
Ha ha.
SO YOU'RE BAD WITH PEOPLE, TOO, HUH?
IF YOU KNOW THAT MUCH, THIS WILL BE MUCH EASIER.
THIS PROBLEM BELONGS TO ME AND MY BROTHER.
EVEN THE GREAT OKITA-SAN CANNOT CHANGE ANYTHING ABOUT THAT.

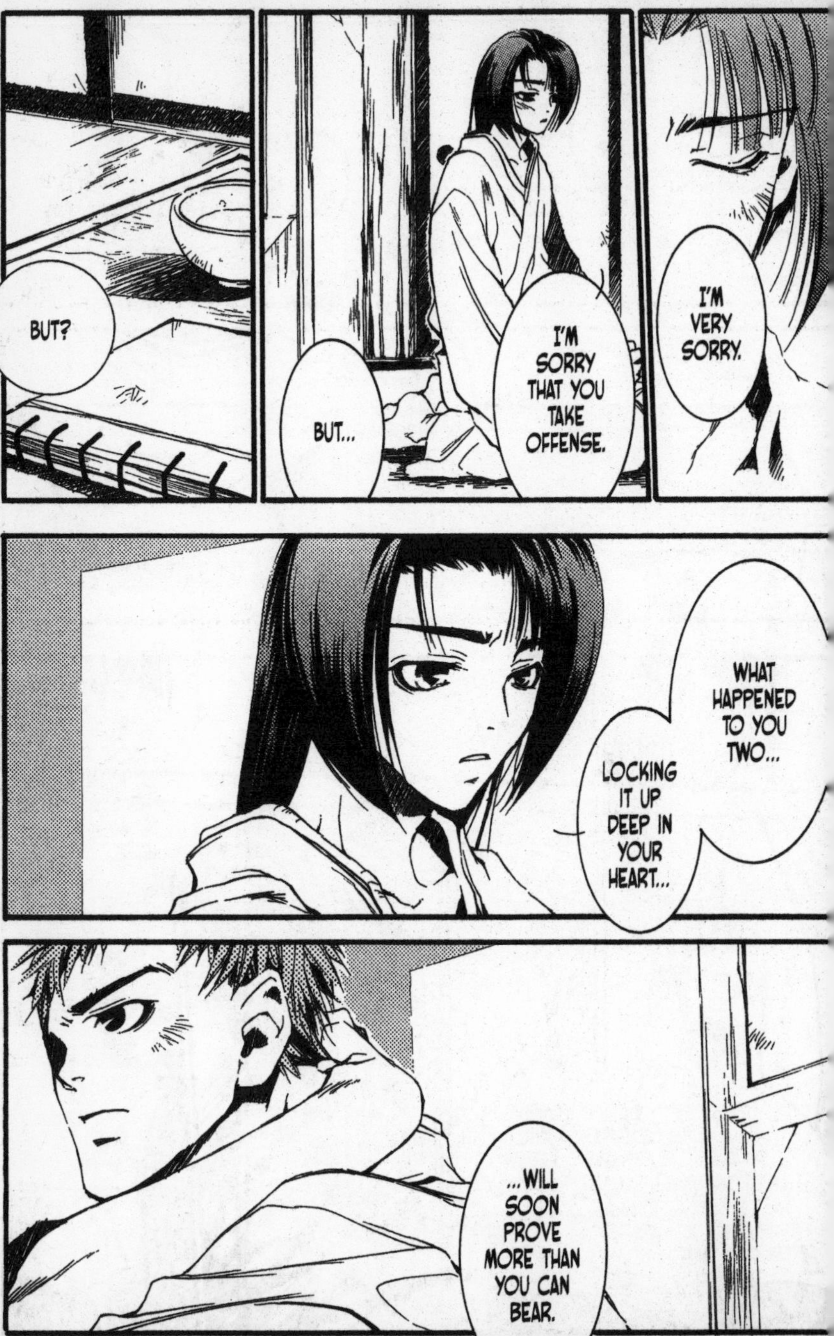
I'M VERY SORRY.
I'M SORRY THAT YOU TAKE OFFENSE.
BUT...
BUT?
WHAT HAPPENED TO YOU TWO...
LOCKING IT UP DEEP IN YOUR HEART...
...WILL SOON PROVE MORE THAN YOU CAN BEAR.

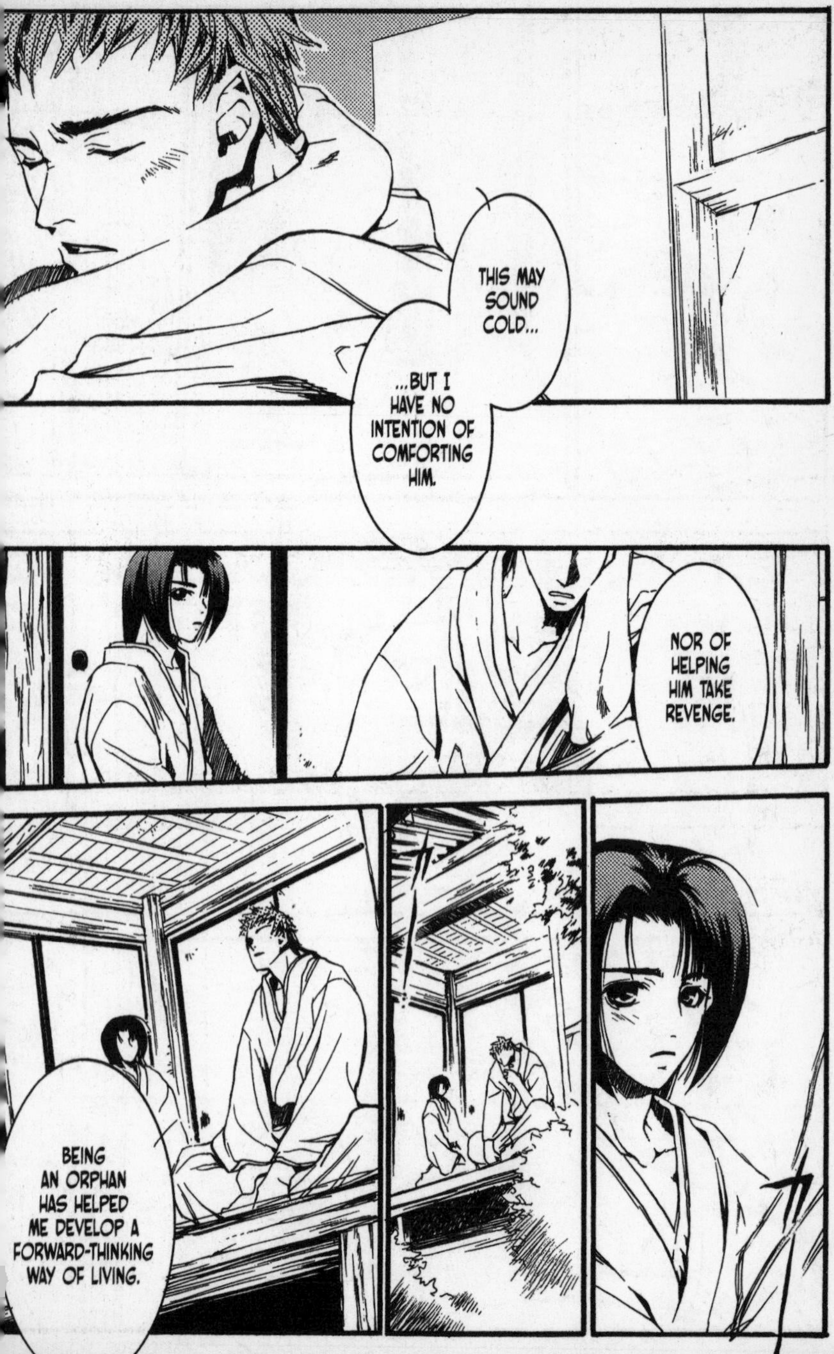
THIS MAY SOUND COLD...
...BUT I HAVE NO INTENTION OF COMFORTING HIM.
NOR OF HELPING HIM TAKE REVENGE.
BEING AN ORPHAN HAS HELPED ME DEVELOP A FORWARD-THINKING WAY OF LIVING.

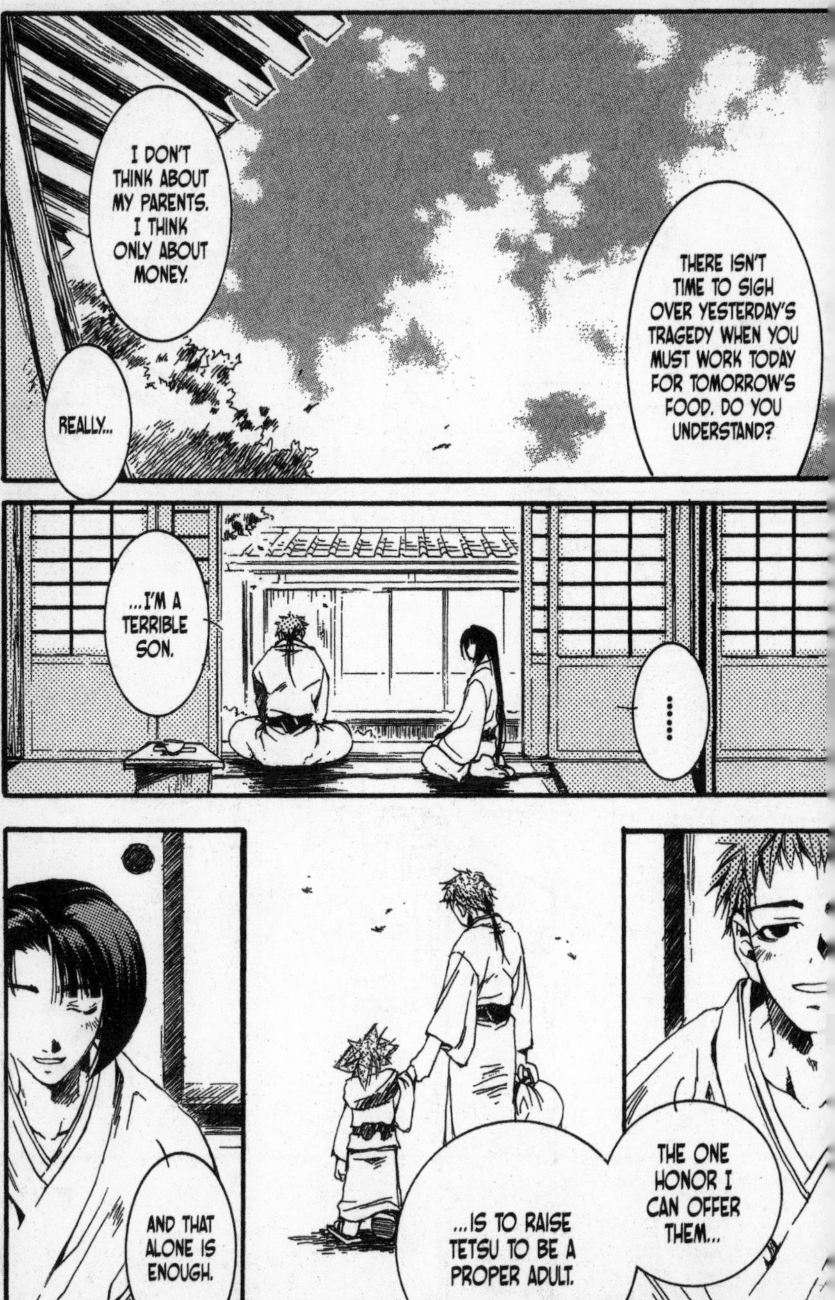
THERE ISN'T TIME TO SIGH OVER YESTERDAY'S TRAGEDY WHEN YOU MUST WORK TODAY FOR TOMORROW'S FOOD. DO YOU UNDERSTAND?
I DON'T THINK ABOUT MY PARENTS. I THINK ONLY ABOUT MONEY.
REALLY...
......
...I'M A TERRIBLE SON.
THE ONE HONOR I CAN OFFER THEM...
...IS TO RAISE TETSU TO BE A PROPER ADULT.
AND THAT ALONE IS ENOUGH.

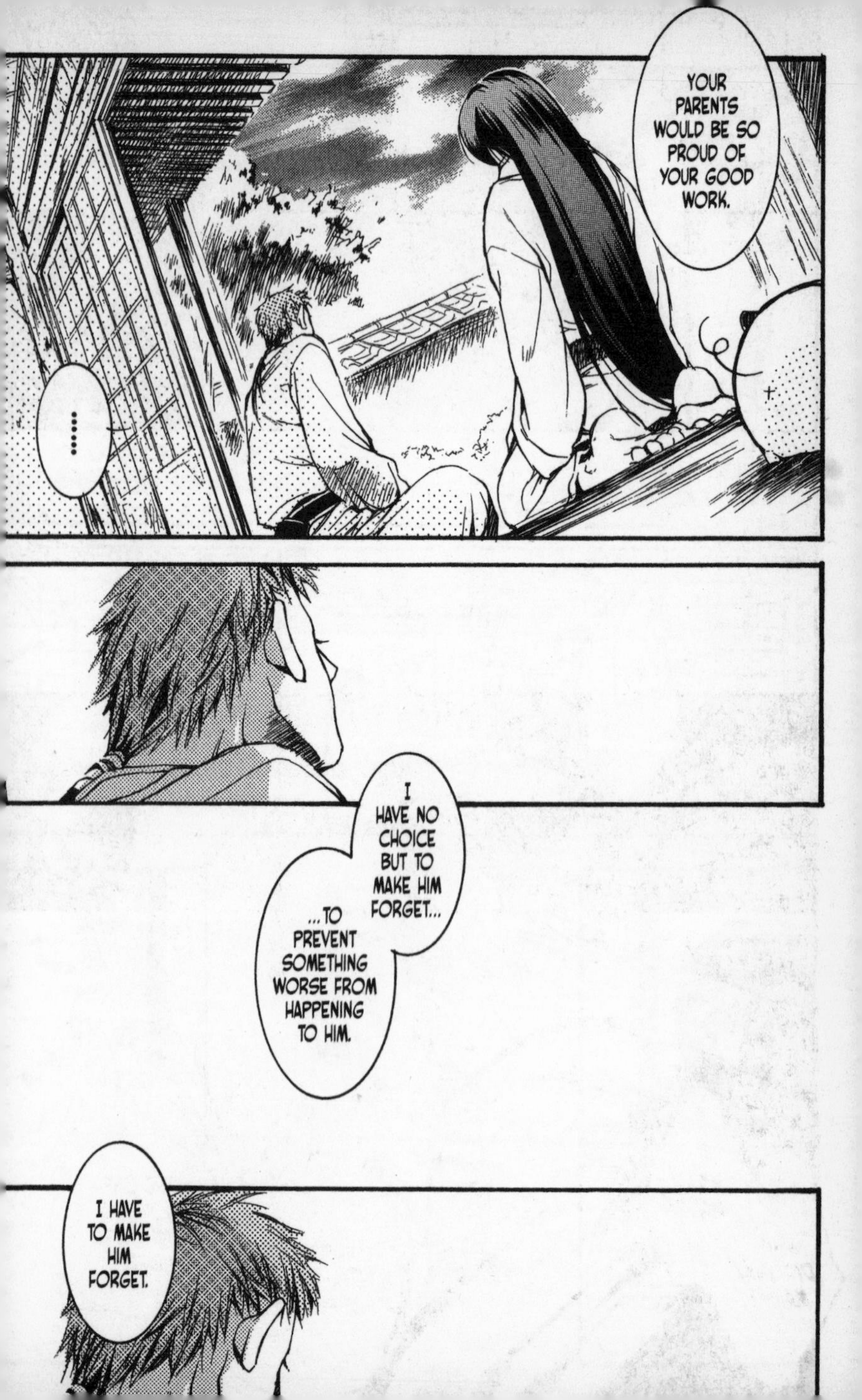
YOUR PARENTS WOULD BE SO PROUD OF YOUR GOOD WORK.
......
I HAVE NO CHOICE BUT TO MAKE HIM FORGET...
...TO PREVENT SOMETHING WORSE FROM HAPPENING TO HIM.
I HAVE TO MAKE HIM FORGET.

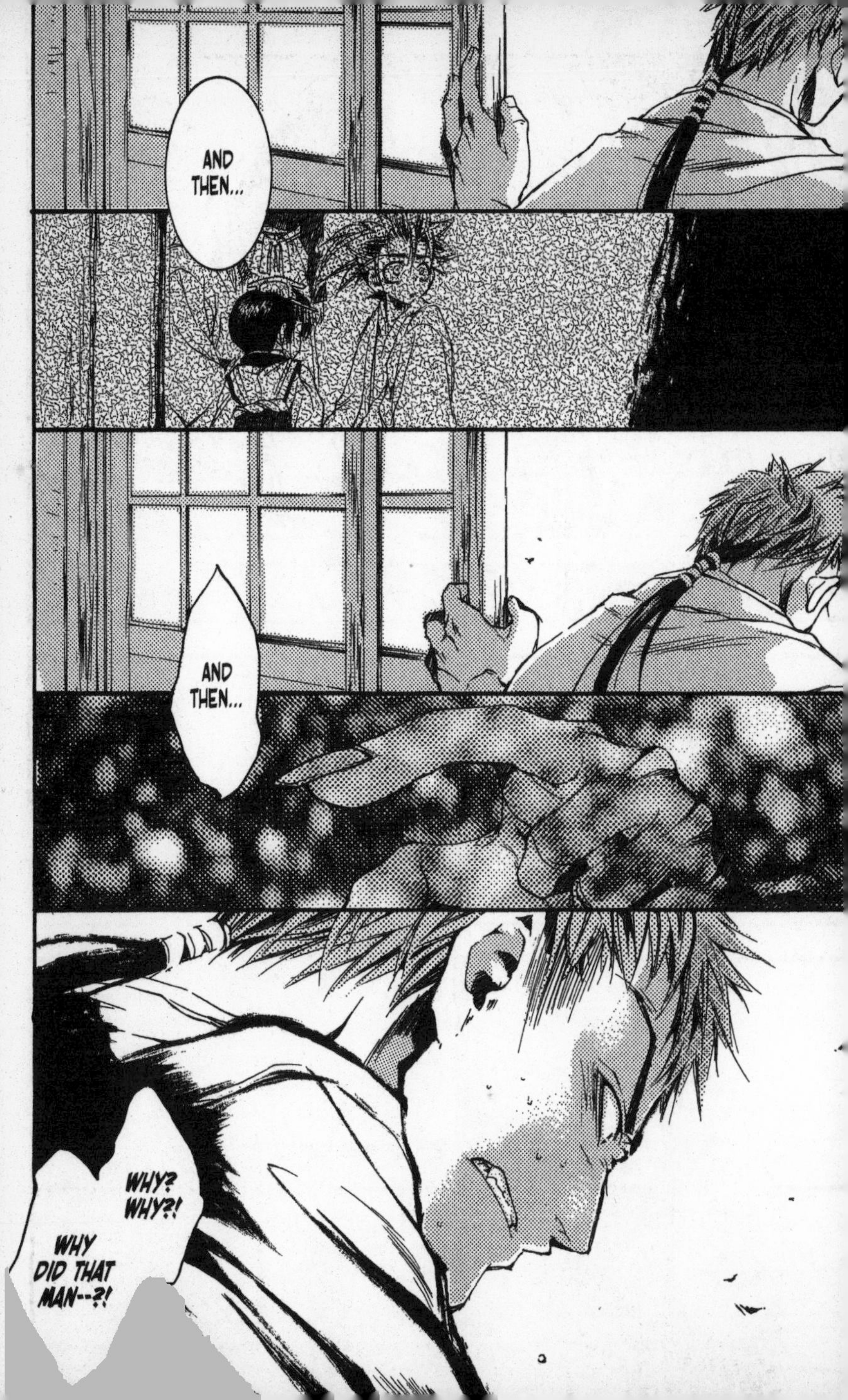
AND THEN...
AND THEN...
WHY? WHY?!
WHY DID THAT MAN--?!

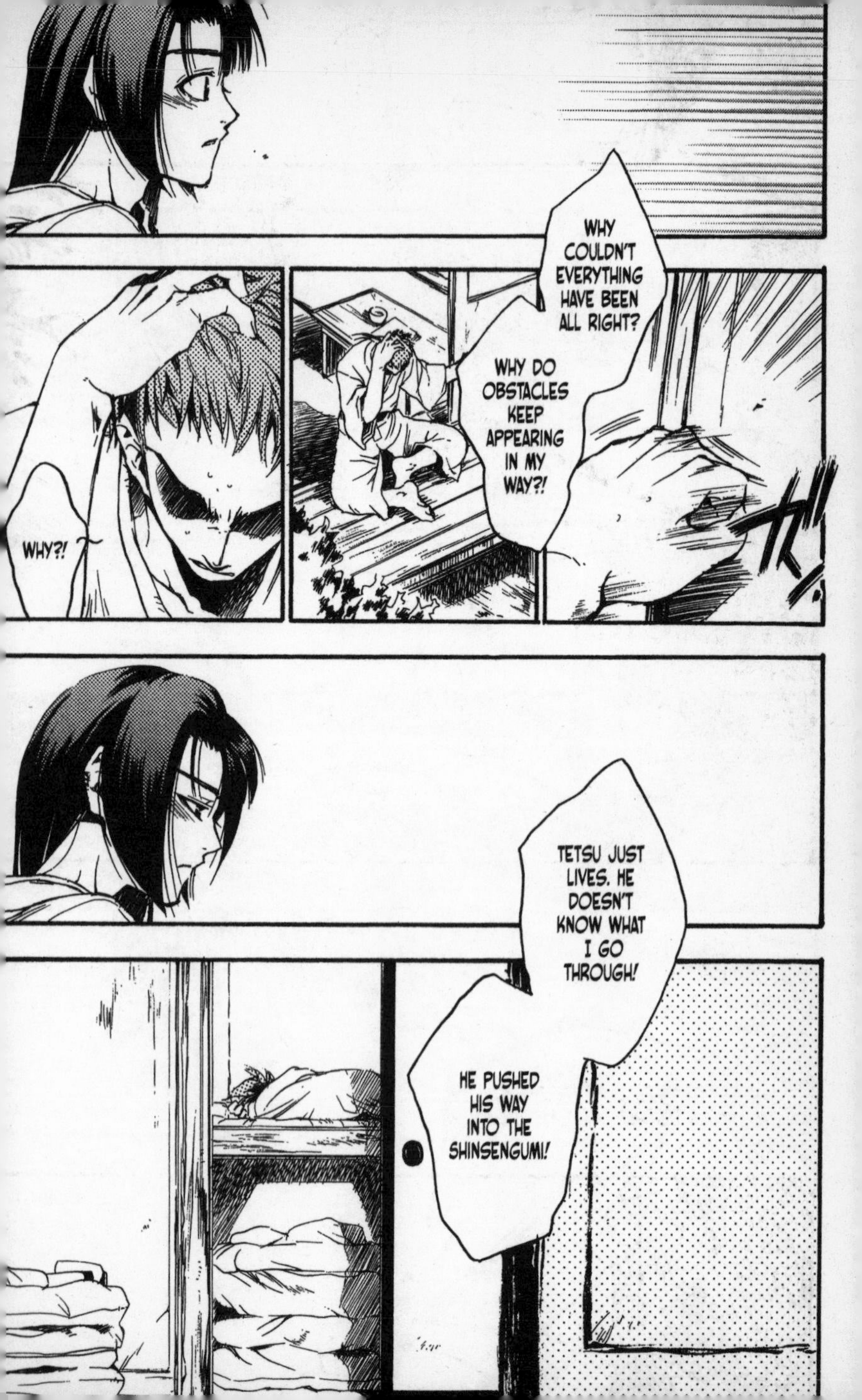
WHY COULDN'T EVERYTHING HAVE BEEN ALL RIGHT?
WHY DO OBSTACLES KEEP APPEARING IN MY WAY?!
WHY?!
TETSU JUST LIVES. HE DOESN'T KNOW WHAT I GO THROUGH!
HE PUSHED HIS WAY INTO THE SHINSENGUMI!

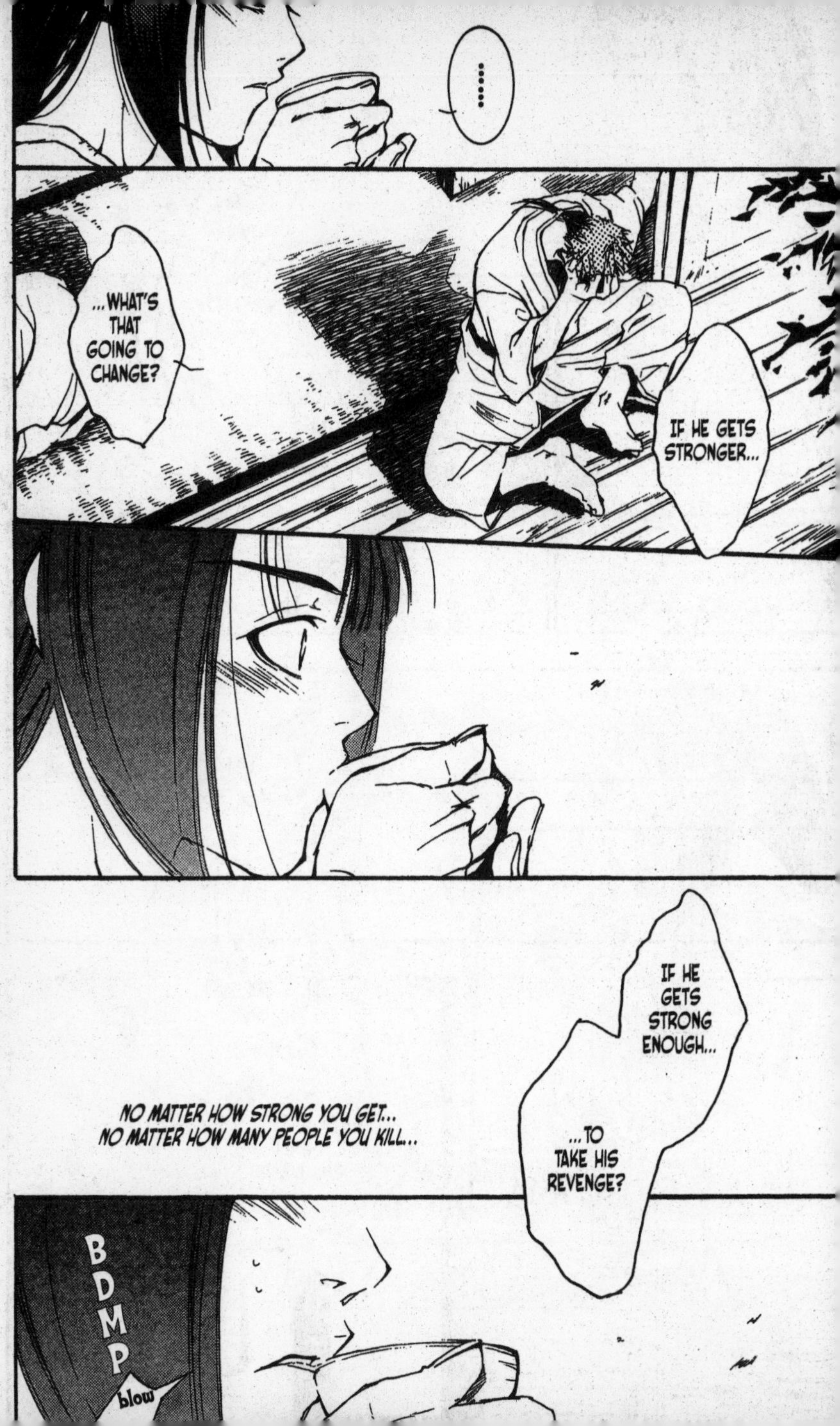
......
IF HE GETS STRONGER...
...WHAT'S THAT GOING TO CHANGE?
IF HE GETS STRONG ENOUGH...
...TO TAKE HIS REVENGE?
NO MATTER HOW STRONG YOU GET...
NO MATTER HOW MANY PEOPLE YOU KILL...
BDMP
blow

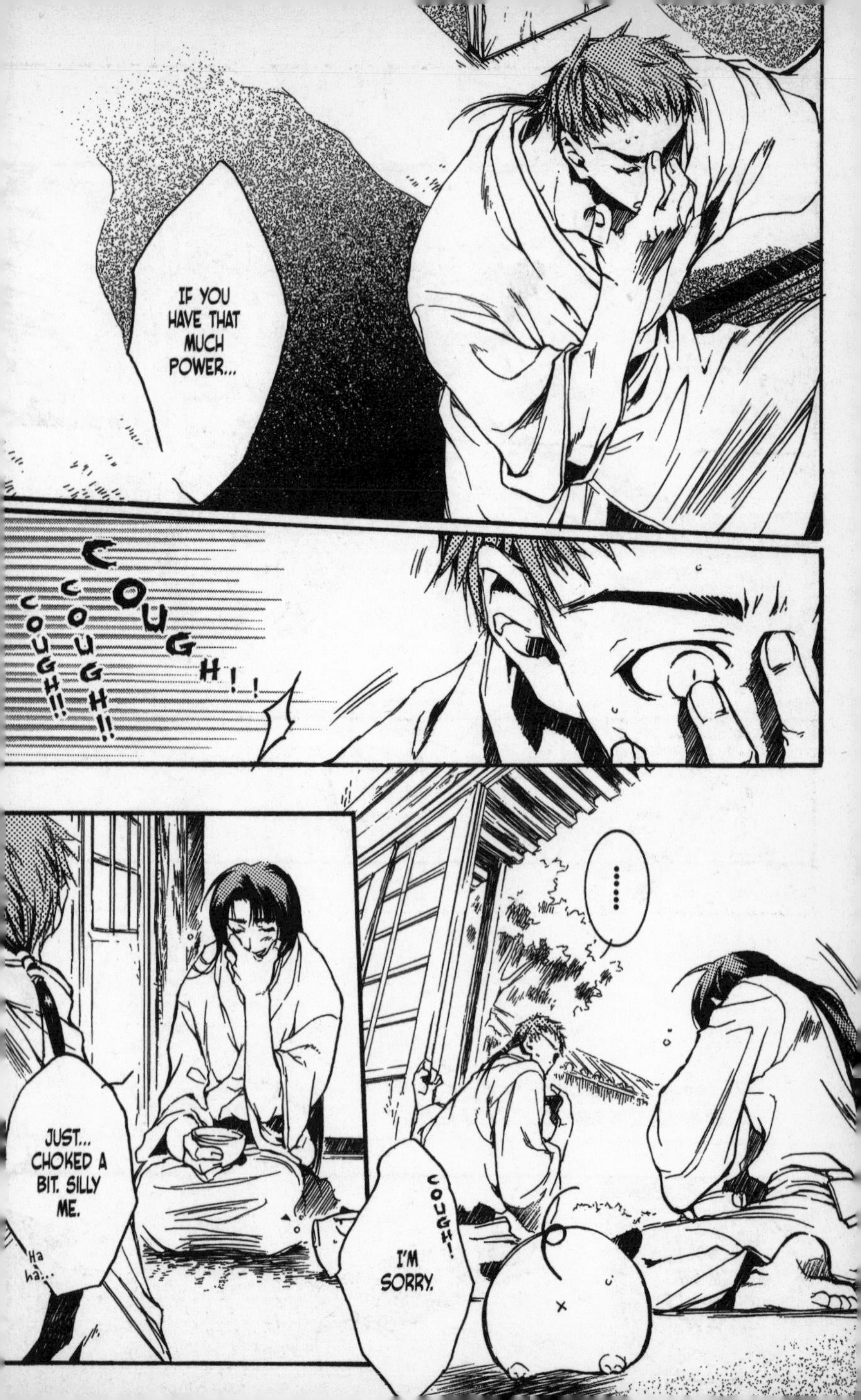
IF YOU HAVE THAT MUCH POWER...
COUGH!!
COUGH!!
COUGH!!
......
COUGH!
I'M SORRY.
JUST... CHOKED A BIT. SILLY ME.
Ha ha...

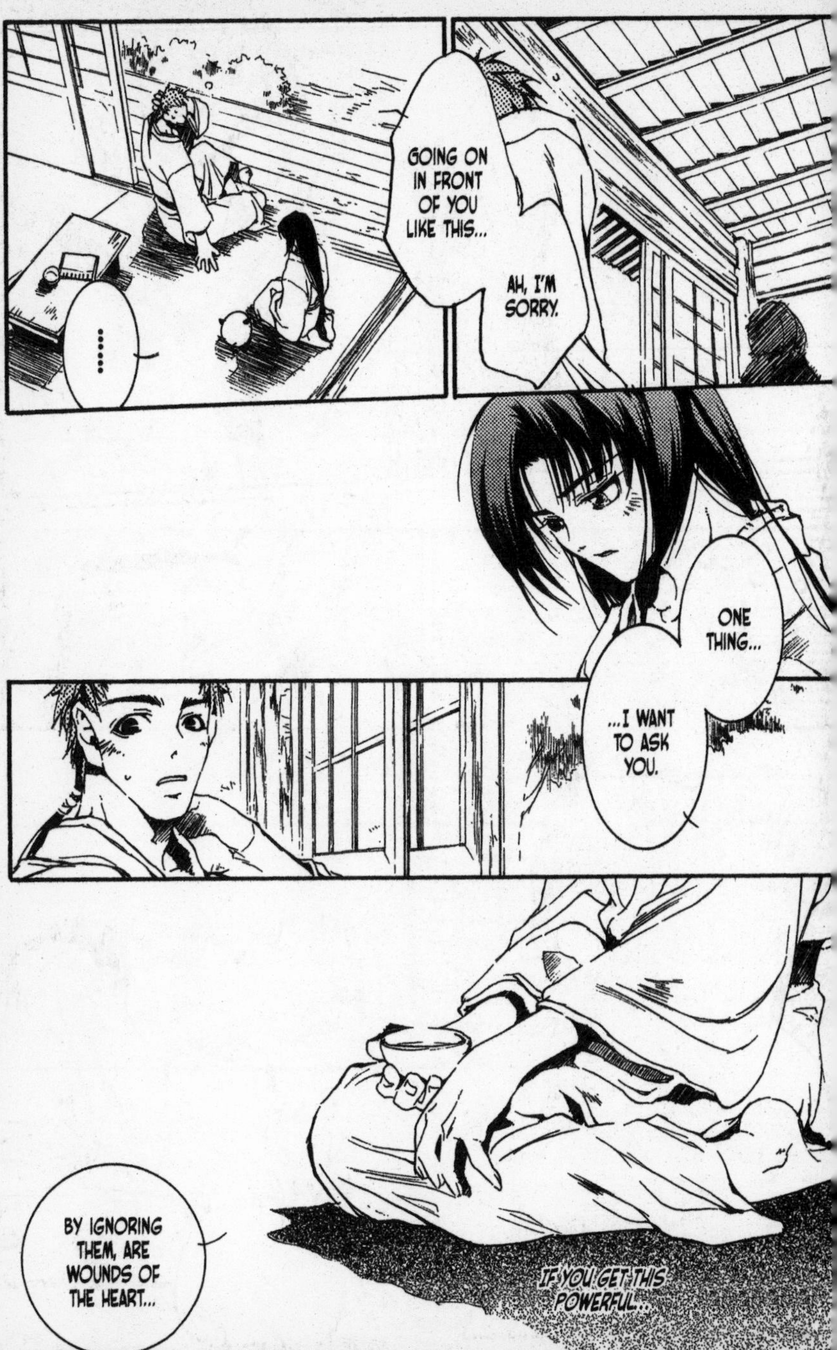
AH, I'M SORRY.
GOING ON IN FRONT OF YOU LIKE THIS...
......
ONE THING...
...I WANT TO ASK YOU.
IF YOU GET THIS POWERFUL...
BY IGNORING THEM, ARE WOUNDS OF THE HEART...

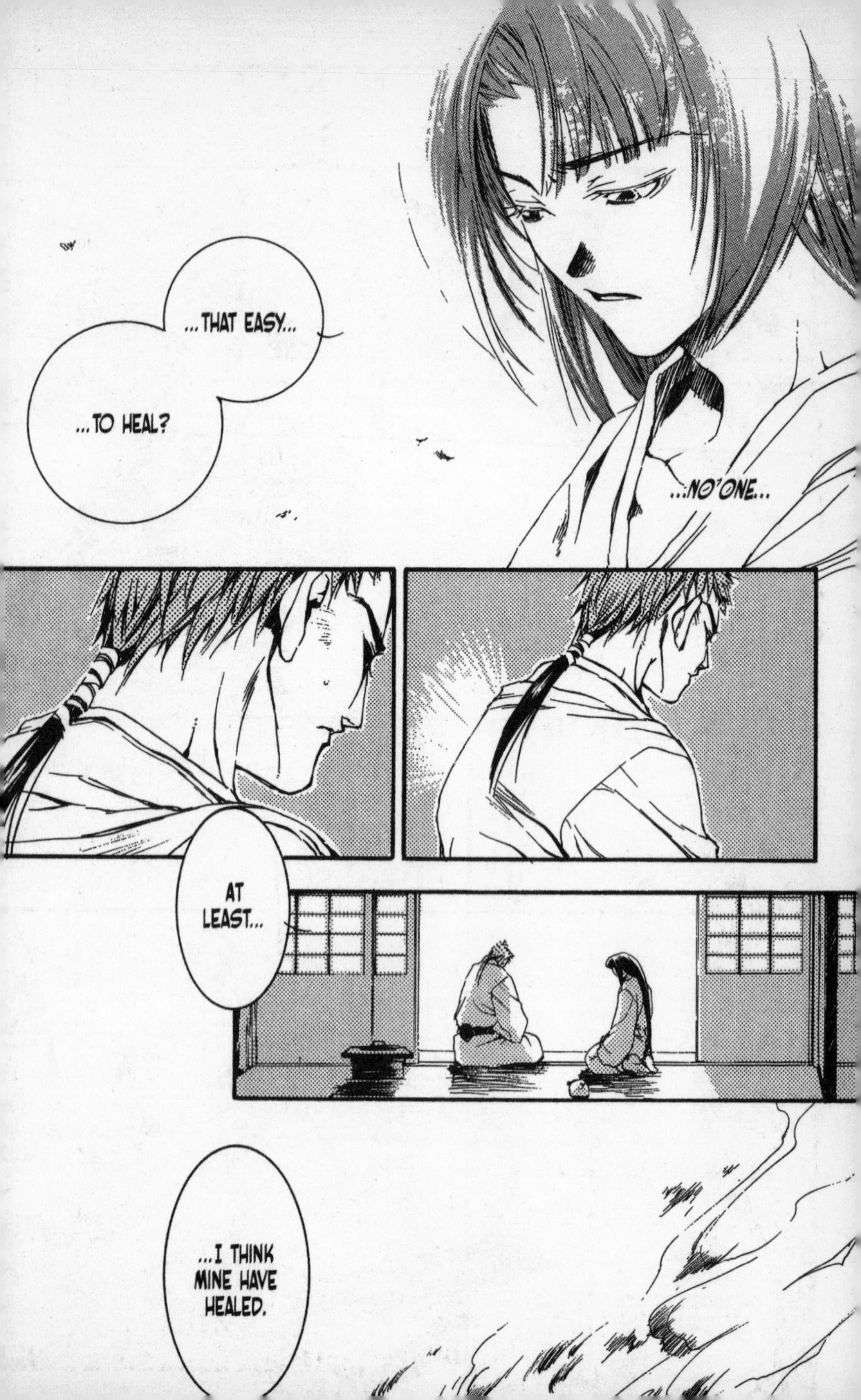
...NO ONE...
...THAT EASY...
...TO HEAL?
AT LEAST...
...I THINK MINE HAVE HEALED.

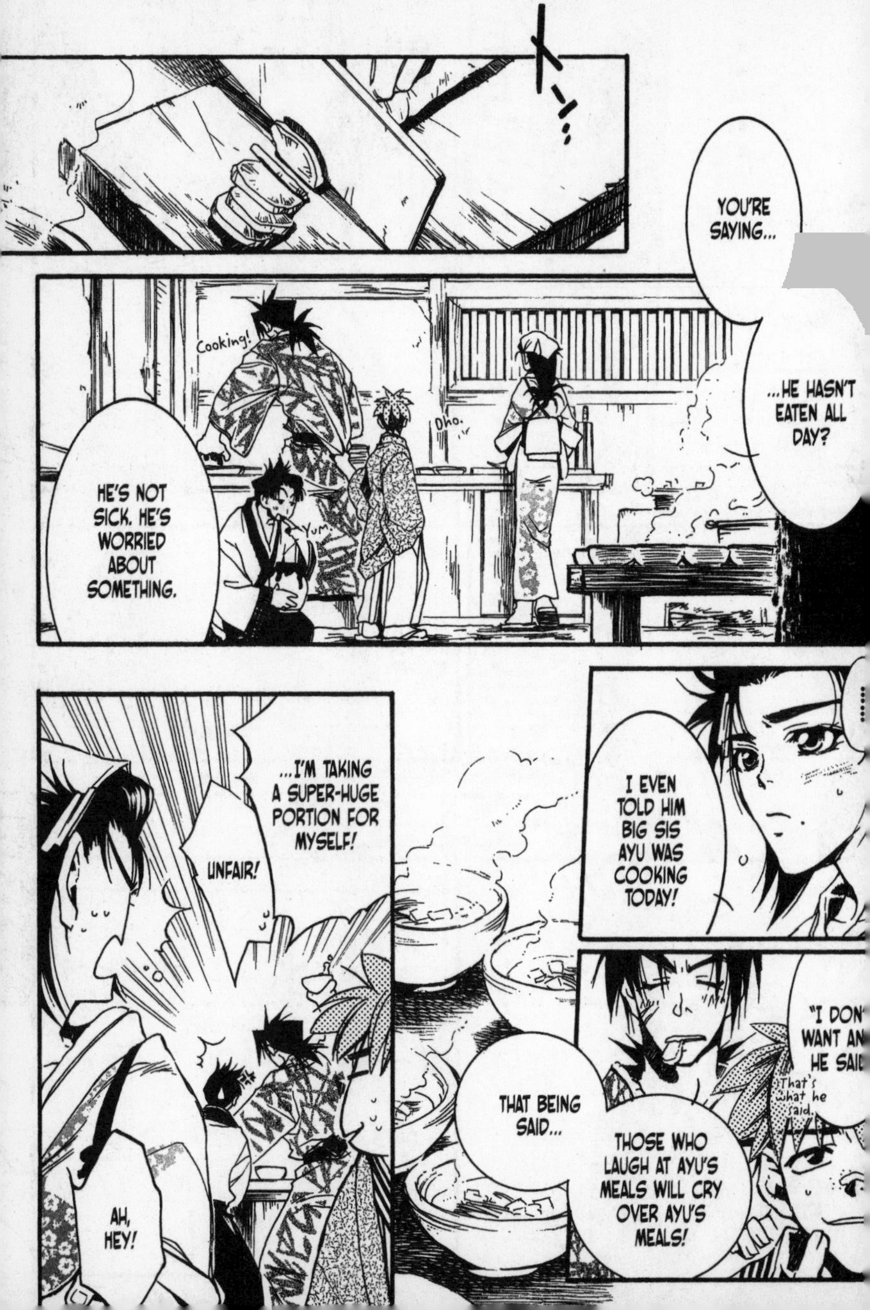
YOU'RE SAYING...
...HE HASN'T EATEN ALL DAY?
Oho.
Cooking!
Yum.
HE'S NOT SICK. HE'S WORRIED ABOUT SOMETHING.
I EVEN TOLD HIM BIG SIS AYU WAS COOKING TODAY!
"I DON WANT AN HE SAI
That's what he said.
THAT BEING SAID...
THOSE WHO LAUGH AT AYU'S MEALS WILL CRY OVER AYU'S MEALS!
...I'M TAKING A SUPER-HUGE PORTION FOR MYSELF!
UNFAIR!
AH, HEY!

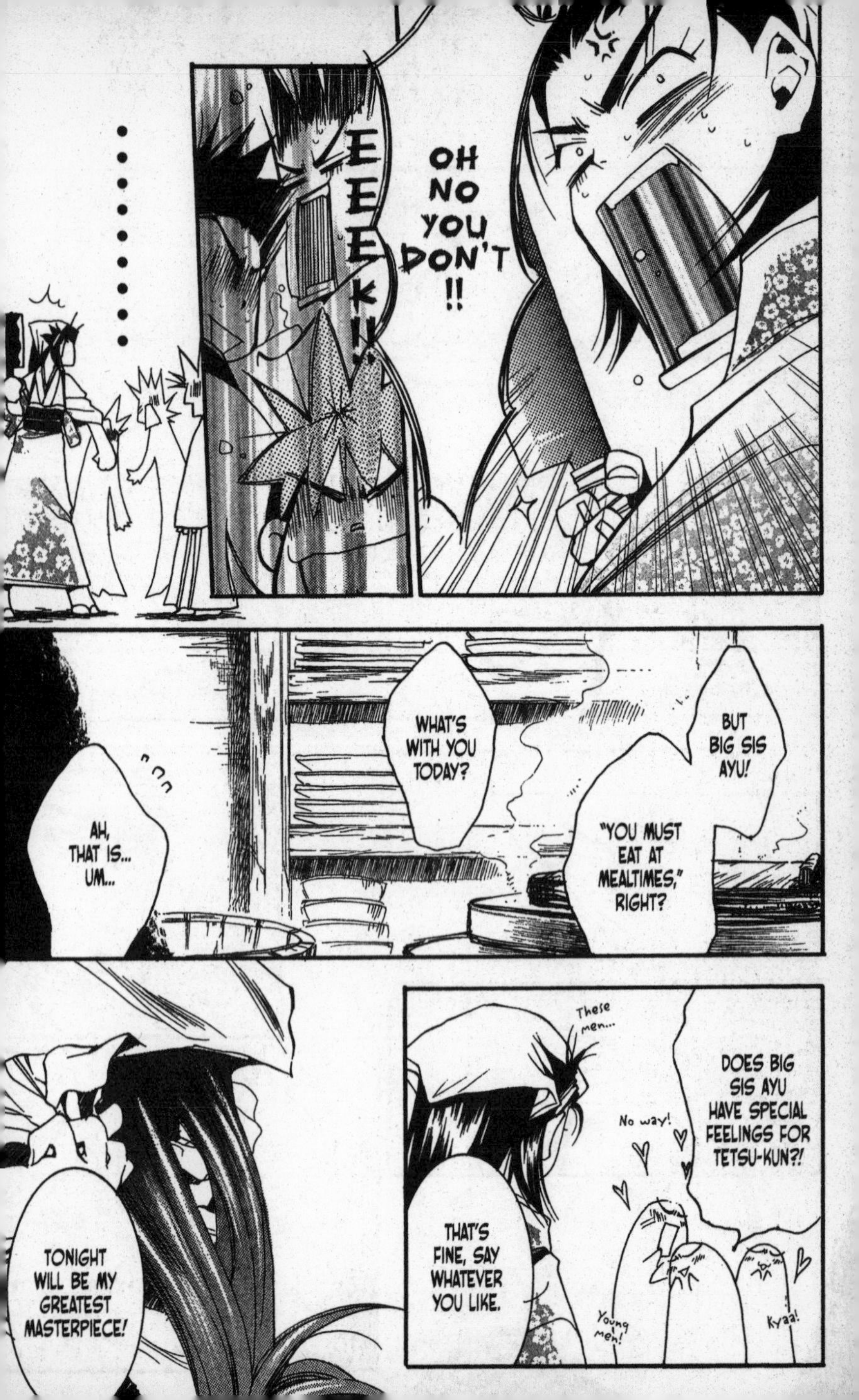
OH NO YOU DON'T!!
EEEEK!!
......
BUT BIG SIS AYU!
"YOU MUST EAT AT MEALTIMES," RIGHT?
WHAT'S WITH YOU TODAY?
AH, THAT IS... UM...
These men...
DOES BIG SIS AYU HAVE SPECIAL FEELINGS FOR TETSU-KUN?!
No way!
THAT'S FINE, SAY WHATEVER YOU LIKE.
Young men!
Kyaa!
TONIGHT WILL BE MY GREATEST MASTERPIECE!

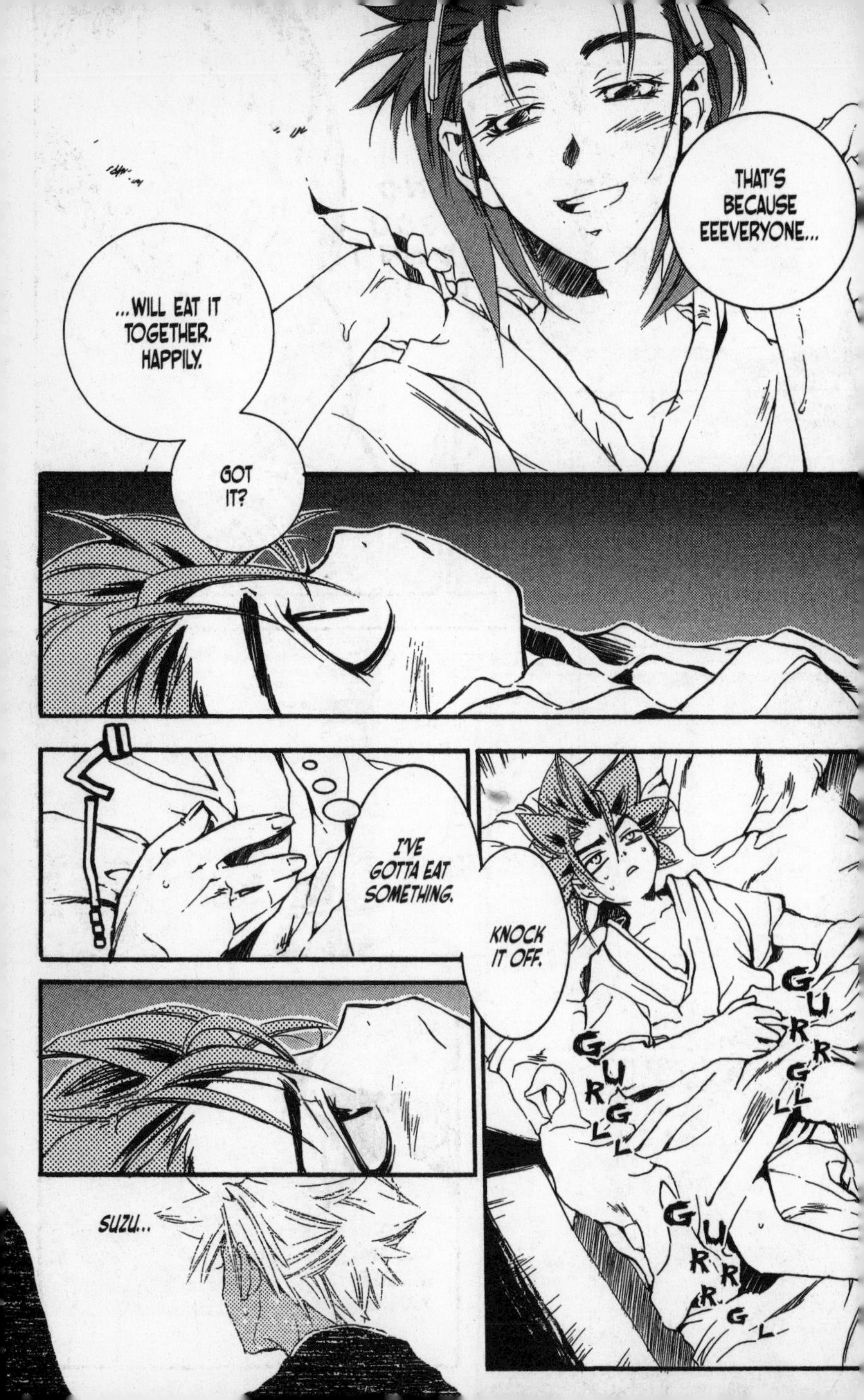
THAT'S BECAUSE EEEVERYONE...
...WILL EAT IT TOGETHER. HAPPILY.
GOT IT?
KNOCK IT OFF.
GURRGLL
GURGLL
GURRRRGL
I'VE GOTTA EAT SOMETHING.
SUZU...

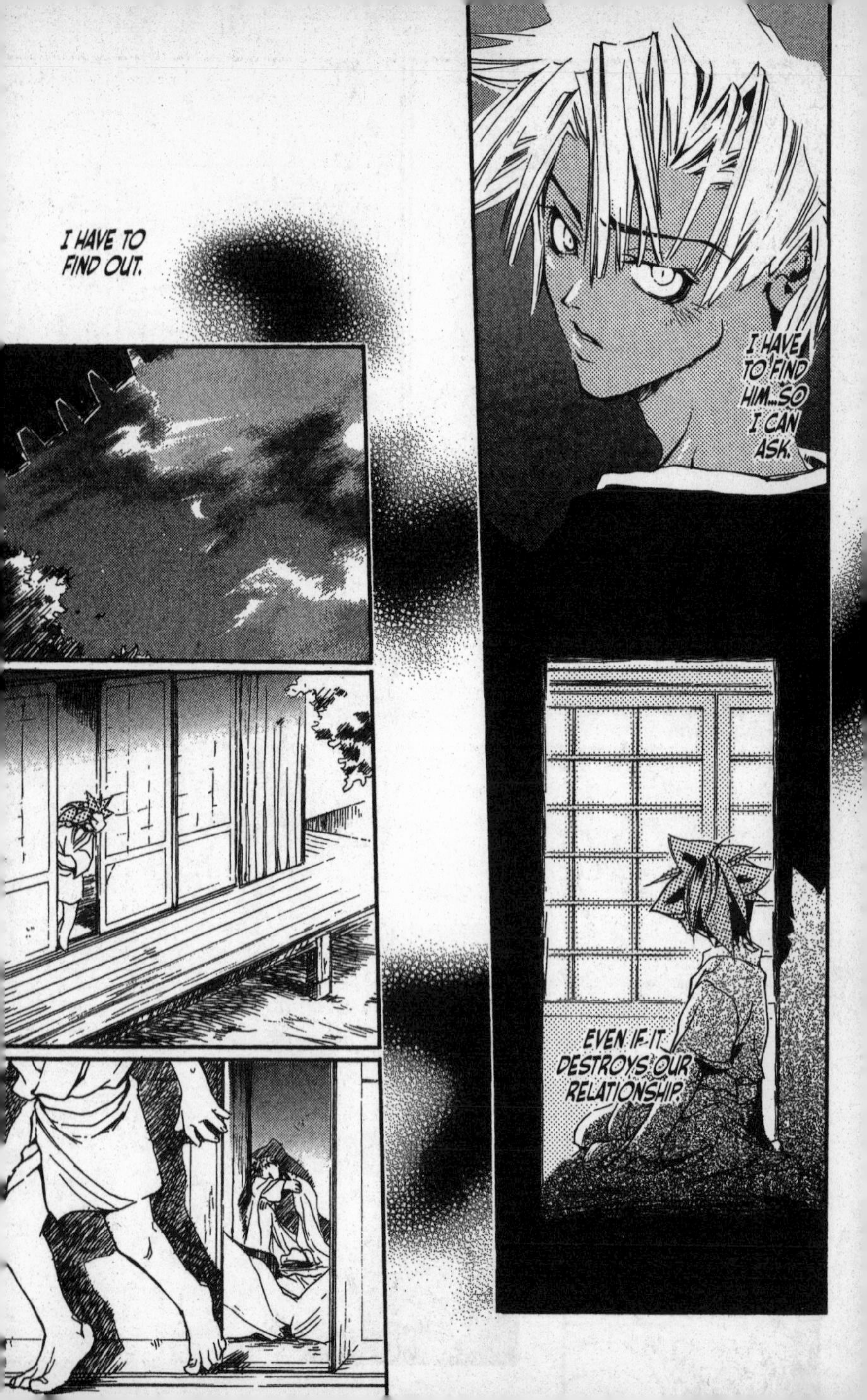
I HAVE TO FIND HIM...SO I CAN ASK.
EVEN IF IT DESTROYS OUR RELATIONSHIP.
I HAVE TO FIND OUT.

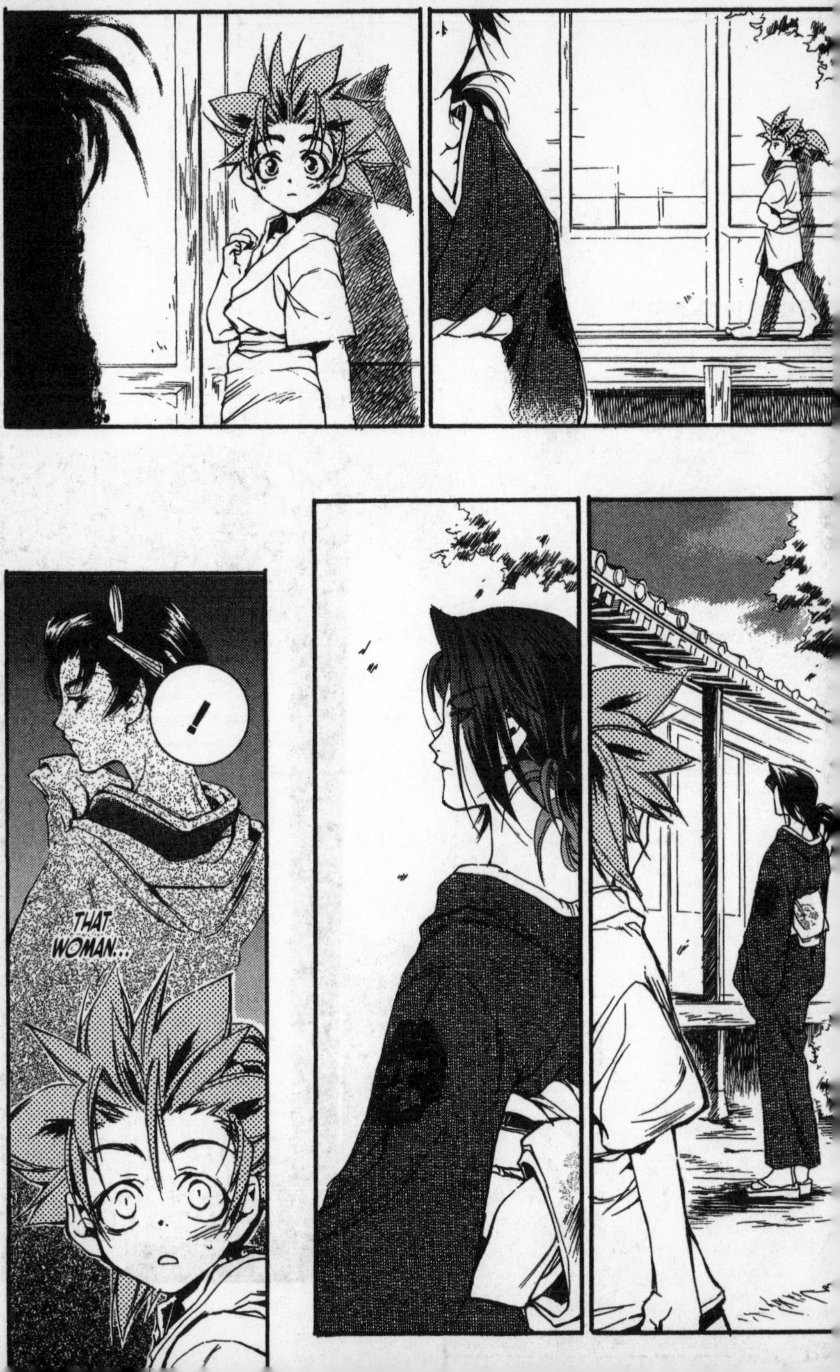
!
THAT WOMAN...

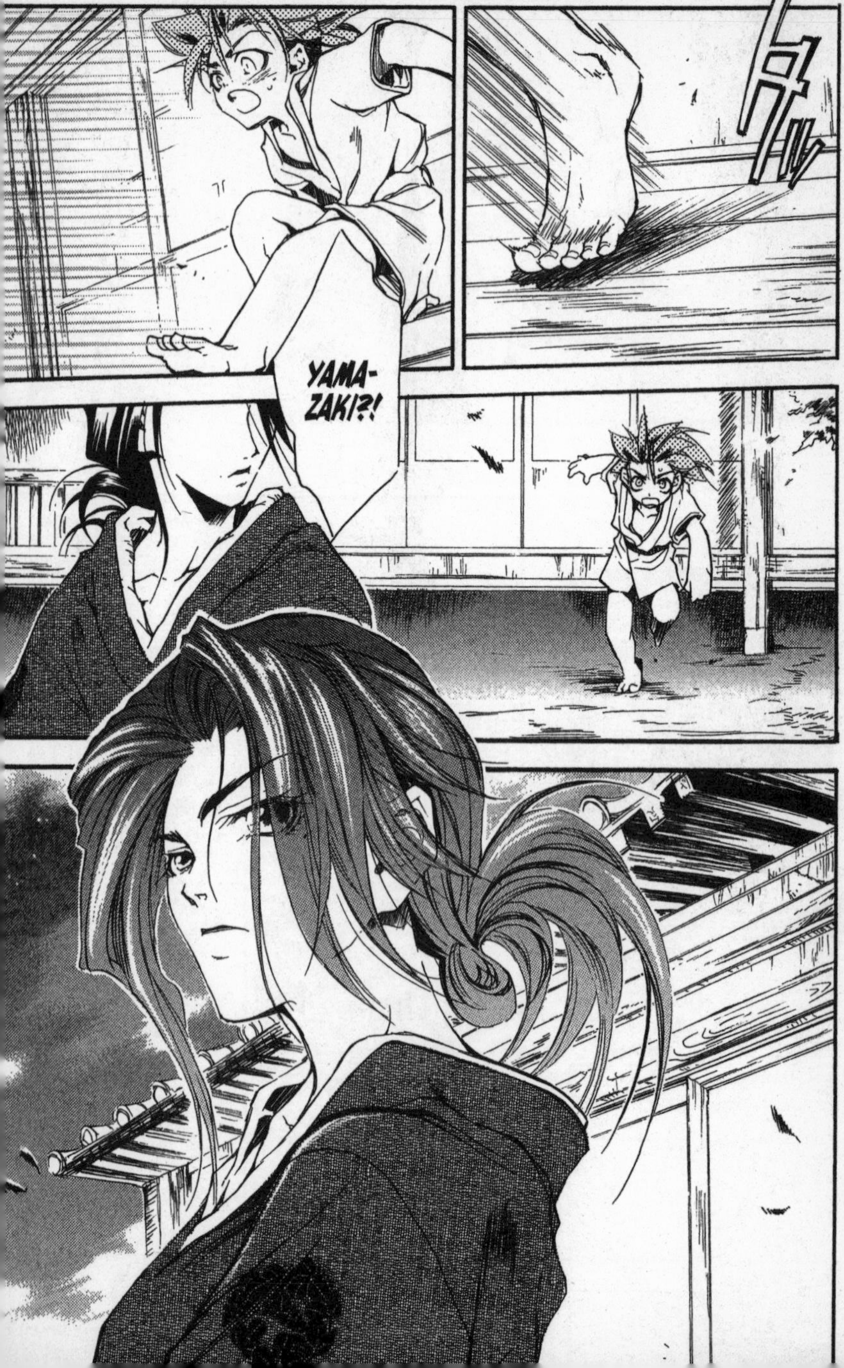
YAMA-ZAKI?!

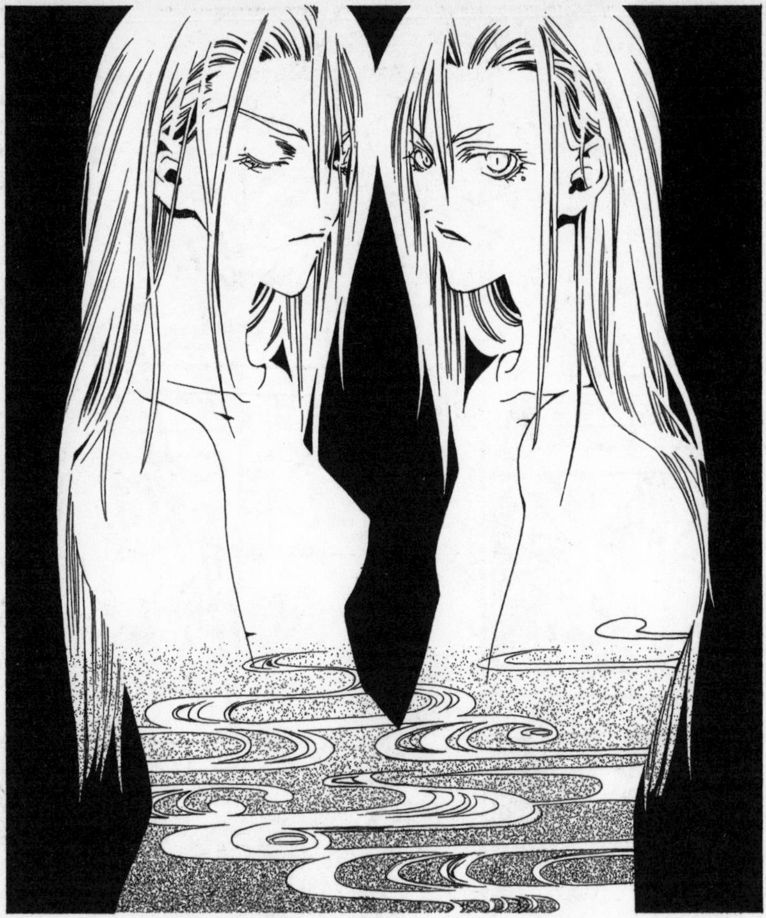

Act.17
I'm Looking Through You

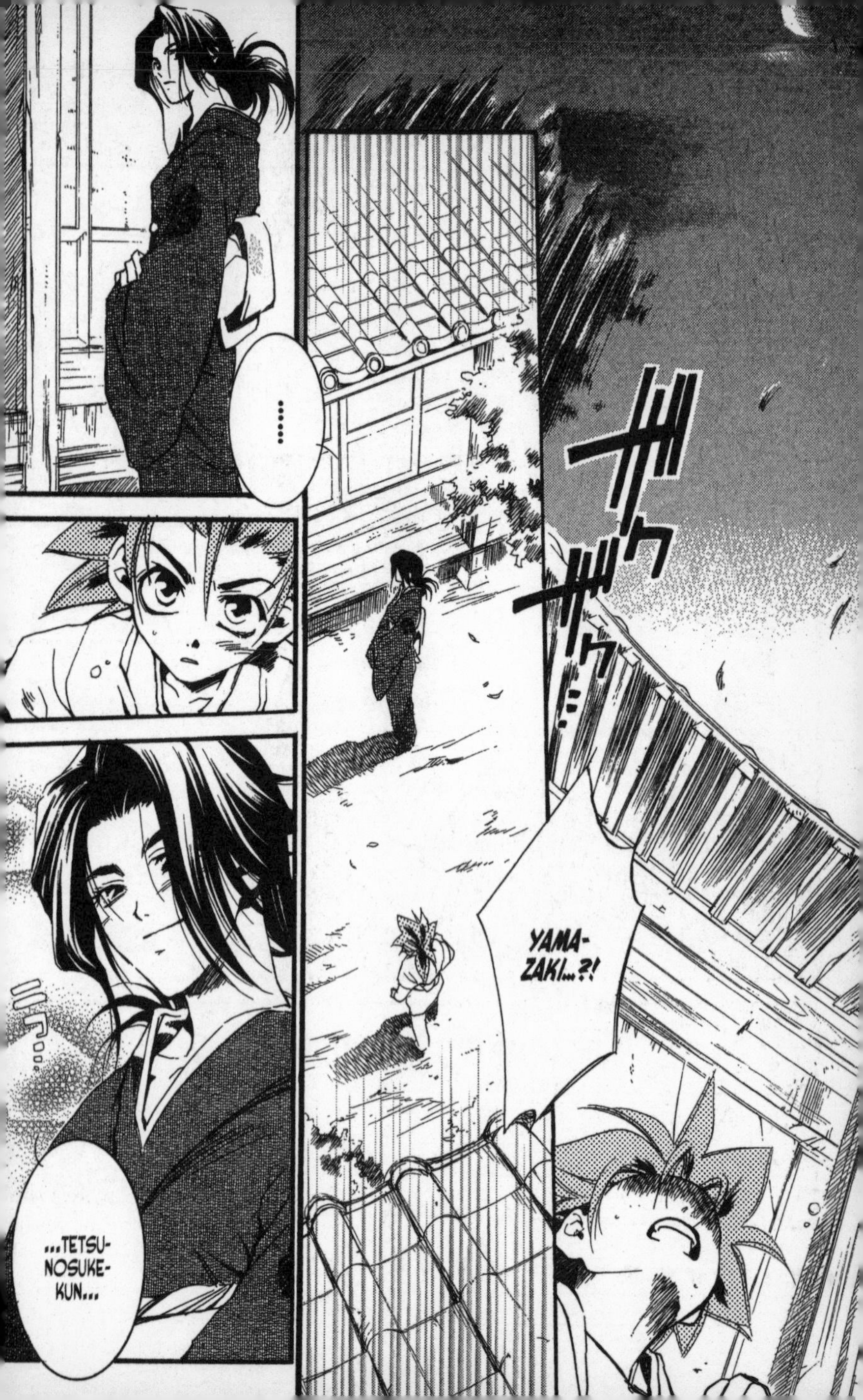
ザクザク…
YAMA-ZAKI...?!
......
ニコッ…
...TETSU-NOSUKE-KUN...

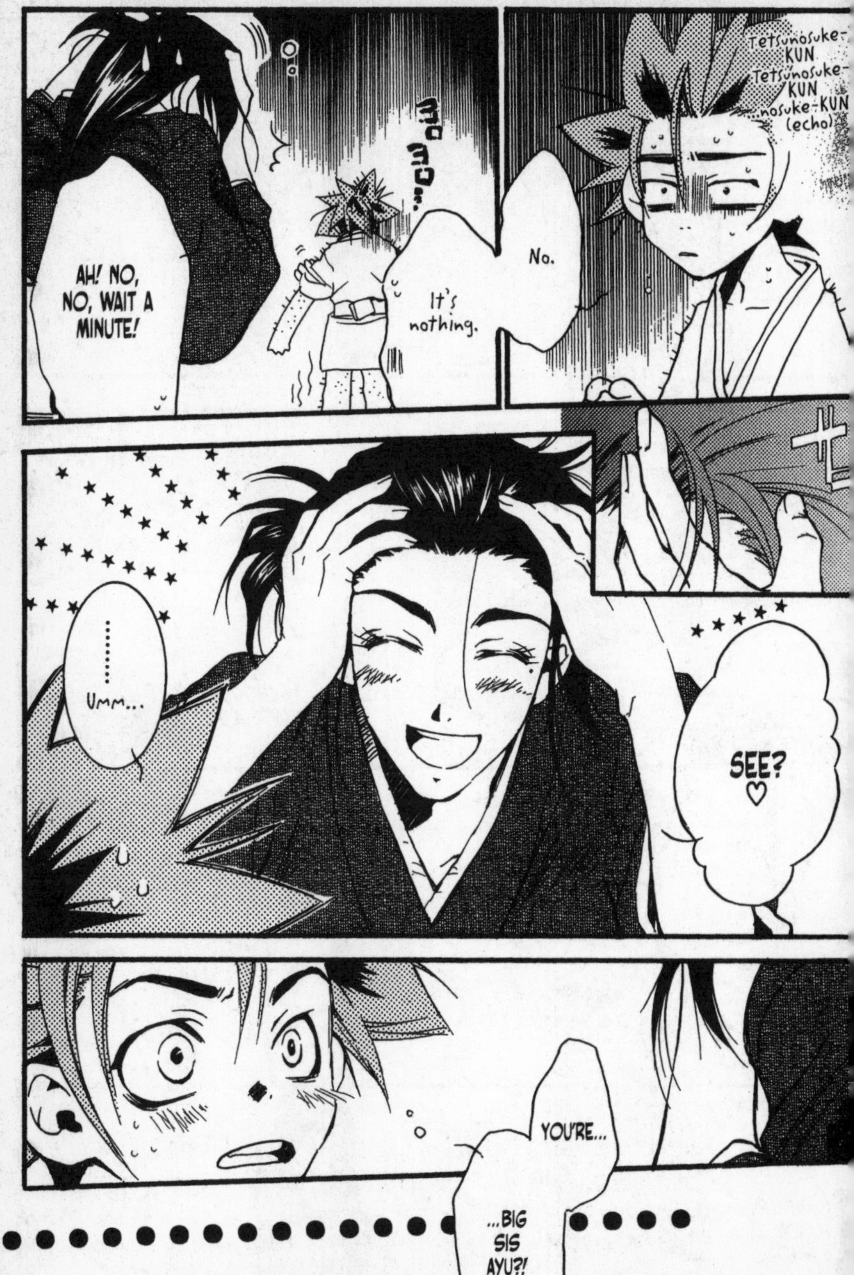
Tetsunosuke-KUN Tetsunosuke-KUN ...nosuke-KUN (echo)
No.
It's nothing.
AH! NO, NO, WAIT A MINUTE!
SEE? ♡
......
Umm...
YOU'RE...
...BIG SIS AYU?!

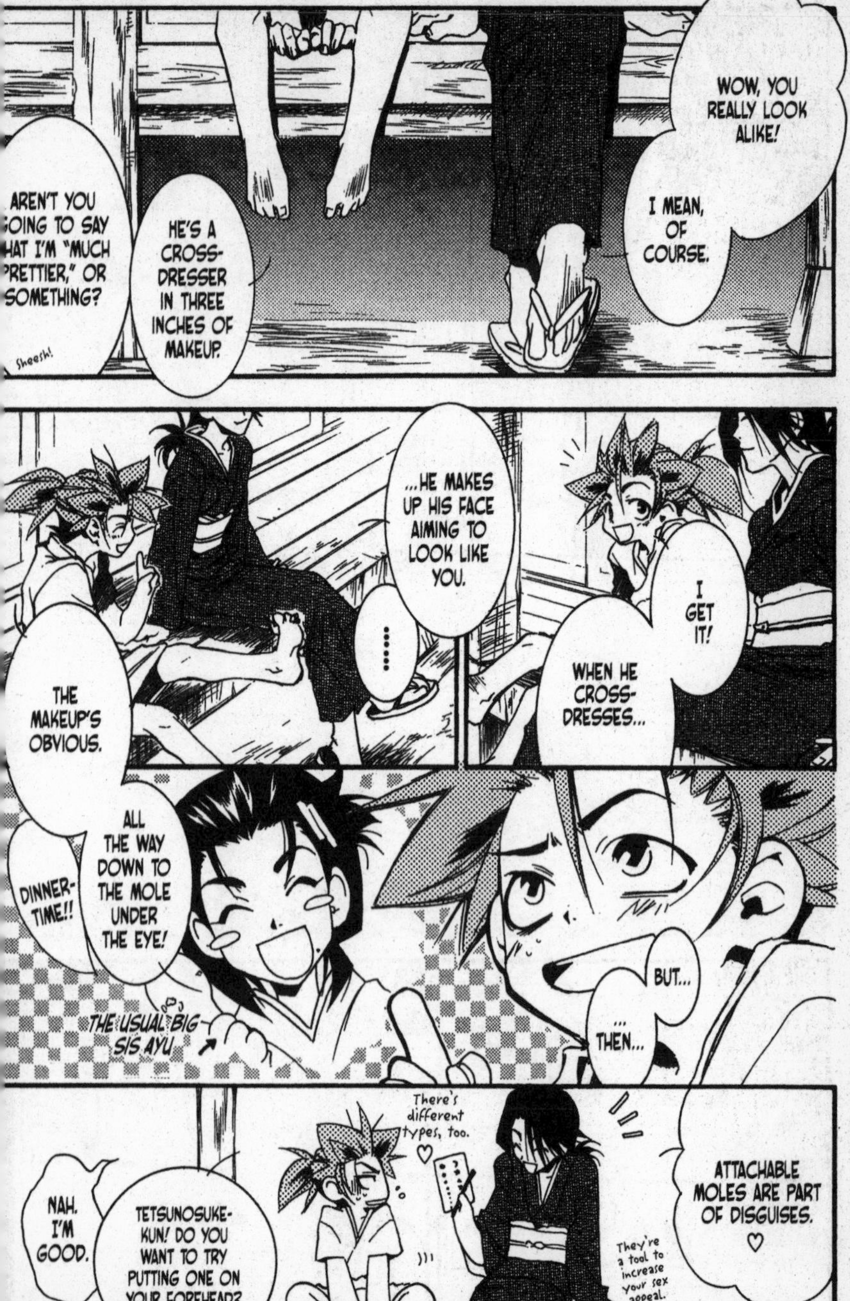
WOW, YOU REALLY LOOK ALIKE!
I MEAN, OF COURSE.
HE'S A CROSS-DRESSER IN THREE INCHES OF MAKEUP.
AREN'T YOU GOING TO SAY HAT I'M "MUCH PRETTIER," OR SOMETHING?
Sheesh!
I GET IT!
WHEN HE CROSS-DRESSES...
...HE MAKES UP HIS FACE AIMING TO LOOK LIKE YOU.
......
THE MAKEUP'S OBVIOUS.
BUT...
...THEN...
ALL THE WAY DOWN TO THE MOLE UNDER THE EYE!
THE USUAL BIG SIS AYU
DINNER-TIME!!
ATTACHABLE MOLES ARE PART OF DISGUISES. ♡
They're a tool to increase your sex appeal. ♡
There's different types, too. ♡
TETSUNOSUKE-KUN! DO YOU WANT TO TRY PUTTING ONE ON YOUR FOREHEAD?
NAH. I'M GOOD.

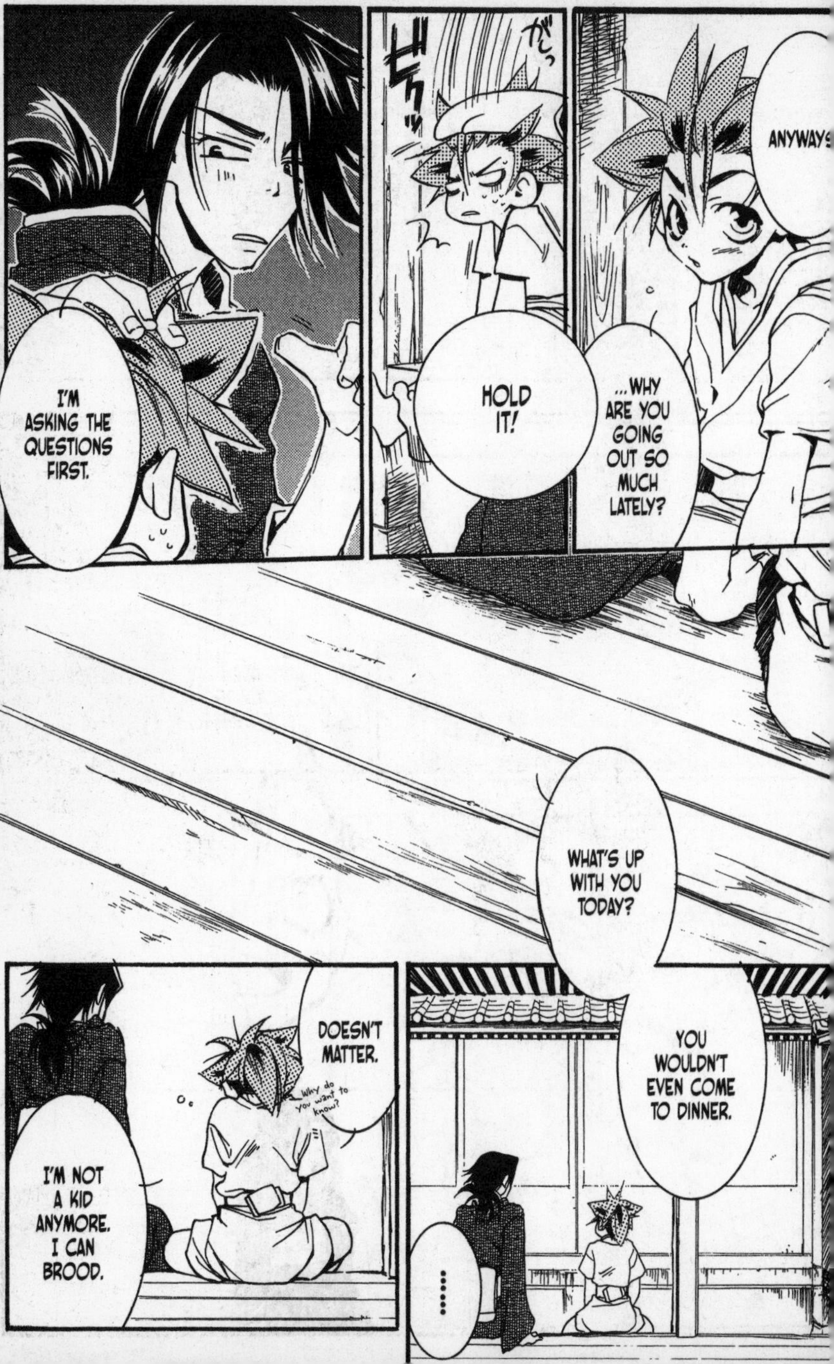
ANYWAYS
...WHY ARE YOU GOING OUT SO MUCH LATELY?
がしっ
ビクッ
HOLD IT!
I'M ASKING THE QUESTIONS FIRST.
WHAT'S UP WITH YOU TODAY?
YOU WOULDN'T EVEN COME TO DINNER.
......
DOESN'T MATTER.
Why do you want to know?
I'M NOT A KID ANYMORE. I CAN BROOD.

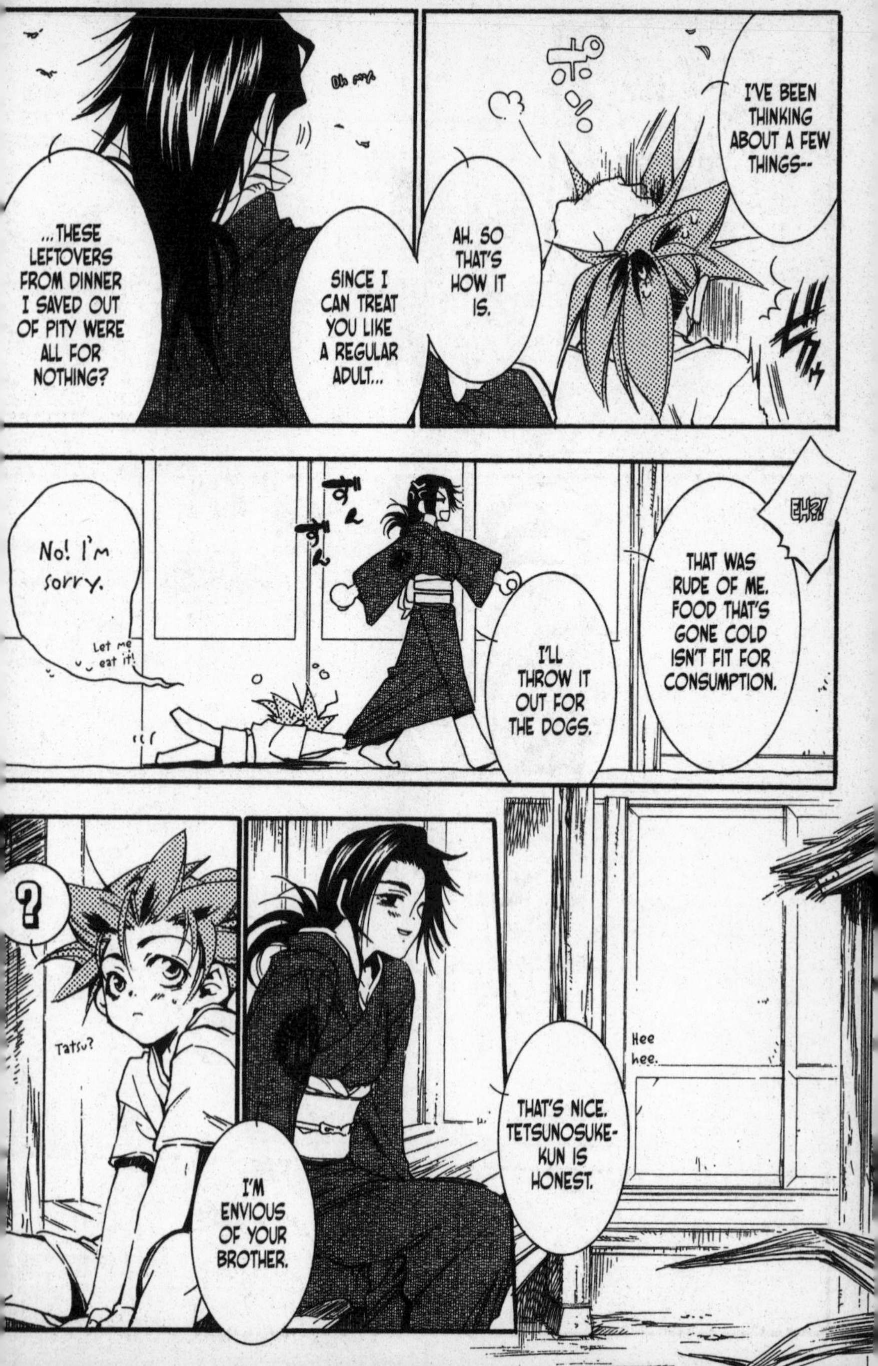
I'VE BEEN THINKING ABOUT A FEW THINGS--
AH. SO THAT'S HOW IT IS.
Oh my.
SINCE I CAN TREAT YOU LIKE A REGULAR ADULT...
...THESE LEFTOVERS FROM DINNER I SAVED OUT OF PITY WERE ALL FOR NOTHING?
EH?!
THAT WAS RUDE OF ME. FOOD THAT'S GONE COLD ISN'T FIT FOR CONSUMPTION.
I'LL THROW IT OUT FOR THE DOGS.
No! I'm sorry.
Let me eat it!
Hee hee.
THAT'S NICE. TETSUNOSUKE-KUN IS HONEST.
I'M ENVIOUS OF YOUR BROTHER.
?
Tatsu?

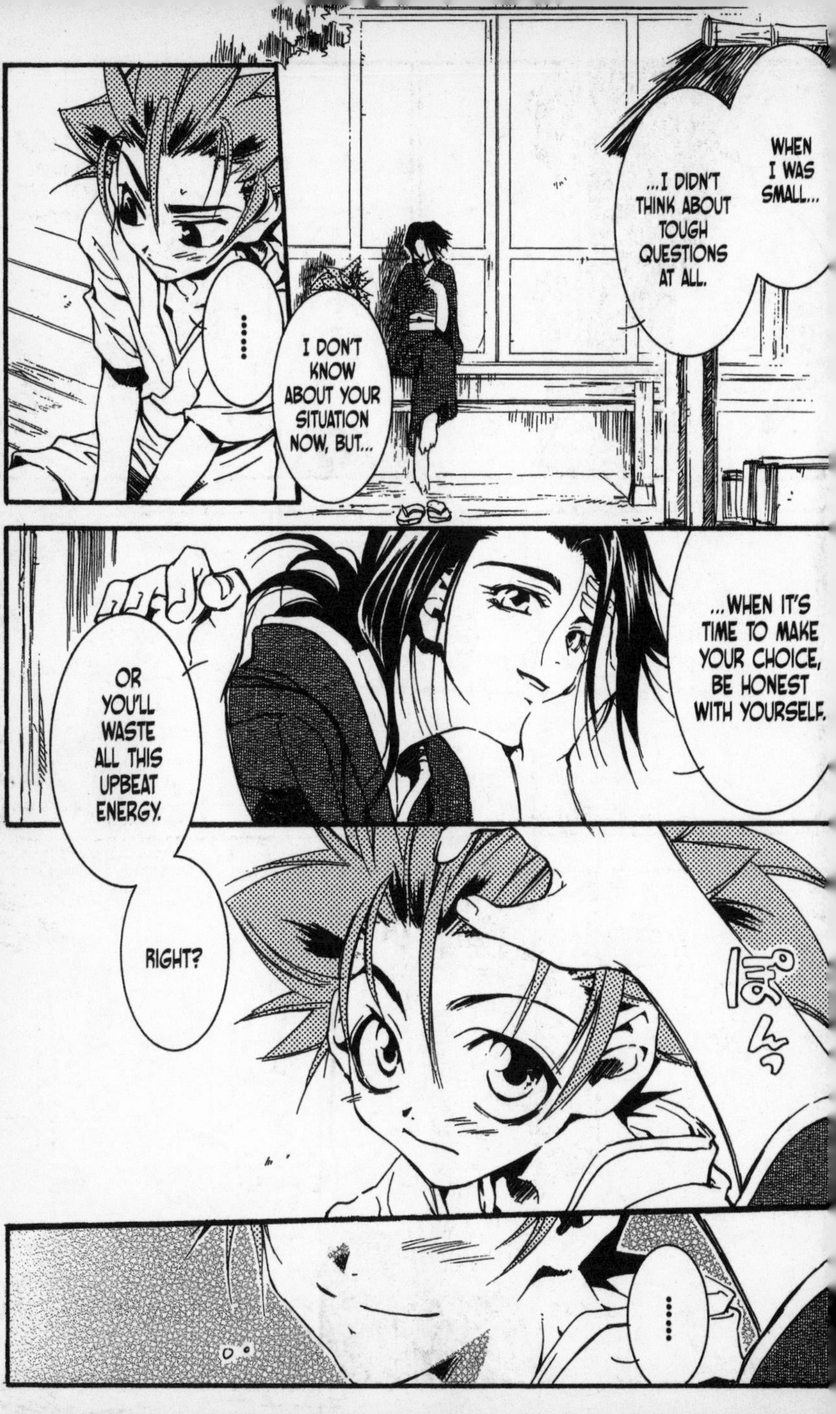
WHEN I WAS SMALL...
...I DIDN'T THINK ABOUT TOUGH QUESTIONS AT ALL.
I DON'T KNOW ABOUT YOUR SITUATION NOW, BUT...
......
...WHEN IT'S TIME TO MAKE YOUR CHOICE, BE HONEST WITH YOURSELF.
OR YOU'LL WASTE ALL THIS UPBEAT ENERGY.
RIGHT?
ぽんっ
......

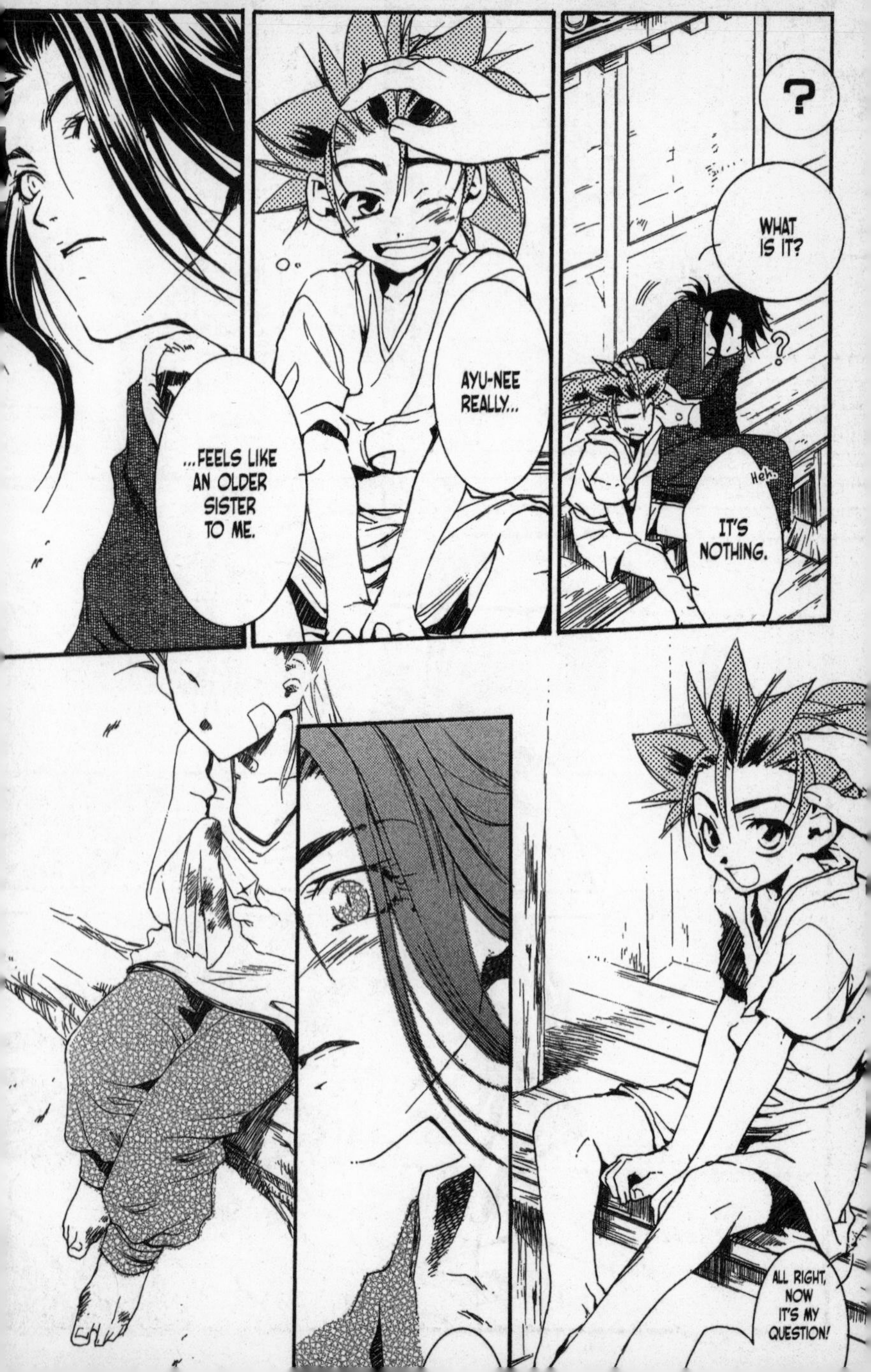
?
WHAT IS IT?
Heh.
IT'S NOTHING.
AYU-NEE REALLY...
...FEELS LIKE AN OLDER SISTER TO ME.
ALL RIGHT, NOW IT'S MY QUESTION!

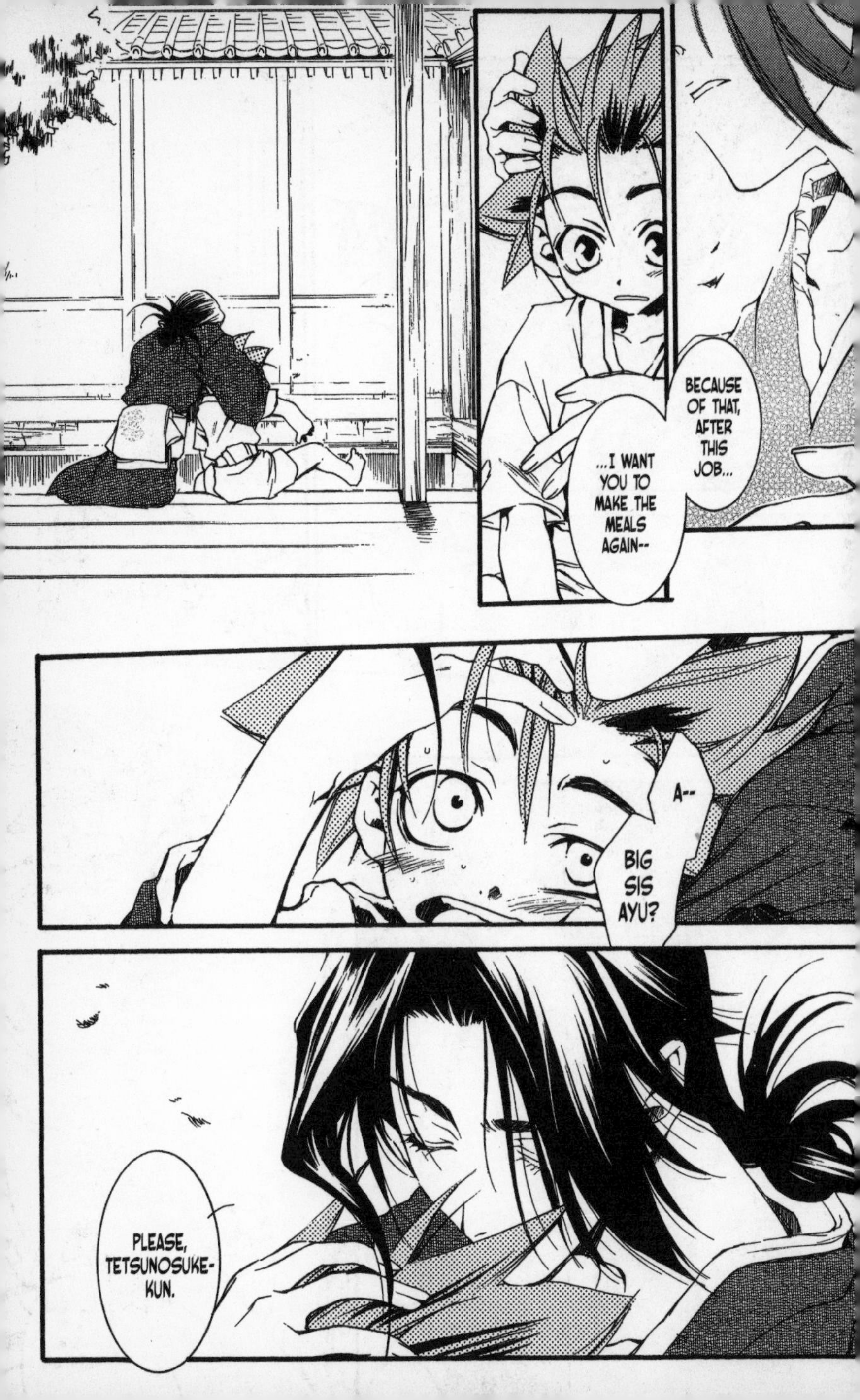
BECAUSE OF THAT, AFTER THIS JOB...
...I WANT YOU TO MAKE THE MEALS AGAIN--
A--
BIG SIS AYU?
PLEASE, TETSUNOSUKE-KUN.

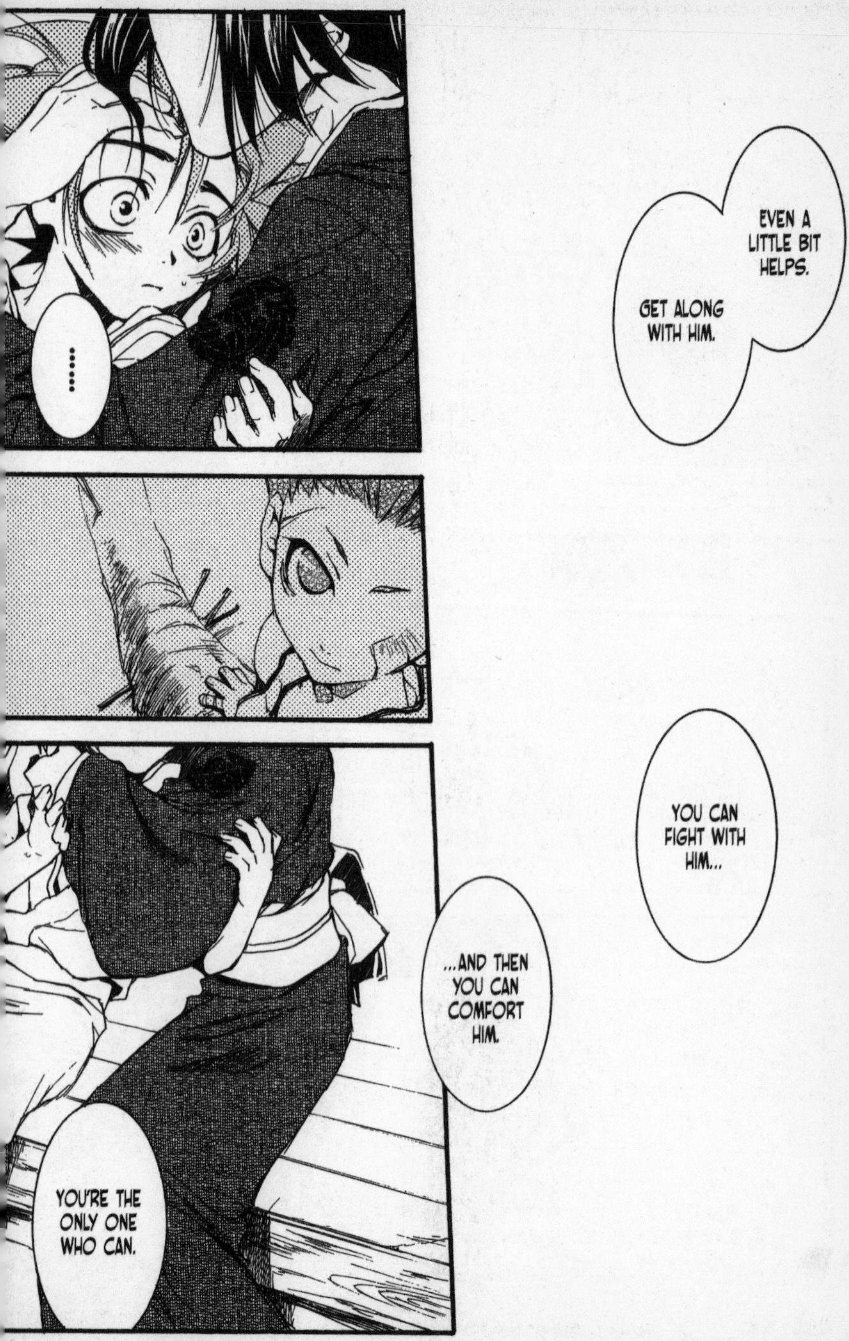
EVEN A LITTLE BIT HELPS.
GET ALONG WITH HIM.
......
YOU CAN FIGHT WITH HIM...
...AND THEN YOU CAN COMFORT HIM.
YOU'RE THE ONLY ONE WHO CAN.

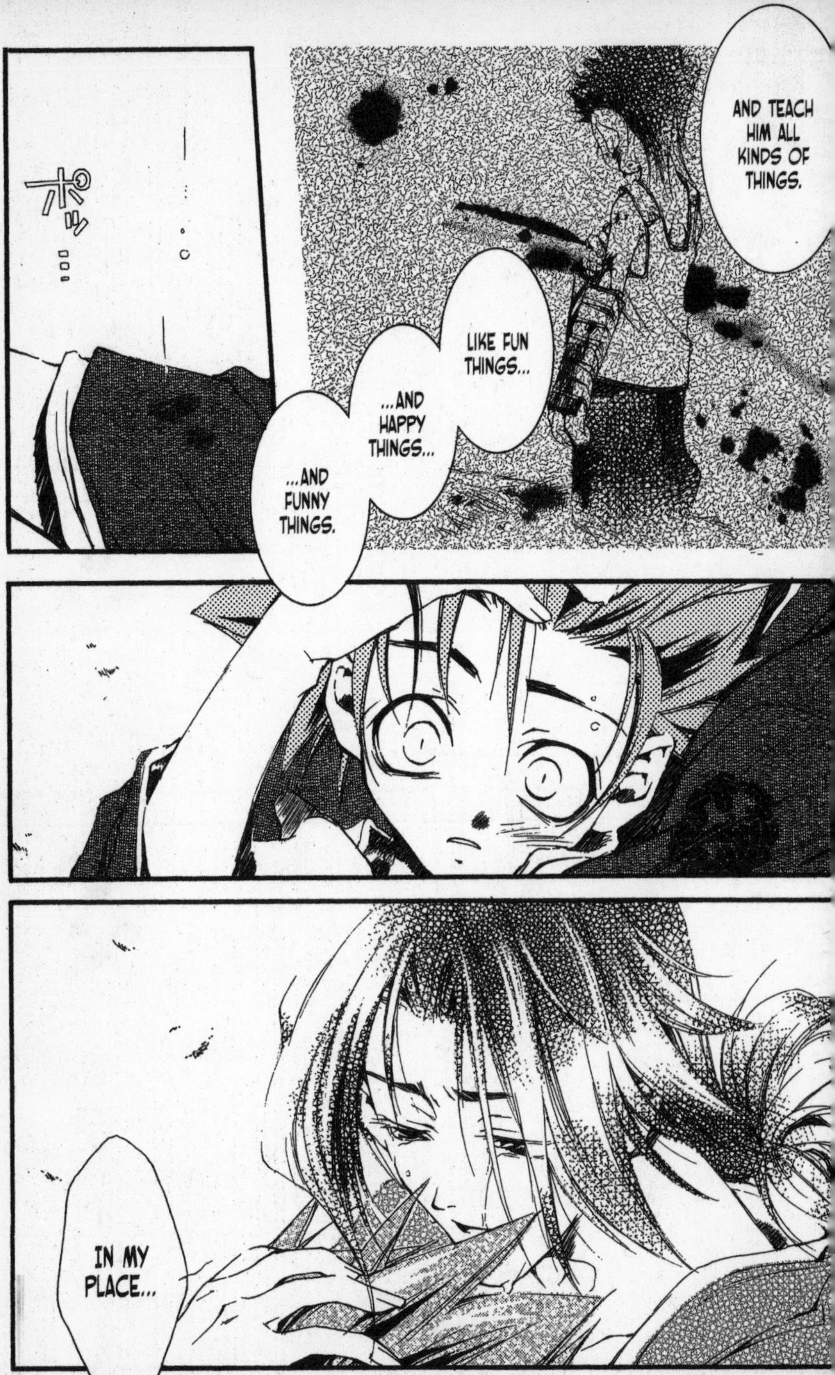
AND TEACH HIM ALL KINDS OF THINGS.
LIKE FUN THINGS...
...AND HAPPY THINGS...
...AND FUNNY THINGS.
ポッ...
IN MY PLACE...

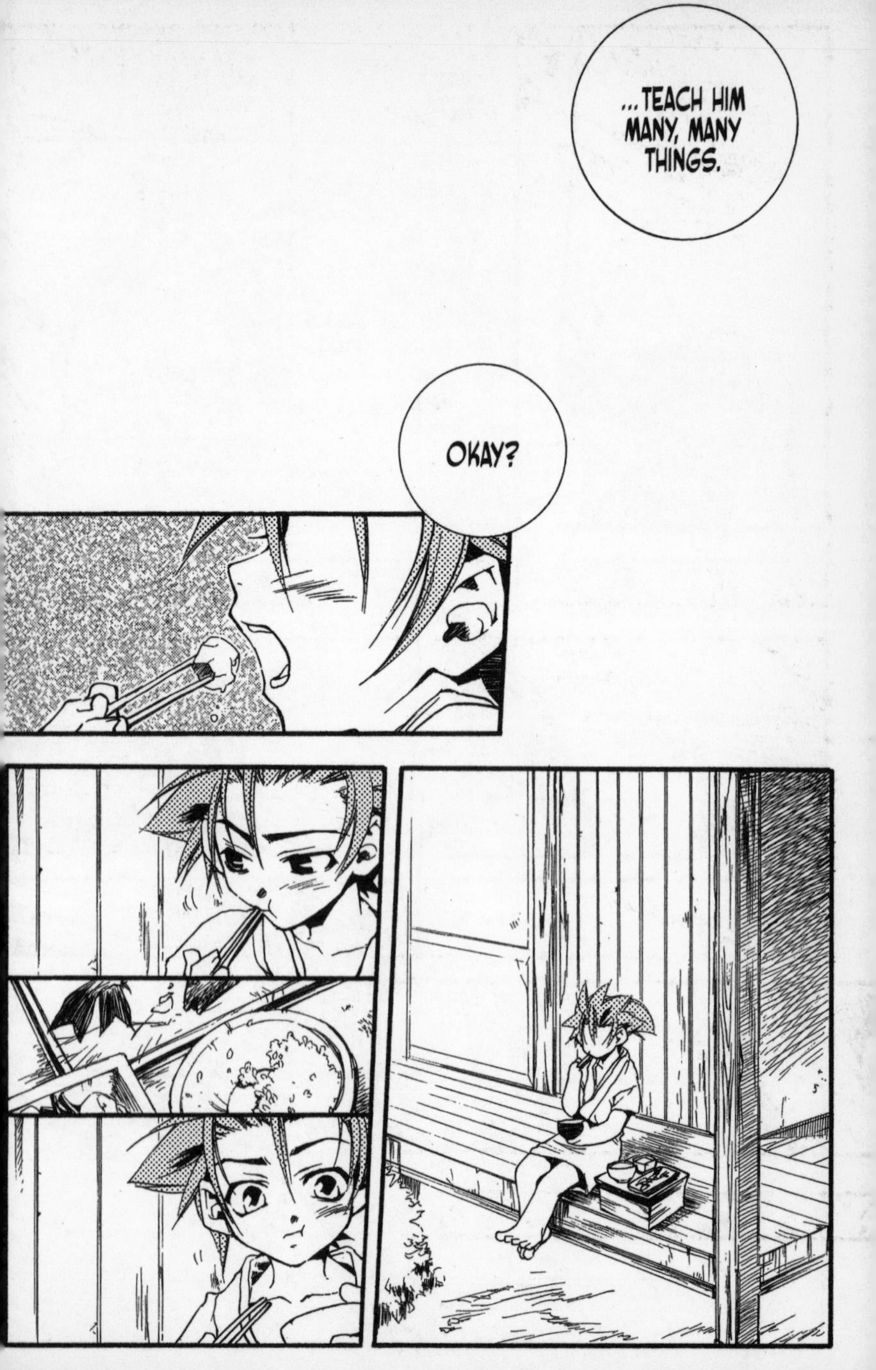
...TEACH HIM MANY, MANY THINGS.
OKAY?

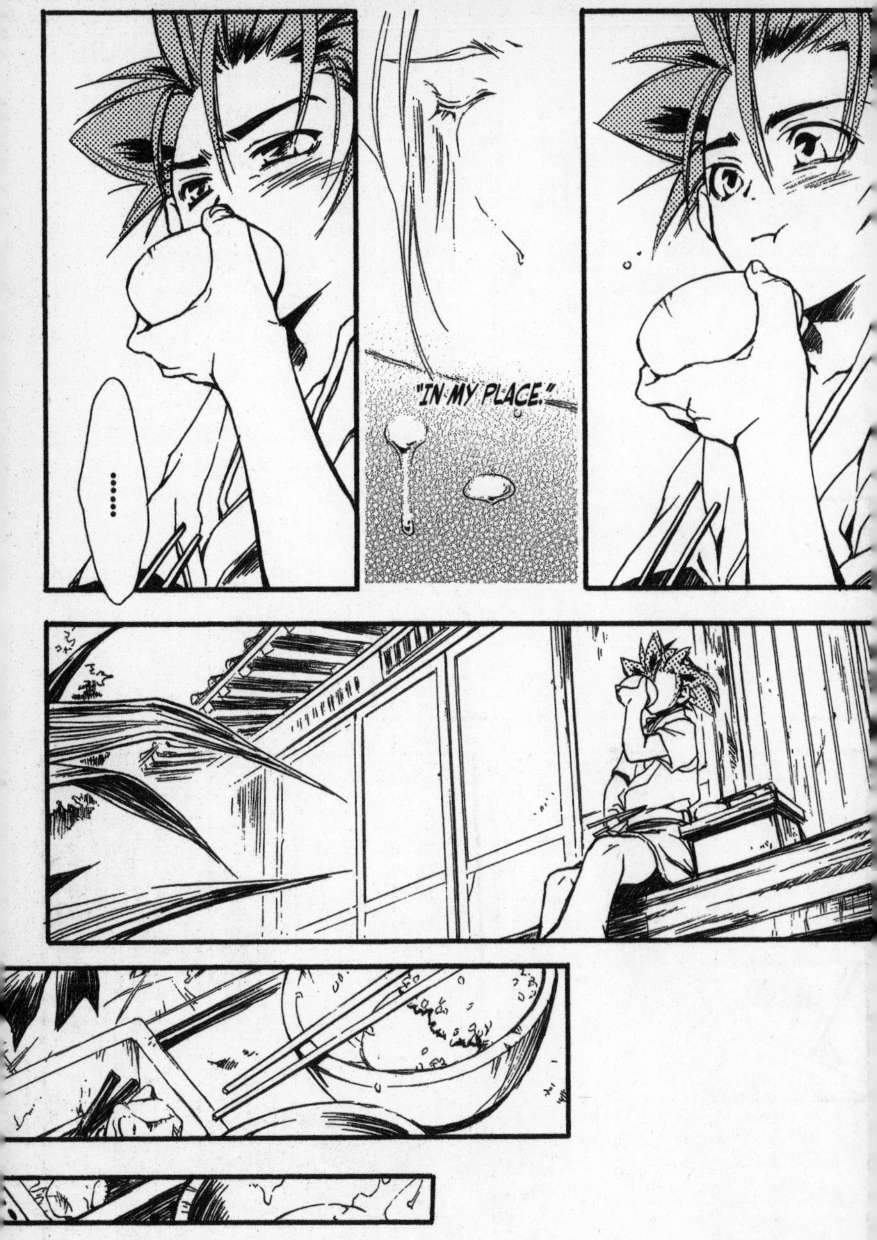
"IN MY PLACE."
......

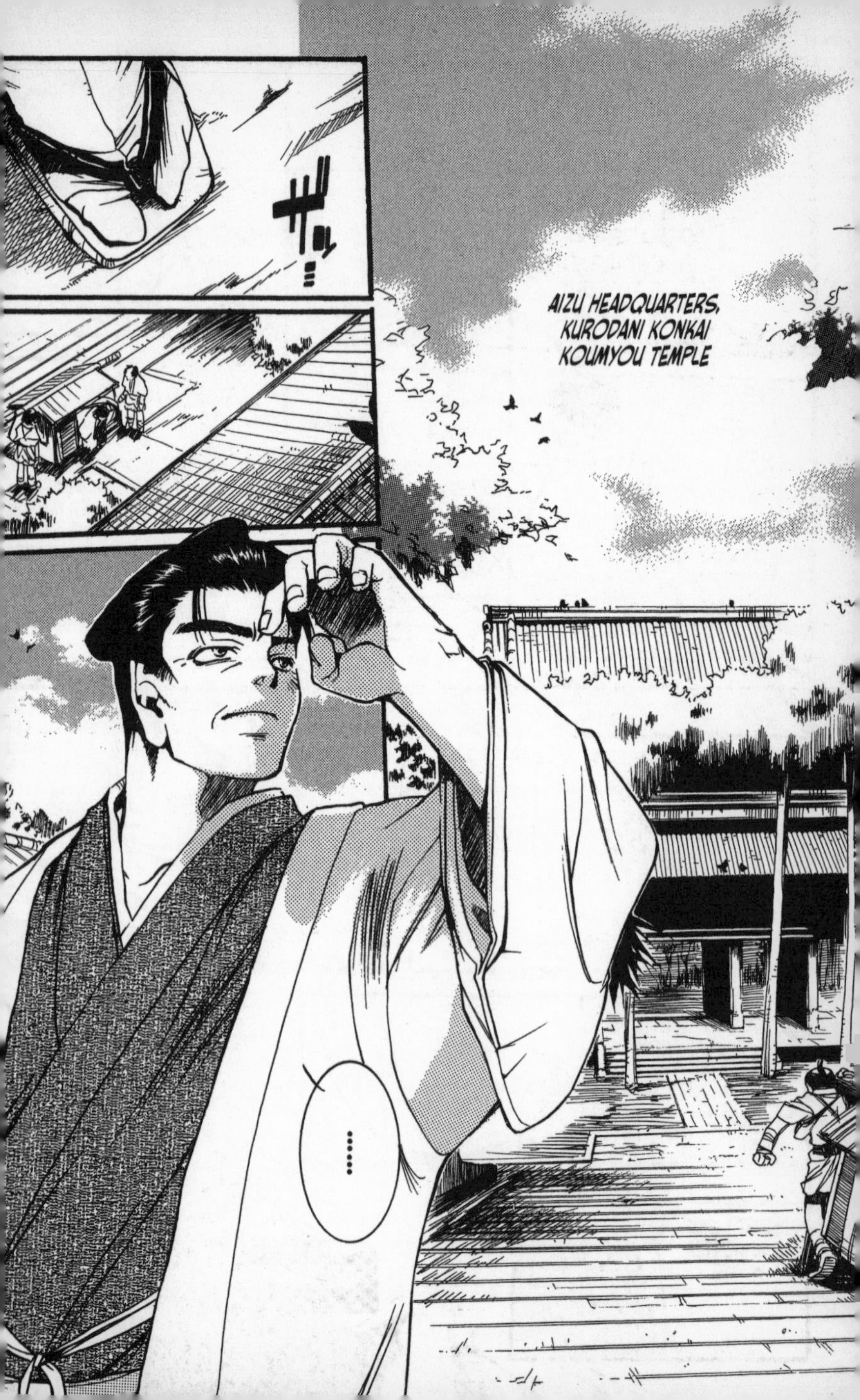
AIZU HEADQUARTERS, KURODANI KONKAI KOUMYOU TEMPLE
ザッ
......

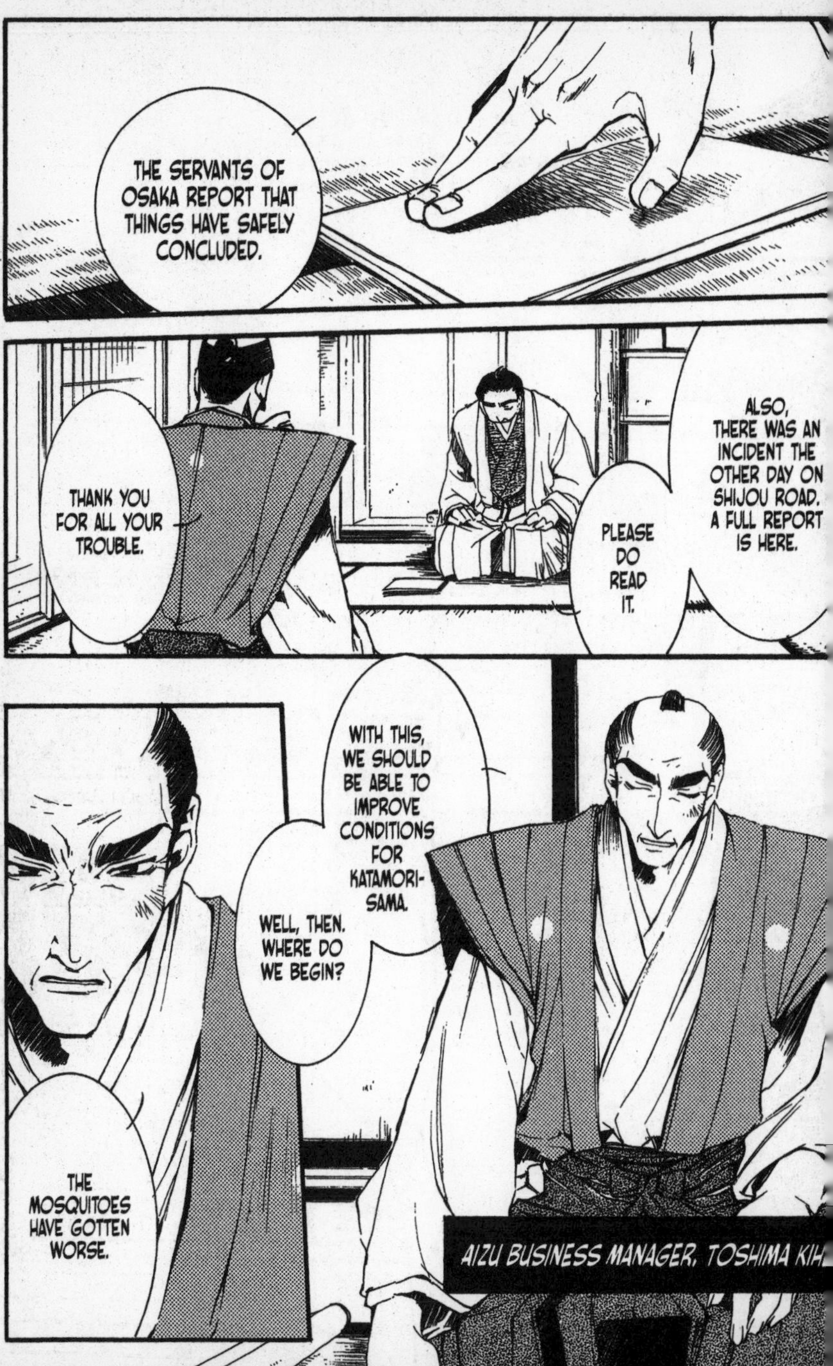
THE SERVANTS OF OSAKA REPORT THAT THINGS HAVE SAFELY CONCLUDED.
ALSO, THERE WAS AN INCIDENT THE OTHER DAY ON SHIJOU ROAD. A FULL REPORT IS HERE.
PLEASE DO READ IT.
THANK YOU FOR ALL YOUR TROUBLE.
AIZU BUSINESS MANAGER, TOSHIMA KIH
WITH THIS, WE SHOULD BE ABLE TO IMPROVE CONDITIONS FOR KATAMORI-SAMA.
WELL, THEN. WHERE DO WE BEGIN?
THE MOSQUITOES HAVE GOTTEN WORSE.

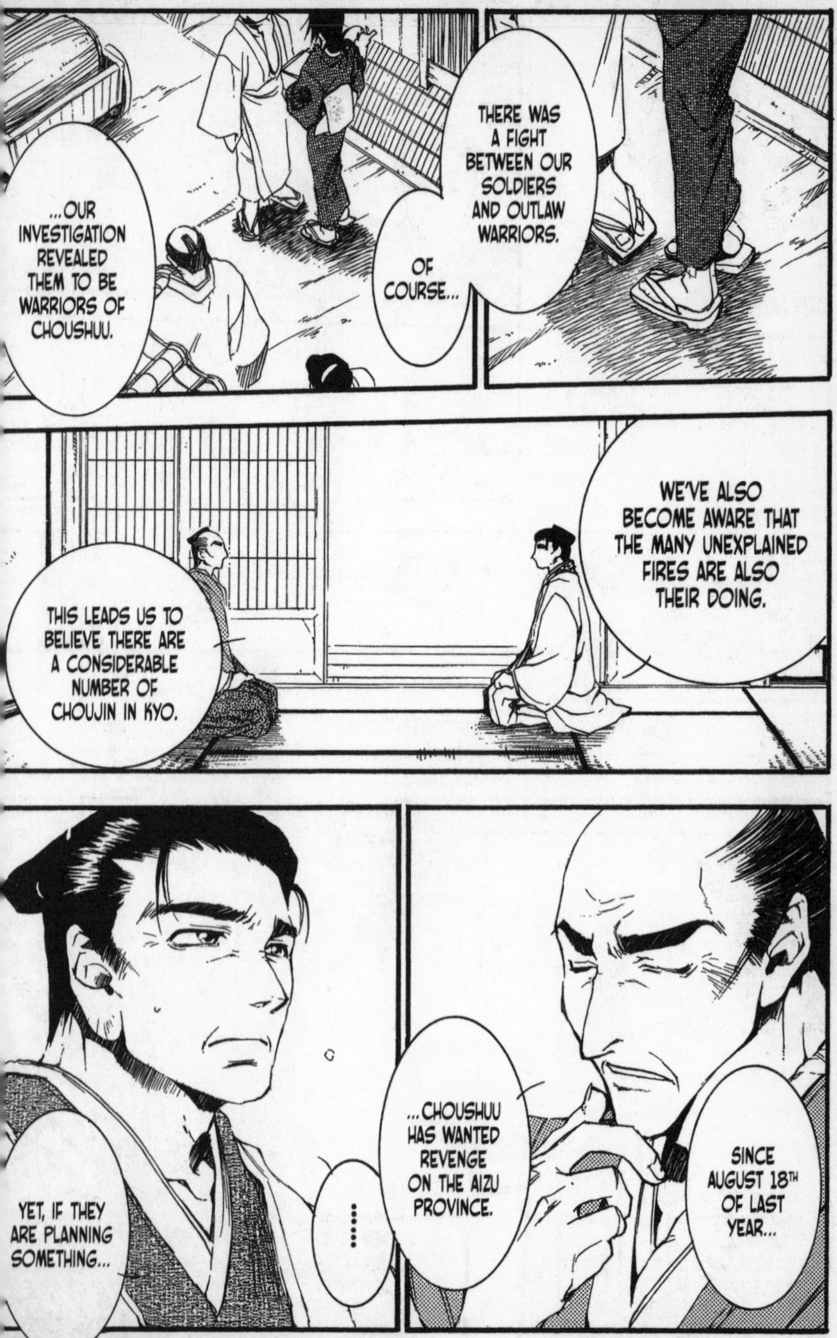
THERE WAS A FIGHT BETWEEN OUR SOLDIERS AND OUTLAW WARRIORS.
OF COURSE...
...OUR INVESTIGATION REVEALED THEM TO BE WARRIORS OF CHOUSHUU.
WE'VE ALSO BECOME AWARE THAT THE MANY UNEXPLAINED FIRES ARE ALSO THEIR DOING.
THIS LEADS US TO BELIEVE THERE ARE A CONSIDERABLE NUMBER OF CHOUJIN IN KYO.
SINCE AUGUST 18TH OF LAST YEAR...
...CHOUSHUU HAS WANTED REVENGE ON THE AIZU PROVINCE.
......
YET, IF THEY ARE PLANNING SOMETHING...

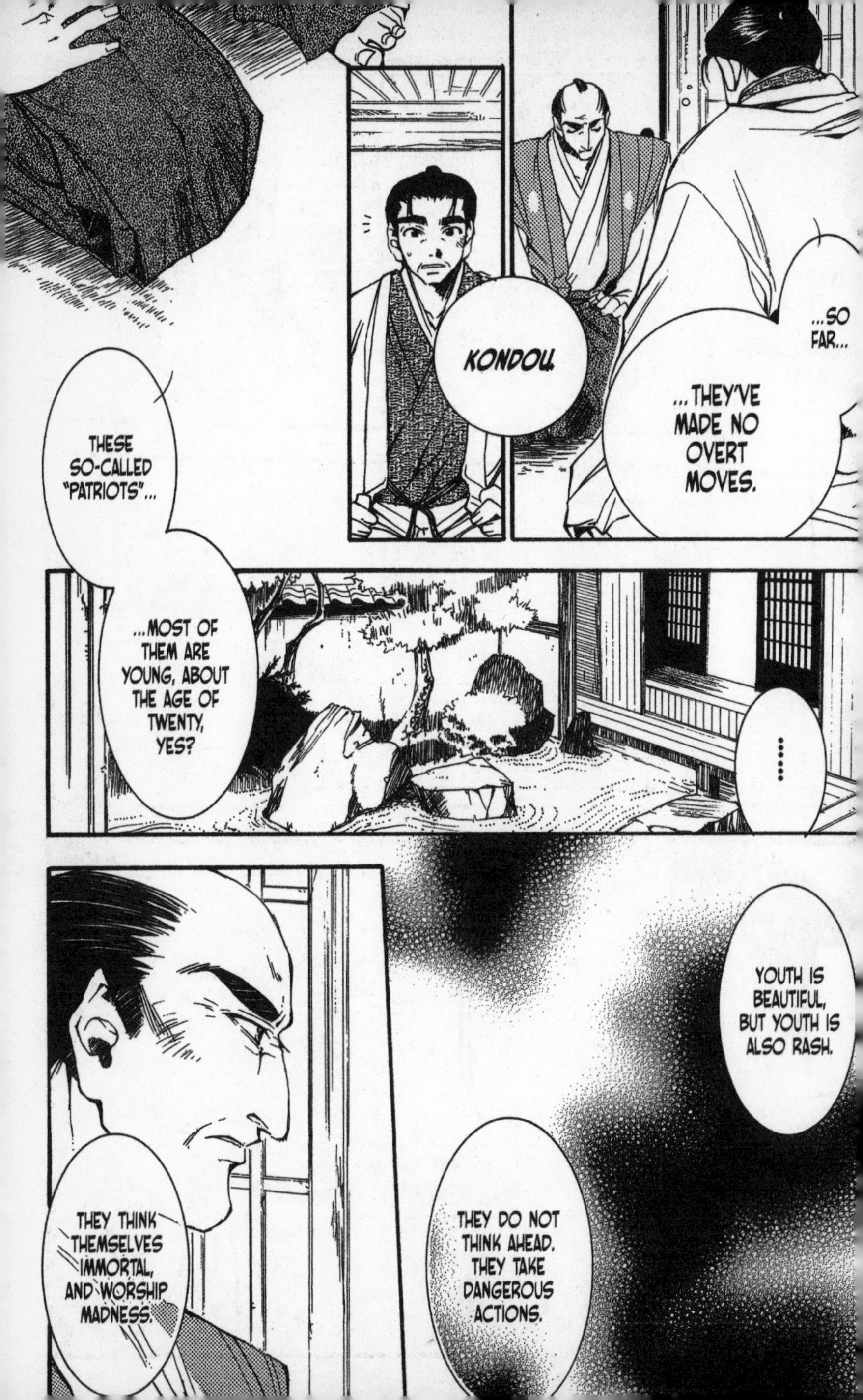
...SO FAR...
...THEY'VE MADE NO OVERT MOVES.
KONDOU.
......
THESE SO-CALLED "PATRIOTS"...
...MOST OF THEM ARE YOUNG, ABOUT THE AGE OF TWENTY, YES?
YOUTH IS BEAUTIFUL, BUT YOUTH IS ALSO RASH.
THEY DO NOT THINK AHEAD. THEY TAKE DANGEROUS ACTIONS.
THEY THINK THEMSELVES IMMORTAL, AND WORSHIP MADNESS.

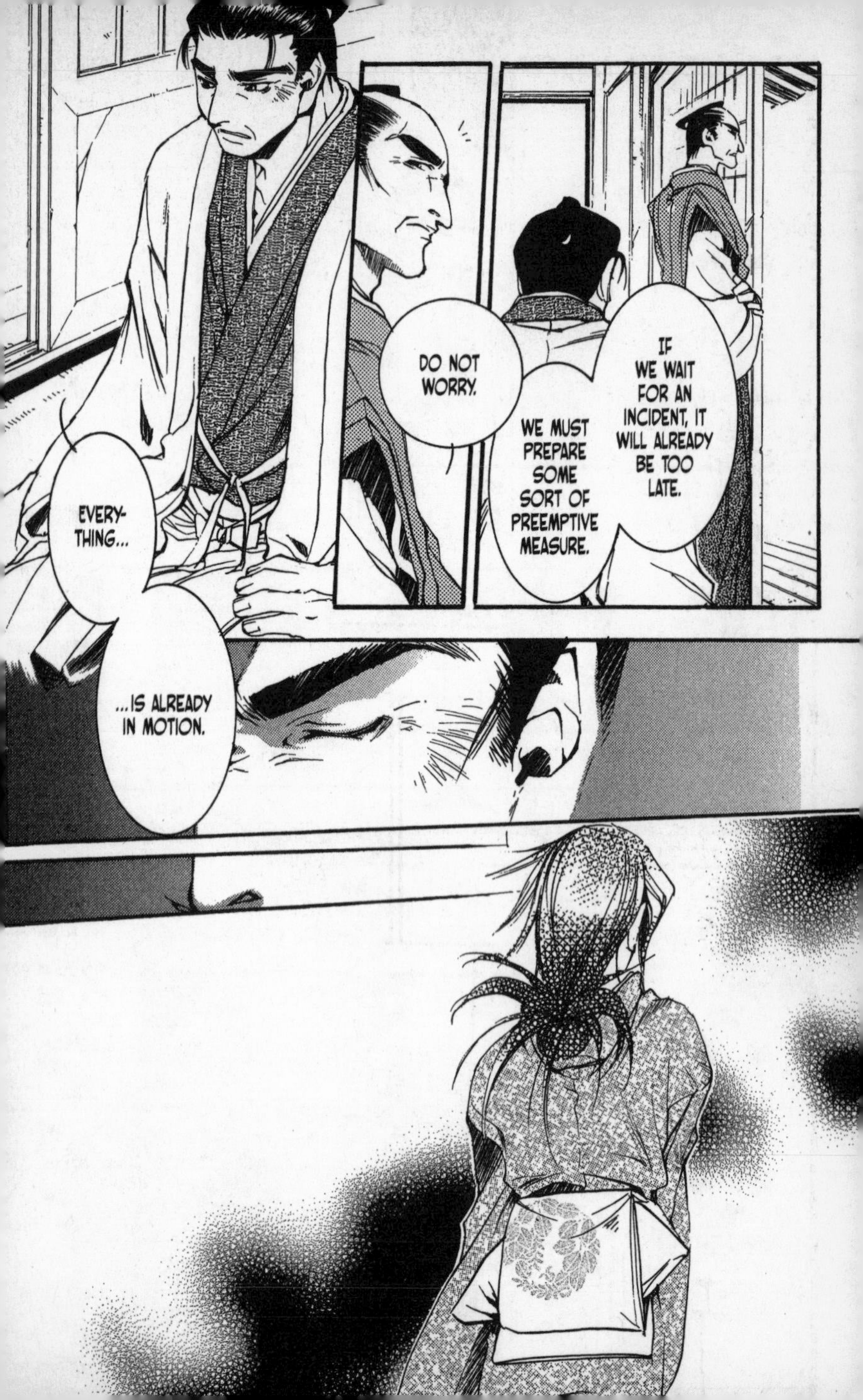
IF WE WAIT FOR AN INCIDENT, IT WILL ALREADY BE TOO LATE.
WE MUST PREPARE SOME SORT OF PREEMPTIVE MEASURE.
DO NOT WORRY.
EVERY-THING...
...IS ALREADY IN MOTION.

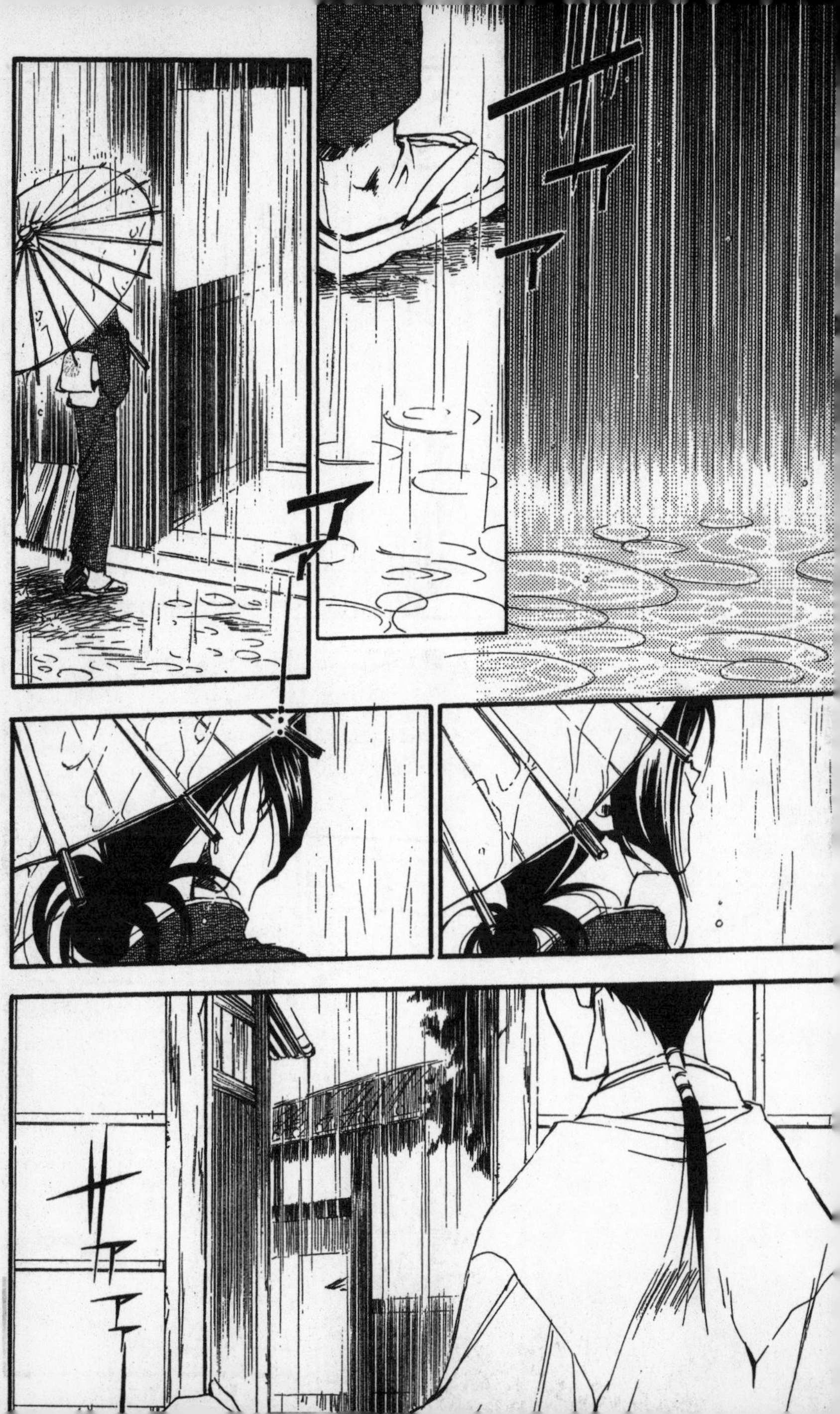
ザァァ
ァァ
ザァァ

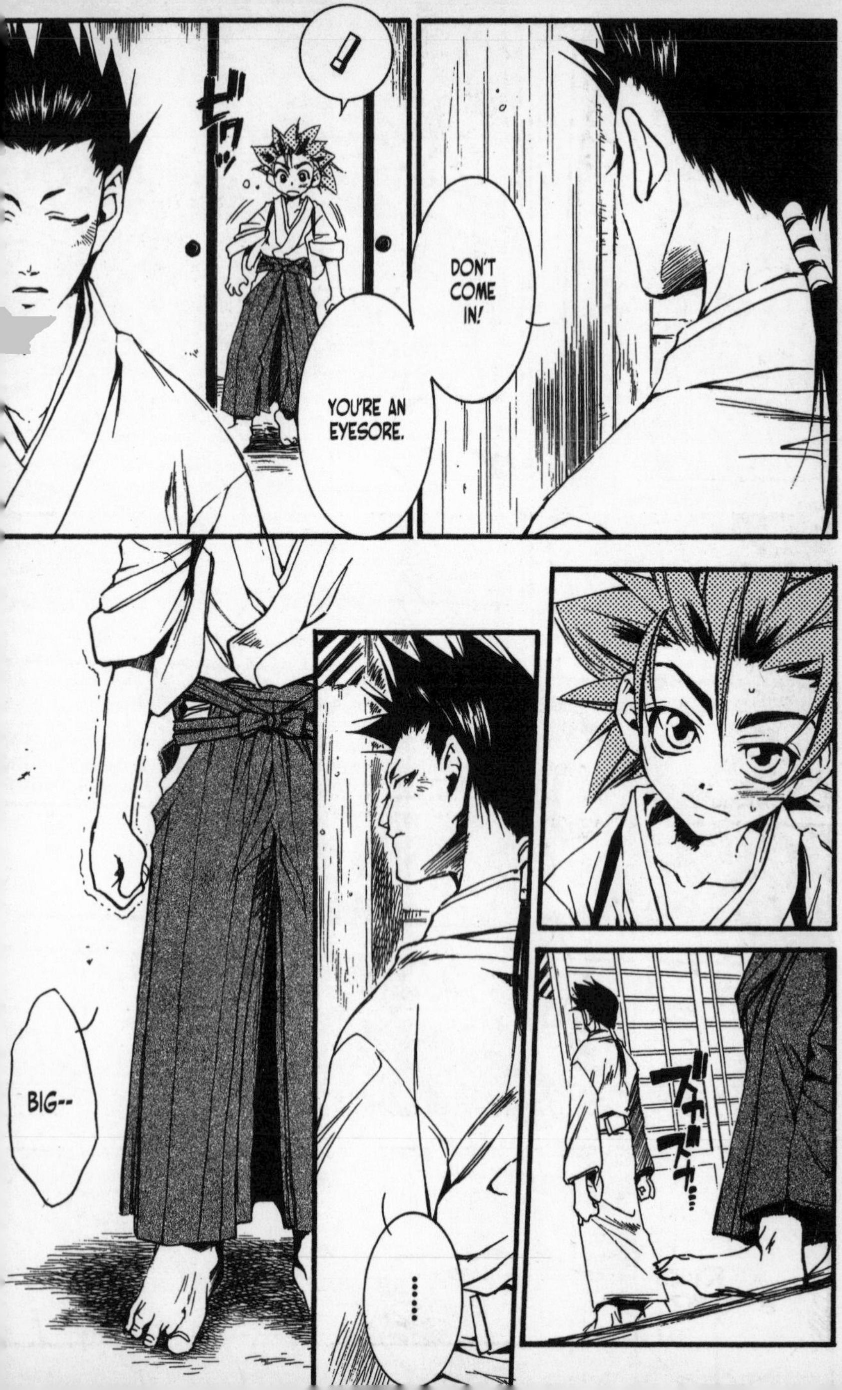
DON'T COME IN!
YOU'RE AN EYESORE.
!
ビクッ
ズカズカ...
......
BIG--

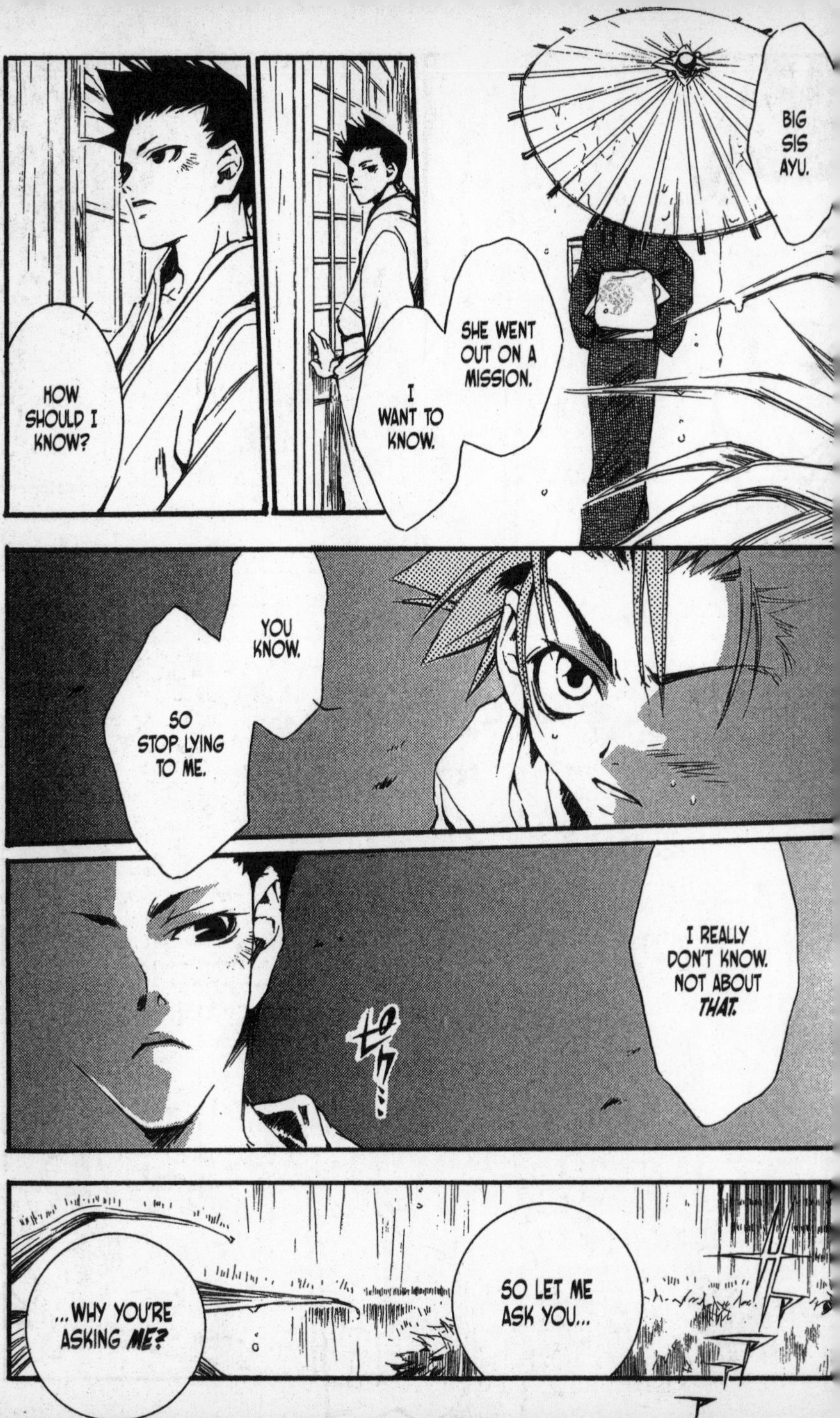
BIG SIS AYU.
SHE WENT OUT ON A MISSION.
I WANT TO KNOW.
HOW SHOULD I KNOW?
YOU KNOW.
SO STOP LYING TO ME.
I REALLY DON'T KNOW. NOT ABOUT *THAT.*
SO LET ME ASK YOU...
...WHY YOU'RE ASKING *ME?*

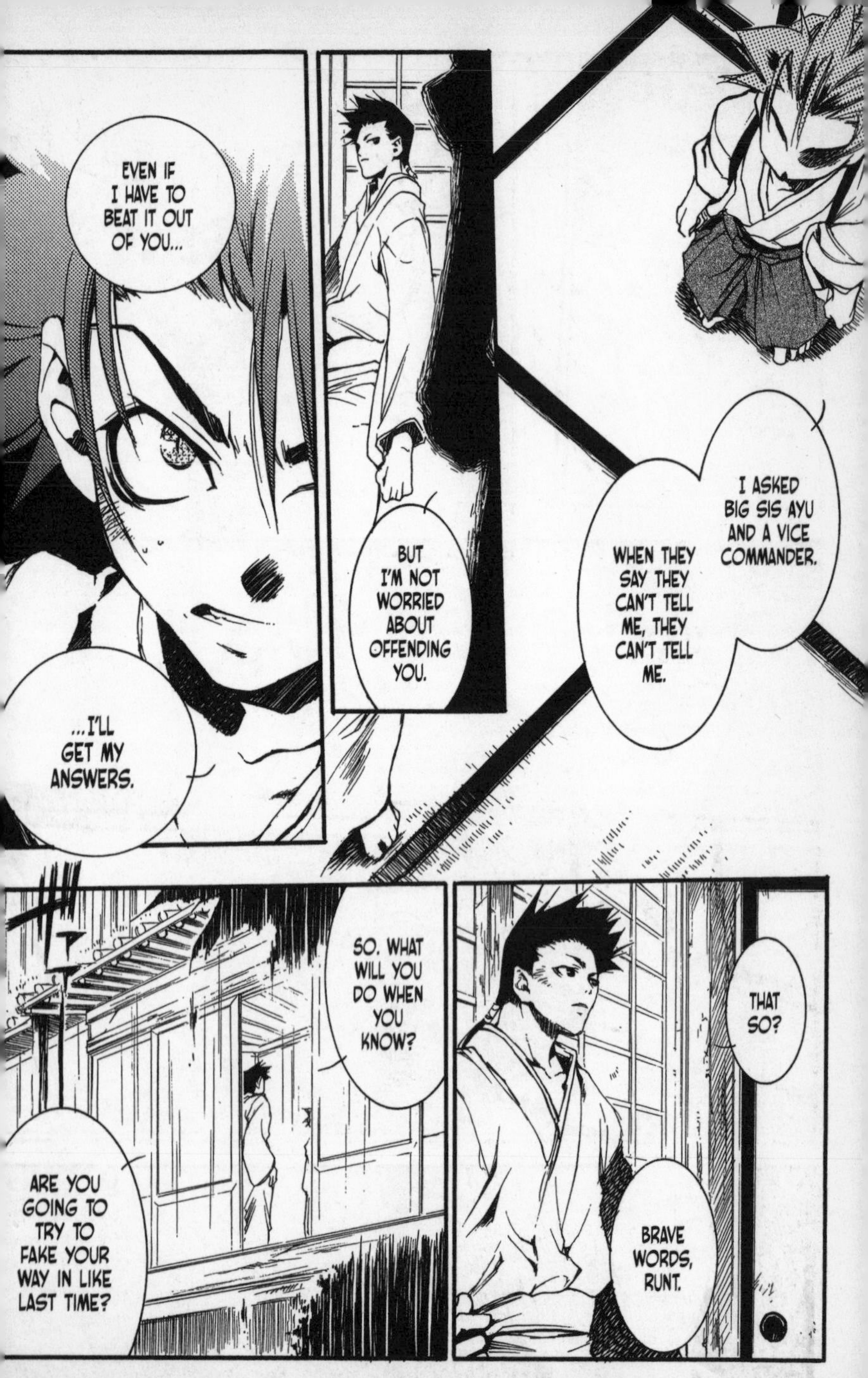
I ASKED BIG SIS AYU AND A VICE COMMANDER.
WHEN THEY SAY THEY CAN'T TELL ME, THEY CAN'T TELL ME.
BUT I'M NOT WORRIED ABOUT OFFENDING YOU.
EVEN IF I HAVE TO BEAT IT OUT OF YOU...
...I'LL GET MY ANSWERS.
THAT SO?
BRAVE WORDS, RUNT.
SO. WHAT WILL YOU DO WHEN YOU KNOW?
ARE YOU GOING TO TRY TO FAKE YOUR WAY IN LIKE LAST TIME?

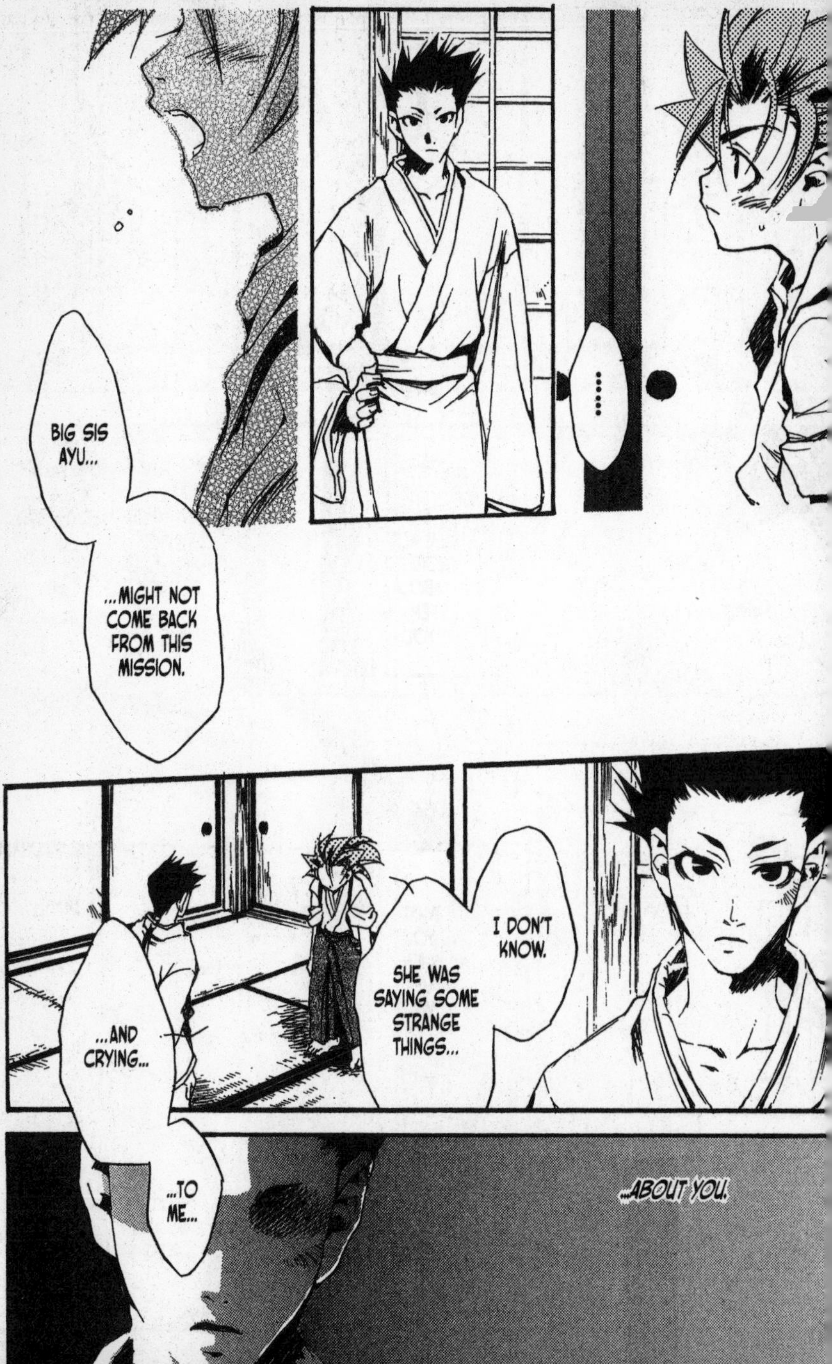
......
BIG SIS AYU...
...MIGHT NOT COME BACK FROM THIS MISSION.
I DON'T KNOW.
SHE WAS SAYING SOME STRANGE THINGS...
...AND CRYING...
...TO ME...
...ABOUT YOU.

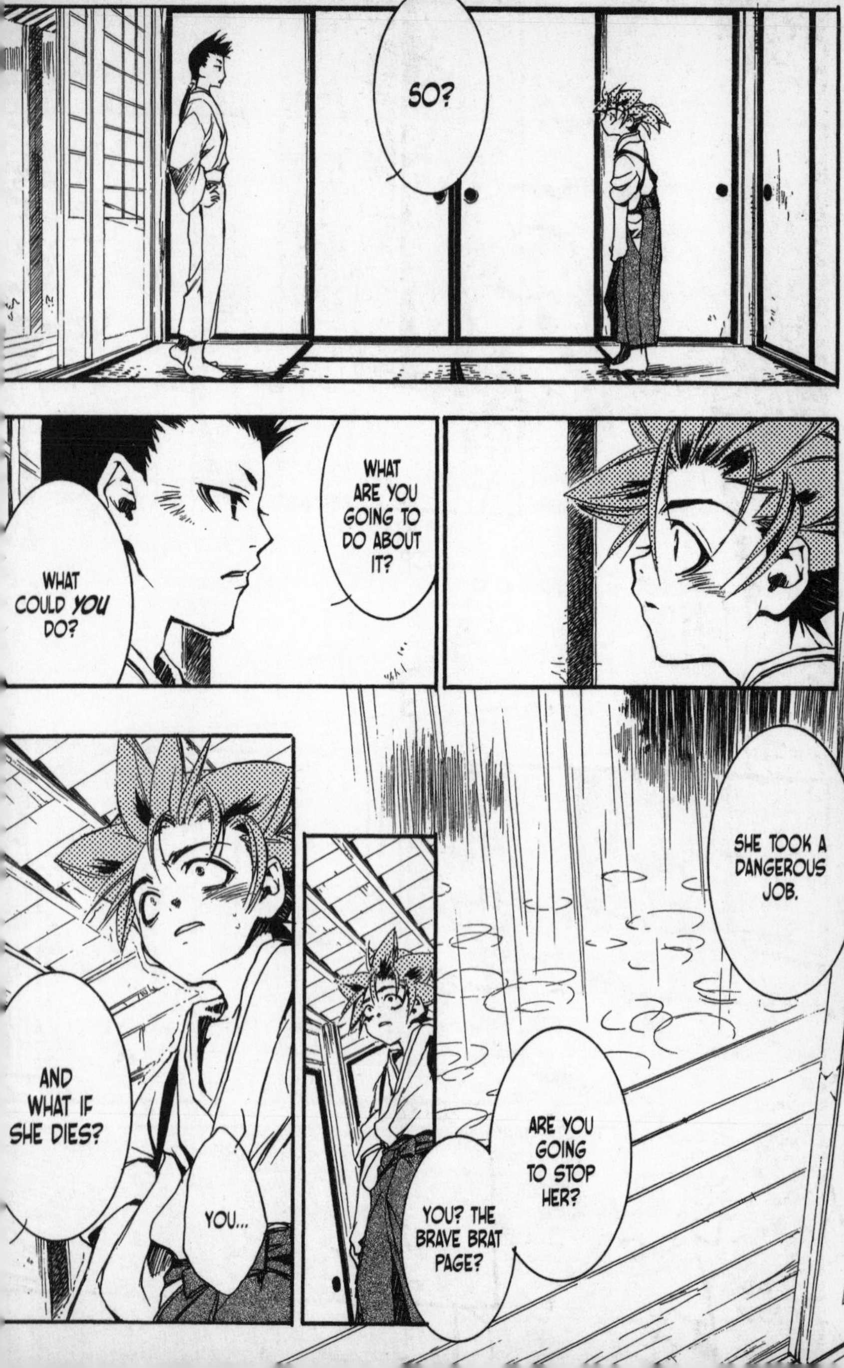
SO?
WHAT ARE YOU GOING TO DO ABOUT IT?
WHAT COULD *YOU* DO?
SHE TOOK A DANGEROUS JOB.
ARE YOU GOING TO STOP HER?
YOU? THE BRAVE BRAT PAGE?
AND WHAT IF SHE DIES?
YOU...

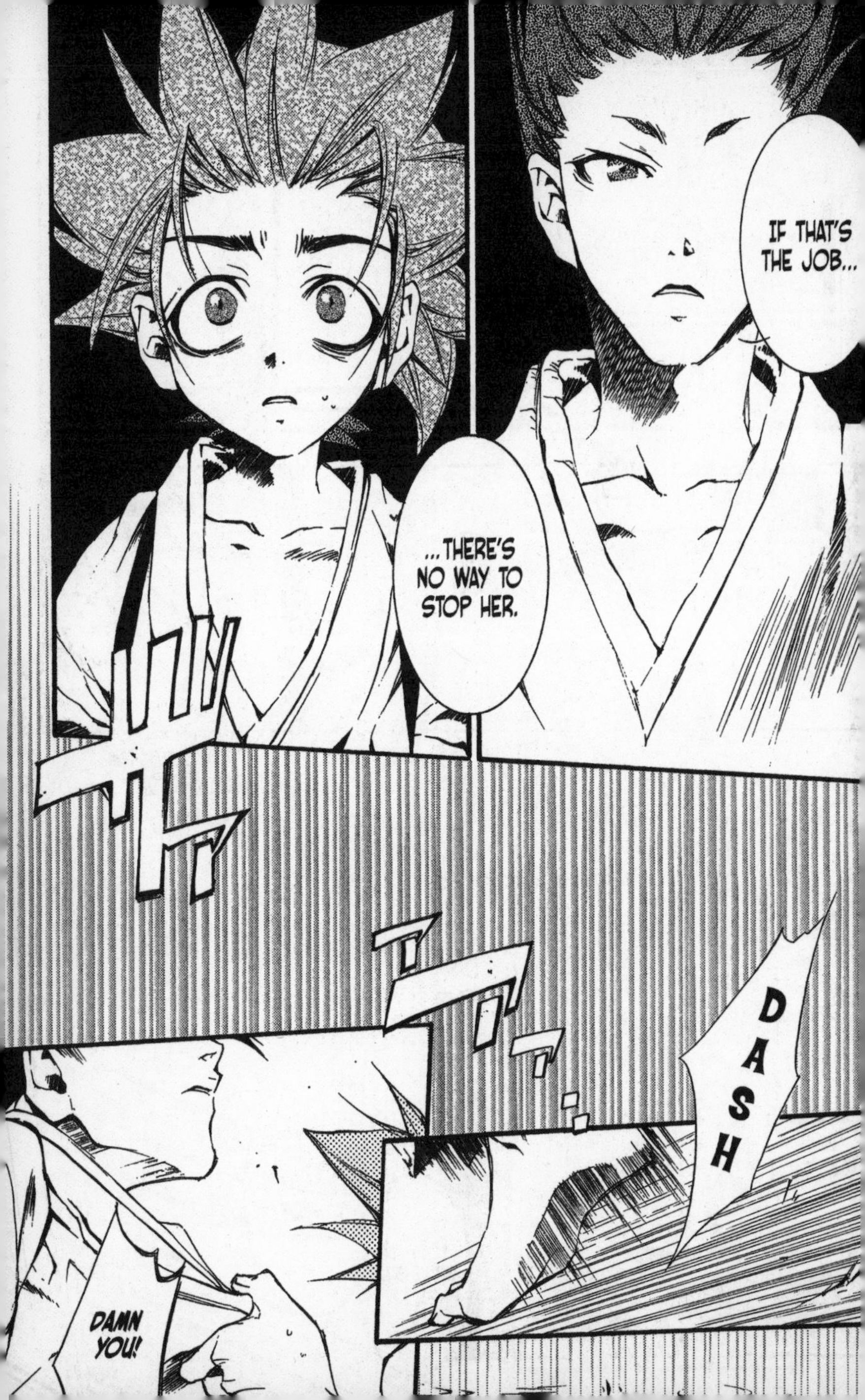
IF THAT'S THE JOB...
...THERE'S NO WAY TO STOP HER.
DASH
DAMN YOU!

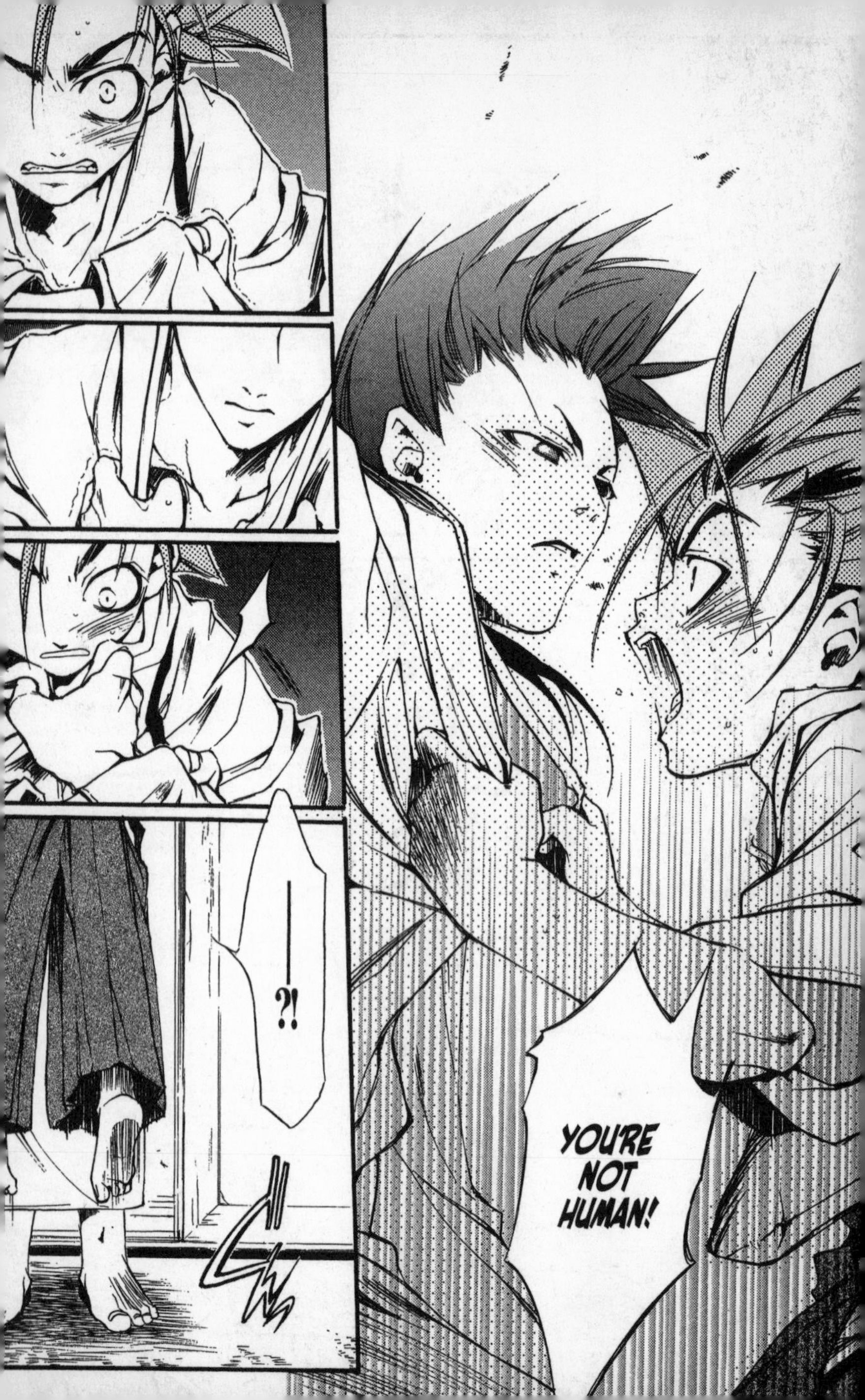
YOU'RE NOT HUMAN!
—?!

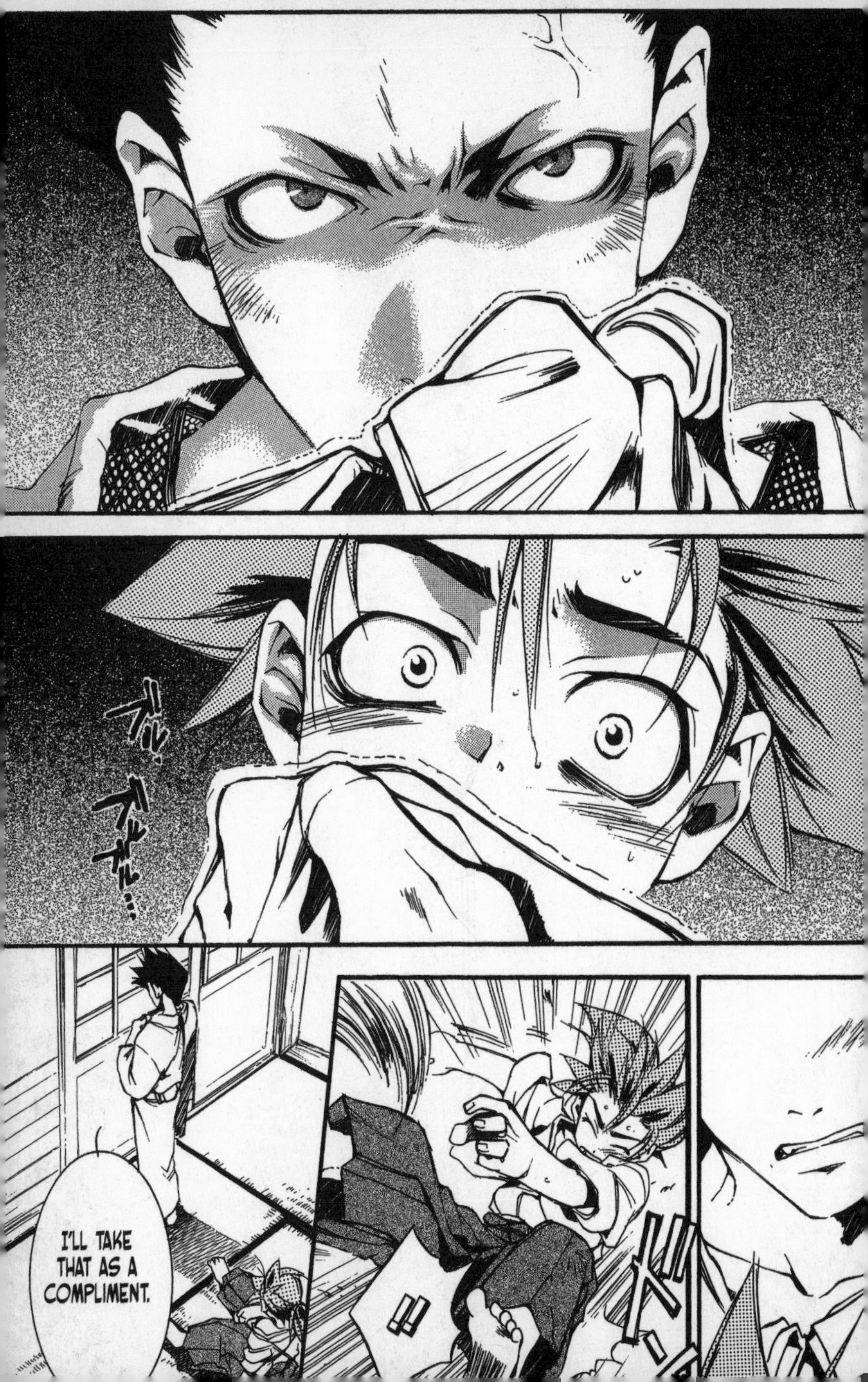
I'LL TAKE THAT AS A COMPLIMENT.
!!

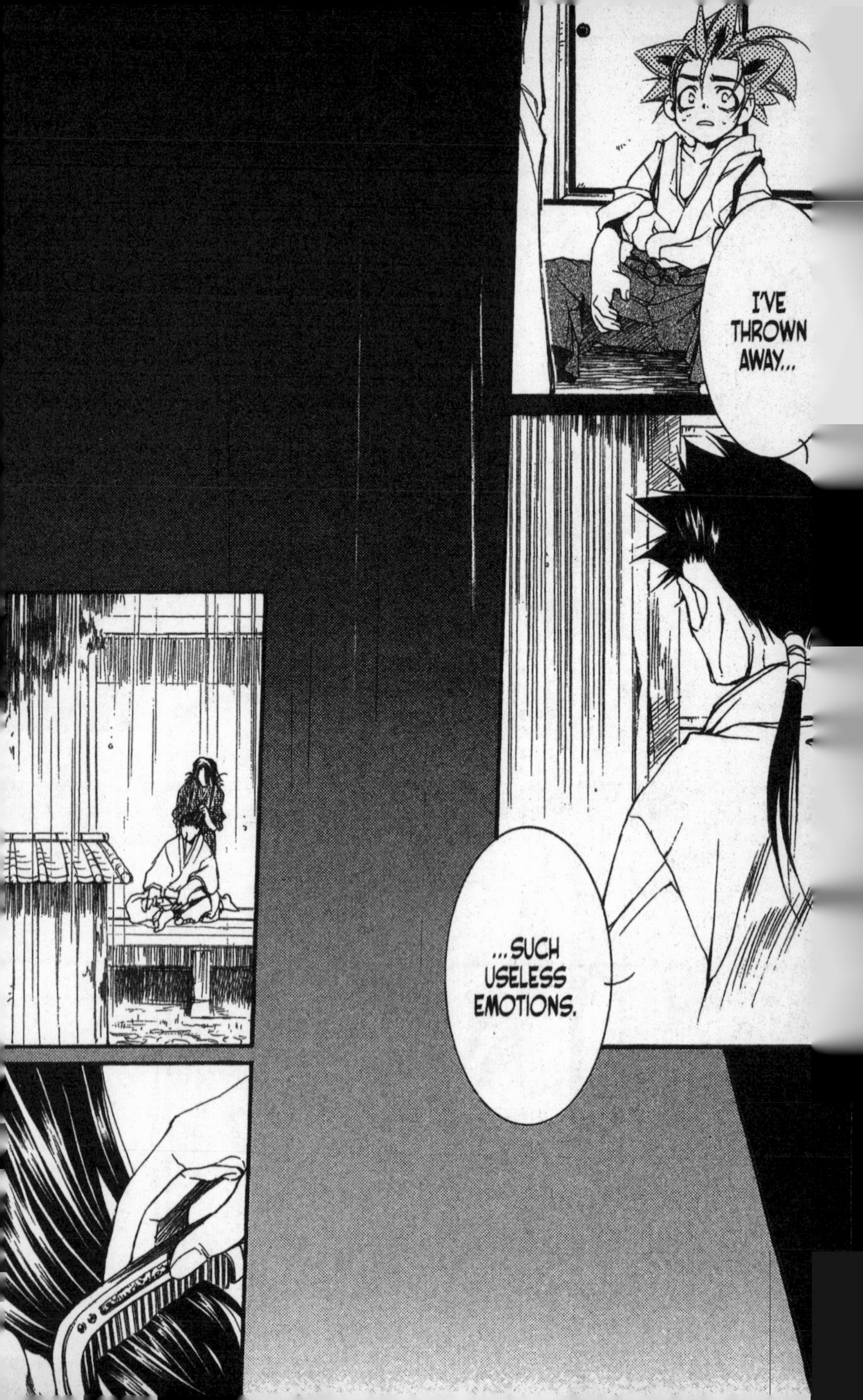
I'VE THROWN AWAY...
...SUCH USELESS EMOTIONS.

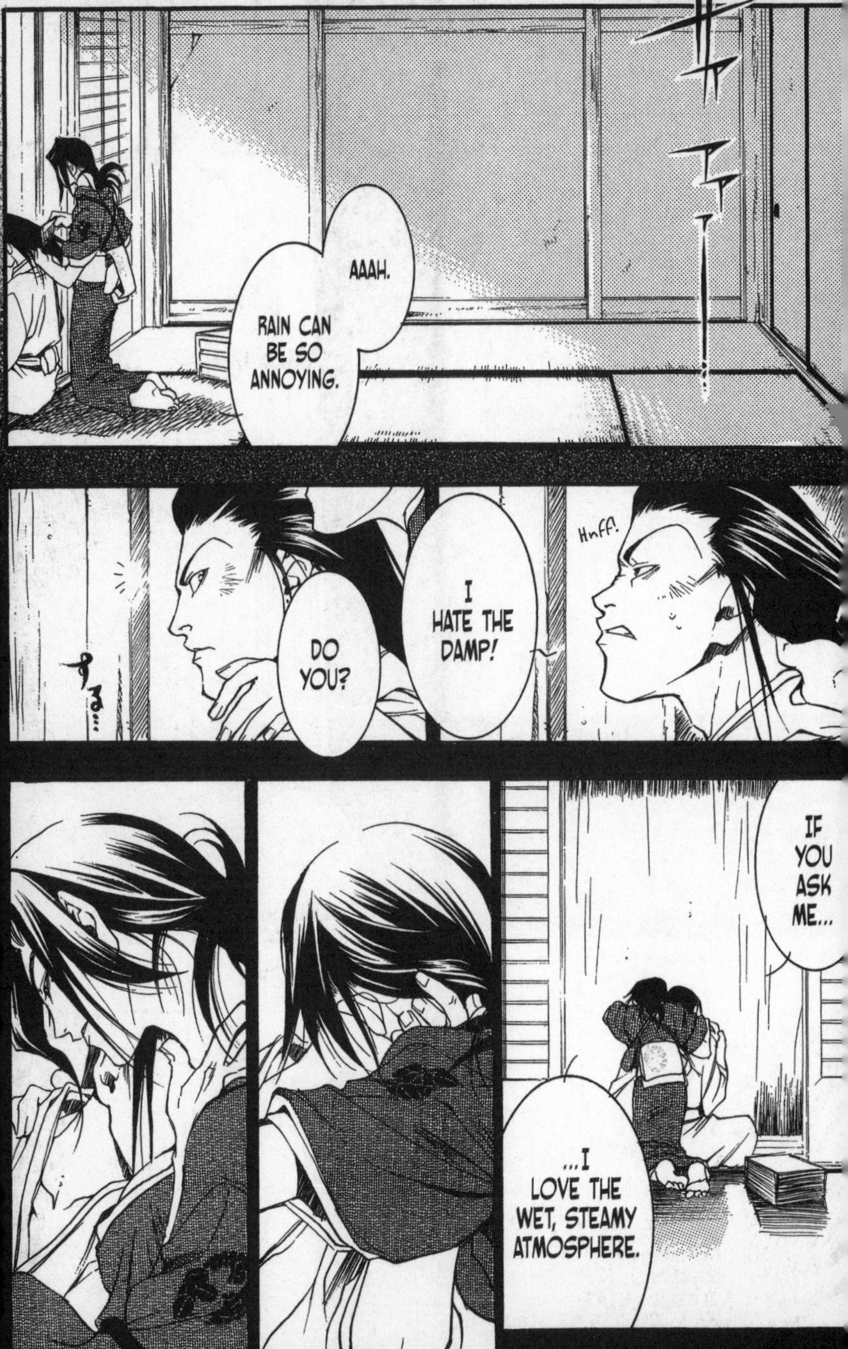
AAAH.
RAIN CAN BE SO ANNOYING.
Hnff!
I HATE THE DAMP!
DO YOU?
IF YOU ASK ME...
...I LOVE THE WET, STEAMY ATMOSPHERE.

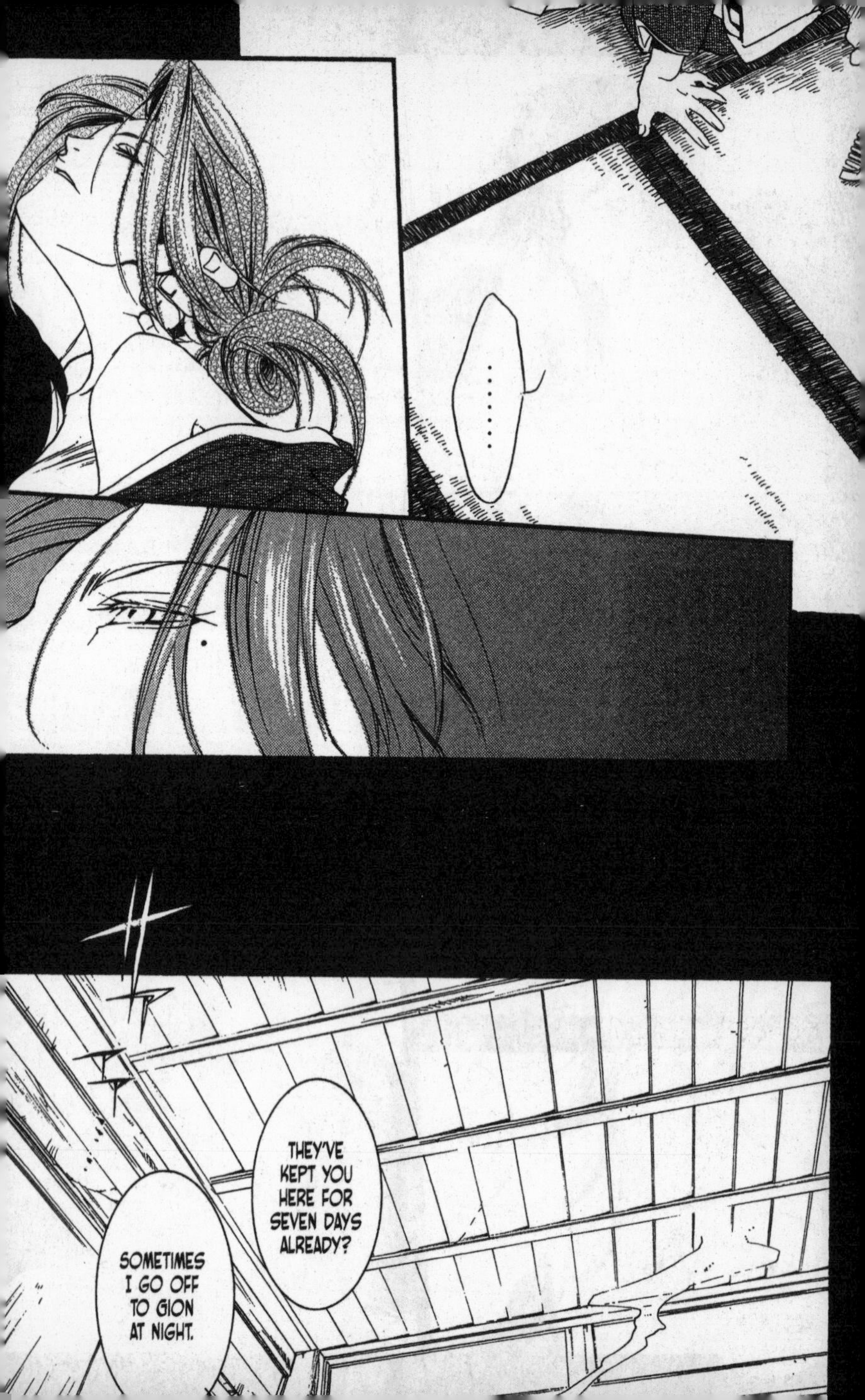
......
THEY'VE KEPT YOU HERE FOR SEVEN DAYS ALREADY?
SOMETIMES I GO OFF TO GION AT NIGHT.

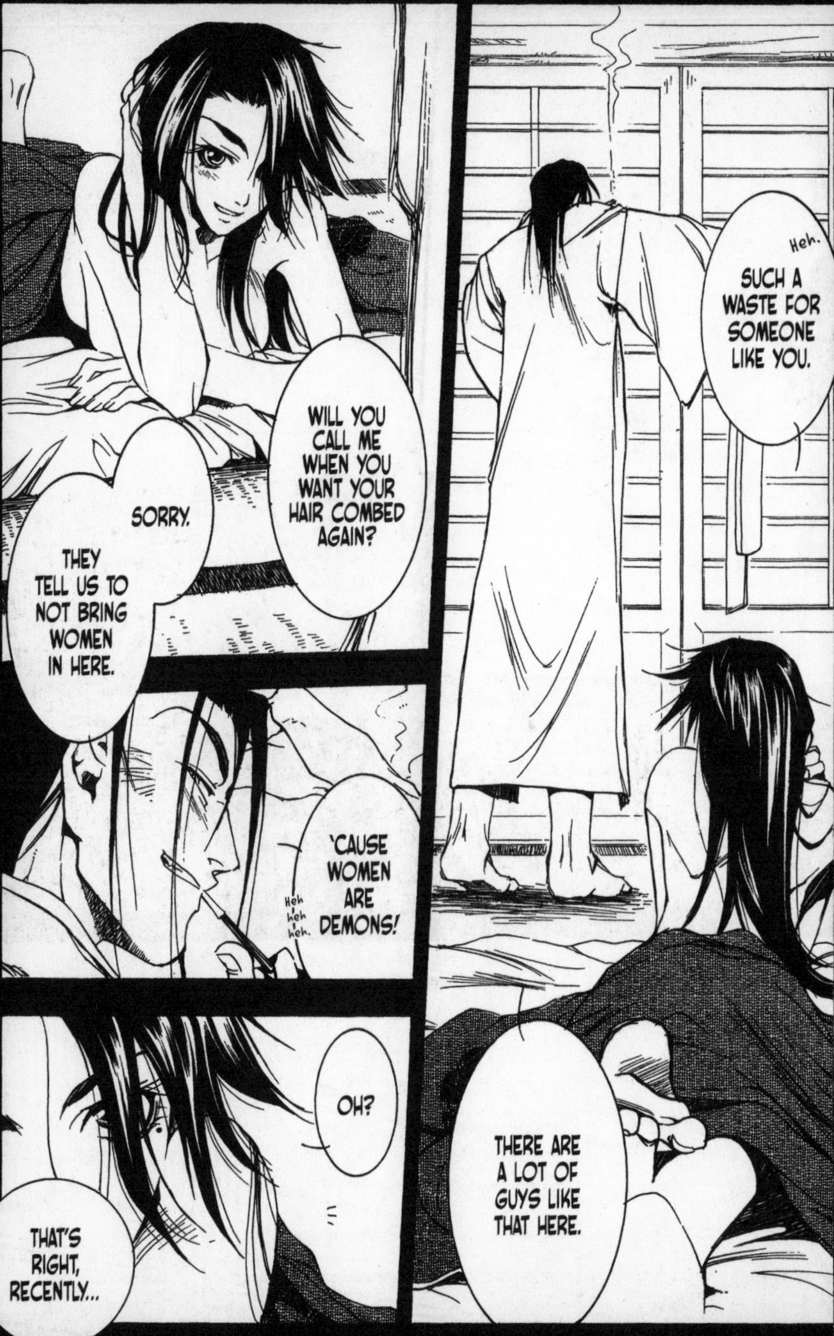
Heh.
SUCH A WASTE FOR SOMEONE LIKE YOU.
WILL YOU CALL ME WHEN YOU WANT YOUR HAIR COMBED AGAIN?
SORRY.
THEY TELL US TO NOT BRING WOMEN IN HERE.
'CAUSE WOMEN ARE DEMONS!
Heh heh heh.
THERE ARE A LOT OF GUYS LIKE THAT HERE.
OH?
THAT'S RIGHT, RECENTLY...

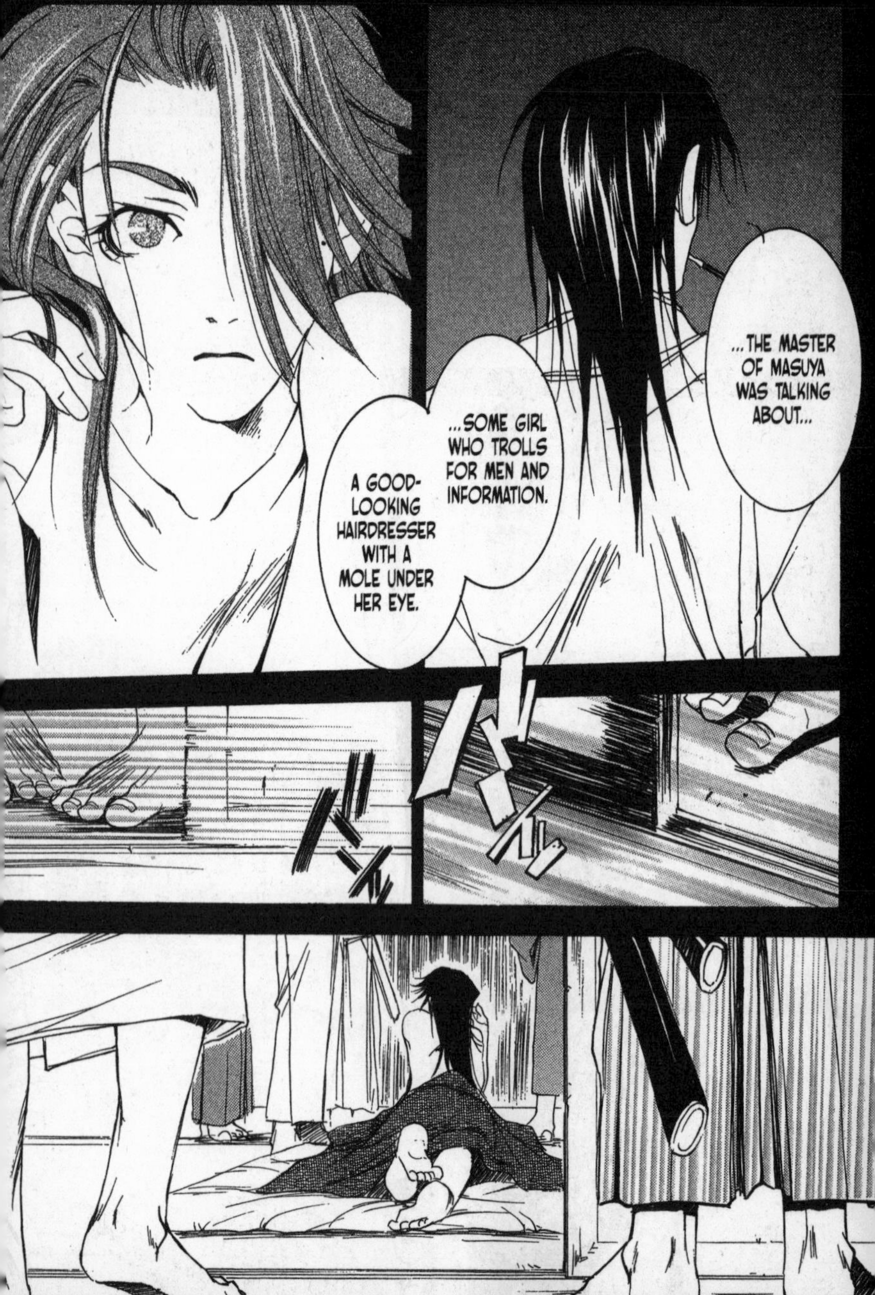
...THE MASTER OF MASUYA WAS TALKING ABOUT...
...SOME GIRL WHO TROLLS FOR MEN AND INFORMATION.
A GOOD-LOOKING HAIRDRESSER WITH A MOLE UNDER HER EYE.

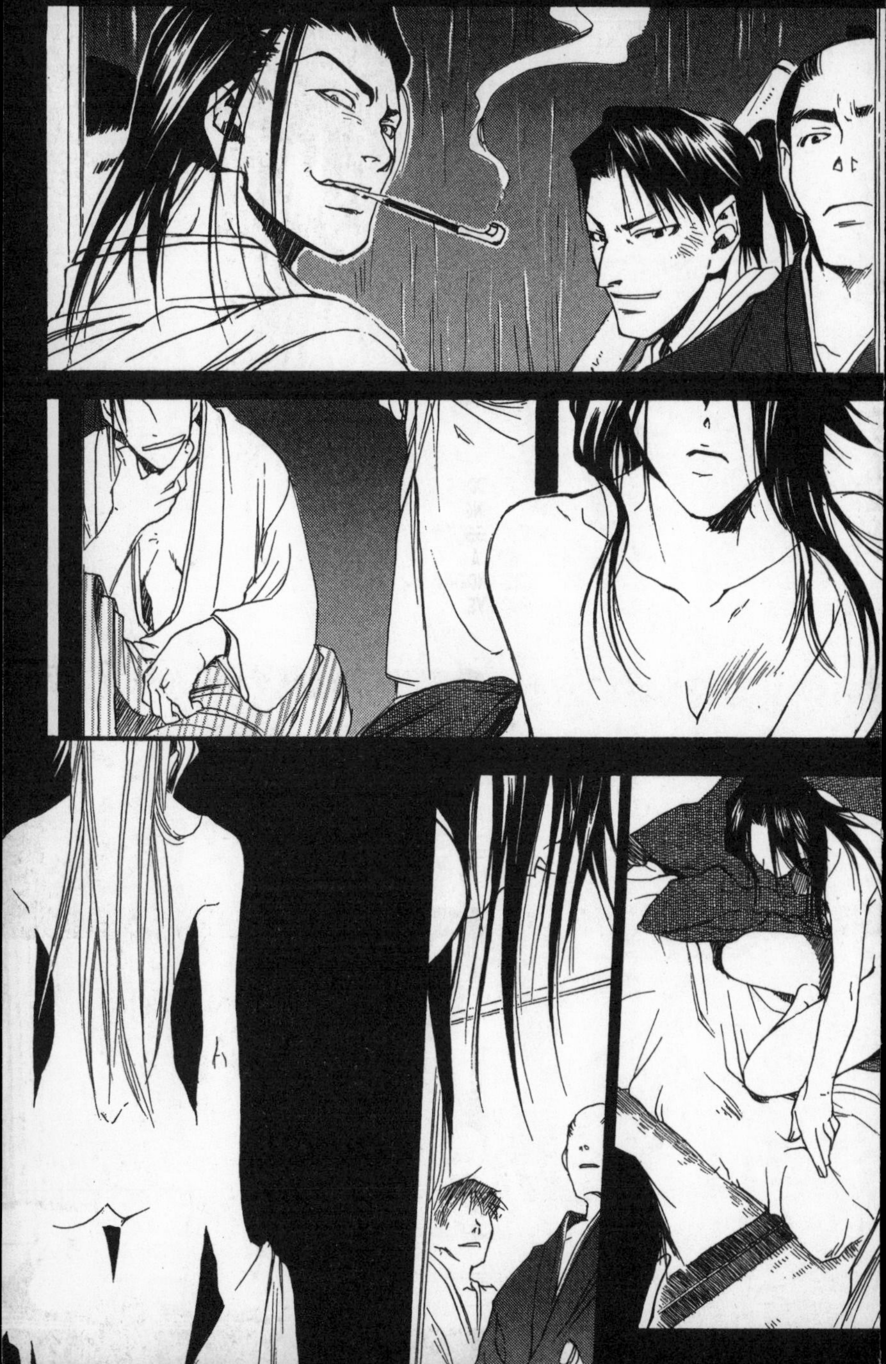

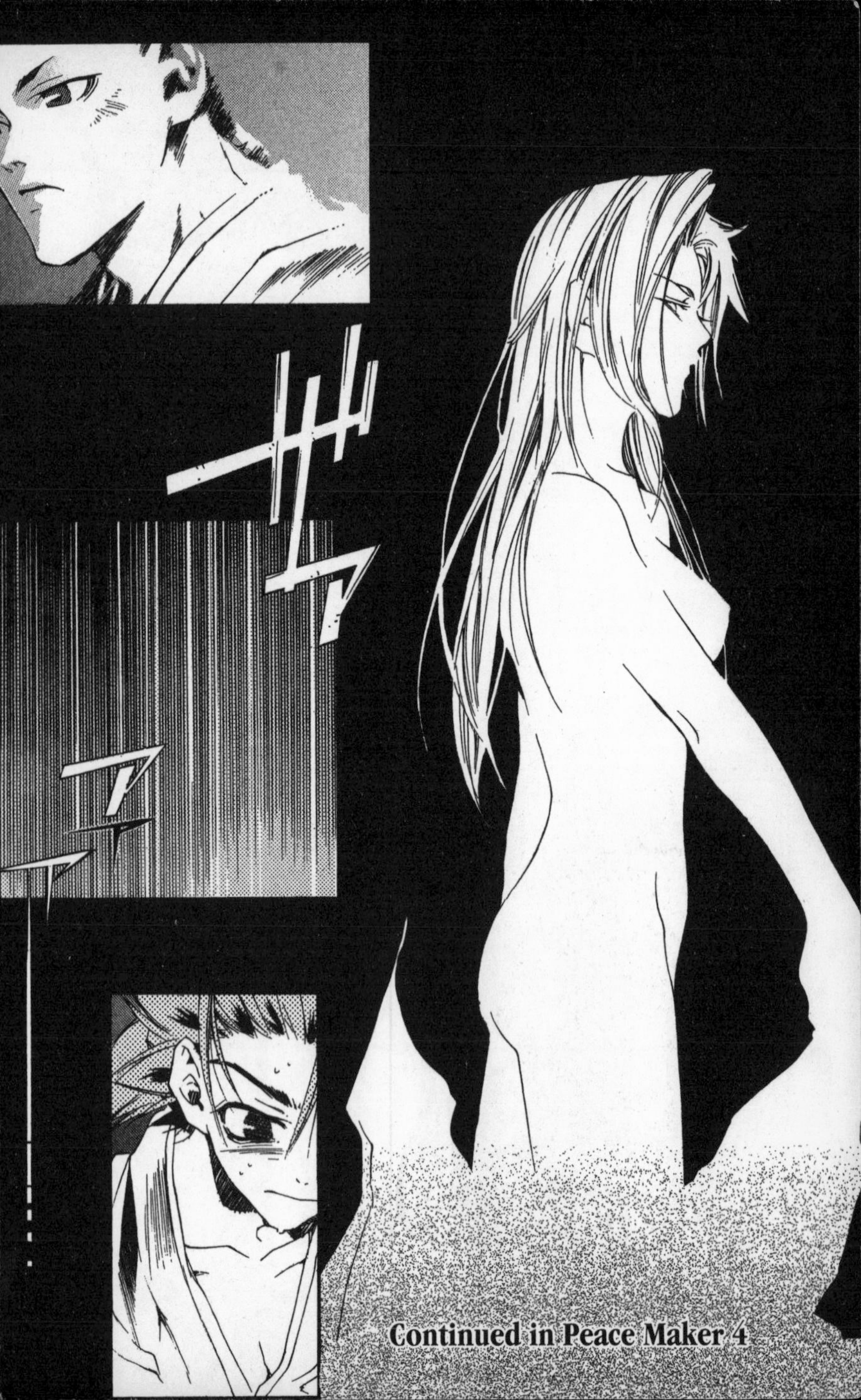

Continued in Peace Maker 4

In the Next

PEACE MAKER
ピースメーカー

With a sister lost,
Now two brothers seek revenge
While the arson laughs.

Coming Soon!

A GUIDE TO THE HISTORICAL ERA OF *PEACE MAKER*

SHIMABARA WAS THE *HANAMACHI* ("FLOWER-TOWN"), OR COURTESAN'S DISTRICT OF KYOTO DURING THE TOKUGAWA SHOGUNATE. IT WAS FOUNDED IN 1640 WITH THE OPENING OF A BROTHEL BY HARA SABUROEMON, AND CLOSED IN 1958 WHEN PROSTITUTION WAS MADE ILLEGAL THROUGHOUT JAPAN. DURING THE EDO PERIOD, IT WAS ALSO CALLED "THE QUARTER," REFERRING TO SHIMABARA'S REPUTATION AS THE PLACE TO FIND CLEAN, CLASSY AND LICENSED PROSTITUTES (AS OPPOSED TO UNLICENSED STREET WALKERS WHO WORKED IN OTHER PARTS OF KYOTO). PROSTITUTION WAS PREVALENT DURING THE EDO PERIOD, AND WAS RESTRICTED TO ONE DISTRICT BY ORDER OF THE TOKUGAWA SHOGUNATE TO EXERCISE CONTROL OVER THE TRADE. *KABUKI* AND *BUNRAKU* THEATRES WERE SIMILARLY CONFINED TO CERTAIN DISTRICTS, NOT OUT OF A RELIGIOUS OR MORAL OPPOSITION TO SEX WORK OR THEATRE, BUT TO COMPARTMENTALIZE THE TRADES WITHIN THE CITY OF KYOTO.

IT IS IMPORTANT TO REMEMBER THAT THE PROSTITUTES WORKING IN SHIMABARA WERE NOT *GEISHA*. GEISHA WERE TRAINED FEMALE ENTERTAINERS WHO TOOK THEIR COMPANY TO THE VERY EDGE OF INNUENDO; THEY WERE MASTERS OF CREATING A FANTASY OF A RELATIONSHIP THAT COULD NEVER BE. GEISHA NEVER ENGAGED IN PAID SEX WITH CLIENTS. HIGH-CLASS COURTESANS WERE CALLED *OIRAN*. THOUGH THEY WERE ALSO TRAINED IN THE ARTS OF ILLUSION AND PLEASURE, AND WORE ELABORATE HAIRSTYLES AND WHITE MAKEUP LIKE THE GEISHA, OIRAN WERE LICENSED TO ENGAGE IN PAID SEX. A MAN OF THE EDO PERIOD COULD TELL THE DIFFERENCE BETWEEN THE TWO IN ONE GLANCE: OIRAN WORE THEIR *OBI* (THE SASH PART OF THE KIMONO) TIED IN THE FRONT. THE OIRAN OFFERED FAR MORE THAN A QUICK SEXUAL ENCOUNTER, ENGAGING THEIR VERY WEALTHY AND PROMINENT CLIENTS IN INTELLECTUAL DISCUSSION AND ENTERTAINING THEM WITH MUSIC, DANCE, CALLIGRAPHY, SPOKEN VERSE AND WITTY CONVERSATION.

JUST AS THE SHINSENGUMI USED MILITARY RANK AND APPRENTICES (OR "PAGES"), THE OIRAN HAD ASSISTANTS, OR GIRLS-IN-TRAINING. HANA AND SAYA WOULD HAVE BEEN GIVEN THE EXTENSIVE EDUCATION NECESSARY TO BECOME OIRAN WHILE PROVIDING HELP TO AKESATO AT THE BROTHEL.

-CHRISTINE BOYLAN

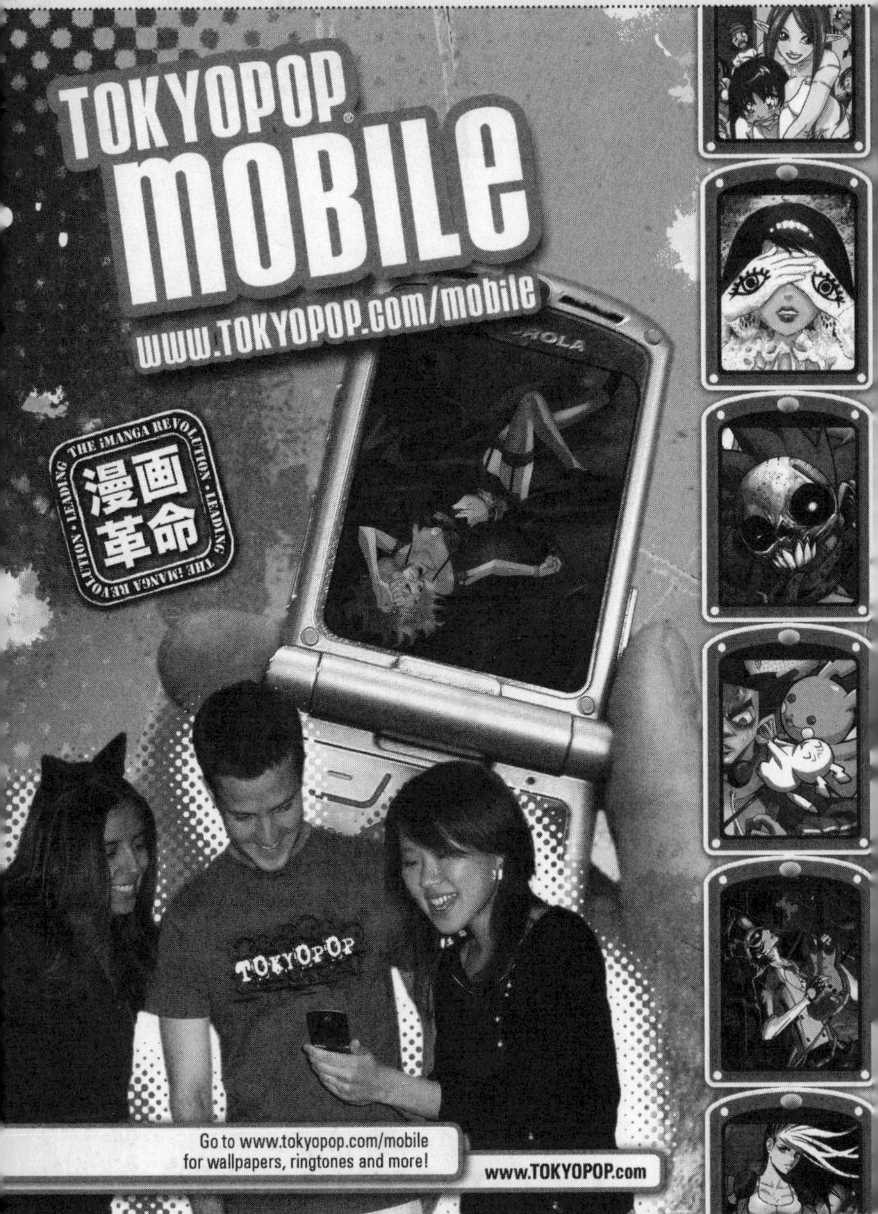
TOKYOPOP® MOBILE
www.TOKYOPOP.com/mobile
THE iMANGA REVOLUTION · LEADING · THE iMANGA REVOLUTION · LEADING
漫画革命
TOKYOPOP
Go to www.tokyopop.com/mobile
for wallpapers, ringtones and more!
www.TOKYOPOP.com

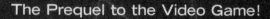

This is the back of the book.
You wouldn't want to spoil a great ending!

This book is printed "manga-style," in the authentic Japa____ ___ ___ ___ft format. Since none of the artwork has been flipped or alt____ __ ___ get to experience the story just as the creator intended. ___ __ asking for it, so TOKYOPOP® delivered: authentic, hot-o___ ___p__ and far more fun!

DIRECT___NS

If this is your first ___ ___ reading manga-st___ ___'s a quick guide to hel___ ___ understand how it ___ ___

It's easy... just sta__ __ ___ ___ right panel and fol___ ___ __ numbers. Have fun, and look for more 100% authentic manga from TOKYOPOP®!